John Skinner

The book of the prophet Isaiah

Chapters XL - LXVI

John Skinner

The book of the prophet Isaiah
Chapters XL - LXVI

ISBN/EAN: 9783337041946

Printed in Europe, USA, Canada, Australia, Japan

Cover: Foto ©ninafisch / pixelio.de

More available books at **www.hansebooks.com**

The Cambridge Bible for Schools and Colleges.

THE BOOK OF THE PROPHET

ISAIAH,

CHAPTERS XL.—LXVI.

London: C. J. CLAY AND SONS,
CAMBRIDGE UNIVERSITY PRESS WAREHOUSE,
AVE MARIA LANE.
Glasgow: 263, ARGYLE STREET.

Leipzig: F. A. BROCKHAUS.
New York: THE MACMILLAN COMPANY.
Bombay: E. SEYMOUR HALE.

The Cambridge Bible for Schools and Colleges.

GENERAL EDITOR FOR THE OLD TESTAMENT:—
A. F. KIRKPATRICK, D.D.

THE BOOK OF THE PROPHET
ISAIAH,
CHAPTERS XL.—LXVI.

WITH INTRODUCTION AND NOTES

BY

THE REV. J. SKINNER, D.D.

PROFESSOR OF OLD TESTAMENT EXEGESIS IN THE PRESBYTERIAN
COLLEGE, LONDON.

EDITED FOR THE SYNDICS OF THE UNIVERSITY PRESS.

CAMBRIDGE:
AT THE UNIVERSITY PRESS.
1898

[*All Rights reserved.*]

Cambridge:
PRINTED BY J. & C. F. CLAY,
AT THE UNIVERSITY PRESS.

PREFACE

BY THE

GENERAL EDITOR FOR THE OLD TESTAMENT.

THE present General Editor for the Old Testament in the Cambridge Bible for Schools and Colleges desires to say that, in accordance with the policy of his predecessor the Bishop of Worcester, he does not hold himself responsible for the particular interpretations adopted or for the opinions expressed by the editors of the several Books, nor has he endeavoured to bring them into agreement with one another. It is inevitable that there should be differences of opinion in regard to many questions of criticism and interpretation, and it seems best that these differences should find free expression in different volumes. He has endeavoured to secure, as far as possible, that the general scope and character of the series should be observed, and that views which have a reasonable claim to consideration should not be ignored, but he has felt it best that the final responsibility should, in general, rest with the individual contributors.

A. F. KIRKPATRICK.

CAMBRIDGE,
August, 1896.

CONTENTS.

		PAGES
GENERAL INTRODUCTION.		
Chapter I.	Contents of the Prophecy	ix
,, II.	Historical Background of the Prophecy	xvii
,, III.	The Prophet's Theological Conceptions	xxii
,, IV.	Date and Authorship of the Prophecy	xxxix
,, V.	Unity of the Prophecy	liii
	Chronological Table	lxi
	TEXT AND NOTES	1—232
	APPENDIX	233—244
	INDEX	245—251

The Text adopted in this Edition is that of Dr Scrivener's *Cambridge Paragraph Bible*. A few variations from the ordinary Text, chiefly in the spelling of certain words, and in the use of italics, will be noticed. For the principles adopted by Dr Scrivener as regards the printing of the Text see his Introduction to the *Paragraph Bible*, published by the Cambridge University Press.

INTRODUCTION.

CHAPTER I.

CONTENTS OF THE PROPHECY.

THE division of the Book of Isaiah into two parts at the end of ch. xxxix., although indicated by no superscription, is at once suggested by the intervention of the narrative section, chs. xxxvi.—xxxix., and is fully justified by the character of the last 27 chapters. Whether these chapters form a single continuous prophecy, or whether, as some think, the work of different hands can be distinguished, they are pervaded by a unity of spirit and aim which separates them from the undisputed prophecies of Isaiah. It is this part of the book which has gained for that prophet the name of the Evangelist of the Old Testament, and whoever the author may have been, that designation aptly characterises the tendency of the chapters. Critical writers, as is well known, generally assign them to an anonymous prophet, living in the latter part of the Babylonian Exile; and the grounds on which this conclusion rests will naturally have to be stated at some length in this Introduction. They will be found to be all of the nature of what is called *internal evidence*, being drawn from indications furnished by the book itself of the circumstances in which it was composed. It would, however, be a mistake to allow this critical question to dominate the enquiry into the nature and teaching of the prophecy. The proper course obviously is first of all to gain as clear an idea as possible of the prophecy itself, and then to consider what light is thereby thrown on its origin. Accordingly, the substance of this and the two following chapters will be independent of the controversy as to authorship and date, and will for the most part represent views in which critics of all shades of opinion are agreed. If it should be necessary occasionally to refer to points of agreement or disagreement with the earlier part of Isaiah, this will be only for the sake of illustration, or to avoid repetition, and certainly not from any desire to prejudge the issue whether the author be Isaiah or another.

The prophecy may be conveniently divided into three nearly equal sections: chs. xl.—xlviii., xlix.—lv., and lvi.—lxvi.[1]

(A) Chs. xl.—xlviii. The Restoration of Israel through the instrumentality of Cyrus.

(1) The Prologue (ch. xl. 1—11) is a magnificent composition, setting forth in striking imagery and in language of exquisite beauty the theme of the whole discourse. The opening words, "Comfort ye, comfort ye my people," which have been finely compared to "the first ripples of light in a cloudless dawn[2]," contain the burden of the prophet's message.

---

[1] The well-known division into three parts of nine chapters each was first proposed by Friedrich Rückert in 1831, and has found its way into many commentaries. It is based on the observation that the words, "There is no peace, saith the Lord (or, my God), to the wicked" recur at the end of ch. xlviii. and lvii., and that the last verse of ch. lxvi. expresses a similar thought. But the idea that these words were introduced by the author *as a refrain* is not borne out by an examination of the structure of the prophecy. Between ch. lvii. and lviii. there is no break, but a very close connexion, and the supposed refrain completes in the most natural manner the idea of the previous verse. In ch. xlviii. 22, on the other hand, the words are so alien to the context that to some commentators they strongly suggest the hand of a compiler. The division as a whole, therefore, must be dismissed as "entirely superficial, and worth nothing except as an aid to the memory" (A. B. Davidson, *Expositor*, 2nd Series, Vol. VI. p. 88). At the same time many of the best critics agree with Rückert in regarding chs. xl.—xlviii. as the first great section of the volume. A large number of characteristic ideas (see p. 79), as well as a few peculiarities of style, are confined to these chapters, and if the last verse was inserted by an editor to mark the close of a division he appears to have been guided so far by a sound instinct. In the remainder of the prophecy it is not so easy to fix on any particular point as marking more than others a fresh departure in the argument; but on the whole the greatest break seems to occur at the end of ch. lv. (so Duhm and Cheyne, and many of the latest writers).

[2] G. A. Smith, *Exposition*, Vol. II. p. 72.

They mean that the night of Israel's affliction is far spent and the day of deliverance is at hand (*vv*. 1, 2). The prophet hears the music of heavenly voices, telling him of spiritual agencies already in motion which will issue in the restoration of the exiles to their own land (*vv*. 3—5); assuring him also that all human resistance must fail before the eternal energy of the Divine word (*vv*. 6—8). The return from captivity is conceived (as throughout these first nine chapters) as a triumphal march of Jehovah through the desert at the head of His ransomed people; and the prelude ends with the arrival of the ideal messengers who call upon Jerusalem and the cities of Judah to behold their God (*vv*. 9—11).

(2) The following paragraph (*vv*. 12—31) introduces a theme frequently recurring in the first nine chapters, the incomparable power, the unsearchable wisdom, in a word, the *infinity* of Israel's God. In order to remove the despondency which has settled on the minds of his fellow-exiles (*vv*. 27—31) the writer dwells at length on the evidences of Jehovah's might and wisdom, to be observed especially in the works of creation (*vv*. 12—17, 26), and takes occasion to shew the inherent absurdity of idolatry (*vv*. 18—20), in proof that such gods as those of Babylon are powerless to thwart the purposes of the one true God.

(3) In ch. xli. the prophet touches for the first time on the historical situation which is to be explained by the truths just unfolded. (*a*) The sudden appearance of Cyrus as a great world-conqueror engrosses the attention of mankind. This fact is splendidly dramatised, in the conception of a great assembly of the nations, to whom Jehovah propounds the questions, Who has raised him up? Who has given him such astonishing success (xli. 1—7)? (*b*) Turning aside for a moment to assure Israel, Jehovah's servant, that he has nothing to fear from these political convulsions, which on the contrary shall issue in his final deliverance and victory (*vv*. 8—20), the prophet (*c*) resumes and completes the argument left unfinished at *v*. 7 (*vv*. 21—29). That Jehovah, and not any of the heathen gods, has raised up Cyrus is proved to demonstration by the fact that He

alone has foreseen and predicted the event; this *argument from prophecy* is another prominent feature of chs. xl.—xlviii.

(4) (*a*) Ch. xlii. 1—4 is the first of four portraits of Jehovah's *ideal* Servant which are amongst the most remarkable passages in the book. This great personage is here introduced as the object of Jehovah's peculiar regard, and as endowed with the Divine spirit for the accomplishment of his mission, which is to teach the true religion to the world (*v.* 1). His manner of working is described as unobtrusive and gentle and helpful; yet he fails not nor is discouraged until his labours are crowned with complete success (*vv.* 2—4). (*b*) In the next verses (5—9) the portrait just sketched is made the ground of encouragement to Israel, Jehovah, as it were, pledging His Godhead to the fulfilment of the ideal in the people's experience. (*c*) The prophet's thoughts being thus led forward to the redemptive act through which Israel's destiny will be realised, he breaks into a short lyric outburst of praise (*vv.* 10—12); after which Jehovah Himself is represented as arousing Himself from His long inactivity to bring about the deliverance of His people (*vv.* 13—17). (*d*) In contrast with the ideal of *vv.* 1—4, the condition of Israel, Jehovah's *actual* servant, is next described (*vv.* 18—25). Blind and deaf, ignorant of the meaning of its own history, it has utterly mistaken its true calling, and as a consequence has been overwhelmed by the immeasurable calamity of the Exile, and been brought to the verge of destruction. (*e*) Yet the Divine election stands immutable; Israel is still Jehovah's servant, and precious in His sight; it shall be ransomed at the cost of the most opulent and powerful nations of the world, and its scattered members shall be brought together from all parts of the earth (xliii. 1—7).

(5) (*a*) But there is at least one function which Israel with all its failures and defects is still capable of performing: it is Jehovah's *witness* to the fact that He has foretold the events that are happening. This thought is again dramatised in a judgement-scene, where the idols are challenged to bring forward, if they can, any similar attestation of their divinity; it would seem also that, in the very act of witness-bearing, Israel's

eyes are at length opened to the significance of this great truth and the character of its God (*vv.* 8—13). (*b*) In xliii. 14 the first explicit announcement of the impending fate of Babylon occurs, introducing a description of the marvels of the new Exodus, for which the way is thus prepared (*vv.* 14—21). (*c*) Israel, indeed, has not merited this deliverance, but Jehovah for His own sake blots out its transgressions and promises to remember them no more (*vv.* 22—28). (*d*) The reconciliation is final and complete; a brilliant future lies before the nation, in which strangers shall esteem it an honour to attach themselves to the religion and the people of Jehovah (xliv. 1—5).

(6) Ch. xliv. 6—23 repeats the argument from prophecy for the sole deity of Jehovah (*vv.* 6—8); confirms this by the most elaborate and sarcastic exposure of the irrationalities of idolatry that the book contains (*vv.* 9—20); and appeals to the Israelites to lay these truths to heart and cleave to the God who forgives sin and is alone able to deliver (*vv.* 21—23).

(7) The passage ch. xliv. 24—xlv. 25 is an important series of oracles dealing mainly with the mission of Cyrus and its effects in the universal diffusion of the worship of Jehovah. (*a*) The subject is led up to in xliv. 24—28, a majestic period, where Jehovah, describing Himself as the God of creation and prophecy, at last announces His commission to Cyrus to rebuild Jerusalem and the Temple. (*b*) Cyrus is next addressed in person by Jehovah, who bestows on him the title of His anointed (*Messiah*), and promises him an uninterrupted course of victory, at the same time declaring that it is only in the interest of Israel that he is thus honoured (xlv. 1—7). (*c*) After a short poetic interlude (*v.* 8) the prophet turns to rebuke the murmurs of dissent which this novel announcement calls forth among some of his fellow-exiles (*vv.* 9—13). (*d*) And now at length he reaches what may be regarded as the highest flight of his inspired imagination. As a consequence of the signal exaltation of Israel, achieved through the victories of Cyrus, the conquered nations renounce their idols and do homage to Israel as the people of the one true God (*vv.* 14—17). (*e*) But further, this disclosure of the character and Godhead of Jehovah

becomes the source of salvation to the world at large. What He has always been to Israel,—a God revealing Himself in clear unambiguous oracles,—that the heathen shall recognise Him to be; and all the ends of the earth shall look unto Him and be saved (*vv.* 18—25).

(8) The next two oracles deal with the fall of Babylon. In ch. xlvi. the principal subject is the collapse of the Babylonian state-religion. A striking contrast is drawn between the ignominious flight of the discredited idols, on the back of "weary beasts," and the unchanging strength of Him who sustains the fortunes of His people through all ages of their history.

(9) Ch. xlvii. is a Taunt-song on the humiliation of the imperial city, personified as a "tender and delicate" woman, reduced from wealth and luxury and power to the lowest depth of degradation.

(10) Ch. xlviii. is largely a recapitulation of arguments unfolded in previous chapters, although these are interspersed with rebukes of the obstinacy of the people, more severe than any hitherto uttered. It closes with a jubilant summons to the exiles to depart from Babylon and proclaim to all the world the story of their redemption.

(B) Chs. xlix.—lv. The work of Jehovah's Servant and the glorification of Zion.

In the second division of the prophecy several lines of thought, which have been very prominent in the first, entirely disappear. The references to Cyrus and the prediction of the fall of Babylon, the appeal to past prophecies now fulfilled, the polemic against idolatry and the impressive inculcation of the sole deity of Jehovah, all these now familiar topics henceforth vanish from the writer's argument. But one great conception is carried over from the first part to the second, and forms an important link of connexion between them. This is the figure of Jehovah's ideal Servant, of which there are three further delineations in ch. xlix. 1—6, l. 4—9, and lii. 13—liii. 12. In xlix. 1—6 the Servant himself addresses the nations of the world, expressing his own consciousness of the mission entrusted to him by Jehovah (see xlii. 1—4) and his sense of disappointment

INTRODUCTION.

at the apparent fruitlessness of his labour in the past, but relating also how his misgivings have been removed by a fresh disclosure of Jehovah's ultimate purpose in raising him up, viz. to be the organ of His revelation to the whole human race. The passage is followed (as in xlii. 5 ff.) by a promise of the restoration of Israel, based on the portrait just given of the Servant.—Ch. l. 4—9 is again a soliloquy of the Servant, describing his entire self-surrender to the guidance of the Divine word, his voluntary acceptance of the persecution which he had to endure in the discharge of his mission, and his unwavering confidence in the triumph of his righteous cause through the help of Jehovah.—Ch. lii. 13—liii. 12, the last and greatest of the four "servant-passages," is an account of the sufferings and death of Jehovah's Servant, and a prediction of his future glory. The impression made by his death on the minds of his contemporaries leads them at length to recognise his true mission and produces in them a sense of guilt and sorrow for sin which removes the barrier that had separated them from God.

The other conception which chiefly occupies the mind of the prophet in this section of his discourse is that of Zion, figured as a woman now desolate and bereaved, or drunken with the cup of Jehovah's displeasure, but soon to be clothed in beauty and comforted by reunion to her divine Husband and by the return of her children. This image is developed in a series of passages: ch. xlix. 14—26, li. 17—lii. 6, and liv. There are also exhortations to individual Israelites to prepare themselves for the coming salvation, and lay aside the fears which naturally beset them: l. 1—3, li. 1—16, lv.; while lii. 7—10 gives a second description of the arrival of the herald of salvation at Jerusalem (cf. xl. 9 f.). It will be seen that the whole division continues to unfold the programme sketched in outline in the Prologue (xl. 1—11).

(C) Chs. lvi.—lxvi. The future blessedness of the true Israel contrasted with the doom of the apostates.

The third section of the book is less homogeneous in its composition than the two others. In passing from ch. lv. to ch. lvi. the reader is at once sensible of a change of manner and circumstance, which becomes still more manifest as he proceeds.

(1) Ch. lvi. 1—8 is a short independent oracle on the admission of foreigners and eunuchs to the new Israel,—a matter of administrative detail, altogether unlike the lofty idealism of the previous chapters.

(2) Then follows, in lvi. 9—lix. 21, a series of discourses in which the strain of prophetic rebuke predominates over the note of comfort and encouragement. (*a*) Ch. lvi. 9—lvii. 2 is a strongly worded denunciation of the worthless rulers through whose selfish greed the nation has been left a prey to its enemies. (*b*) Ch. lvii. 3—13 is addressed to an idolatrous community, perpetuating the illegal worship of pre-exilic Israel, and practising in addition many strange and outlandish superstitions. (*c*) This is followed in lvii. 14—21 by a promise of forgiveness and redemption to the true people of God. (*d*) Ch. lviii. states the moral conditions on which the fulfilment of this promise depends, and censures in particular the solemn mockery of the customary fasts, combined as they were with avarice and high-handed oppression. (*e*) In ch. lix. the prophet in the name of the community confesses the great social evils which prevail within it, and utters a promise that Jehovah will speedily interpose to make an end of unrighteousness and perform the gracious word which He has spoken concerning His people.

(3) Chs. lx.—lxii. form a group by themselves, more akin to the spirit of the earlier section of the prophecy, and having a special resemblance to ch. liv. The theme is the felicity of the ideal Zion of the future, which is depicted with a marvellous wealth of imagery and illustration. The material splendour of the restored city, the righteousness of its inhabitants, the subservience of the Gentiles, and the return of the exiles from all parts of the earth, are the features of Zion's glory which bulk most largely in the eye of the prophet.

(4) In ch. lxiii. the tone again changes. *Vv.* 1—6 are a detached oracle,—one of the most graphic pieces of word-painting in the Old Testament,—the subject being Jehovah's return from a great slaughter of His assembled foes in the land of Edom.

(5) Ch. lxiii. 7—lxiv. 12 is a long prayer and confession put

in the mouth of Israel, the most pathetic and plaintive passage in the whole prophecy.

(6) Chs. lxv. and lxvi. contain an alternation of threats and promises, corresponding to the distinction between two classes of hearers which we have already recognised in ch. lvii. The contrast is pushed to the utmost extreme: the true believers are assured of an abiding inheritance in the Holy Land, and an existence of more than natural blessedness in the new heavens and the new earth which Jehovah is about to create; while the apostates are threatened with final destruction, leaving their name for a formula of imprecation, and their dishonoured corpses for an everlasting spectacle to the worshippers in the new Temple.

CHAPTER II.

HISTORICAL BACKGROUND OF THE PROPHECY.

1. AT the time when this prophecy opens Cyrus has appeared on the stage of history and has gained many important victories. In order to determine more precisely the period thus indicated it will be sufficient to bear in mind the following events in the career of this hero, as elucidated by two inscriptions first published in the year 1880[1]. In these Cyrus appears first as king of Ansan, in Elam, the country adjoining Babylonia on the east. Although connected with the royal house of Persia, the particular branch of the family to which he belonged does not appear to have reigned over Persia proper; at all events it is not till the year 546 that he is named as king of Persia. Some years previously he had ascended the throne of Ansan, and speedily gave proof of the commanding ability and energy which were soon to raise him to the front rank among the conquerors of the East. Through the defeat of Astyages in 549

---

[1] See Sayce, in *Records of the Past*, New Series, Vol. v. pp. 144—176.

he annexed Media to his dominions, and laid the foundation of the great Medo-Persian empire which controlled the destinies of Western Asia for more than 200 years. His next great success was the overthrow of Crœsus, the wealthy king of Lydia, whose capital of Sardis, with its fabulous treasures, fell into the hands of Cyrus in B.C. 540[1]. After some months spent in reducing the tribes of "Upper" Asia[2] Cyrus gathered his forces for the attack on Babylon. This crowning enterprise of his life was carried to a successful issue in 538. "In the month Tammuz [June] when Cyrus in the city of Rutu [?], on the banks of the river Nizallat, had delivered battle against the soldiers of Akkad [Northern Babylonia], when the men of Akkad had delivered (battle) the men of Akkad raised a revolt: (some) persons were slain. On the 14th day (of the month) Sippara was taken without fighting; Nabonidus [last king of Babylon] fled. (On) the 16th day Gobryas [general of Cyrus], the governor of the country of Gutium, and the soldiers of Cyrus without fighting entered Babylon." Such is the unvarnished record of the so-called "Annalistic Tablet" of Cyrus[3]; the religious aspect of the event is expressed in remarkable language in his "Cylinder Inscription": "Merodach...appointed also a prince who should guide aright the wish of the heart which his hand upholds, even Cyrus, the king of the city of Ansan; he has proclaimed his title; for the sovereignty of all the world does he commemorate his name...Merodach, the great lord, the restorer of his people, beheld with joy the deeds of his vicegerent, who was righteous in hand and heart. To his city of Babylon he summoned his march; he bade him also take the road to Babylon; like a friend and comrade he went at his side. The weapons of his vast army, whose number, like the waters of a river, could not be known, were marshalled in order, and it spread itself at his side. Without fighting and battle (Merodach) caused him to enter into Babylon; his city of Babylon he spared; in a hiding-place Nabonidus the king, who revered him not, did he give into his hand[4]."

---

[1] Herodotus, I. 73—84.
[2] *Ibid.* I. 177.
[3] Sayce, *loc. cit.*, p. 162.
[4] *Loc. cit.*, pp. 165 f.

The allusions to Cyrus in the prophecy make it perfectly certain that the time to which it refers lies between 549 and 538. Cyrus is mentioned as one already well known as a conqueror, and one whose brilliant victories have sent a thrill of excitement through the world. He is spoken of as having been "raised up from the east" (xli. 2, 25; cf. xlvi. 11), or "from the north" (xli. 25), as one whom "victory attends at every step" (see on xli. 2), who "comes upon rulers as upon mortar, and as the potter treadeth clay" (xli. 25), who "pursues them and passes on in safety," whose movements are so rapid that he appears not to "touch the path with his feet" (xli. 2, 3). Now Cyrus could not have been recognised under such descriptive allusions prior to the conquest of Astyages in 549, when he first became a prominent actor in the political arena. But indeed the language employed is so striking and emphatic as to suggest an even later date, and to make it probable that the prophet has in view the impression created by the first intelligence of the memorable victory over Crœsus in the year 540.

On the other hand, the capture of Babylon is still in the future. Cyrus has not yet reached the climax of his success; "the doors of brass and the bolts of iron" have still to be broken before him; "treasures of darkness, the hidden riches of secret places" are still to be given to him (xlv. 2, 3). It is he who "*shall* execute Jehovah's purpose on Babylon" (xlviii. 14), who "*shall* rebuild My city and let My exiles go free" (xlv. 13; cf. xliv. 28). But this final conquest, bringing in its train the sovereignty of the world (xliii. 3, xlv. 14, li. 5), is imminent; "Jehovah has made bare His holy arm in the eyes of all the nations" (lii. 10) and the decisive blow is about to be struck. The standpoint of the prophecy, therefore, is certainly intermediate between 549 and 538, and most probably about 540 B.C.

2. In perfect harmony with these references to Cyrus are those to the circumstances of Israel. The nation is in exile, but on the eve of deliverance. Jerusalem has undergone a period of hard servitude on account of her sins, but the term of it has now expired; her punishment has been more than adequate (xl. 2). Israel is a people robbed and spoiled, snared in

holes and hid in prison-houses (xlii. 22); the captive crouches in the dungeon (li. 14); the people are repeatedly spoken of as prisoners or bound (xlii. 7, xlix. 9). Such expressions are no doubt largely metaphorical, but the metaphors can denote nothing but a national captivity. The oppressing power is Babylon, the imperial city, still called "mistress of kingdoms" (xlvii. 5), who has laid her yoke very heavily on the aged (*v.* 6). She has said to Israel, "Bow down that we may go over," and caused her to make her back as the ground and as the street to them that go over (li. 23); and it is from Babylon that the exiles are summoned to make good their escape (xlviii. 20, cf. lii. 11 f.). Meanwhile Palestine is a waste and ruined land (xlix. 8, 19, li. 3, lii. 9); Jerusalem is frequently likened to a widowed and bereaved mother mourning the loss of her children, though now comforted with the promise of their restoration (xlix. 14 ff., li. 17 ff., lii. 1 f., liv.). No such calamity as these accumulated allusions imply had ever befallen Israel except in the half century that followed the destruction of the state by the Chaldæans (B.C. 586).

3. One other fact may be noticed, as shewing how completely the prophet's point of view is identified with the age of the Exile. Amongst the arguments most frequently adduced for the deity of Jehovah and against idolatry is the appeal to prophecies fulfilled by the appearance of Cyrus (xli. 26, xlii. 9, xliii. 8—10, xlv. 21, xlvi. 10). What prophecies are referred to is a question of some difficulty, which need not detain us here. It is obvious that whatever they were the argument has no force except as addressed to persons for whom the fulfilment was a matter of experience. To the men of an earlier age such an appeal could only appear as confusing and fallacious, being an attempt to illustrate *ignotum per ignotius*; hence we must conclude that the prophecy was directly intended for the generation of the Exile, and could produce its full effect only on them. It must be observed that neither the appearance of Cyrus nor the captivity of Israel is ever *predicted* in this prophecy; they are everywhere assumed as facts known to the readers. Predictions do occur of the most definite kind, but they are of events

subsequent to those mentioned and lying in advance of the standpoint which the prophet occupies. A distinction is often made by the writer between "former things," which have already come to pass, and "new things" or "coming things" (xli. 22, xlii. 9, xliii. 9, 18 f., xliv. 7, xlv. 11, xlvi. 9, xlviii. 3—8), and in some cases it seems clear that by "former things" he means the fulfilment of earlier prophecies concerning Cyrus, while the "new things," now first announced, are such events as the triumph of Cyrus, the salvation of Israel, and the conversion of the world to the worship of Jehovah. Even on the supposition that the chapters were written by Isaiah, 150 years before any of these occurrences, it still remains true that he does not formally predict the rise of Cyrus, but addresses himself to those who have witnessed it and only require to be told what developments will result from it in the unfolding of Jehovah's purpose[1].

[1] The passages cited above in illustration of the circumstances presupposed by the prophecy are all, it will be observed, taken from the first two divisions (chs. xl.—lv.). It would be possible to supplement the references in some particulars from the later chapters. Not, indeed, with regard to Cyrus, or the argument from prophecy based on his conquests, for these topics are never introduced after ch. xlviii.; but undoubtedly with regard to the desolation of the country (lviii. 12, lxi. 4, lxii. 4, lxiv. 10) and a return of exiled Jews (lvi. 8, lx. 4, 8, lxvi. 20). The reason for not treating these passages as quite on the same footing with those cited in the text is that in the later chapters (lvi.—lxvi.) there are allusions of an opposite character which seem to imply that those there addressed are the Jewish community of Palestine after the Return. Hence there is some uncertainty whether expressions which at first sight seem altogether of a piece with those of the earlier sections have not in reality a different bearing. In fact, it will be found that with scarcely an exception they are more or less ambiguous in their terms. The desolation of the land, for example, must have continued for some time after the first Return; and it is possible that only the condition of the rural districts is described in lviii. 12, lxi. 4 and lxii. 4. The only place where Jerusalem itself is spoken of as desolate is ch. lxiv. 10 f., and this no doubt raises a certain presumption that the capital is *included* in the parallel expressions. But the passage lxiii. 7 —lxiv. 12 presents so many peculiar features that it may be unsafe to generalize from it to the bulk of chs. lvi.—lxvi. In like manner the mention of a restoration of exiles is not inconsistent with the hypothesis of post-exilic origin. The reference may be to the wider dispersion over the civilised world of Israelites whose ingathering continued to be an object of aspiration long after the Jewish state had been reestablished. Even in the verses beginning, "Go through, go through the gates" (lxii.

CHAPTER III.

THE PROPHET'S THEOLOGICAL CONCEPTIONS.

THE religious teaching of chs. xl.—lxvi. has to be considered in the light of the situation sketched in the previous chapter. Although the writer's manner of thinking is more distinctly theological than that of many other prophets, he is nevertheless before all things a prophet, that is, an inspired Interpreter of Jehovah's action in a great crisis of history. No part of the prophetic literature answers more fully to the conception of prophecy implied in the words of Amos: "Surely the Lord Jehovah will do nothing, but he revealeth His secret unto his servants the prophets" (Am. iii. 7). The great event in which this prophet recognises the hand of Jehovah, and of which the secret has been revealed to him, is, as has been already indicated, the advent of Cyrus. Just as the teaching of Amos and Isaiah is dominated by the appearance of the portentous Assyrian power, or that of Jeremiah by the approach of the Chaldæans, so the thoughts of this writer crystallise around the historic figure of Cyrus and the astonishing series of victories which have distinguished his career. It is true he is the first prophet who discerns in the signs of the times a Divine purpose which is from the first a purpose of grace towards Israel. His predecessors had all looked on the world-power as the instrument of Jehovah's chastisement of His people, and had anticipated a happy issue only as a second step, after the earthly instrument had been broken and thrown away. But the writer of these chapters has the word "comfort" constantly on his lips; the whole burden of his message is one of consolation and good

10 f.), so closely resembling xlviii. 20 and lii. 10 f., there is nothing to shew clearly that the gates of Babylon are meant. (See, moreover, Zech. ii. 6, 7,—a post-exilic passage).—The question is perhaps one on which it would be premature to offer a positive opinion, and of course this is not the place to discuss it. But since it was impossible to ignore it in the notes, it is right that attention should be called to the difficulty here. Some further observations will be found in Chapter v. below.

tidings; and he views Cyrus as the chosen agent of Jehovah, not merely in crushing obstacles to the execution of His purpose, but as lending active support in the establishment of His kingdom. Nevertheless the author lives his prophetic life in a time of perplexity and disquietude, when men's hearts failed them for fear; and it is in the disentanglement and solution of a situation which was to all others a hopeless mystery that he realises his vocation as a prophet.

Like other prophets, too, he sees in the events of the time the immediate precursors of Jehovah's everlasting kingdom of righteousness. The final consummation of God's purposes with humanity lies in germ in the appearance of Cyrus; in the writer's own graphic phrase, it already "sprouts" before men's eyes (xlii. 9, xliii. 19). And thus he is led to a prophetic construction of the outward course of events in which many things are left obscure, but of which the salient features are as follows: This Cyrus whom Jehovah has raised up to do His pleasure on Babylon is the destined instrument of Israel's emancipation. He shall let the captives go free; they shall return to Jerusalem in triumphal procession, with Jehovah Himself as their Shepherd,—the wilderness breaking forth before them into springs of water and a luxuriant forest vegetation. The story of this redemption resounds through the world, and the nations, already impressed by the victory of Cyrus, and now convinced that he has been raised up by Jehovah for the sake of Israel, renounce their idolatries and find salvation in the knowledge of the one true God.

The prophet is aware, however, that his hearers are not in a mood to be easily cheered. References to their state of mind are numerous, and nowhere do we find any indication of an enthusiastic response to the prophet's joyful proclamation. When Jehovah came there was no man, when He called there was none to answer (ch. l. 2). Among the exiles were some who are described as "stouthearted, far from righteousness" (xlvi. 12), who rejected the prophet's message and took exception in particular to his designation of Cyrus as the chosen instrument of Israel's release (xlv. 9—13). But the prevalent mood was one of utter weariness and despondency. Israel said, "My way is hid from Jehovah, and my right passes from my God" (xl. 27; cf. xlix. 14). Dismayed by the might of Babylon, and fearing continually because of the oppressor (li. 13), confronted on every hand by the monuments of a vast system of idolatry, the exiles had given way to gloomy thoughts and doubts of the power or willingness of Jehovah to redeem. To counteract this despairing mood something more was needed than a bare announcement of deliverance. The first requisite was to revive their consciousness of God, to impress them with a sense of His infinite power and resources, and the immutability of His word; and also to impart to them a new and inspiring view of their own mission and destiny as a nation. And to this task the writer addresses himself with all the impassioned and persuasive eloquence of which he is an unrivalled master.

JEHOVAH, THE GOD OF ISRAEL.—The prophet's doctrine of God is, accordingly, the fundamental element of his teaching. The book, it has been well said, "is a structure based upon and built out of the Monotheistic conception, the idea that Jehovah, God of Israel, is the true and only God[1]." The author does not differ from earlier prophets in being a monotheist, but he differs remarkably in this that he inculcates the principle almost as an abstract truth of religion, and strives to bring it home to the reason and imagination of his readers. It is perhaps not strictly accurate to say that he sets himself to *prove* any positive truth about Jehovah, although some passages read to us like demonstrations. The existence of Jehovah is assumed, as are also the facts that He is the Creator of the universe and the Disposer of the events of history; and what is built on these assumptions is an attempt to elevate and purify the conceptions of the Israelites and convey to them some worthy idea of what Deity involves. But if anything is made a matter of demonstration, it is the negative conclusion that the idols are not gods, that their helplessness in the face of the facts of history shews them to lack the attributes of Deity, that in short, as there is room for only

[1] A. B. Davidson, *Expositor*, 2nd Series, Vol. VI. p. 81.

one God, the God of Israel has alone made good His right to be so regarded.

The prophet's conceptions of what God is in Himself are most fully set forth in the meditation which immediately follows the Prologue (ch. xl. 12—26). The chief thought is contained in the repeated question, "To whom will ye liken God?" (*vv.* 18, 25). It is the *incomparableness* of Jehovah which the writer seeks to expound and illustrate. This is enforced first of all by an appeal to the works of creation. What sort of Being must He be who "measured the waters in the hollow of His hand, and meted out heaven with the span, and comprehended the dust of the earth in a measure, and weighed the mountains in scales, and the hills in a balance?" (*v.* 12). "Lift up your eyes on high and see! Who hath created these [the starry host]? bringing out their host by number, calling them all by name; because of Him who is great in might and strong in power not one is missing" (*v.* 26). In comparison with such a Being, how insignificant and inappreciable is every form of finite existence! He "sitteth over the circle of the earth and the inhabitants thereof are as grasshoppers" (*v.* 22); "the nations are as a drop from the bucket, and are counted as the small dust of the balance" (*v.* 15). His purposes in history cannot be thwarted by any political combinations, however powerful; for He "bringeth princes to nothing, and maketh the judges of the earth as vanity; hardly have they been planted; hardly have they been sown;...when He bloweth upon them and they wither, and the whirlwind taketh them away as stubble" (*vv.* 23 f.). And if men, singly and collectively, are thus helpless before Him, what shall be thought of those so-called gods which are the work of men's hands? The idol is sufficiently discredited by a description of the process of its manufacture (*vv.* 18—20); it is not merely a "nonentity" (as Isaiah called it), it is a *reductio ad absurdum* of the very conception of deity.

Thoughts similar to these run through the prophecy, especially the first nine chapters. The question, "To whom will ye liken me?" recurs in xlvi. 5; Jehovah's creative activity is touched upon in xlii. 5, xlv. 7, 12, 18, xlviii. 7, liv. 16, lxv. 17 f.

&c. The argument against idolatry is developed in a series of passages (xli. 7, xliv. 9—20, xlvi. 6 f., comp. xli. 23 ff., xlii. 17, xlv. 16, 20, xlvi. 1 f., xlviii. 5) which at once arrest attention by their scathing irony and scorn. Idolatry is as it were laughed out of court, treated as an effete delusion which the world ought long to have outgrown. The consciousness of unique Godhead is attributed to Jehovah in such utterances as, "Before me there was no God formed, neither shall there be after me" (xliii. 10), or "I am God, and there is none else" (xlvi. 9; cf. xliv. 8, xlv. 6, 14, 18, 21 f.). The same truth is expressed when He is called *Qâdôsh* (Holy) absolutely, almost as a proper name (xl. 25); meaning that He alone possesses the attributes that constitute divinity[1]. He is the "First and the Last" (xli. 4, xliv. 6, xlviii. 12), unchanging through all ages, an "Everlasting God," inexhaustible in power and wisdom (xl. 28).

But though Jehovah is thus transcendently exalted, His relation to the world and men upon it is not one of negation or indifference. He did not create the earth for a waste, but to be inhabited (xlv. 18); He is present in all ages of history, calling the generations from the beginning (xli. 4), and moulding their destinies in accordance with His world-wide purpose of salvation. In pursuance of His far-reaching and unsearchable designs He has raised up Israel, calling it from the ends of the earth (xli. 9) to be the organ of His revelation, and now He has raised up the Persian king Cyrus to be the instrument of His final victory over heathenism. In connexion with this unceasing activity of Jehovah in the affairs of men, great stress is laid upon His knowledge of the future and His habit of predicting it. The heathen gods are repeatedly challenged to prove their claim to deity by instances of unambiguous predictions subsequently verified (xli. 22 f., xliii. 9, xliv. 7); while Israel, on the other hand, is appealed to as a witness that Jehovah has foreseen and foretold the future (xliii. 10, xliv. 8). This peculiar test of divinity might appear to be a concession to the mode of thought of the heathen, whose religion consisted in great part in the search for divine prognostications of coming

---

[1] See Vol. I. pp. xlv f.

events. But it has also a positive value for the prophet's own mind, as evidence that events are prearranged by Jehovah in accordance with a fixed and intelligible plan whose goal is the redemption of Israel and the manifestation of the Divine glory to all mankind.

Of the moral (as distinguished from the metaphysical) attributes of God, the most important is His *righteousness*. The prophet's use of this word is somewhat difficult, and it appears to denote more than one aspect of the Divine character[1]. It is plain enough that what is called retributive righteousness, or dealing with men according to their strict deserts, is far too narrow an idea to explain some of its most striking applications. Righteousness is the quality displayed in the raising up of Cyrus (xlv. 13), in the sustaining of Israel, which is ascribed to Jehovah's "right hand of righteousness" (xli. 10), and in the calling of the ideal Servant of the Lord (xlii. 6). But further it is exhibited in Jehovah's manner of revealing Himself; He is One who "speaks righteousness" (xlv. 19); One who in contrast with the false gods is approved as righteous by the verification of His prophecies (xli. 26); a word goes forth from His mouth in righteousness and shall not return (xlv. 23). The general idea suggested by these various usages is perhaps trustworthiness in word and deed, and particularly in the perfect correspondence between word and deed. This implies that Jehovah's actions are all regulated by a consistent and firmly maintained principle, so that when He speaks He but reveals the inner principle which is the true motive of His action; and when He is said to uphold Israel or to raise up Cyrus "in righteousness" the meaning is that He does so in pursuance of a steadfast purpose which He may be relied on to carry through. And since His purpose is ultimately a purpose of salvation, we can understand how so frequently in the prophecy the idea of righteousness tends to become merged in that of salvation. It would, of course, be a paradox to speak of salvation as a divine *attribute*, although the paradox would very nearly represent an important element in the prophet's idea of God. The power and readiness to save men is a standing characteristic of

---

[1] See Appendix, Note II.

Jehovah, which can be predicated of no other god; He is a "righteous and saving God" (xlv. 21); besides Him there is no Saviour (xliii. 11; cf. xlv. 15, 21; xlix. 26). But, speaking strictly, salvation is the outward act which gives effect to Jehovah's purpose; and so we find several passages where righteousness itself ceases to be an attribute and becomes a name for the external manifestation in which the attribute embodies itself (xlvi. 13, li. 6, 8, lvi. 1 b). The same truth is expressed in the frequent application to Jehovah of the verb "redeem" or the epithet "Redeemer" (xli. 14, xliii. 1, xliv. 6, 22 f., 24, &c.; see p. 20). "Salvation," however, is a term of wider import than "redemption." The latter expresses what Jehovah does for His own people of Israel; but the former, although used in the first instance of the deliverance of Israel from Babylon, is a spiritual blessing in which all mankind have an interest. "Israel is saved in Jehovah with an everlasting salvation" (xlv. 17); and the heathen, recognising this, are invited to avail themselves of the same privilege: "Look unto me and be ye saved, all the ends of the earth, for I am God, and there is none else" (v. 22)[1].

[1] The idea of salvation has an instructive history. In Arabic the root *wasiʻa* means to be wide, roomy, spacious, &c.; and hence the Hebr. verb "to save" (which is the causative of this) means primarily "to make room for one," "to give one freedom or space to move in." Even in this form the word contains the germ of a valuable religious idea, salvation being essentially freedom for the normal expansion of man's true life. In the O.T., however, it is always used with express reference to some pressure or impediment, the *removal* of which constitutes the essence of the act called salvation or the state of salvation which results from it (יֵשַׁע, יְשׁוּעָה, תְּשׁוּעָה). In the earlier literature these names have mostly a secular and political application, denoting "succour" in a military sense, or (more frequently) "victory." The religious sense grew naturally out of this. At all times it was recognised that Jehovah is the source of deliverance or victory; but at least from the time of the Exile the centre of gravity of the idea was shifted from the temporal act of deliverance to the partly spiritual blessings which were secured by it. Salvation becomes (as in this prophecy) a comprehensive term for that decisive vindication of Israel's cause which was the foundation of all national well-being. At the same time "these words seldom, if ever, express a spiritual state exclusively; their common theological sense in Hebrew is that of a material deliverance attended by spiritual blessings" (see Driver, *Notes on Samuel*, p. 90).

These are perhaps the most characteristic features in the idea of God as presented in these chapters. It is after all an imperfect statement of the Prophet's conception of God, which is indeed so rich and full as almost to baffle analysis. "Jehovah is to him a living moral Person, possessing all the powers of personality in a degree transcending conception, and shewing all the activities of moral being in perfection[1]." "It would be easy to find in the prophet proof-texts for everything which theology asserts regarding God, with the exception perhaps of the assertion that He is a spirit, by which is meant that He is a particular kind of substance. Neither the prophet nor the Old Testament knows anything of a Divine essence. It does not say that God is spirit, but that He has a spirit; and by spirit is not meant a substance, but an efficiency. The spirit of God is God operating in any way according to the ineffable powers which He possesses as a moral person[2]."

It may be remarked in contrast to what was said of Isaiah in Vol. I. p. l, that the divine tenderness receives full and emphatic expression, as was to be expected from the character of this prophecy. "In an outburst of wrath I hid my face from thee for a moment, but with everlasting kindness will I have mercy upon thee" (liv. 8). Jehovah is compared to a shepherd, gathering the lambs in His arms and carrying them in His bosom, and gently leading those that give suck (xl. 11); and the pathos of this image is even exceeded by one of the latest in the book: "as a man whom his mother comforteth, so will I comfort you" (lxvi. 13). These expressions shew that with all the prophet's insistence on the transcendent perfection of Jehovah, there is no diminution of the vivid sense of His personal being. These chapters contain anthropomorphisms as bold and striking as any to be found in the Old Testament. Jehovah is described as a man of war eager for the fray, as crying like a travailing woman, as gasping and panting with suppressed fury (xlii. 13 f.). He arms Himself for conflict with His enemies, putting on righteousness as a breastplate, clothing

[1] A. B. Davidson, *Expositor*, 2nd Series, Vol. VIII. p. 255.
[2] *Ibid.* p. 253.

Himself with zeal as a cloke, &c. (lix. 16—18). In lxiii. 1—6 He is represented coming up from a great slaughter of His foes, striding in the greatness of His might, and speaking of the day of vengeance that was in His heart. Such delineations are no doubt imaginative, but the images express a truth, and belong as much to the prophet's conception of God as the more abstract and lofty ideas which stand side by side with them in the book.

ISRAEL, THE SERVANT OF JEHOVAH. Remarkable as is the prophet's contribution to the Biblical doctrine of God, it is surpassed in importance and originality by his teaching with regard to the mission of Israel. The very grandeur and universality of his conception of Jehovah appears to necessitate a profounder interpretation of Israel's place in history than any previous prophet had explicitly taught. It might readily appear that a Being so exalted and glorious as Jehovah is here represented to be could not enter into special relations with any particular people of the earth, and that Israel could be no more to Him than the children of the Ethiopians (Am. ix. 7). This inference, which for a special purpose the prophet Amos seemed almost ready to draw, would obviously be fatal to the religion of revelation. It is little to say that this prophet does not accept the conclusion suggested; he repudiates it in the most direct and emphatic manner, declaring that since Israel was precious in His sight, Jehovah gives Egypt as its ransom, Ethiopia and Seba in its stead (xliii. 3). And whether he was conscious of the problem latent in his conceptions or not, it is certain he has provided a solution of it, which lies in the thought that Israel is *elect for the sake of mankind.* Jehovah, as we have already seen, cherishes a purpose of grace towards the whole human race (xlv. 18 ff.), and the meaning of His choice of Israel is that He uses it as His instrument in the execution of that world-wide purpose of salvation.

This view of Israel's position amongst the nations is expressed in the title "Servant of Jehovah," which is applied to the people in passages too numerous to quote (xli. 8, xlii. 19 ff., xliii. 10, 12, xliv. 1 f., 21, xlv. 4, xlviii. 20). In most of these places there is no room for doubt as to the subject which the writer has in his mind. It is the historic nation of Israel, represented in the present chiefly by the community of the Exiles, but conceived throughout as a moral individual whose life and consciousness are those of the nation. The personification is at times extremely bold; as when Israel is said to have been formed "from the womb" (xliv. 1 f.), or when Jehovah speaks of it as having been "borne from the womb," and promises to carry it "even unto old age and hoar hairs" (xlvi. 3, 4); at other times the collective nature of the conception is suffered to appear (xliii. 12, &c.). Still no one who reads the passages can suppose for a moment that anything else than the actual people of Israel is intended. Nor is the writer of these chapters the first who employs the name "servant" in this sense. It is used by Ezekiel in ch. xxviii. 25, xxxvii. 25, where Jehovah speaks of "the land that I have given to Jacob my servant[1]," and it is found also in Jer. xxx. 10, in a sentence which might have been written by our prophet: "Fear thou not, O Jacob my servant, saith Jehovah, neither be dismayed, O Israel," &c. (So also Jer. xlvi. 27.) In itself the designation might mean much or little. As expressing the relation between the people and its national deity, it might mean simply "worshipper" (see Josh. xxiv. 29; Neh. i. 10; Job i. 8; Dan. vi. 20 and often); and this is certainly included; Israel is the Servant of Jehovah as His worshipper, His client, through whom His name is perpetuated among men. But as certainly the prophet's idea goes far beyond this. Comparing the different connexions in which the name occurs, we find the thoughts associated with it to be these two: *first*, that Israel has been adopted by Jehovah of His free grace and brought into a peculiar relation to Himself. The words used are many: "called," "chosen," "created," "formed," "made"; but all these refer to one fact, the formation of the people at the time of the Exodus from Egypt or (it may be) the call of Abraham from Chaldæa. The *second* thought is that of a mission entrusted to the nation of Israel by Jehovah. This is naturally suggested by the word "servant"; and it is made still

---

[1] It is possible, however, in these passages, to understand the expression of Jacob as the ancestor of the nation.

clearer by ch. xlii. 19: "Who is blind but my servant? or deaf as *my messenger that I send?*" and other passages. In so far as the historic Israel is concerned, this mission is fulfilled more by experiences in which it is passive than by its voluntary activity. It has proved itself "blind" and "deaf"; i.e. spiritually unfit for its high vocation (xlii. 19, 20, xliii. 8). Yet as the prophetic nation it has already served an important purpose; it is Jehovah's *witness* to the truth of His prophecy, and through this to the reality of His divinity (xliii. 10, 12, xliv. 8). And this function shall be still more fully realised when the great deliverance through Cyrus has taken place, and the nations of the world shall behold this crowning demonstration of Jehovah's Godhead, and turn to Israel with the confession, "Surely God is in thee; and there is none else, there is no God" (xlv. 14 ff.). In that day Israel shall not be wholly a passive instrument of Jehovah's great purpose; for "I will pour my spirit upon thy seed and my blessing upon thine offspring....One (i.e. from among the heathen) shall say, I am Jehovah's, and another shall call himself by the name of Jacob; and another shall inscribe on his hand 'To Jehovah,' and be titled by the name of Israel" (xliv. 3—5).

But there is another class of passages where this application of the title "Servant of Jehovah" to the actual Israel does not suffice (xlii. 1—4, xlix. 1—6, l. 4—9, lii. 13—liii. 12). We must not overlook the close resemblance between these passages and those spoken of in the last paragraph. The ideas included in the term "servant" are precisely the same in the two cases. New features are added to the description which are inapplicable to the nation as a whole, but still the conception of the office of the ideal Servant does not go beyond the two elements of an election by Jehovah, and a commission to be discharged in His service. What makes it impossible in the last group of passages to suppose that the Servant means Israel simply, is not so much the intense personification of the ideal (although that is very remarkable, and weighs with many minds); it is rather the character attributed to the Servant and the fact that he is distinguished from Israel by having a work to do on behalf of

INTRODUCTION. xxxiii

the nation. He is to raise up the tribes of Jacob and restore the preserved of Israel (xlix. 8), to open blind eyes, to bring out the prisoners from the dungeon (xlii. 7); to "raise up the land, to make them inherit the desolate heritages; to say to them that are bound, Go forth; to them that are in darkness, Shew yourselves" (xlix. 8, 9). That is, he is to be the agent in Jehovah's hand of effecting the release of Israel from captivity and of restoring it to its own land. Nay more, he endures persecution and opposition from his own countrymen (l. 6—9), and dies the death of a martyr at their hands (liii. 1—9). His sufferings and death constitute an atonement for the sins of his people, so that with his stripes they are healed (liii. 4—6, 8). He is one also who is in conscious and perfect sympathy with Jehovah's purpose in raising him up; he is neither blind nor deaf, but alert and sensitive and responsive to the divine voice (l. 4, 5). So conscious is he of his mission and so eager to succeed in it, that he speaks of himself as depressed and discouraged by its apparent failure so long as it was limited to the conversion and instruction of his own people (xlix. 4), and correspondingly cheered when it is revealed to him that his work has a larger scope, even the gathering of the whole race into the fold of the true religion (xlix. 5, 6). To this wider outlook there is attached the assurance of a signal success (xlii. 1, 4), which shall excite the astonishment of the nations and potentates of the world (xlix. 7, lii. 13—15, liii. 10—12).

The question, who is meant by the Servant of Jehovah in these delineations is perhaps the most difficult problem in the exposition of these chapters. Of the many views that have been propounded (see Appendix, Note I.) there are but two which call for consideration here.

1. A large number of expositors hold that the term "Servant of Jehovah" always, in some sense, denotes Israel. They regard it as inconceivable that the prophet should apply the same title to two distinct subjects without so much as a hint that there is a double application in his mind. It is all the more difficult to suppose that this should be the case, because the predicates associated with the title are essentially identical in all

its uses. The Servant is throughout one called and upheld by Jehovah, and destined to be the organ through whom He carries out His purpose of establishing His universal kingdom. It is true that the subject of the personification cannot in every case be the actual Israel, or the nation *en masse*, for it has been shewn that the characteristics of the Servant are in some instances the opposite of those displayed by the bulk of the people. But if the Servant cannot in such passages be the literal historic nation, he may still be Israel according to its true vocation and destiny, the ideal Israel which has existed in the mind of God from the beginning, and which would yet emerge on the stage of history in the nation purified and redeemed from the sorrows of the Exile. It may be urged against this theory that the Servant is represented as one who has an experience and a history behind him (xlix. 4 ff., l. 6, liii. 1—9); and to many it may appear a contradiction that an ideal should have a history of the kind depicted. A still more serious difficulty is thought to lie in the fact that the Servant labours and suffers for the good of Israel, and in particular is the agent of its deliverance from captivity. These objections are forcible, but they are partly met by the consideration that the ideal has been approximately realised in a section of the people who had worked for the conversion of their nation, and on whose minds there had dawned the more glorious hope of being a light to the Gentiles. The conception is not free from difficulty, but there is nothing unnatural in the supposition that the experiences of this godly kernel of Israel should be ascribed to the ideal which is partly manifest in them or that this ideal when personified should be called by the name of Israel. And the fact that he is the agent of the people's redemption may be explained in a similar way: the ideal stands for the destiny of the nation, and since it is for the sake of the ideal embodied in the Servant that Jehovah in His providence brings to pass the redemption of Israel, the whole process of deliverance might, in the personification, be ascribed to the Servant.

2. Other writers, however, are not satisfied with this explanation, and think that the Servant of Jehovah must in some cases

be an individual yet to arise, who shall embody in himself all the characteristics that belong to the divine idea of Israel. It is a question of inferior importance whether the figure be a modification of the conception of the Messianic king, or an independent creation, which was only shewn by the fulfilment to be identical with the Messiah of other prophets. Now such a conception is in itself perfectly intelligible and natural. We might suppose, for example, that the author took up the expression, "Servant of Jehovah," and under the guidance of the Spirit of God threw out a portrait of what the ideal Servant of the Lord must be, and that there was imparted to him the conviction that an individual answering to this portrait would appear in the immediate future. But in the connexion in which the idea occurs in this prophecy, the explanation is encumbered by certain difficulties. Besides the exegetical difficulty arising from the application of the same title to subjects entirely different, there is this further objection that the course of events as conceived by the prophet does not appear to afford space for the evolution which it is necessary to suppose. The Servant on the hypothesis has yet to appear (for it is impossible to think that the writer speaks of a contemporary known to him), has to be misjudged, rejected, maltreated and put to death by his countrymen; then the thoughts of his generation concerning him have to undergo a revolution (ch. liii. 9); and only after all this has taken place can the people look for his resurrection and the deliverance from exile which he is to effect. The process described obviously demands time, and we cannot help asking whether it is credible that this should be the meaning of the prophet who penned the hasty summons to escape from Babylon (xlviii. 20, lii. 11, 12) and gives many another indication that he regards the deliverance as imminent. If, on the other hand, the Servant be a personification of the ideal of Israel, the greater part of the process lies already behind the prophet. The popular misapprehension of the Servant's mission, his persecution, his martyrdom, have been accomplished in the persons of those Israelites in whom the ideal of Israel was partly exhibited; the revulsion of feeling, so profoundly conceived and described in ch. liii., is perhaps a process which the prophet sees taking place around him; and all that remains for the future is the Servant's rising from the dead, which is, on this theory, but a figure for the national restoration.

Each hypothesis, therefore, has its own peculiar attractions and difficulties; and it is natural that commentators should differ as to which furnishes on the whole the most satisfactory solution. Perhaps the point that requires most to be insisted on as a matter of fair historical interpretation is that in the prophet's mind the crisis of the Servant's career is somehow bound up with the fortunes of Israel in the age of the Exile. "Not to raise the question of the Servant here, whether he be Israel or another, the way in which the prophet himself takes up his own words towards the end of his prophecy, and, speaking of Israel restored, says, 'The Gentiles shall come to thy light' (lx. 3), shews that at any rate the Servant shall come into communion with the Gentiles through Israel redeemed, and in this way become their 'light.' Any missionary enterprises of individuals, however exalted, could not occur to the prophet. Like all prophets of the Old Testament he operates with nations and peoples. And if the nations are to receive 'light' through Israel, it will be through Israel, again an imposing people before the world's eyes, just as the Law goes forth from Zion and the word of the Lord from Jerusalem (Isa. ii.)[1]."

The value of the conception as a prophetic delineation of the character and work of our Lord is in no way affected by the view we may be led to adopt regarding its inception in the mind of the prophet. All Christian interpreters agree that the ideal has been fulfilled but once in history, in the person of Jesus Christ, in whom all the features of the divine ideal impressed on Israel have received adequate and final expression. Perhaps we may go further and say that to us it is clear that the ideal could only be realised in a personal life at once human and divine; only, we have no right to say that this must have been equally evident to the prophet in his day. The significance of his teaching does not lie in any direct statement that in some future age an individual should arise bearing this image,—a

---

[1] A. B. Davidson, *Expositor*, 2nd Series, VII. p. 91.

statement which he never makes—; it consists in the marvellous degree in which he has been enabled to foreshadow the essential truths concerning the life and mission of the Redeemer. This is a fact which nothing can obscure, and which is attested for us, if it needed attestation, by the application of these passages to Christ in the New Testament. But just as it is certain that the prophecy was not fulfilled in the precise way that the writer expected (viz., as an element of Israel's restoration from Babylon), so it is a legitimate question for historical exegesis what kind of basis the ideal had in his thoughts,—"a real or an ideal man, a man of flesh and blood, who, as he foresaw, would appear in the world, or an ideal man, in one sense the creation of his own mind, though in another sense existing from the moment of Israel's call and creation, all down its history, and to exist for ever[1]."

ISRAEL AND THE GENTILES.—The state of things which follows the redemption of Israel is an age of universal salvation in which all nations share in the blessings that flow from a knowledge of the true God. That Israel is to enjoy a religious primacy among the peoples of the world might be assumed from the general position of the Old Testament on this subject, and is expressly asserted in ch. lxi. 5, 6, where the Jews are spoken of as the future priesthood of humanity. The manner in which the world is to be converted to the religion of Israel and of Jehovah is variously represented. In the first place, it is the direct result of the victories of Cyrus, the "Anointed" of Jehovah. For this purpose Jehovah has raised him up, "that men may know from the rising of the sun and from the west, that there is none beside Me" (xlv. 6). The effect on the heathen nations is described in vv. 14—17 of the same chapter; and it is noteworthy that it is not merely a negative effect, leading them to repudiate their false gods, but involves some positive revelation of the character of the God of Israel. "Only in thee (Israel) is God, and there is none else; there is no God. Verily thou art a God that hidest thyself, O Saviour-God of Israel" (vv. 14, 15). Of the same nature are passages where the forthputting of Jehovah's

---

[1] A. B. Davidson, *Expositor*, VIII. p. 450.

might is spoken of as the means of convincing men of His Godhead: "mine arms shall judge the peoples; the isles shall wait for me, and on mine arm shall they trust" (li. 5; cf. lii. 10, lxvi. 19, &c.). In the second place, the conversion of the heathen is the work of Jehovah's ideal Servant, and is accomplished partly by his doctrine ("the isles wait for his teaching," xlii. 4) and the prophetic word which is placed in his mouth (xlix. 2), partly by the spectacle of his startling elevation from extreme abasement to the highest influence and glory (lii. 13—15). He is thus set for a "light to the Gentiles," to be God's salvation to the ends of the earth (xlix. 6); he "shall not fail nor be discouraged, till he have set judgement (i.e. true religion) in the earth" (xlii. 4). The attitude towards the Gentiles expressed in these "servant-passages" is singularly sympathetic and even appreciative. They are likened to "crushed reeds" and "smoking wicks" (xlii. 3); that is, they are conceived as possessing some natural virtue, which is ready to expire for lack of a true faith, but which the Servant's tender and helpful ministry will strengthen and fan into a glowing flame. Once more, in the later chapters of the prophecy, the salvation of the heathen is ascribed to the impression made by the unimagined splendour of the new Jerusalem, which is the one centre of light in a benighted world. "For, behold, darkness shall cover the earth, and gross darkness the peoples; but upon thee shall Jehovah arise and his glory shall be seen upon thee. And nations shall come to thy light, and kings to the brightness of thy rising" (lx. 2, 3). The conception of the future kingdom of God becomes perhaps on the whole less ideal and more material towards the end of the book than in the early chapters. The blessedness of Israel contains moral and spiritual elements (lx. 21, lxi. 3, 11, lxii. 2, lxv. 24, lxvi. 10— 13, &c.); but great stress is laid on its external magnificence and prosperity; on the architectural beauties of Jerusalem (liv. 11 f., lx. 13, 17), on its wealth (lx. 5—7, 9, 13, 16, lxi. 6, lxvi. 12) and security in the enjoyment of temporal blessings (lvii. 13, lxii. 8 f., lxv. 9 f., 21 ff.), and its abundant population (xlix. 17 ff., liv. 1 ff., lxvi. 7 ff.). So the relation of the Gentiles to the true God is represented as one of subservience to Israel, the people of God:

they shall "bow down to thee with their faces to the earth, and lick the dust of thy feet" (xlix. 23; cf. lx. 14), placing their wealth at the disposal of Israel (lx. 6 f., 11, 16, lxi. 6, lxvi. 12) and performing menial offices in its service (lx. 10, lxi. 5). But the subjection is on the whole represented as a voluntary one on the part of the nations, as is shewn by their goodwill in escorting the exiles back (xlix. 22, lx. 4, 9, lxvi. 20), and the honourable function assumed by them as guardians of the new community (xlix. 23, lxvi. 12). They are animated by a sincere desire to share in the religious privileges which are dispensed through Israel, and willingly acknowledge the superior position belonging to it, as the seed which the Lord hath blessed (lxi. 6, 9). The thought expressed by these images is still the universal diffusion of the true religion; the Temple becomes a "house of prayer for all peoples" (lvi. 7), and "all flesh" comes to worship before Jehovah at Jerusalem (lxvi. 23).

CHAPTER IV.

Date and Authorship of the Prophecy.

An attempt must now be made to present a summary of the evidence for and against the Isaianic authorship of chs. xl.—lxvi.[1] In doing so it is right to begin with the arguments that have led a majority of critics to regard the prophecy as a work composed towards the close of the Exile[2]. Tradition has its prescriptive

[1] The present chapter is largely indebted to Driver's admirable (and of course much fuller) statement of the evidence in his *Isaiah*[2], pp. 185—212.

[2] Döderlein, in 1775, was the first modern scholar who took up this position. Before then the traditional view does not seem to have been questioned except by the Jewish commentator Aben Ezra († 1167 A.D.), who, in very obscure language, appears to hint that the title of the book does not guarantee the authorship of every part of it, any more than in the case of the books of Samuel, of which Samuel himself could only have written the first 24 chapters (his death being recorded in 1 Sam. xxv. 1). Döderlein has been followed, among others, by Gesenius, Ewald, Hitzig, Knobel, Umbreit, de Wette, Bleek, Bunsen, Cheyne, Kuenen, Reuss, Duhm, Oehler, A. B. Davidson, Orelli, König, Driver,

rights, and its assertions are not to be questioned except on adequate grounds. But where, as in the present case, it is challenged by a large body of critical opinion, it is necessary to form some estimate of the value of this opinion before proceeding to test the traditional view which opposes it. Following the example of Driver we may arrange the internal evidence under three heads: (1) that derived from the historical presuppositions of the prophecy; (2) that furnished by the prophet's conceptions; and (3) that of his style and language.

1. The most important element in the critical argument is the inference to be naturally drawn from the *historical situation* presupposed by the prophecy, as described in Chapter II. It is impossible here to add anything to what was there said; and it is the less necessary to do this, since the case is freely admitted by the ablest opponents of the critical position to be as stated[1]. It may therefore be taken as proved that the prophet's apparent position is in the Captivity, and it only remains to be considered

---

G. A. Smith, Kirkpatrick, Delitzsch (in the 4th Ed. of his *Comm.* 1890), &c. Amongst the defenders of the Isaianic authorship the best-known names are those of Hengstenberg, Hävernick, Drechsler, Delitzsch (down to about 1880), Stier, Rutgers, Kay, Nägelsbach, Douglas, &c.

[1] Delitzsch, writing in 1857 as a defender of the Isaianic authorship, says: "The author of Isa. xl.—lxvi. finds himself amongst the exiles, and preaches to them with a pastor's most particular concern for their varied moral circumstances.... If the author had another situation actually present before him, he is as it were completely detached from it. In vain one looks in the course of these 27 chapters for an indication that the prophet distinguishes his ideal from his actual present, that he turns back from Babylon, where he is in spirit, to the yet undestroyed Jerusalem, where he receives his message, that his consolation and admonition ever turn aside from the people of the Exile to the people of the Holy Land, from the future generation to his own contemporaries. This nowhere happens; he lives and moves entirely in the Exile, there and nowhere else is the home of his thoughts" (Drechsler's *Isaiah*, III. p. 389). Hengstenberg's admissions are less sweeping, but perhaps on that account all the more significant. "The prophet, in the whole of the second part, assumes his standpoint *as a rule*...in the time when Jerusalem was conquered by the Chaldaeans, &c....In this period he thinks, feels and acts; it has become to him the present, from which he looks out into the future, yet in such a manner that he *does not everywhere maintain this ideal standpoint*" (*Christologie*, II. 193). Similar testimonies could be quoted from other writers.

whether it is credible that his actual position should be different from this.

No question is here raised of the *possibility* of such a projection of the prophetic standpoint into the remote future as is implied in the assumption that Isaiah wrote these chapters. The only question is whether the phenomenon be probable, judged by the analogy of prophecy itself. Now it is perfectly true that the prophets do sometimes take up an ideal standpoint from which events really future are spoken of as if they were past. But no passage can be found which presents any real parallel to the case before us if Isaiah be the writer of this prophecy. In all other instances the adoption of a future standpoint is but a sudden and transient flight of the prophet's imagination, from which he speedily reverts to his actual present; no example can be produced of a prophet immersing himself, as it were, in the future, and gathering round him all the elements of a definite and complex historical situation, and forecasting from it a future still more distant. Moreover, none of the alleged parallels violate the invariable rule that the prophets address themselves in the first instance, and chiefly, to the men of their own time. Their descriptions of the future are meant for the instruction and guidance of their own contemporaries, whether the tenses used be past or future. But if Isaiah wrote these chapters he absolutely ignores his contemporaries, alluding to circumstances of which they were not cognisant, and using arguments (p. xx above) which had no force for them. There is therefore nothing in the nature of prophecy to lessen the inherent improbability that the prophet's actual standpoint is at variance with what is acknowledged to be his ideal standpoint. Nothing seems left for the consistent upholders of the traditional theory but to admit that the phenomenon is unique, and to urge (as Stier does) that there are other unique facts in history which no one dreams of questioning. That again is perfectly true, and if the fact were established no one would have a right to disbelieve it merely because nothing like it could be found elsewhere. But so long as the probability of the fact in itself is under discussion, to admit that it is unique is virtually to concede the whole matter in dispute.

By some, however, it is denied that the exilic standpoint is consistently maintained[1], and expressions are cited (principally from chs. lvi.—lix.) which are thought to shew that the writer lived before the Exile. These passages have an important bearing on the unity of the prophecy, a point on which something will have to be said in Chapter V.[2] In the present argument the unity of the book must be assumed, for obviously if that be abandoned the passages in question will speak only for themselves, and will not affect the authorship of the much more important parts of the prophecy where no such references occur. Let us suppose, then, that the allusions are really to the age of Manasseh, and that Isaiah was then alive and might have witnessed the state of things there described; what we have to consider is, For whose benefit are these descriptions penned? If it were seriously maintained that they are directly addressed to the contemporaries of Isaiah's old age, there would be some plausibility in the contention that he is the writer of them. But this is not said by any believer in the unity of the prophecy. It is admitted that, like the rest of the book, they are spoken to the generation of the Exile. And if this be so, it is at least as likely that they were written by a prophet living in the Exile (who may have availed himself of older written material) as that they were prepared for this purpose beforehand by Isaiah himself. In either case the implication must be that the exiles shared the guilt of their forefathers' idolatries, as not having disowned them by a genuine repentance; and that idea is perhaps more natural, certainly not less natural, in the mind of an exilic prophet, than in the mind of one living five generations before.

Another argument is based on the repeated allusions in the prophecy to predictions already fulfilled. Strangely enough it has been supposed that these predictions must be those of the prophecy itself, and from this assumption the inference is deduced that it must have been written long before the fulfilment in the age of the Exile. This is almost as much as to say

---

[1] See the quotation from Hengstenberg on p. xl, above.
[2] See pp. lv ff.

that the prophecy must have been written before it was written. It makes the book to be at once a prediction and an appeal to the fulfilment of its own prediction in proof of its divine authority, a thing which is certainly without analogy in the prophetic literature. The writer is responsible for no such confusion. He nowhere says or implies that the fulfilled predictions were uttered by himself, still less that they are contained in this book. He distinguishes in the clearest manner between the predictions that have come to pass and those that still await their verification[1]. He himself claims to be the medium of new prophecies concerning the deliverance of Israel and the glorious future to follow, but he does not claim to be the author of those to which he triumphantly appeals as evidences of the Divine foreknowledge. What prophecies they were that he had in view we cannot now determine, but they were predictions of the rise and conquests of Cyrus, and these are events which he himself never predicts but always assumes as known.

The reader must be left to form his own judgement on the considerations thus far submitted. But unless they can be neutralised by evidence from some other quarter it is difficult to resist the conclusion that they constitute a strong presumption in favour of the exilic authorship of the prophecy.

2. We have next to compare the *leading ideas* of the prophet's theology, as described in Chapter III., with those characteristic of Isaiah (Vol. I. pp. xliii—lxiii). Arguments from this source may seem to many less cogent than either those derived from historical allusions or those based on a comparison of language. It may be thought that a prophet's ideas, being communicated to him through divine inspiration, are independent of the ordinary laws of human thinking. Or, again, it may be said that the ideas in the second part of the book are the development of those in the first, and that it is impossible to distinguish the development which takes place in a single mind from that which is wrought out in the course of several generations. But a thoughtful reader of the Old Testament would be slow to entertain the first of these suggestions, because it is absolutely

---

[1] See p. xxi above.

certain that the prophetic inspiration was not an influence which suppressed the human individuality of the writers or suspended the normal operations of their minds. And when every allowance is made for the possibility of development within the limits of the individual mind, it still remains in some degree improbable that a prophet like Isaiah, who through a long life operates with one set of distinctive conceptions, should in the end abandon them, and adopt others of a different character.

There is a difference, (*a*) first of all, in the conception of God as presented in the two parts of the book. The writer of chs. xl. ff. loves to expatiate on the infinitude and eternity of Jehovah, on His incomparableness, on the fact that He is the universal Creator, the bestower of Life, the omnipresent ruler of history. Universality, indeed, may be said to be the distinctive feature in the writer's thoughts about God. These truths are no doubt implicitly contained in Isaiah's idea of God, but we search his undisputed prophecies in vain for any direct inculcation of them. If they do not belong of necessity to a later stage of revelation, they are at least more intelligible in an age when Israel's views of the world had been expanded by the breaking up of the political system in which Isaiah's life was spent, and by direct contact with the power and civilisation of the greatest empire of the world. (*b*) Again, one of Isaiah's most characteristic doctrines is that of the elect remnant of Israel, which is to survive the judgement and inherit the promise of the future. This doctrine is not, indeed, wholly absent from the later chapters (see lix. 20, lxv. 8, 9), but it occupies a very insignificant and subordinate place and "is not more prominent than it is in the writings of many later prophets[1]." (*c*) On the other hand, the mission and destiny of Israel as a whole are expounded in these chapters in a manner to which there is no parallel in the uncontested writings of Isaiah. (*d*) To take one more example, perhaps the most striking of all, the central position occupied by the Messianic King in the writings of Isaiah is assumed in chs. xl. ff. by the entirely distinct figure of the Servant of Jehovah. It

---

[1] Driver (*Isaiah*[2], p. 206), who instances Am. v. 15, ix. 9; Mic. ii. 12, v. 7 f.; Zeph. iii. 13; Jer. iv. 27, xxx. 11, xxxi. 7.

is possible (though denied by most expositors) that there is a single allusion to the Messianic King in ch. lv. 3, 4. But even if this be the case, it only illustrates the wholly secondary position which the idea holds in the writer's thinking. Nor can it be supposed that the figure of the Servant of Jehovah is a form into which that of the Messiah might have developed at a late stage in Isaiah's career; it is a new creation, resting on different analogies, an idealisation not of the King, but of the Prophet. Many other points of difference might be adduced, if space permitted; but these are perhaps sufficient. They relate to features which are distinctive, on the one side or the other, and there are no conceptions at all distinctive in which the two sections of the book agree. Whatever weight, therefore, may be assigned to these considerations, it is at least undeniable that they point rather to diversity than to identity of authorship.

3. The evidence of *style* and *language* is very decidedly against the probability that Isaiah is the author of chs. xl.—lxvi. The general style of these chapters presents in many respects a strong contrast to that of Isaiah. The difference is one to be felt rather than described; and it may readily be felt, even through the medium of a translation. Speaking broadly, it may be said that Isaiah's style is distinguished by force and compression, while that of the later chapters is profuse and flowing, with a marked tendency to amplification and repetition. Isaiah, with the exception of a few favourite and graphic phrases, rarely repeats himself, and never dilates, but the writer of chs. xl.—lxvi. constantly reverts to a few fixed themes, in language which might be monotonous if it were not always impressive. In illustration of this full and expansive manner of expression, two stylistic peculiarities may be mentioned, to neither of which is there any strict parallel in Isaiah: (1) the duplication of the opening word of a sentence or of some other emphatic word (xl. 1, xliii. 11, 25, xlviii. 11, 15, li. 9, 12, 17, lii. 1, 11, lvii. 6, 14, lxii. 10, lxv. 1); and (2) the habit of attaching a series of descriptive participial (or relative) clauses to the name of God, or Israel, or Cyrus (see xl. 22 f., 28 f., xli. 8 f., 17, xlii. 5, xliii. 16 f., xlv. 7, 18, xlvi. 10 f., &c., and especially the splendid passage xliv. 24—28).

A corresponding difference of imaginative quality may also be detected: each writer is gifted in an unusual degree with the sense of the sublime; but the sublimity of Isaiah's images is that of concentrated (often destructive) energy, while the later writer's imagination revels chiefly in the thought of physical magnitude (the spacious heavens, the innumerable starry host, the mountains, the coast-lands, &c.). There is besides a strain of pathos in the imagery of the later part of the book which is absent from that of Isaiah (see Driver, *Isaiah*[2], pp. 182 ff.).

But the linguistic argument is capable of being brought to a definite test by a comparison of the words and phrases characteristic of the two portions of the book. There is of course a large number of expressions common to both, and imposing lists of such expressions have been drawn up for the purpose of shewing that the style is the same. But on examination these lists shrink to very insignificant dimensions, and really prove little more than that both sections are written in good Hebrew[1]. The only coincidences which arrest attention are the three following: (1) Isaiah's designation of Jehovah as "the Holy One of Israel," which occurs fourteen times in chs. xl.—lxvi., and only five times outside the book of Isaiah. This is undoubtedly an important link of connexion. But it has to be observed that a phrase like this, expressing an important theological idea, is just one of those likely to be borrowed by one writer from another, and therefore, unless supported by other resemblances, it hardly counts in the argument for unity of authorship. (2) The

---

[1] For example, a list of 34 such words is given by Cheyne (not of course with the object of proving identical authorship) in his *Introduction*, pp. 251 ff. If the reader will take the trouble to go through this list, and strike out (1) words which are found in chs. i.—xxxix. only in passages probably not written by Isaiah, and (2) those found only once in either part of the book, and therefore not as a rule distinctive of its style, he will find that not more than *six* remain. These are "*seek Jehovah*," *Jacob*, "*house of Jacob*," "*high and lifted up*," *tôrâh* (= instruction), and a rare form of the preposition *from*. All these except the fourth are frequent in other writings. A list of 7 divine titles (*ibid.* p. 254) is equally indecisive, except as regards "*the Holy One of Israel*," which is discussed above.

divine title "Mighty One ('*ăbîr*) of Israel (or Jacob)" occurs in ch. i. 24, xlix. 26, and lx. 16 (also in Gen. xlix. 24; Ps. cxxxii. 2, 5). The coincidence is not important, since the phrase is obviously borrowed by the various writers from the blessing of Jacob (Gen. xlix. 24). Moreover ch. lx. 16 is clearly a quotation from xlix. 26. (3) The formula "saith Jehovah," with the imperfect tense instead of the usual perfect. This is found in ch. i. 11, 18, xxxiii. 10, xl. 1, 25, xli. 21, lxvi. 9; also in Ps. xii. 5. It must be admitted that this is a stylistic peculiarity *of the kind* which would establish literary identity, but being an almost solitary instance, it has little weight, and is more than counterbalanced by the contrary evidence now to be adduced.

Over against this somewhat slender array of coincidences we have to set a large number of characteristic expressions in which the two writings differ. König[1] justly remarks that in this discussion special importance attaches to those slighter and less significant elements of discourse where one word might indifferently be substituted for another, so that a marked preference for any particular idiom can only be due to the literary habit of the author or his age. He instances the following cases of this kind as characteristic of the second part of Isaiah (the list is here slightly abridged and corrected in some points):—

(1). '*aph* (=also, with various shades of meaning): twenty-two times in chs. xl.—xlviii.; never in undisputed portions of Isaiah (?xxxiii. 2).

(2) *bal* (negative particle): eight times; never in Isaiah (unless ch. xxxiii. 20—24 be written by him).

(3) *hēn* (=behold): about twenty-one times; twice in Isaiah (xxiii. 13, xxxii. 1; ?xxxiii. 7).

(4) *zû* (relative pronoun): xlii. 24, xliii. 21; never in Isaiah.

(5) *lĕma'an* (=in order that): sixteen times; once in Isaiah (v. 19).

(6) *mĕ'ōd* (=very): xlvii. 9, lvi. 12, lxiv. 9, 12; in Isaiah xxxi. 1.

(7) *pĕ'ullāh* (=work, reward): xl. 10, xlix. 4, lxi. 8, lxii. 11, lxv. 7; nowhere in Isaiah.

(8) *çedeq* (=righteousness): about seventeen times; in Isaiah only i. 21, 26, xi. 4 f., xxxii. 1.

---

[1] *Offenbarungsbegriff des A. T.* Vol. I. pp. 211 f.; *Einleitung*, p. 322.

(9) *sûs, sasôn, masôs* (=rejoice, joy): some fourteen times; three times in Isaiah.

(10) *tōhû* (=chaos, nothingness): about eight times; in Isaiah once (xxix. 21).

(11) *lĕ'ôlām* (=for ever): xl. 8, xlvii. 7, li. 6, 8, lx. 21; and *tāmîd* (=continually): xlix. 16, li. 13, lii. 5, lviii. 11, lx. 11, lxii. 6, lxv. 3. Isaiah uses *lānéçaḥ* (xxviii. 28), and *lĕ'ad* (xxx. 8).

(12) *'ôth* is written for *'eth* (=with) in liv. 15, lix. 21;—a mark of late style.

(13) *lāmô* (an unusual suffix): xliii. 8, xliv. 7, 15 (?liii. 8).

To these should be added:

(14) *yaḥad, yaḥdāv* (=together): a peculiar pleonastic idiom illustrated by xli. 19, 20, and occurring some fifteen times in chs. xl.—lxvi.

The following is a list of more expressive words and phrases, more or less characteristic of the later chapters, and occurring either not at all or only once in the undisputed portions of Isaiah[1]:—

(15) *all flesh*: xl. 5, 6, xlix. 26, lxvi. 16, 23, 24.

(16) *'ônîm* (=strength): xl. 26, 29.

(17) *'epheṣ* (=nothing): xl. 17, xli. 12, 29, xlv. 6, 14, xlvi. 9, xlvii. 8, 10, lii. 4, liv. 15. In Isaiah only v. 8.

(18) *'iyyîm* (=coast-lands): xl. 15, xli. 1, 5, xlii. 4, 10, 12, 15, xlix. 1, li. 5, lix. 18, lx. 9, lxvi. 19. In Isaiah only the sing. *'îy*, in its proper restricted signification, xx. 6, xxiii. 2, 6.

(19) *ends* (or *end*) *of the earth*: xl. 28, xli. 5, 9, xlii. 10, xliii. 6, xlv. 22, xlviii. 20, xlix. 6, lii. 10, lxii. 11.

(20) *gā'al* (=redeem): verb and participle are used over 20 times.

(21) *bārā'* (=create): about sixteen times; in Isaiah only iv. 5, —a doubtful passage.

(22) *choose, chosen* (of Israel or the Servant of Jehovah): twelve times.

(23) *Lift up (your) eyes* &c.: xl. 26, xlix. 18, li. 6, lx. 4.

(24) *ḥēpheṣ* (=pleasure), liv. 12, lxii. 4: (=purpose), xliv. 28, xlvi. 10, xlviii. 14, liii. 10: (=business), lviii. 3, 13.

---

[1] This list and the next are for the most part abridged from the three given in Driver's *Isaiah*[2], pp. 194—199, which the reader should by all means consult. The dependence was inevitable; the object being to present but a few of the clearest cases, a more judicious selection than Driver's could not be made.

INTRODUCTION.

(25) *pā'ēr* (=deck) and *hithpā'ēr* (=deck oneself): xliv. 23, xlix. 3, lv. 5, lx. 7, 9, 13, 21, lxi. 3. In Isa. only x. 15.

(26) *break out* into singing: xliv. 23, xlix. 13, lii. 9, liv. 1, lv. 12.

(27) *hillēl* and *tĕhillāh* (=praise, vb. and subst.), *hithhallēl* (=exult): xli. 16, xlii. 8, 10, 12, xliii. 21, xlv. 25, xlviii. 9, lx. 6, 18, lxi. 3, 11, lxii. 7, 9, lxiii. 7, lxiv. 11 [10].

(28) *ḥāshāh* (qal and hiph. = be silent): xlii. 14, lvii. 11, lxii. 1, 6, lxiv. 12, lxv. 6.

(29) *çe'ĕçā'îm* (=offspring): xlii. 5, xliv. 3, xlviii. 19, lxi. 9, lxv. 23. Isa. only xxii. 24.

(30) *çāmaḥ* (=sprout): xliv. 4, xlv. 8, lv. 10, lviii. 8, lxi. 11. Note the unique metaphorical application to an event coming to pass, in xlii. 9, xliii. 19.

(31) *Holy City*: xlviii. 2, lii. 1 (cf. lxiv. 10).

(32) *rāçôn* (=favour): xlix. 8, lvi. 7, lviii. 5, lx. 7, 10, lxi. 2.

(33) *from the first* (*mērōsh*): xl. 21, xli. 4, 26, xlviii. 16.

(34) *lay to heart*: xlii. 25, xlvii. 7, lvii. 1, 11.

Still more suggestive is a list of Isaiah's characteristic expressions, not found at all in chs. xl.—lxvi. The following examples (from Driver) must suffice:—

(1) *The Lord, Jehovah of Hosts*: i. 24, iii. 1, x. 16, 33, xix. 4.

(2) *'elîlîm* (=nonentities, of idols): ii. 8, 18, 20, x. 11, xix. 1, 3, xxxi. 7.

(3) *mirmās* (=trampling): v. 5, vii. 25, x. 6, xxviii. 18.

(4) *glory* (of a nation): v. 13, viii. 7, x. 16, 18, xvi. 14, xvii. 3, 4; (of an individual), xxii. 18.

(5) *smear* (of the eyes): vi. 10, xxix. 9, xxxii. 3.

(6) *siksēk* (=incite): ix. 11, xix. 2 (nowhere else).

(7) *shĕ'ār* (=remnant): vii. 3, x. 19, 20, 21, 22, xvi. 14, xvii. 3, xxviii. 5.

(8) *final and decisive work*: x. 23, xxviii. 22.

(9) the figure of the *scourge*: x. 26, xxviii. 15, 18.

(10) *flying sāraph*: xiv. 29, xxx. 6 (nowhere else).

(11) *kabbîr* (=numerous, mighty, &c.): xvi. 14, xvii. 12, xxviii. 2. Only seven times in Job besides.

(12) *mĕbûsāh* (=treading down): xviii. 2, 7, xxii. 5 (nowhere else).

(13) *çābā'* (=to war): xxix. 7, 8, xxxi. 4 (uncommon).

(14) *zérem* (=streaming rain): xxviii. 2 *bis*, xxx. 30, xxxii. 2.

(15) *briers and thorns*: v. 6, vii. 23, 24, 25, ix. 18, x. 17. Except in xxvii. 4, xxxii. 13, neither word occurs elsewhere.

(16) *miz'ār* (=a little): x. 25, xvi. 14, xxix. 17.

It is impossible to pursue the subject further. The evidence of style is as conclusive as could be desired, and amply confirms the deduction to be naturally drawn from the historical setting of the prophecy and its leading conceptions. The resulting impression is so strong that probably few will hesitate to acquiesce in the statement that "if the great prophecy of Israel's redemption and glorification now included in the Book of Isaiah had come down to us as an independent and anonymous document, no reasonable doubt could have been entertained as to the time at which it was written. Internal evidence would be regarded as fixing its date with remarkable precision towards the close of the Babylonian Exile[1]."[2]

The only question that remains is whether all these considerations can fairly be held to be outweighed by the circumstance that the prophecy *does* form part of the book of Isaiah, or by the all but unbroken tradition in favour of the Isaianic authorship. That tradition is unquestionably very ancient. It is attested by Jesus the son of Sirach (ch. xlviii. 22—25)[3], by several New

---

[1] Kirkpatrick, *Doctrine of the Prophets*[2], p. 353.

[2] With regard to the *place* where the author wrote, little can be said except that it is most reasonably to be assumed that he lived in Babylonia. That was probably the only country where he could have had any considerable audience of exiled Israelites; and that he was actually in direct touch with an audience can hardly be doubted, in view of the eager and passionate pleadings in which the book abounds. Allusions to Babylonia are as numerous as could be expected (see xliv. 27, xlv. 1 f., 3, xlvi. 1 f., xlvii. 8—15, &c.), and quite as specific as those to be found in Ezekiel, who lived there; although they are perhaps hardly definite enough to determine the matter absolutely by themselves. The view of Ewald and Bunsen, that the book was written in Egypt, rests on no solid grounds, and Duhm's arguments in favour of Phœnicia are equally unconvincing. The idea that it was composed in Judæa has a certain plausibility as far as some of the later chapters are concerned, but is wholly inconsistent with the allusions of chs. xl.—xlviii. It is, of course, *conceivable* that the author might have returned to Palestine with Zerubbabel in 536, and that parts of the prophecy might be subsequent to that event. (See Appendix, Note III.)

[3] *Vv.* 24 f. "He saw by an excellent spirit what should come to

Testament writers (Matt. iii. 3 and parallels, viii. 17, xii. 17; Luke iv. 17; John i. 23; Acts viii. 28; Rom. x. 16, 20) and by Josephus (*Archaeol.* XI. 1, § 2; cf. X. 2, § 2)[1]; and is unhesitatingly accepted by subsequent Jewish and Christian opinion. Yet it may be doubted if all this weight of authority really adds any evidence whatever to the fact that the prophecy stands in the Canon under the name of Isaiah. It is not an unreasonable assumption that the belief that Isaiah is the author rested originally on nothing else than the canonical title of the book, and was simply transmitted without examination from one generation to another. This possibility would be admitted readily enough in the case of the secular writers that have been referred to. To many it may seem that the New Testament writers, in virtue of their inspiration, stand on a different footing. But this is surely to press the doctrine of inspiration to a dangerous extreme. In no single instance is it material to the purpose for which the quotation is made, whether the author be Isaiah or a prophet of the Exile; and to say that an inspired writer may not use the current language of his time in referring to a book of Scripture without imperilling the veracity of the author of Revelation, is a position to which no wise man would wish to be committed.

What weight, then, is to be assigned to the fact that the prophecy is included in the book of Isaiah? The view taken by critical scholars is the very simple one that the incorporation was the work of an editor of the prophetical literature,—a point, by the way, which seems to be imperfectly apprehended by those writers who so persistently impute to critics the imaginary crime of "sawing Isaiah asunder." Critics do not profess to know who the editor was, or what were the precise motives by which he was guided; it is enough to know that the operation is perfectly conceivable, and that a variety of reasons might easily be suggested for it[2]. Nor is it an isolated instance

pass at the last; and he comforted them that mourned in Zion. He shewed the things that should be to the end of time, and the hidden things or ever they came." See Vol. I. p. lxxiii.

[1] See Note on ch. xliv. 28.

[2] Kirkpatrick (*Doctrine of the Prophets*[2], p. 363), suggests that "a partial explanation [of the position of the prophecy] may be found in

in the history of prophetic writings. In Jeremiah li. 64 we find a note (evidently the work of an editor), "thus far are the words of Jeremiah"; and it is practically certain that the book of Zechariah contains the work of three separate prophets. Whether, therefore, the editor supposed the prophecy to be a genuine work of Isaiah, or whether for some other reason he decided to add it to the collection of his prophecies, the fact that it stands there is far from being a conclusive proof that Isaiah is the author. And since a chain is no stronger than its weakest link, it cannot be held that even a tradition of 2,000 years is sufficient to invalidate the critical arguments for the late date of the prophecy.

It is but fair to notice another kind of external evidence to which considerable importance is attached by some scholars, viz., the alleged use by certain pre-exilic prophets of the last twenty-seven chapters of Isaiah. This is thought to be proved by a comparison of parallel passages, of which the clearest examples are: Jer. x. 1—16 with ch. xliv. 12—15, &c.; Jer. xxx. 10 f. (=Jer. xlvi. 27 f.) with ch. xliii. 1—6, &c.; Jer. xxxi. 12 with ch. lviii. 11; Jer. xxxi. 35 with ch. li. 15; Jer. xxxiii. 3 with ch. xlviii. 6; Jer. l. 2, 8 with xlvi. 1, xlviii. 20; Nah. i. 15 with lii. 7; Nah. iii. 4, 5 with xlvii. 3, 9; Nah. iii. 7 with li. 19; Zeph. ii. 15 with xlvii. 8, 10. In some of these cases the resemblance is slight, and may be accidental, but in others it is so close as to create an irresistible impression of literary dependence, on one side or the other. In no instance, however, can it be pronounced with confidence on *which* side the priority lies, the supposition that the second Isaiah borrowed from his predecessors being, in itself, just as reasonable as that pre-exilic prophets borrowed from him. In three of the parallels there is perhaps a certain presumption that the Isaianic passage is the original; these are Jer. x. 1—16, xxx. 10 f., and Nah. i. 15; but each of these passages is suspected on independent grounds of being an

---

the form of ancient books. The prophecy was annexed to Isaiah i.—xxxix., in order to form a volume approximately equal to those of Jeremiah, Ezekiel, and the Minor Prophets. If it was anonymous it would soon come to be ascribed to Isaiah."

interpolation in the pre-exilic book where it stands. In any event, the presumption is not strong enough to counterbalance any decided probability in the opposite direction. Moreover, the force of the argument from verbal parallelisms would seem to be neutralised by the fact that no pre-exilic writer betrays any knowledge that the end of the Babylonian Exile had been distinctly foretold by Isaiah the son of Amoz. It would be a very singular and unaccountable thing if the latter part of Isaiah had been studied by a succession of prophets with such care that its phrases passed into their style, while none of them ever suffers it to appear that he had assimilated the contents of the book. It cannot be too strongly insisted that the whole discussion is a balancing of probabilities, and it will generally be found that the argument from parallel passages can be used on either side to strengthen that conclusion which on other grounds seems most probable.

CHAPTER V.

UNITY OF THE PROPHECY.

THE most difficult of the current critical questions in regard to the second part of Isaiah are those concerning the unity or integrity of the volume. Whether the prophecy is the work of a single writer, whether it was composed wholly before the close of the Exile, or in part after the Return, whether the writer has adopted fragments from earlier prophecies into his own work, these are matters on which the utmost diversity of opinion exists among recent scholars. And although it is neither desirable nor possible in this place to enter fully into the discussion of them, there are two questions of such magnitude and importance that a few pages must be devoted to their consideration[1].

1. The first relates to the genuineness of the so-called "Servant-passages" (xlii. 1—4, xlix. 1—6, l. 4—9, lii. 13—liii. 12).

[1] There are of course numerous passages supposed, with more or less reason, to be interpolated, but these have to be considered in detail.

Ewald, in 1841, was the first great critic who expressed the opinion that ch. lii. 13—liii. 12 was borrowed by the prophet from an earlier composition (which he assigned to the age of Manasseh); and similar views have been advocated with regard to this passage by several subsequent writers. More recently the tendency has been to recognise a close affinity between the four great descriptions of the Servant of Jehovah, and to apply the same critical methods to them all. Thus the question raised, in its most general form, is whether these four passages form an integral part of the exilic prophecy of chs. xl. ff., or whether they are the work of another writer, who may have lived either before or after that date.

It may be remarked that so long as the negative theory is held in the form in which it was propounded by Ewald, the question has but a secondary interest for the interpreter. "The question he asks is not what may possibly have been the original meaning of ch. liii. but what is its meaning now as it stands an integral part of the magnificent production of which it is the crown[1]." If it be admitted that the disputed passages passed through the mind of the exilic author, and were by himself incorporated in his work, it matters comparatively little whether he originally wrote them or drew them from an independent source; they form an essential element of his teaching, and for all practical purposes may be treated as if they were his own work. It is only when they are classed as real interpolations, inserted without the knowledge of the author and after his book was completed, that the issue becomes of serious consequence. This is the position assumed by some writers, notably by Duhm, who thinks that the fragments may have been inserted by an editor, almost at hap-hazard, where there chanced to be a convenient space in the manuscript; an almost incredible hypothesis, which, at least in this extreme form, is not likely to be sustained. Some who follow Duhm, such as Kosters[2], have perceived that the first three passages cannot be lifted from their places without carrying some of the succeeding

---

[1] Davidson, *Expositor*, 2nd Series, Vol. VI. p. 87.
[2] *Theologisch Tijdschrift*, 1896, pp. 588 ff.

verses with them, and find accordingly that the interpolations must be more extensive than Duhm supposed. But this kind of criticism is exceedingly hazardous when applied to a work like the second Isaiah, where one has only to read on far enough to obtain a new point of connexion with something that has gone before. For the rest, the present writer must be content to express his general agreement with the conclusion of Cheyne, which is that while it cannot be shewn that the "Servant-passages" have sprung immediately from the preceding context, "they have in general exercised such an influence on the following sections that they cannot well have been inserted by anyone but II. Isaiah himself[1]"; and further that it is not "at all impossible that they may be the work of II. Isaiah himself[2]."

2. Another critical question of some importance arises in connexion with the later chapters of the prophecy. Certain peculiarities of these chapters (particularly lvi.—lix., lxiii.—lxvi.) have for a long time engaged the attention of critics. Their style differs considerably from that of the earlier part of the volume; their tone is much less hopeful and buoyant, they lay far greater stress on the externals of religion (e.g. Sabbath-observance and the Temple ritual), they appear to be addressed to a Jewish community possessing a certain measure of political independence, and the allusions to natural scenery indicate that this community was settled in Palestine. These circumstances conspire to render the literary unity of the second Isaiah very difficult of belief; and those who hold that the book is on the whole the work of a single author have usually sought to explain them by two assumptions: first, that the exilic author has

---

[1] *Introduction*, p. 307. In Cheyne's view, the latter statement is only partially true of ch. lii. 13—liii. 12, which he regards as an insertion made by the author *after* the completion of the work, and therefore without direct influence on the succeeding context.

[2] *Ibid.* p. 309. The suggestion is that they were composed by the prophet at an earlier period of his life. Even this concession does not seem to me necessary. If it be the practice of the writer "to take up one of the Servant-passages as a suggestive theme" for a fresh start in his argument, there can be no great difficulty in supposing that he wrote them for that purpose along with the rest of the prophecy.

embodied fragments of pre-exilic prophecies in his work, adapting them to his own purpose; and secondly, that some portions may have been written after the high hopes with which he started had been damped, and possibly after he had returned to Palestine. Of late years, however, and especially since the appearance of Duhm's commentary in 1892, the idea has gained favour in many quarters that the whole of the third division of the prophecy (chs. lvi.—lxvi.) is of post-exilic origin, and was written by one or more prophets living in Jerusalem about the time of Nehemiah.

It cannot be denied that this theory has much to recommend it. The condition of the people during the first century after the Restoration is very imperfectly known, but the state of things revealed by the books of Ezra and Nehemiah and the prophecies of Haggai, Zechariah[1], and Malachi embraces several features which correspond to the allusions of chs. lvi.—lxvi. The following are some of the circumstances which are appealed to in support of the post-exilic authorship of this part of the prophecy:—(1) The existence of the Temple appears to be presupposed in ch. lvi. 7, lx. 7, lxii. 9, more clearly in lxv. 11, lxvi. 6. It is quite possible to interpret the first three references of a Temple yet unbuilt, but this suggestion cannot be so readily entertained with regard to the two remaining cases. If the impression that an actually existing Temple is referred to be correct, the date of the passages would be fixed as later than B.C. 515 (Ezra vi. 15, &c.). (2) Ch. lvi. 8 seems to imply that a partial gathering of exiled Israelites has taken place, and promises that others shall yet be gathered. None of the other allusions to a restoration of exiles (lx. 4, 8, lxvi. 20) contain anything inconsistent with this; they can all be naturally understood of the Dispersion that remained after the first return from Babylon. (3) The social conditions dealt with in the prophecy are in accordance with those which are known

[1] It must be remembered, however, that Haggai and Zechariah are separated from the time of Nehemiah by an interval of nearly 80 years (see Chronological Table, p. lxi). Any illustrations drawn from their writings are of value only in so far as they reveal a state of things likely to have persisted through that long space of time.

to have existed after the Exile. Oppression of the poor by the rich or of slaves by their masters (lviii. 3—6, 9, lix. 3 f., 13 ff.) is attested by Neh. v. and Mal. iii. 5. The description of the leaders of the community as worthless, greedy and self-indulgent (lvi. 10—12) is illustrated by the conduct of the worldly-minded priests who sought their advantage in family alliances with their half-heathen neighbours (Ezra ix. 1, 2; Neh. xiii. 4, 28), or the hireling prophets who tried to undermine the influence of Nehemiah (Neh. vi. 10—14). There are also traces of that cleavage into two parties,—one strict, fearing Jehovah and trembling at His word, the other lax and indifferent to all religious interests—which the book of Malachi proves to have existed in the first century after the Restoration (see ch. lvii. 1, 15, 20, lix. 4—8, 18, lxv. 8, 13 ff., lxvi. 5; and comp. Mal. iii. 5, 15—18). These facts, taken together, seem to imply a date either earlier or later than the Exile, and the parallels in post-exilic writings go to shew that the latter alternative is at least as probable as the former. (4) There are repeated allusions in these chapters to a section of the population addicted to idolatrous practices of a very peculiar kind (lvii. 3—13, lxv. 1—7, 11 f., lxvi. 3 f., 17). It is an interesting suggestion of Duhm's that these passages refer to the mixed population (of Israelites, Ammonites, Arabians, &c.) which had settled in the land during the Exile, particularly the half-caste Samaritans, who had at first sought a share in the building of the Temple (Ezra iv. 1 ff.), but afterwards, on being repulsed, did their utmost to weaken the hands of the strictly religious party in Jerusalem. The persons spoken of are described as "brethren" of the God-fearing Jews (lxvi. 5) and at the same time as the most bitter enemies of the Temple-community (lvii. 4, lxvi. 5); they pride themselves on their "righteousness" (lvii. 12), although they have been unfaithful to Jehovah (lvii. 8) and "forgotten" His holy mountain (lxv. 11); the comparison of ch. lvii. 3 certainly gains in force if understood of a hybrid race like the Samaritans. These things could not be said of pure heathen; they *might* no doubt be said of a section of the Israelites themselves, but perhaps their fittest application is to the community of whom it is recorded that "they feared Jehovah and served their own gods" (2 Ki. xvii. 33). (5) The prophet gives utterance to a feeling which prevailed amongst the post-exilic Jews when he complains that the promised redemption is delayed, and finds the explanation of the delay in the moral condition of the people (ch. lix. 1—15). Such a feeling is never expressed in the earlier part of the book (with the doubtful exception of ch. xlviii. 17—19); and it is difficult to believe that it could have arisen in the interval between the appearing of the prophet and the close of the Exile. (6) In addition to all this, the theory of Duhm is recommended by its comparative simplicity. It has the merit of applying a single explanation to a large number of congruous phenomena; and this is more than can be said for any tenable form of the theory that the whole material has passed through the hands of the principal author. The idea that a writer so original as the second Isaiah should have copied long passages from earlier prophets in order to convey his own message to his countrymen is not a natural one; and if the literary unity of the prophecy is only to be saved by such expedients as that, it is a question whether the problem is not really simplified by ascribing the later chapters to an independent author, addressing a different audience.

These arguments are, of course, not decisive, and may not be such as to overcome the natural reluctance to carry the disintegration of the prophetic books further than can be proved absolutely necessary. And there are some considerations on the other side which must not be overlooked. (1) Chs. lx.—lxii. so closely resemble the work of the second Isaiah that it may seem hardly reasonable to assign them to a different author. The question may fairly be raised whether the resemblance is more than superficial, and whether a close examination of chs. lx.—lxii. does not shew that the existence of the Temple and the Jewish State is there presupposed. Still the presumption that this is the case can scarcely be said to be much stronger than in the similar descriptions of chs. xlix.—liv., which only a few critics have supposed to be written in Palestine. (2) A large number of coincidences, both of thought and expression, are to be found distributed over the whole prophecy, and form an important link of connexion between the two parts. Compare, for example, ch. lvi. 1 with xlvi. 13; ch. lvii. 14, lxii. 10 with xlviii. 20, lii. 11, 12; lviii. 12, lxi. 4 with xlix. 8; lix. 16, lxiii. 5 with l. 2; lix. 17 with xlii. 13; lix. 21 with xliv. 3; lx. 14, 16, lxvi. 11 with xlix. 23; lxi. 1—3 with the Servant-passages; lxi. 2 with xlix. 8; lxi. 11 with xlv. 8; lxii. 11 with xl. 10; lxv. 17, lxvi. 22 with li. 6; lxvi. 8 with liv. 1;—a list which might be extended. It is difficult to determine whether such affinities indicate unity of authorship or only the influence of one author on another, or, in some instances, direct quotation of the earlier by the later. (3) Although there is no unambiguous declaration that the release from Babylon is still future, yet the two passages lvii. 14 and lxii. 10 ff. so much resemble ch. xl. 3, xlviii. 20, and lii. 11 f. as to suggest that they refer to that event. Duhm thinks that in these cases (as in others) the post-exilic writer has adopted the idea from his predecessor, but applied it figuratively, to the removal of spiritual obstacles to the redemption of Israel, a suggestion which may strike some minds as over-subtle. (4) The change in the prophet's attitude (as compared with chs. xl.—lv.) might be fully explained if we knew anything at all of the circumstances of the Jews in Babylon towards the close of the Exile. It is indeed conceivable that many features of their social and religious condition might furnish an even more satisfying explanation of the allusions in the prophecy than the parallels drawn from the meagre post-exilic records.  Thus, the earlier part of the book contains indications of a division of parties, and it is not unlikely that the cleavage might have been accentuated as the deliverance drew near. Still, there are not many scholars who hold that *all* the phenomena of the prophecy can be thus accounted for; some parts are generally allowed to be so manifestly Palestinian in their colouring that, if not post-exilic, they must be based on pre-exilic documents. (5) The supposed references to the Samaritans, while instructive and plausible up to a certain point, yet lack the definiteness which was to have been expected and which is necessary to produce complete conviction. Moreover, they differ in some important particulars from what is otherwise known of that community and its relations with the Jews (see esp. on lxv. 2)[1].

Whatever view be adopted regarding the literary integrity of the prophecy, there is a deeper unity in it which is not impaired by any critical theory of its authorship. If chs. lvi.—lxvi. were not written by the same author as chs. xl.—lv. they were at least written by one who was imbued with the teaching of his predecessor, and consciously built on the foundations which he had laid. The brilliant promises of the second Isaiah had received but a meagre fulfilment in the return of the first colony of exiled Jews to Palestine; and the century that followed was in large measure a period of disenchantment, when "the prophecies, being read literally, proved a heritage of woe[2]." The existing state of things was one in which believing minds found it impossible to acquiesce. The restoration of the Jewish state might be a solid gain to the cause of religion, but it did not realise the glorious hopes that had been cherished with regard to it. It had not ushered in the everlasting salvation of which the prophet had spoken; it had not even brought great prosperity to Israel. The glory of the Lord had not been revealed so that all flesh could see it, and there were no signs of any movement of the Gentile world towards the true religion. Hence the great question that exercised the minds of devout Jews of this period was, Why does the Lord delay His coming? What hinders the complete fulfilment of His word? We know of some prophets who were raised up in the post-exilic age to answer that question, and to keep alive the faith in the ultimate triumph of Jehovah's kingdom. And if it should prove that one prophet (or even more than one) has devoted himself to supplementing the work of the second Isaiah by presenting his ideals in fresh forms suited to the altered circumstances of the time, there is certainly nothing in that view which will cause disquietude to any unprejudiced student of Revelation, while there may be much to throw light on an interesting, though very obscure, portion of sacred history.

[1] See further, Appendix, Note III.
[2] Davidson, *The Exile and the Restoration*, p. 86.

CHRONOLOGICAL TABLE.

B.C.	
604.	Battle of Carchemish.
	NEBUCHADNEZZAR, King of Babylon.
597.	First deportation of Jewish Captives to Babylonia, with Jehoiachin.
586.	Destruction of Jerusalem, and second deportation of Jews, with Zedekiah.
561.	EVIL-MERODACH succeeds Nebuchadnezzar.
559.	NERIGLISSAR.
555.	NABONIDUS.
549.	CYRUS conquers Media.
540.	Defeats Crœsus and captures Sardis.
538.	Capture of Babylon.
	Return of exiles under Zerubbabel.
529.	CAMBYSES.
521.	DARIUS HYSTASPIS.
520.	Haggai.
520—518.	Zechariah.
520—516.	Building of the Second Temple.
490.	Battle of Marathon.
485.	XERXES.
480.	Battles of Thermopylæ and Salamis.
464.	ARTAXERXES I. (Longimanus).
458.	Return of exiles under Ezra.
	Malachi (?).
445.	Nehemiah appointed Governor of Judæa.
444.	Introduction of the Law.
432.	Nehemiah's second visit to Jerusalem.

THE BOOK OF THE PROPHET
ISAIAH.

Ch. XL. 1—11. The Prologue.

This first proclamation of glad tidings to Zion (see ch. xli. 27) is a passage of singular beauty, breathing the spirit of new-born hope and enthusiasm with which the prophet enters on his work. The announcement of a miraculous restoration of the exiles to their own land is the central theme of his prophecy, and the point around which all the ideas of the book crystallize. As yet the historical fact is but dimly outlined, the writer's mind being occupied with its ideal significance as a revelation of the glory and the gracious character of Jehovah (*vv.* 5, 10 f.). His state of mind borders on ecstasy; his ears are filled with the music of heavenly voices telling him that the night is far spent and the day is at hand; and although his home is with the exiles in Babylon, his gaze is fixed throughout on Jerusalem and the great Divine event which is the consummation of Israel's redemption.—The prologue consists of two parts:

i. *vv.* 1, 2.—Proclamation of forgiveness and promise of deliverance to the exiled nation.

ii. *vv.* 3—11. An imaginative description of the process by which the promise is to be fulfilled,—Jehovah's return with His people to their ancient abode. This second division contains three sections:—

(1) *vv.* 3—5. A voice is heard calling on unseen agencies to prepare a way for Jehovah through the desert. The idea expressed is that already the spiritual and supernatural forces are in motion which will bring about the return of the captives and a revelation of the Divine glory to all the world.

(2) *vv.* 6—8. A second voice calls on the prophet to proclaim the fundamental truth on which the realisation of his hope depends,—the perishableness of all human power, and the enduring stability of the word of the Lord.

(3) *vv.* 9—11. The prophet himself now takes up the strain; he summons a company of ideal messengers to announce to Zion and the cities of Judah the advent of Jehovah with His ransomed people.

40 Comfort ye, comfort ye my people, saith your God.
2 Speak ye comfortably to Jerusalem, and cry unto her,
That her warfare is accomplished,
That her iniquity is pardoned:

1, 2. The term of Jerusalem's servitude is accomplished; she has suffered the full penalty of her transgressions.

Comfort ye] The repetition of an emphatic opening word is characteristic of the writer's style; cf. ch. xliii. 11, 25, xlviii. 11, 15, li. 9, 12, 17, lii. 1, 11 etc. (see Introd. p. xlv). It is rather idle to enquire who are the persons addressed; they might no doubt be prophets (as the clause is paraphrased by the Targ.) or the prophetically minded among the people, but certainly not the priests, as is suggested by the Sept. addition of ἱερεῖς at the beginning of *v*. 2.

saith your God] The verb differs in tense from the usual prophetic formula, being an impf. either of continued or of incipient action (see Introd. p. xlvii, and Driver, *Tenses*, § 33 (*a*) Obs.). To translate it by a future and take this as a proof that the words were written by Isaiah 150 years before is quite unwarranted.

2. *speak ye comfortably to*] Lit. "speak to the heart of." To "speak to one's own heart" is to whisper or meditate (1 Sam. i. 13); to speak to the heart of another is to soothe, or persuade, or comfort. For the meaning of the phrase, see Gen. xxxiv. 3; Jud. xix. 3; 2 Sam. xix. 7; Hos. ii. 14; and esp. Gen. l. 21; and Ruth ii. 13, where it is parallel to "comfort" as here.

Jerusalem] an ideal representation of the people, like Zion in *v*. 9; cf. xlix. 14 ff., li. 16 f., lii. 1 ff. 7 ff. That there was an actual population in the ruined city during the Exile is of course not to be inferred from this figure. There are two standing personifications of Israel in this prophecy, the other being the "Servant of the Lord." These, however, are not interchangeable; Zion represents the nation on its receptive side; she is the mother of the people, the recipient of the blessings of salvation; while the Servant represents the historic Israel, past, present and future, in its religious aspect, with a Divine mission to fulfil for humanity.

her warfare is accomplished] The word for "warfare" is that rendered "appointed time" in A.V. of Job vii. 1, xiv. 14. It means properly a term of military service; then figuratively any period of irksome toil or endurance which a man longs to reach the end of; such as life itself had become to Job. The reference here is of course to the Exile. Render: **time of service** (R.V. marg.).

her iniquity (better, **her guilt**) *is pardoned*] The expression for pardon is rare. The verb commonly means "to be pleased with"; in a few places it means (as here) "to pay off a debt to the satisfaction of the creditor" (see Lev. xxvi. 34, 41, 43, and cf. 2 Chron. xxxvi. 21). For the idea see ch. l. 1.

for she hath received...double] i.e. "double penalty for her sins" (cf. Jer. xvi. 18, xvii. 18; Rev. xviii. 6), not "(she *shall* receive) double

For she hath received of the LORD's hand double for
all her sins.

The voice of him that crieth in the wilderness, 3
Prepare ye the way of the LORD,
Make straight in the desert a highway for our
God.
Every valley shall be exalted, 4
And every mountain and hill shall be made low:
And the crooked shall be made straight,

favour for her previous punishment." It is difficult to say whether the clause is subordinate to the two preceding (as in A.V.) or co-ordinate with them, as in R.V. (reading **that** instead of *for*). The idea that Jerusalem's punishment had been greater than her sin required is not to be pressed theologically; but the idea that Jehovah's penal purpose can be satisfied by a temporary chastisement is of the essence of the O.T. notion of forgiveness. It must be remembered, however, that in the view of this prophet, Israel includes the Servant of Jehovah, and the unmerited sufferings of the Servant form the atoning element in the punishment which has fallen on the nation as a whole (ch. liii.).

3—5. The prophet hears a voice calling on angelic powers to prepare the way of the Lord. It is doubtful whether Duhm is right in regarding this as a case of true prophetic "audition"; it is more naturally understood as a flight of poetic imagination.

3. *The voice of him that crieth*] The word "voice" here and often has the force of an interjection; render accordingly: **Hark! one crying.** The voice is not that of God (on account of the following "our God"), neither is it a human voice; it comes from one of the angelic ministers of Jehovah and is addressed to beings of the same order. The words *in the wilderness* should be joined with *prepare ye* etc., in accordance with the accents (R.V.). A.V. agrees with LXX. and Vulg. and the N.T. citations (Matt. iii. 3; Mark i. 3; Luke iii. 4); but sense and parallelism alike shew that the Heb. accentuation is right.

Prepare] strictly "clear of obstacles" (see Gen. xxiv. 31; Lev. xiv. 36; Ps. lxxx. 9; cf. ch. lvii. 14, lxii. 10; Mal. iii. 1). The figure is taken from the well-known Eastern practice of repairing the roads for a royal journey. It may be difficult to say how far the representation is ideal. Allusions to the march through the desert are too constant a feature of the prophecy (ch. xl. 10 f., xli. 18 f., xlii. 16, xliii. 19 f., xlviii. 21, xlix. 9 ff., lv. 12 f.) to be treated as merely figurative; the prophet seems to have expected the deliverance to issue in a triumphal progress of Jehovah with His people through the desert between Babylonia and Palestine, after the analogy of the exodus from Egypt. But all such passages probably look beyond the material fulfilment and include the removal of political and other hindrances to the restoration of Israel.

4. *and the crooked...plain*] More literally: **and the uneven shall**

>   And the rough places plain:
> 5 And the glory of the LORD shall be revealed,
>   And all flesh shall see *it* together:
>   For the mouth of the LORD hath spoken *it*.
> 6 The voice said, Cry.
>   And he said, What shall I cry?
>   All flesh *is* grass,
>   And all the goodliness thereof *is* as the flower of the field:
> 7 The grass withereth, the flower fadeth:
>   Because the spirit of the LORD bloweth upon it:

become a plain, and the rugged places a valley. *rough places* is a word of somewhat uncertain sense, which does not occur elsewhere. *straight* and *plain* are nouns in the original.

5. In place of *it together* LXX. has "the salvation of God," borrowing apparently from ch. lii. 10. See Luke iii. 6.

for the mouth...it] This prophetic formula is nowhere else used by second Isaiah. The whole verse is deleted as a gloss by Duhm and Cheyne, but on grounds which seem insufficient.

6—8. The second voice proclaims the double truth: all earthly might is transitory, the word of God is eternal. Logically the section interrupts the connexion between *v.* 5 and *v.* 9, and is itself a prelude to *vv.* 12 ff. But to transpose *vv.* 6—8 and 9—11, as is done by the two commentators just named, is hardly advisable; logical sequence is not the principle on which the book is arranged.

6. *The voice said, Cry*] Render (as before) **Hark! one saying**, Cry. "Cry" here evidently means "prophesy" as in *v.* 2, ch. xliv. 7, lxi. 1 f.; Jer. vii. 27. Hence the response, **and one said** (R.V.) will naturally come from a prophet, the call being from the same quarter as in *v.* 3. There is no need to suppose that an ideal person is meant, the most probable interpretation is that it is the prophet himself who replies to the voice. It is better, therefore, to change the vowels and read with LXX. and Vulg. "and I said"; in spite of the fact that the author usually keeps his own personality in the background. The other reading does not sufficiently express the distinction between the call and the answer; hence A.V. seems to refer both to the same speaker.

all flesh is grass] The answer to the question, "What shall I cry?" Cf. ch. xxxvii. 27; Job viii. 12, xiv. 2; Ps. xxxvii. 2, ciii. 15, and esp. Ps. xc. 5 f. *goodliness*] The Heb. word is nowhere else used in this sense. It signifies "lovingkindness" or "grace" (of God to men). The transition from the one meaning to the other is illustrated by the Greek χάρις, and there is no reason to suspect the text.

7. *the spirit of the LORD*] Better as R.V. **the breath of the LORD**, i.e. the wind (Ps. ciii. 16), specially the scorching east-wind (Hos. xiii. 15) or Sirocco, which blows chiefly in the spring, blighting the fresh vegetation (see Smith, *Hist. Geog. of Palestine*, pp. 67 ff.).

Surely the people *is* grass.
The grass withereth, the flower fadeth: 8
But the word of our God shall stand for ever.

O Zion, that bringest good tidings, get thee up into 9
the high mountain;
O Jerusalem, that bringest good tidings, lift up thy
voice with strength;
Lift *it* up, be not afraid;
Say unto the cities of Judah, Behold your God.

surely the people is *grass*] "The people," used absolutely, must apparently mean "humanity"; although there are no strict parallels to this sense. To understand it of Israel is opposed to the prophet's general teaching and misrepresents his meaning here. It is not Israel, but the enemies of Israel, whose perishableness he is concerned to assert. The words at best are a flat repetition of *v.* 6 and should probably be removed as a marginal gloss. The LXX., indeed, omits all from *because* in *v.* 7 to *fadeth* in *v.* 8: but this proves nothing, as it is evidently an oversight caused by the homœoteleuton. The resumption of the leading thought is a very effective introduction to the contrasted idea in the end of *v.* 8.

8. *the word of our God*] is the word spoken by the prophets to Israel, the announcement of Jehovah's immutable purpose in the world; this is the one permanent factor in human history. It is a mistake to limit the reference to the word of promise just declared by the prophet; the statement is general, although the implied argument is that as the threatening predictions of earlier prophets have been fulfilled, so this new word of comfort shall stand, because it proceeds from the same God, who can dissolve the mightiest combinations of human power (*v.* 23).

9—11. The prophet announces the triumphal approach of Jehovah to Zion.

O Zion...tidings] R.V. has **O thou that tellest good tidings to Zion**. Either translation is grammatically admissible; but the second is to be preferred, (1) because of the analogous passages xli. 27 and lii. 7, and (2) because Zion always in this prophecy represents the community as the passive recipient of salvation. The other rendering might seem to be recommended by the apparent distinction between Jerusalem and *the cities of Judah*, but this is probably not intended; Zion itself is included among the cities of Judah. The verb employed (*mĕbassĕreth*) is the Hebrew basis (through the LXX.) of the N.T. εὐαγγελίζειν; the fem. partic. is collective, denoting an ideal band of messengers (less probably the company of prophets). These Evangelists are bidden to "go up to a high mountain" to see from afar the coming of Jehovah, then to "lift up their voice without fear" (of being put to shame) and proclaim the glad tidings.

10   Behold, the Lord GOD will come with strong *hand*,
    And his arm *shall* rule for him:
    Behold, his reward *is* with him,
    And his work before him.
11 He shall feed his flock like a shepherd:
    He shall gather the lambs with his arm,
    And carry *them* in his bosom,
    And shall gently lead those that are with young.

10, 11. These words are spoken by the prophet in his own person.

10. *with strong* hand] R.V. **as a mighty one**; lit., "in (the capacity of) a strong one" (*Bêth essentiae*). The chief ancient versions vocalised the word as an abstract noun *běhōzeq* ("with strength"), which yields an even better sense.   *and his arm* shall *rule*] or **His** arm ruling;—the "arm," the symbol of strength.

For *work* render **recompence** (as R.V.) (see Lev. xix. 13). The idea is somewhat uncertain. It might mean, (1) the reward (lit. "hire") which Jehovah has *earned* by His victory over the Chaldæans, in which case the redeemed exiles themselves are the reward, which He brings with Him through the desert (*v.* 11). Or (2) it may refer to the reward which Jehovah is prepared to *bestow* on His people,—the blessings of His salvation. The last is perhaps the better sense, and is supported by the similar passage, ch. lxii. 11.

11. Jehovah as the Good Shepherd: an ideal picture of the homeward journey of the exiles, hardly of the permanent relations of Jehovah to His people in the final dispensation. The same image is used of the Restoration in Jer. xxiii. 1 ff., xxxi. 10; Ezek. xxxiv. 11 ff.; Isa. xlix. 9; cf. lxiii. 11.

those that are with young] Render, with R.V., **those that give suck**. cf. Gen. xxxiii. 13.

CH. XL. **12—31.** JEHOVAH, GOD OF ISRAEL, THE INCOMPARABLE,

is the title suggested by Dr Davidson[1] for this great passage. It is a meditation or homily on the immeasurable greatness and power and wisdom of Jehovah, the Creator, as displayed in the works of nature and in the government of the world; an expansion of the idea of *vv.* 6—8. The argument from Creation is handled with a boldness of conception and freedom of imagination to which there is nothing equal in the earlier literature, and the frequent appeal to it on the part of this prophet may be held to mark a distinct advance in Israel's consciousness of God, coinciding generally with the period of the Exile. The practical aim which the writer has in view appears from *vv.* 27 ff.; it is to counteract the unbelief and despondency of his fellow-countrymen and to inspire them with some true sense of the infinitude of Jehovah,

---

[1] *Expositor*, Second Series, Vol. VII. p. 96.

Who hath measured the waters in the hollow of his 12
hand,
And meted out heaven with the span,

their own God, who has addressed to them the consolations of *vv.* 1—11. The passage may be divided as follows:—

i. The argument, *vv.* 12—26.
(1) *vv.* 12—17. The greatness of Jehovah is illustrated by the magnitude of His operations as Creator (*v.* 12), by the perfection and self-sufficiency of His knowledge (*vv.* 13, 14), and by the insignificance in comparison with Him of all that exists (*vv.* 15—17).
(2) *vv.* 18—20. The thought of the transcendent greatness of Jehovah "suggests the idol, which also bears the name of God....The magnitude of the true God suggests the littleness of the idol-god. *He is* incomparable; *it* is by no means so. Its genesis and manufacture are known. It is a cast metal, gilt article, upheld with chains, lest it should totter and tumble to the ground. Or it is a hard-wood tree fashioned into a block by a cunning workman[1]." This is the first of several sarcastic passages in which the processes of an idol factory are minutely described: xli. 6, 7, xliv. 9—20, xlvi. 6—8.
(3) *vv.* 21—26. The thought of *vv.* 12—17 is now resumed and completed. The intelligent contemplation of nature (*vv.* 21 f.) or of history (*vv.* 23 f.) is enough to dispel the glamour of idolatry, and force the mind back on the Incomparableness of Him who is the Creator and Ruler of the world (*v.* 25 f.).

ii. The application, *vv.* 27—31. If such be the God of Israel, how can the exiles think that He is either unobservant of their fate or indifferent to it? Their God is an everlasting God; His strength is unfailing, His understanding unsearchable; and they who wait on Him shall find in Him an inexhaustible source of life and energy.

12—14. The argument for the infinitude of God opens with a series of rhetorical questions, not needing to be answered, but intended to raise the thoughts of despondent Israelites to the contemplation of the true nature of the God they worshipped. For a different purpose, namely, to humble the pride of human reason, the Almighty Himself addresses a similar series of interrogations to Job (xxxviii. 4 ff.).

12. Who can vie with Jehovah *in power?* The point of these questions lies in the smallness of the measures figured as being used by Jehovah in creating the universe,—the hollow of the hand, the span, etc. Logically, the questions are not quite on the same line as those in *vv.* 13 f. There the answer required is a simple negative: "No one"; here the meaning is, "What sort of Being must He be who actually measured" etc.

meted out] Lit. "weighed out" (as Job xxviii. 25); see on "directed," (*v.* 13). The word for *comprehended* has in New Hebr. and Aram. the sense of "measure" and is probably so used here,—the only instance in the O.T.

---

[1] Davidson, *Ibid.* p. 101.

And comprehended the dust of the earth in a measure,
And weighed the mountains in scales,
And the hills in a balance?
13 Who hath directed the spirit of the Lord,
Or *being* his counseller hath taught him?
14 With whom took he counsel, and *who* instructed him,
And taught him in the path of judgment,

a measure] means "a third part," **a tierce**, but obviously a small measure, probably a third of an ephah.

scales and *balance* might be better transposed; the first word denotes probably a "steelyard," the second the ordinary pair of scales.

The conception of the universe as measured out by its Creator appears to include two things. There is first the idea of order, adjustment and proportion in Nature, suggesting intelligence at work in the making of the world. But the more important thought is that of the infinite power which has carried through these vast operations as easily as man handles his smallest instruments of precision. The passage is not a demonstration of the existence of God, but assuming that He exists and is the Creator of all things, the prophet seeks to convey to his readers some impression of His Omnipotence, which is so conspicuously displayed in the accurate determination of the great masses and expanses of the material world.

13. From the *power* of Jehovah, the writer passes to expatiate on His perfect and self-sufficing *wisdom*.

Who hath directed] The verb is the same as "meted out" in the previous verse, and the transition from the literal to the metaphorical use is somewhat uncertain. From the idea of "weighing out" according to a fixed scale we get the notion of "regulating" or "determining"; cf. Ez. xviii. 25 (and pars.) "the way of Jehovah is not weighed out," regulated, i.e. is arbitrary. Or, on the other hand, the meaning might be "rightly estimated," "searched out" (as Prov. xvi. 2, xxi. 2). The first sense suits the context best; whether we render "direct" or "regulate" or "determine." LXX. probably read a different word; its τίς ἔγνω νοῦν Κυρίου is verbally cited in 1 Cor. ii. 16.

the spirit of the Lord] denotes here the organ of the Divine intelligence (see 1 Cor. ii. 11). This is more likely than that the spirit is personified and then endowed with intelligence. The idea, however, does not appear to be found elsewhere in the O.T. The Spirit of God is ordinarily mentioned as the life-giving principle emanating from Jehovah, which pervades and sustains the world, and endows select men with extraordinary powers and virtues.

or being...*him*] Better, perhaps: **and was the man of His** counsel **who taught Him.** "His" and "Him" refer of course to Jehovah, not the Spirit.

14. *and* who *instructed*] Or, **so that he instructed.**

path of judgment] **path of right** (*mishpāṭ*). See ch. xxviii. 26, where the word means orderly procedure; here the reference is to the order

And taught him knowledge,
And shewed to him the way of understanding?
Behold, the nations *are* as a drop of a bucket,   15
And are counted as the small dust of the balance:
Behold, he taketh up the isles as a very little thing.
And Lebanon *is* not sufficient to burn,   16
Nor the beasts thereof sufficient *for* a burnt offering.
All nations before him *are* as nothing;   17
And they are counted to him less than nothing, and vanity.

To whom then will ye liken God?   18
Or what likeness will ye compare unto him?

of nature, or else the transition is already made from creation to providence (*v.* 15).

way of understanding] Or, **way of insight**. The intermediate clause *and taught him knowledge* is omitted by the LXX., and since it disturbs the parallelism, and repeats the verb just used, it may be a gloss.

15—17. The insignificance of collective humanity before Jehovah. The meditation passes from Nature to History, with the same design of encouraging those who doubted Jehovah's power to save.

a drop of a bucket] Rather: **a drop from the bucket**; which falls away without appreciably lessening the weight.

the small dust &c.] which does not turn the scale.

the isles] a characteristic word of the second half of Isaiah, occurring 12 times (see Introd. p. xlviii). In the general usage of O.T. it denotes the islands and coastlands of the Mediterranean (comp. the use of the singular by Isaiah in ch. xx. 6). Etymologically it probably means simply "habitable lands"; and this prophet uses it with great laxity, hardly distinguishing it from "lands" (see esp. ch. xlii. 15).

as a very little thing] "a grain of powder," used of the manna, Ex. xvi. 14.

16. So infinitely great is Jehovah that the forests of Lebanon would not yield fuel enough, nor its wild animals victims enough, for a holocaust worthy of Him.

17. *less than nothing*] Better: **of nought**; "belonging to the category of nothingness" (Cheyne).

vanity] The Hebr. is *tōhû*, a word which means primarily "a waste," and is applied in Gen. i. 2 to the primeval chaos (A.V. "without form"). See on ch. xxix. 21, xxxiv. 11. Here and in many other cases it is a synonym for nonentity.

18—20. "To whom will ye liken God?" This question introduces the second distinct theme of the argument, the folly of idolatry. Although the prophet has in his mind the difficulties of Jews impressed by the fascinations of idolatry, his words are addressed not to them directly, but to men in general. The error he exposes is not the

19　The workman melteth a graven image,
And the goldsmith spreadeth it over with gold,
And casteth silver chains.
20　He that *is* so impoverished that he hath no oblation chooseth a tree *that* will not rot;

worshipping of Jehovah by images, but the universal error of thinking that the Deity (*ēl*) can be represented by the works of human hands. His point of view is that of Paul's speech to the Athenians: "we ought not to think that the Godhead is like unto gold or silver or stone, graven by art and device of man" (Acts xvii. 29). In order to see how absurd this is, one has but to observe how the images are manufactured; and the various processes are described with an unmistakeable irony. After *v.* 19 Duhm and Cheyne (following out a hint of Lagarde's) insert *vv.* 6 and 7 of the next chapter. The description would then fall into two unequal parts; first, the construction of a metal idol (*v.* 19, xli. 6, 7), and second, that of a wooden idol (*v.* 20); each ending naturally with the fastening of the image to its pedestal.

19. *melteth a graven image*] R.V. **The graven image, a workman melted it.** The word *pésel* means strictly a "graven image," but is used several times as here of an image in general.

overlayeth it *with gold*] The idol consists of a core of brass which is cast by the "workman," and then handed over to the goldsmith to be covered with a plating of gold (see ch. xxx. 22).

and casteth silver chains] A perplexing clause, which the LXX. omits. The word rendered "casteth" is the same as that for "goldsmith" (strictly "assayer"), the participle being translated by a finite verb. But such a construction is incorrect: and besides the *verb* is never used except in the sense of "test" or "purify." It is only when the partic. has become a noun that it assumes the general sense of worker in metal. Hence Dillmann proposes to render "and with silver chains a smelter (sc. covers it)." But this is exceedingly harsh. The word for "chains" is also of doubtful meaning, and altogether the clause must be pronounced hopelessly obscure.

20. *He that* is *so...oblation*] R.V. **He that is too impoverished for such an oblation** (lit. impoverished with respect to an oblation). If the text be sound this seems the only possible interpretation, although the whole sense turns on the word "such" which is in no way expressed. Moreover the technical *tĕrûmāh* (temple-oblation) has no appropriateness here. The LXX. appear to have read *tĕmûnāh* (ὁμοίωμα), which looks more promising, but leaves the word for "impoverished" (מְסֻכָּן) more unintelligible than ever. Jerome gives the information that *mĕsukkān* is a durable kind of wood (see Vulg. "lignum imputribile"); and this has led some to connect it with an Assyrian word, *musukkânu* (= palm-tree). The Targ. gives "he cutteth down a laurel-tree," apparently taking מסכן as a denominative from סַכִּין (= knife). This shews at least that there was no reliable Jewish tradition as to the meaning of the word. Duhm, combining the hints of the Targ. and the LXX., obtains a

He seeketh unto him a cunning workman
To prepare a graven image, *that* shall not be moved.

Have ye not known? have ye not heard? 21
Hath it not been told you from the beginning?
Have ye not understood *from* the foundations of the earth?
It is he that sitteth upon the circle of the earth, 22
And the inhabitants thereof *are* as grasshoppers;
That stretcheth out the heavens as a curtain,
And spreadeth them out as a tent to dwell in:

reading which is as good as any that can be suggested: "He who carves an image." The transition from the metal to the wooden idol is thus more distinctly expressed.

a tree that *will not rot*] Such as those named in ch. xliv. 14. A weak parody of Eternity!

that *shall not be moved*] **that will not totter.** See 1 Sam. v. 3, 4; cf. Wisd. Sol. xiii. 15 f.

21. The next section (21—26) again commences with a series of questions driving home the force of the whole previous argument. The appeal seems to be still to mankind at large.

have ye not heard? Rather: **Do ye not know? Do ye not hear?** The two avenues by which the knowledge of God reaches the mind are reflexion on the facts of nature and history, and external testimony.

told you from the beginning) i.e. from the beginning of the world, by an unbroken tradition.

from *the foundations*] The preposition "from" might easily have been accidentally omitted in the Heb. The LXX., indeed, and other Versions take "foundations" as obj. to "understood." The parallelism seems to require the phrase to be taken in a temporal sense (cf. Rom. i. 20), but there is no other case where the word has the sense of *fundatio* (properly, = *fundamenta*).

22, 23. The majesty of the God who reveals Himself in Creation and Providence is described in interjectional participial clauses, the force of which should not be blunted by the superfluous "It is" of E.V.

upon (rather: above, R.V. marg.) *the circle of the earth*] i.e. the horizon, where earth and heaven meet (see Prov. viii. 27), "at the confines of light and darkness" (Job xxvi. 10). The earth with its surrounding ocean is conceived as a flat disc, on which the arch of heaven comes down. The rendering "on the vault of the earth" (see Job xxii. 14, "vault of heaven," the same word) is possible, though not so good.

and (**so that**) *the inhabitants thereof* are *as grasshoppers*] Comp. for the expression Num. xiii. 33, and for the thought Ps. cxiii. 5 f.

as a curtain] **like gauze** (lit. fine cloth).

a tent to dwell in] i.e. simply "a habitable tent."

23 That bringeth the princes to nothing;
    He maketh the judges of the earth as vanity.
24 Yea, they shall not be planted;
    Yea, they shall not be sown:
    Yea, their stock shall not take root in the earth:
    And he shall also blow upon them, and they shall wither,
    And the whirlwind shall take them away as stubble.
25 To whom then will ye liken me, or shall I be equal? saith the Holy One.
26 Lift up your eyes on high,
    And behold who hath created these *things*,
    That bringeth out their host by number:

23, 24. The majesty of God displayed in Providence.

princes] **dignitaries** (a poetic word), "potent, grave and reverend signiors."   *as vanity*] "as nothingness," lit. "chaos"; see on *v.* 17. For *he maketh*, render **who maketh**.

24. *Yea, they shall not be...*] Render: **Scarcely have they been planted, scarcely have they been sown, scarcely has their stock struck root in the earth, when he bloweth** etc. (see R.V. marg.).

their stock] The same word as "stem" in ch. xi. 1, but in a different sense. See the note there.

25, 26 form the peroration of a passage of striking elevation. The writer makes a final appeal to the imagination of his audience by pointing to the nightly pageant of the starry hosts mustered at the command of Him who is Jehovah of Hosts.

25. *To whom then*] Exactly as in *v.* 18, and following a similar idea. *or shall I be equal?*] Or, as R.V., "that I should be equal *to him*?" *the Holy One*] Qādôsh, without the art., almost like a proper name. So Job vi. 10; Hab. iii. 3, and perhaps Ps. xxii. 3.

26. *and behold who hath created*] Better as R.V. marg.: **and see: who hath created these?** The word "create" occurs fifteen times in ch. xl.—lv. and five times in the chapters which follow; perhaps not more than nine times in the whole of the *earlier* literature. No other language possesses a word so exclusively appropriated to the Divine activity. Although it may not express the metaphysical idea of creation *ex nihilo*, it certainly denotes the effortless production, by a bare volition, which is the manner of God's working. Its frequent use in these chapters is significant not only of the writer's theology, but of the great movement of religious thought in Israel about the time of the Captivity. See Introd. pp. xliv, xlviii.

For *these things* render simply **these**, i.e. "these (stars) yonder" which you see when you lift your eyes on high. The stars are likened to a great army, a host of living, intelligent beings, which every night Jehovah marshals and leads across the sky.

that bringeth out] a participial clause like those of *vv.* 22 f.

He calleth them all by names
By the greatness of *his* might, for that *he is* strong in power;
Not one faileth.

Why sayest thou, O Jacob, and speakest, O Israel,   27
My way is hid from the LORD,
And my judgment is passed over from my God?
Hast thou not known? hast thou not heard,   28
That the everlasting God, the LORD,
The Creator of the ends of the earth,
Fainteth not, neither is weary?
There is no searching of his understanding.
He giveth power to the faint;   29

he calleth...names] Better: **calling them all by name**, i.e. not "bestowing names on them," but calling each forth by his name. Cf. Ps. cxlvii. 4, 5.

by the greatness ..faileth] Render as a single sentence: **On account of Him who is great in might and strong in power not one is missing**; none dares to leave its post vacant when it hears the summons of the Almighty. A slight change of pointing (*mērab* for *mērōb*) seems necessary to make the epithet "great in might" correspond with "strong in power." For the latter cf. Job ix. 4.

27—31. The prophet now turns to his own people, drawing the lesson of hope and encouragement which lies in the true doctrine of God. Jehovah, whom Israel still calls "my God" (*v.* 27), is eternal and unchangeable, of infinite power and discernment (28), and the source of strength to those who have none in themselves (29) if only they will wait on Him in faith (31).

27. *My way*] i.e. my circumstances, my lot (Ps. xxxvii. 5). Israel feels that its hard lot is overlooked or ignored by Jehovah; far harder is the complaint of Job (iii. 23) that God Himself has hidden his way, setting a hedge across it.

my judgment...God] **my right passes from my God**,—escapes His notice. In all its consciousness of guilt before God, the nation retained the consciousness of having "right" on its side against its oppressors. (See Appendix, Note II.).

28. that *the everlasting God, the LORD*] Better: **An everlasting God is Jehovah**.   **He** *fainteth not*] a new sentence.

there is no searching...] Therefore it must be for wise reasons that

> Deep in unfathomable mines
>   Of never-failing skill
> He treasures up His bright designs, etc.

29 should be joined in one verse with the last two lines of *v.* 28.

And to *them that have* no might he increaseth strength.
30 Even the youths shall faint and be weary,
    And the young men shall utterly fall:
31 But they that wait upon the LORD shall renew *their* strength;
    They shall mount up *with* wings as eagles;
    They shall run, and not be weary;
    And they shall walk, and not faint.

Not only is Jehovah never weary, but He gives strength to them who are weary.

30. *Even the youths shall faint…*] Better: **And though youths faint and are weary and choice young men stumble** (the protasis to *v.* 31). Natural strength at its best is exhausted, but—

31. *they that wait upon the LORD* (shall) *renew* (lit. "exchange" cf. ch. ix. 10) their *strength*.

mount up with *wings*] although an excellent sense, is doubtful grammatically. The authorities are divided between the Targ. on the one hand, and LXX. and Vulg. on the other. The former has "lift up (their) wings"; the latter "put forth (lit. "cause to grow") pinions" (LXX. πτεροφυήσουσιν). The second is by far the best. An allusion to the popular notion that the eagle renews his feathers in his old age (Cheyne) is not probable; it is even doubtful if the idea of *renewal* is in the metaphor at all. It is rather a description (and a very fine one) of the new kind of life which comes to him who waits on the Lord; he is borne aloft on wings of faith and hope.

CH. XLI. THE APPEARANCE OF THE CONQUEROR CYRUS, A PROOF THAT JEHOVAH PRESIDES OVER THE DESTINIES OF ALL NATIONS.

The prophet here touches the soil of contemporary history. Although he is more of a theologian than earlier prophets, he is nevertheless like them an interpreter to Israel of the signs of the times, and the great historical fact which was the occasion of his message is the rise of the new Persian Power. The victories of Cyrus have already challenged the attention of the world. He conquered Media in 549; he overthrew Croesus, king of Lydia, in 540, and captured Babylon in 538. The stand-point of the prophecy is obviously somewhere in this career of conquest, certainly subsequent to 549, when the Medo-Persian empire was consolidated, and most probably subsequent to the defeat of Croesus in 540, the most signal success of Cyrus prior to the occupation of Babylon, which of course is still in the future. See Introd. pp. xvii ff.

In form the chapter is dramatic. Two great debates are imagined: the first (*vv.* 1—7) between Jehovah and the nations; the second (*vv.* 21—29) between Jehovah and the idols, the subject of both being the appearance of Cyrus. In the intervening passage (*vv.* 8—20) Jehovah encourages His servant Israel in view of this great crisis of history.

Keep silence before me, O islands; **41**
And let the people renew *their* strength:

The chapter accordingly may be analysed as follows:—
i. *vv*. 1—7. The proof of Jehovah's sovereignty in the form of a discussion between Him and the nations.
(1) *vv*. 1—4. The nations are summoned into the presence of Jehovah, that it may be seen whether they can produce an explanation of the rise of Cyrus (1). The problem is propounded: who has raised him up? who is leading him from victory to victory? (2 f.); to which the answer follows in the end of *v*. 4.
(2) *vv*. 5—7. In their consternation the nations are represented as betaking themselves to the fabrication of new idols to reassure themselves against the advance of the conqueror. (But see the notes below.)
ii. *vv*. 8—20. Turning from the nations, Jehovah addresses Israel with words of encouragement and consolation.
(1) *vv*. 8—10. Israel is Jehovah's servant or client, chosen in the person of Abraham to be the organ of the true religion and never since cast off; hence it is upheld through all its history by the strength of its Almighty Protector.
(2) *vv*. 11—16. Israel need not fear (in the coming convulsions) for by the help of Jehovah it shall put to shame all its enemies, and annihilate mountains of opposition.
(3) *vv*. 17—20. But Israel, in the distress and misery of the Exile, needs first of all refreshment; and this shall be abundantly and miraculously provided. The figures are suggested by the thirsty march through the desert: but, as in ch. xl. 3 f., the material becomes a symbol of the spiritual,—of Jehovah's all-sufficient grace for the needs of His people.
iii. *vv*. 21—29. The argument for Jehovah's Divinity is resumed; but this time the parties to the debate are the true God and the idols.
(1) *vv*. 21—24. The question is first stated in general terms: what proof can the false gods produce of their own divinity? Has any articulate prediction of theirs anticipated the great events that are happening? Or will they *now* undertake to foretell the issue of those events? They cannot; and their pretensions are dismissed as unworthy of serious consideration.
(2) *vv*. 25—29. Then the appearance of Cyrus is adduced as an instance in which they might have been expected to exercise the divine function of foreknowledge. But while Jehovah has called and strengthened Cyrus and announced it beforehand, *they* have not even foreseen that He would do so.

1. Jehovah calls the heathen nations to a disputation concerning the appearance of Cyrus.

Keep silence before me] A pregnant constr. in the Heb. = **Listen in silence unto me.** On *islands*, see on ch. xl. 15.

renew their *strength*] The words are somewhat suspicious, as they are repeated from ch. xl. 31, and the thought is hardly suitable at the beginning of an argument. Job xxxviii. 3 is not an exact parallel. Possibly the eye of a scribe may have wandered to the previous verse.

> Let them come near; then let them speak:
> Let us come near together to judgment.
> 2 Who raised up the righteous *man* from the east,
> Called him to his foot,
> Gave the nations before him, and made *him* rule over kings?
> He gave *them* as the dust *to* his sword,
> *And* as driven stubble *to* his bow.
> 3 He pursued them, *and* passed safely;
> *Even by* the way *that* he had not gone with his feet.

judgment] (*mishpāṭ*) is used in the same sense as in Mal. iii. 5 (="judicial process.") Cf. Jud. iv. 5.

2, 3. The marvellous career of Cyrus is vividly described in highly poetical language. That the reference is to Cyrus (who is first named in ch. xliv. 28) is unquestionable; although the Jewish exegetes (with the exception of Aben Ezra), and even Calvin, follow the Targ. in applying the verses to Abraham, and his victory over the four kings (Gen. xiv.).

2. *Who* **hath stirred** *up...foot*] A much-disputed clause. Two points may be regarded as settled; (1) that the abstract noun *çédeq* cannot be rendered "righteous man" (A.V. following Vulg.); and (2) that it is not to be treated as obj. to "stirred up" (A.V., LXX., Vulg.), but belongs to the second member of the sentence (Heb. accentuation). On the whole the most satisfactory translation is: **Who hath stirred up from the sun-rising (him whom) victory meets at** every step? (lit. "at his foot" cf. Gen. xxx. 30). Comp. R.V. marg. The Heb. verbs for "meet" and "call" are distinct in origin, but closely resemble each other; and the forms are constantly interchanged. The bare sense of "victory" is perhaps an extreme use of *çédeq* (=righteousness) but it is in the line of the prophet's characteristic use of the expression. It means the outward manifestation that one is in the right, and when, as here, the tribunal is the battle-field, right is equivalent to victory (see Appendix, Note II). If the ordinary sense of "righteousness" is to be retained, the word must be taken as adv. acc., as in R.V.: **Who hath raised up one from the east, whom he calleth in** righteousness **to his foot?**

gave] **giveth.** *made* him *rule over*] It is perhaps necessary (with Ewald or Hitzig) to change the vowels, rendering, subdueth (as in ch. xlv. 1).

he gave them *as the dust* to *his sword*] The words would naturally read, "he maketh his sword as dust." But this is an unnatural figure for the swiftness of Cyrus's conquests; we must either take "his" as equivalent to "their" (which is obviously objectionable), or with the LXX. change the suffix to plur., **he maketh their sword** as dust. So the next clause: **their bow as driven stubble.**

3. *by the way...feet*] The easiest and most acceptable rendering is:

Who hath wrought and done *it*, 4
Calling the generations from the beginning?
I the LORD, the first,
And with the last; I *am* he.
The isles saw *it*, and feared; 5
The ends of the earth were afraid,
Drew near, and came.
They helped every one his neighbour; 6
And *every one* said to his brother, Be of good courage.
So the carpenter encouraged the goldsmith, 7
And he that smootheth *with* the hammer him that smote the anvil,

the path **with his feet he does not tread**,—a picture of the celerity of his movements. Other interpretations, such as: "by a path which he had not gone (before) with his feet," or, "disdaining made roads," or "not returning on his tracks," are forced, if not impossible.

4. The answer.

calling the generations from the beginning] i.e. guiding the destinies of the nations from the origins of human history. The clause should be connected with what follows: it belongs to the answer, not to the question ("He that calleth").

I am he] Cf. ch. xliii. 10, 13, xlvi. 4, xlviii. 12, also Ps. cii. 27. The sense which best suits the various passages is, "I am the same." There is probably an allusion to the explanation of the name Jehovah in Ex. iii. 14 ff. Jehovah is "the First," existing before history began to run its course, and He is "with the last," an ever-present, unchanging God.

5—7. The alarm of the nations leads to the production of fresh images. The view that *vv.* 6 and 7 form part of ch. xl. 18—20 has already been mentioned. With regard to the suitability of the verses in their present connexion, opinions differ. While some consider the scene an appropriate sequel to *vv.* 1—4, and its irony exquisite and well-timed, others find the irony overstrained, and doubt if even the most benighted idolaters could be represented as seeking to arrest the advance of Cyrus by making "a particularly good and strong set of gods." And it must be admitted that the transition from an assembly of peoples to the inside of an idol factory is extremely abrupt. The view in question gives a somewhat different turn to *v.* 6 and probably necessitates the excision of *v.* 5.

5. At the end of the verse LXX. seems to have read "and came together to judgment" (in accordance with *v.* 1).

6. *they helped*] i.e. the nations. But if the verse stood originally after xl. 19, "they" refers to the two classes of workmen there mentioned. **Each helps the other, and says to his fellow, Cheer up!**

7. *the carpenter*] stands here for the same word as **workman** in xl. 19: it denotes an "artificer" either in metal or wood or stone.

he that smootheth with *the hammer*] probably the man who fits on the

Saying, It *is* ready for the sodering:
And he fastened it with nails, *that* it should not be moved.

8 But thou, Israel, *art* my servant,
Jacob whom I have chosen,
The seed of Abraham my friend.

golden covering (xl. 19). The translation *anvil* is doubtful, the Targ. has "him that striketh with the mallet."

saying...sodering] Render as R.V.: **saying of the soldering, It is good.** that *it should not be moved*] See ch. xl. 20.

8—20, coming between *vv.* 1—4 and 21 ff., reads like a digression or an "aside." But beneath the apparent disconnectedness there is a real continuity of thought running through the chapter. It opens with a discussion between Jehovah and the nations, and closes with another between Jehovah and the heathen gods. But these ideal representations have no reality except in so far as they take concrete form in history; and the historical process of which they are the expression is suggested by *vv.* 8—20. Jehovah's controversy with heathenism is carried on in His Providence, and especially in His vindication of the "right" of Israel against the world. The opposition which Israel encounters from the heathen (*vv.* 11 f.) is a reflection of the antagonism between the true religion and idolatry; and the essential identity of interest between Jehovah and Israel in this conflict of principles is the basis of the message of consolation which these verses convey. Thus we have the true God and His people over against the false gods and their peoples, and there is a fitness in the introduction at this point of Israel in its ideal functions as the organ of Jehovah's historical purpose. His victory must issue in the redemption of His people, and therefore Israel has no reason to fear the advance of Cyrus, who is God's chosen instrument for the overthrow of idolatry.

8—10. Israel is bidden "Fear not," because of its peculiar relation to Jehovah.

But thou, Israel] In opposition to the other peoples (*v.* 1). Omit "art" with R.V.

my servant] Cf. Jer. xxx. 10 f., xlvi. 27 f.; Ezek. xxviii. 25, xxxvii. 25,—the only older passages (if those in Jeremiah be really older) where the name is applied to Israel. The title is used in its simplest and widest sense, being applied to the nation as a whole, although of course in its ideal aspect, as it exists in the mind of Jehovah. The idea, however, is already a complex one, although the writer does not as yet analyse it into its different elements. (See Introduction, p. xxxi.) The one fact emphasized in this passage is the irrevocable choice or election of God, by which Israel was from its origin in Abraham constituted His servant. Cf. ch. xliii. 10, xliv. 1 f., xlix. 7.

seed of Abraham my friend] (cf. 2 Chr. xx. 7) lit. "my lover": but as Duhm remarks Heb. has no single word to express the reciprocal relation of friendship as distinct from companionship. Cf. James ii. 23, φίλος

Thou whom I have taken from the ends of the earth, 9
And called thee from the chief men thereof,
And said unto thee, Thou *art* my servant;
I have chosen thee, and not cast thee away.
Fear thou not; for I *am* with thee: 10
Be not dismayed; for I *am* thy God:
I will strengthen thee; yea, I will help thee;
Yea, I will uphold thee with the right hand of my righteousness.
Behold, all they that were incensed against thee shall 11 be ashamed and confounded:
They shall be as nothing; and they that strive with thee shall perish.
Thou shalt seek them, and shalt not find them, *even* 12 them that contended with thee:

θεοῦ ἐκλήθη. So among the Mohammedans, Abraham is designated *chalîl ullah*, "Friend of God." Note that Abraham is called "my servant" in Gen xxvi. 24.

9. *taken* (better, as R.V., **taken hold of**) *from the ends of the earth*] It is disputed whether the reference is to the call of Abraham, or to the Exodus. It is a little difficult to suppose that Egypt could be described as the "ends of the earth" by a Jew; for although the writer may have lived in Babylonia, he could hardly divest himself of the historic consciousness of his nation, that Egypt was the neighbour of Israel. It is more probable, therefore, that he is thinking of Mesopotamia, and of the choice of Israel as effected in the call of Abraham. For *chief men* render **corners** (R.V.).

cast thee away] rejected **thee**—because of thy smallness.

10. *be not dismayed*] lit. "look not round" in terror.

I will strengthen] The perf. tense used in the original expresses the unalterable determination of the speaker's will; Driver, *Tenses*, § 13.

the right hand of my righteousness] Either "my righteous right hand," or, "my right hand of righteousness." See Appendix, Note II.

11—13. Humanly speaking Israel has cause for fear, being surrounded by opponents; but they shall be put to utter confusion.

11 f. *incensed*] lit. "inflamed," as in ch. xlv. 24; Cant. i. 6. The precise form occurs only in these passages.

they that **strive**...*them that* **contend**...*they that war*] Lit. **men of thy contention**...**strife**...**warfare**; a climax which Delitzsch renders by *adversarii, inimici, hostes*. These expressions are emphatic and stand at the end of their respective clauses, and to each are attached *two* (logical) predicates; hence in *v*. 11 we should read (as R.V. nearly): they shall be **as** nothing, and **shall perish**—**the men** etc.

thou shalt seek and not *find* **them that** &c.] Cf. ch. xxxiii. 18.

They that war against thee shall be as nothing, and
as a thing of nought.
13 For I the LORD thy God will hold thy right hand,
Saying unto thee, Fear not; I will help thee.
14 Fear not, thou worm Jacob, *and* ye men of Israel;
I will help thee, saith the LORD,
And thy redeemer, the Holy One of Israel.
15 Behold, I will make thee a new sharp threshing instrument having teeth:
Thou shalt thresh the mountains, and beat *them* small,

13. *will hold...will help*] **do hold...do help.** For *saying* render: **I who say.**

14—16. Israel itself, in the might of Jehovah, shall be the means of crushing and scattering its foes. The idea, however, is not that of warlike conquest on the part of the Israelites, it is simply that in the contest Israel is as the threshing instrument to the corn, it is armed with an irresistible strength. Cheyne pointed out that in *vv.* 14, 15 *a*, Israel is addressed in the fem., but that is in all probability a mere freak of the punctuators, suggested by the fem. "worm."

thou worm Jacob] Cf. Ps. xxii. 6; Job xxv. 6. *ye men of Israel*] supplies a very weak parallel. It is generally taken as an ellipsis for "ye few men of I." (as if it were מְתֵי מִסְפָּר, Gen. xxxiv. 30 &c.), but that would have to be expressed. We should probably read with Ewald "thou small worm Israel" (רִמַּת for מְתֵי); the two words for "worm" occur together in Job xxv. 6 and also in ch. xiv. 11.

I will help] Render, as before, **I help.**

and thy redeemer, the Holy One] Read with R.V. **and thy Redeemer is the Holy One.** The word for "Redeemer" is *Gōʼēl*, the technical term for the person charged with the duty of buying back the alienated property of a kinsman, of avenging his death, and certain other obligations (see Lev. xxv. 48 f.; Num. xxxv. 19 ff.; Ruth iii. 12 &c.). It is a standing title of Jehovah in the latter part of Isaiah, occurring in 12 passages (the corresponding verb in 6 others). The verb means originally *to assert a right* by purchase: hence fig. *to reclaim, rescue* &c.; Driver, *Introduction*⁶, p. 418.

15. The *threshing instrument* (*mōrāg*) is a heavy sledge studded on its under surface with sharp stones or knives, drawn by oxen over the floor. See the Note in Driver's *Joel and Amos*, pp. 227 f. It is not a different implement from the *ḥārūç* of ch. xxviii. 27. Indeed this word *ḥārūç* is the one here translated "sharp"; and it may be doubted whether it has not intruded into the text as a variant to *mōrāg* (Duhm). The instrument to which Israel is likened is "new" and "many-toothed" (lit. "possessor of mouths" i.e. edges), therefore in the highest state of efficiency.

the mountains...the hills] A figure for formidable enemies; perhaps also for obstacles in general. Comp. ch. xxi. 10; Mic. iv. 13.

And shalt make the hills as chaff.
Thou shalt fan them, and the wind shall carry them 16
away,
And the whirlwind shall scatter them:
And thou shalt rejoice in the LORD,
And shalt glory in the Holy One of Israel.
When the poor and needy seek water, and *there is* 17
none,
And their tongue faileth for thirst,
I the LORD will hear them,
I the God of Israel will not forsake them.
I will open rivers in high places, 18
And fountains in the midst of the valleys:
I will make the wilderness a pool of water,
And the dry land springs of water.
I will plant in the wilderness the cedar, the shittah 19
tree, and the myrtle, and the oil tree;
I will set in the desert the fir tree, *and* the pine, and
the box tree together:

17—20. With great pathos the prophet recalls to mind the miserable condition of Israel in the present, and adapts his glorious promise to their sense of need. He is thus led to a glowing description of the marvels of the desert journey, in which, however, a spiritual meaning is not lost sight of.

When *the poor*...] Better: **The afflicted and needy are seeking water where there is none, their tongue is parched with thirst.** It may be a question whether such a description applies to all the exiles, or only to those, the true Israel, who were conscious of the religious privations of the Captivity.

18. Cf. ch. xxx. 25. *in high places*] R.V. **on the bare heights.** The word occurs only in ch. xlix. 9 and in Jeremiah (iii. 2 &c.). In Num. xxiii. 3 the text is doubtful.

19. The desert itself shall be transformed into a grove of stately and beautiful trees. *I will plant*] Better: **I will place.** The *shittah tree* is the acacia. The *myrtle* is only mentioned in exilic and post-exilic writings; ch. lv. 13; Zech. i. 8, 10 f.; Neh. viii. 15.

the oil tree] Not the olive, but **the oleaster** or wild olive.

the fir tree] Rather: **the cypress** (R.V. marg.). With regard to the two last of the seven trees there is no sure tradition. The first (*tidhar*) is identified by different authorities with the fir, the elm and the plane. The other (*te'ashshûr*) is according to some the box-tree, according to others a species of cedar, probably the sherbîn-tree of the Arabs (*cypressus oxycedrus*). The names occur again only in ch. lx. 13; the last, however, is also disguised in a corrupt reading in Ezek. xxvii. 6.

20 That they may see, and know, and consider, and understand together,
That the hand of the LORD hath done this,
And the Holy One of Israel hath created it.
21 Produce your cause, saith the LORD;
Bring forth your strong *reasons*, saith the King of Jacob.
22 Let them bring *them* forth, and shew us what shall happen:
Let them shew the former *things*, what they *be*,
That we may consider *them*, and know the latter end of them;

20. The ultimate object of this miracle is the demonstration of the creative power of the true God; see ch. xl. 5, lv. 13. The verse seems to shew that the previous description is not *merely* figurative, but that an actual physical transformation of the desert is contemplated.

That they (men in general) *may...consider*] Lit. "lay (to heart)," a common ellipsis. *together* binds the four verbs of the sentence.

21—24. The argument of *vv*. 1—4 is resumed, but now the idols (*v*. 23), not their worshippers, are addressed. Foreknowledge is the test of divinity. Can the idols produce any instance whatever of their power to predict, or indeed any proof of life and activity at all?

21. *your strong* reasons] Lit. "your strengths," a military metaphor transferred to controversy; cf. Job xiii. 12. The related word *'iṣma* is used in the same way in Arabic.

the King of Jacob] (Cf. ch. xliii. 15, xliv. 6), referring back, perhaps, to *vv*. 8 f.,—the King whose "servant" Jacob is.

22. *bring* them *forth and shew*] It is assumed that the "strong arguments" must be predictions.

the former things] i.e. "things past" (from the standpoint of the speaker) as opposed to things still future (*things to come*). The expression (*hā-ri'shônôth*) occurs with great frequency in the first part of this prophecy. Sometimes the stress lies on the event, sometimes on the prediction; but in reality the phrase includes both ideas—"past events as predicted." So here the challenge is to produce past predictions which have been already verified by the event. There is no ground whatever for the view of Delitzsch and others that in this verse *hā-ri'shônôth* refers to events still future, but in the *immediate* future, as opposed to the more remote future ("things to come"). See G. A. Smith, *Exposition*, p. 121, *note*.

the latter end of them] their issue. Sense and parallelism are undoubtedly improved if (with Duhm) we transpose the last two clauses, reading the closing lines thus:

the former things, what they are do ye announce, that we may lay it to heart; or the coming things let us hear, that we may know their issue.

Or declare us *things* for to come.
Shew the *things* that are to come hereafter, 23
That we may know that ye *are* gods:
Yea, do good, or do evil,
That we may be dismayed, and behold *it* together.
Behold, ye *are* of nothing, and your work of nought: 24
An abomination *is he that* chooseth you.
I have raised up *one* from the north, and he shall 25
come:
From the rising of the sun shall he call upon my
name:
And he shall come *upon* princes as *upon* morter,

23. *do good, or do evil*] i.e. "do anything whatever, good or bad" (Jer. x. 5; Zeph. i. 12), give any sign of vitality or intelligence.

that we may be dismayed] Rather: **that we may stare** (in astonishment). (The same word in v. 10.)

24. The silence of the idols settles the controversy.

of nothing...of nought] See on ch. xl. 17. The word '*épha*' here is probably a copyist's error for '*éphes*.

he that chooseth you]—your worshipper.

25—29. The general argument is now brought to bear on the particular case of the raising up of Cyrus.

25. *raised up*] Strictly: **stirred up** (as in v. 2) i.e. "impelled into activity" (Driver).

from the north...from the rising of the sun (cf. v. 2)] Scarcely: "from Media (in the north)" and "from Elam (in the east)." The terms are poetic; the north is the region of mystery, and the east the region of light (ch. xxiv. 15). In point of fact Cyrus came from the north-east.

shall he call upon my name] Render with R.V. **one that calleth** (or, **shall call**) **on my name**. The clause is a relative one, and forms the obj. to "stirred up." The expression can hardly mean less than that Cyrus shall acknowledge Jehovah as God; the meaning "make known everywhere, by his deeds" (Dillmann) is not to be defended. It is true that in ch. xlv. 4 f. it is said that Cyrus *had not known* Jehovah; but it is also said (v. 3) that the effect of his remarkable successes will be "that thou mayest know that I am Jehovah *that calleth thee by thy name*, the God of Israel." There is therefore no difficulty in the idea that Cyrus, who was at first the unconscious instrument of Jehovah's purpose, shall at length recognise that Jehovah was the true author of his success. But the further explanation that Cyrus shall "become conscious of his original religious affinity to the Jews, and act upon that consciousness" (Cheyne) goes beyond the language of the prophet.

come upon *princes*] is a possible construction; but it is better, with many comm. since Clericus, to read "tread" (*yābûs* for *yābô*). The word for "princes" (*sāgān*) is Assyrian (*shaknu*) and occurs first in Ezekiel.

And as the potter treadeth clay.
26 Who hath declared from the beginning, that we may know?
And beforetime, that we may say, *He is* righteous?
Yea, *there is* none that sheweth, yea, *there is* none that declareth,
Yea, *there is* none that heareth your words.
27 The first *shall say* to Zion, Behold, behold them:
And I will give to Jerusalem one that bringeth good tidings.
28 For I beheld, and *there was* no man;
Even amongst them, and *there was* no counseller,
That, when I asked of them, could answer a word.
29 Behold, they *are* all vanity; their works *are* nothing:
Their molten images *are* wind and confusion.

26. He is *righteous*] **He is in the right** (cf. Ex. ix. 27); or, simply, **Right**! (cf. ch. xliii. 9), although the adj. is always used of persons, except in Deut. iv. 8 (of the divine ordinances).

27. *The first...behold them*] A very perplexing sentence: lit. "A first one to Zion, Behold, behold them!" We may render (nearly as R.V.) **(I) first (have said) to Zion, Behold**, etc. Or we may supply the verb from the following line, thus: "I first will give to Zion (one saying) Behold," etc.; or "I will give a first one (i.e. a forerunner) to Zion (saying), Behold, etc." It is difficult to choose. In any case there appears (from the phrase "behold them") to be a reference back to ch. xl. 9 ff.; and the general sense must be that that prediction was the first authoritative declaration of the meaning of the appearance of Cyrus. That Cyrus himself is the "forerunner" (Nägelsbach) is not a probable interpretation.

one that bringeth good tidings] **an evangelist** (see ch. xl. 9).

28. *For I beheld, and* there was] Rather as R.V. **And when I look, there is.** Cf. l. 2.   *even amongst them*] Better: **and among these**, viz., the idols; the previous clause referring to their worshippers.

no counseller] None who can advise in the present crisis.

29. The last word of the argument.

all of them (R.V.)] idols and worshippers together.

their works] are the images of the gods, "the work of men's hands" (parallel to "molten images" below).

confusion] "nothingness"—chaos (see ch. xl. 17).

CH. XLII. THE HIGH DESTINY OF ISRAEL AS THE SERVANT OF JEHOVAH CONTRASTED WITH ITS PRESENT ABASEMENT AND UNFITNESS FOR ITS MISSION.

The two preceding chapters were to some extent introductory to what follows. Nearly all the leading ideas of the prophecy have been already expressed, and all the personages of the drama—Jehovah, Israel, Cyrus, the nations and their gods—have been brought upon the stage, or at least have been mentioned. With this chapter the prophet begins to amplify and develope the various conceptions, already touched upon, by means of which he is enabled to interpret the action of Jehovah in the present crisis of history. And the first which he takes up is the thought of Israel, Jehovah's Servant. Up to ch. xliv. 23, that is the central and recurrent idea; in the end of that chapter the figure of Cyrus comes to the front, and the main theme for several chapters is the mission which he executes in the service of Jehovah. But the treatment is nowhere exhaustive; and although the minor sections are remarkably distinct, sharply defined stages or advances in the general thought can hardly be found. The writer glides rapidly from one theme to another, frequently returning on his track; and while some conceptions are dropped as he proceeds, there are others, and these the most important, which run on to the close.

In the view of many expositors, indeed, an entirely new personage is introduced in the opening verses of this chapter, namely, the Servant of Jehovah, whom these writers hold to be distinct from Israel. This is the deepest problem in the whole prophecy, and is only to be solved by paying the closest attention to the exegesis of the individual passages and the prophet's general scheme of thought. As supplementing the notes on *vv.* 1—4 below, see Introduction, pp. xxxii—xxxvii, and Appendix, Note I.

Ch. xlii. consists of three divisions:

i. *vv.* 1—9. The ideal calling and function of Israel.

(1) *vv.* 1—4. A portrait of Israel as the Lord's Servant from the point of view of Jehovah, who is the speaker.

(2) *vv.* 5—9. The truth embodied in the portrait is held up as a ground of encouragement to Israel; Jehovah, as it were, pledges His Godhead to the fulfilment of the ideal in the experience of the people.

ii. *vv.* 10—17. The prophet's thoughts are thus led forward to the great redemptive act by which Jehovah will raise Israel to the height of its glorious destiny.

(1) *vv.* 10—13 are a poem calling on the whole earth to rejoice in Jehovah's triumph over His enemies.

(2) *vv.* 14—17. Jehovah Himself is then introduced as the speaker, announcing that He will rouse Himself from His long inactivity, to bring about the redemption of His people, and the consequent overthrow of idolatry.

iii. *vv.* 18—25. The prophet addresses himself to Israel in its present state of blindness and wretchedness. He calls on the exiles to reflect on all that they have suffered at the hand of their God, and to recognise in it the effect of their obduracy and unfaithfulness to their calling, their misuse of religious privileges, and their positive transgressions of the law of Jehovah.

1—4. Israel as the Lord's Servant. The features of the portrait are these: (1) It starts from the thought of ch. xli. 8 ff., the *election* by which Israel is constituted the Servant of Jehovah; but this is immediately followed by (2) the *equipment* of the Servant with the Divine

42 Behold my servant, whom I uphold;
Mine elect, *in whom* my soul delighteth;
I have put my spirit upon him:
He shall bring forth judgment to the Gentiles.

Spirit, and (3) the *mission* for which he is raised up, viz., to be the organ of the true religion to the world (*v.* 1). (4) The *manner* and *spirit of the Servant's working* are then described; his unobtrusiveness and tenderness (3 f.). (5) His unflinching *constancy* in the prosecution of his work, and his final and complete *success*. The whole description is singularly elevated, and impressive; Jehovah speaks of His Servant as He sees him, and as he shall yet be revealed to the world.

If the Servant of the Lord here described is Israel, he is obviously not Israel in its actual condition of bondage and inefficiency. He is Israel according to its idea,—the Divine ideal after and towards which Jehovah is fashioning the people. This ideal is personified, and it is the vividness of the personification that leads many readers to think that an individual must be meant. But such impressions are not greatly to be trusted. It is a very hazardous thing to set limits to the possibilities of O.T. personification. The real question is whether the characteristics ascribed to the Servant are capable of being realised by the nation of Israel, or whether they are such as to demand a separate and personal embodiment. Even if it should be found that some details do not readily fall in with the national interpretation it would not at once follow that that interpretation was false; for no one argues that our Lord's parables must be literally true stories, because they contain features to which no spiritual meaning can be attached. But that consideration need not trouble us in this passage, for it will be seen that all that is here said of the Servant is applicable to Israel in the ideal light in which it is here presented. Certainly no historic individual *of that age* can possibly be the subject of the picture.

1. The election, equipment, and mission of the Servant.

Behold my servant] LXX. reads Ἰακὼβ ὁ παῖς μου ("Jacob my servant") and in the next line, Ἰσραὴλ ὁ ἐκλεκτός μου ("Israel my chosen").

whom I uphold] Cf. ch. xli. 10.

mine elect] R.V. **my chosen**. Used of Israel ch. xliii. 20, xlv. 4; cf. the verb in xli. 8 etc.; and Deut. vii. 7 &c.

I have put my spirit upon him] The Servant's function being prophetic, he is, like the prophets, endowed with the spirit of Jehovah. Cf. ch. xi. 2 ff., where the Messiah is endowed with the Spirit for His royal functions.

he shall bring forth (or **send forth**) *judgment to the* nations] This is the ultimate purpose of the Servant's being raised up,—the diffusion of the true religion throughout the world. The word "judgement" (*mishpāṭ*) occurs three times in these few verses, and evidently in a special sense. The plural is often used of the ordinances (lit. "judicial decisions") of Jehovah; these are sometimes viewed as a unity and

He shall not cry, nor lift up,
Nor cause his voice to be heard in the street.
A bruised reed shall he not break,
And the smoking flax shall he not quench:
He shall bring forth judgment unto truth.
He shall not fail nor be discouraged,
Till he have set judgment in the earth:
And the isles shall wait for his law.

described by the sing. (see ch. li. 4; Jer. v. 4, viii. 7). This is the sense here; it means the religion of Jehovah regarded as a system of practical ordinances. All recent commentators instance the close parallel of the Arabic *dîn*, which denotes both a system of usages and a religion. This the Servant shall "send forth" to the nations by his prophetic word. The best commentary on the passage is ch. ii. 1—4.

2 The Servant's unobtrusive manner of working. Not by clamorous self-assertion in the high places of the world, but by silent spiritual influences his great work shall be accomplished. Comp. the striking application in Matt. xii. 17 ff. This feature of the Servant's activity can hardly have been suggested by the demeanour of the prophets of Israel; and for that reason the prophecy is all the more wonderful as a perception of the true conditions of spiritual work. It reminds us of the "still small voice" in which Elijah was made to recognise the power of Jehovah (1 Ki. xix. 12 f.). *nor lift up*] sc. his voice.

3. His gentleness towards the downtrodden expiring good in men. *the smoking flax*] R.V. marg. the dimly **burning wick**. The metaphor (like the preceding) involves a *litotes*: the meaning is that instead of crushing the expiring elements of goodness he will strengthen and purify them. It is an interesting question whether these rudiments of religion are conceived as existing in the heathen world or in the breasts of individual Israelites. The former view is no doubt that to which the national interpretation of the Servant most readily accommodates itself, and is also most in keeping with the scope of the passage as a whole. But in later sections a mission in and to Israel is undoubtedly assigned to the Servant, and a reference to that here cannot be pronounced impossible.

unto truth] i.e. probably, **in accordance with truth**. The rendering of R.V., however, "in truth," may be right.

4. His constancy. The words *fail* and *be discouraged* correspond in the original to "dimly burning" and "broken" in *v.* 3. (See R.V. marg.) The former is used of the failing eyesight of Eli (1 Sam. iii. 2); cf. Ezek. xxi. 7 (R.V. marg.).

for his law] his instruction (see on ch. i. 10), his revelation of the truth. It is doubtful whether the verb of this clause should be rendered "shall wait" or "do wait." If the latter be correct, the remarkable thought may be expressed that already the best of the heathen are dissatisfied with their religious systems and long for a purer faith.

5 Thus saith God the LORD,
He that created the heavens, and stretched them out;
He that spread forth the earth, and that which cometh out of it;
He that giveth breath unto the people upon it,
And spirit to them that walk therein:
6 I the LORD have called thee in righteousness,
And will hold thine hand, and will keep thee,
And give thee for a covenant of the people, for a light of the Gentiles;

5—9. Jehovah's promise to Israel, based on the preceding description.
God] in the Heb. *hā-'ēl*, **the God**,—the God who alone is truly God, who has created and sustains all things.

spread forth] or "made firm." The word means to beat out into a thin surface, and probably (as in the noun "firmament") combines the ideas of density and extension (cf. ch. xliv. 24; Ps. cxxxvi. 6). By a strong zeugma this verb is made to govern a second object, *that which cometh out of it*, which here probably denotes "vegetation" (see on ch. xxxiv. 1).

breath and *spirit* are here nearly identical, the divine principle of life breathed into man at his creation; Gen. ii. 7.

6. *called thee in righteousness*] i.e. in accordance with a stedfast and consistent purpose. See Appendix, Note II, and cf. ch. xlv. 13.

and will keep thee] R.V. marg. ("form thee") derives the verb from a different root; if this sense be taken, it is necessary to read the words in close connexion with what follows: "I will form and appoint thee for a covenant &c."

for a covenant of the people] The expression occurs again in ch. xlix. 8, and is one of the most difficult in this prophecy. The idea is necessarily a pregnant one, and it is nowhere developed in such a way that we can be sure of the exact meaning. The notion of a "national league" must be dismissed, because the Heb. *bĕrîth*, unlike the German "Bund," nowhere means "confederation." To take "people" in the sense of "humanity" is also unsuitable because of xlix. 8, which clearly limits the reference to Israel. Looking at the phrase by itself two constructions are grammatically possible: (*a*) We may render it, "a covenant of a people," or "a covenant people," after the analogy of Gen. xvi. 12, where Ishmael is called "a wild ass of a man" (cf. "Wonder of a Counsellor" in ch. ix. 6). This, however, is somewhat strained. (*b*) The most natural, and on the whole probably the most satisfactory rendering is, "a nation's covenant," i.e. the covenant upon which a nation is constituted, the conception implied being that Israel's future national existence must be based on a new covenant between it and Jehovah (ch. lv. 3; Jer. xxxi. 30—32). The difficulty is thus reduced to the pregnancy of the statement that the Servant *is* or *shall be* this covenant. It is probably to be explained in accordance with such expressions as

To open the blind eyes, 7
To bring out the prisoners from the prison,
And them that sit in darkness out of the prison house.
I *am* the LORD: that *is* my name: 8
And my glory will I not give to another,
Neither my praise to graven images.
Behold, the former *things* are come to pass, 9
And new *things* do I declare :
Before they spring forth I tell you of them.
Sing unto the LORD a new song, 10
And his praise from the end of the earth,
Ye that go down to the sea, and all that is therein;

"thou shalt be a blessing" (Gen. xii. 2). As "blessing" there means "cause of blessing," so here "covenant" may be equivalent to the *ground* or (as most commentators explain) the *mediator* of a national covenant. The idea at all events must be something like this: the Divine ideal represented by the Servant of the Lord becomes the basis of a new national life, inasmuch as it expresses that for the sake of which Jehovah enters into a new covenant relation with His people.

for a light of the **nations**] The ultimate destiny of the Servant; see on *v.* 1.

7. *to open* [the] *blind eyes*] The subject of this and the following verb might be either Jehovah or His Servant, and the point is not quite settled by ch. xlix. 8. The latter, however, seems more probable from xlix. 6. The reference is no doubt to the Servant's work on Israel. The "blindness" spoken of is spiritual (see *vv.* 18—20); imprisonment is a metaphor for the Captivity (*v.* 22); although a spiritual application may be included here also.

8. *my glory...another*] (Cf. ch. xlviii. 11)—the glory of true deity, which would be forfeited if Jehovah were unable to predict the future, or if His predictions should fail (*v.* 9).

9. *the former* things] the things formerly predicted. The reference probably is to prophecies just fulfilled in the successes of Cyrus. The *new things* are the substance of the present prophecy, the exaltation of the Servant, the redemption of Israel, and the conversion of the heathen. (See Introd., p. xxi.)

10—13. The mention of "new things" in *v.* 9 suggests this "new song," in which the creation is called to celebrate Jehovah's redemption of His people. The expression is common in the Psalms (xxxiii. 3, xl. 3, xcvi. 1, xcviii. 1, cxliv. 9, cxlix. 1; cf. Rev. xiv. 3). These Psalmists probably borrowed the term from our prophet, whose use of it bears the stamp of originality. It is a song "such as has never been heard in the heathen world" (Delitzsch). See ch. xxiv. 14—16.

from the end of the earth] means (as in Gen. xix. 4; Jer. li. 31) "from end to end."

ye that go down to the sea] **seafarers**, cf. Ps. cvii. 23. There is some

The isles, and the inhabitants thereof.
11 Let the wilderness and the cities thereof lift up *their voice*,
The villages *that* Kedar doth inhabit:
Let the inhabitants of the rock sing,
Let them shout from the top of the mountains.
12 Let them give glory unto the LORD,
And declare his praise in the islands.
13 The LORD shall go forth as a mighty *man*,
He shall stir up jealousy like a man of war:

awkwardness in the following words: *and all that is therein* (lit. "and the fulness thereof"), which are naturally parallel to "the sea" and not to "those who go down to it." The harshness is removed by a plausible emendation of Lowth, who reads the whole clause in accordance with Ps. xcvi. 11, xcviii. 7 *let the sea roar and the* fulness thereof (יִרְעַם for יוֹרְדֵי).

the isles] See on ch. xl. 15. The mention of the sea and its coasts before the land is one indication of the prominence which the western lands have in the mind of this prophet.

11. *the wilderness and the cities thereof*] The "cities," like the "villages" of the next line, are those in the oases, occupied by the settled Arabs; the former are probably the great centres of the caravan trade, like Tadmor and Petra. *Kedar* (see on ch. xxi. 16) is sometimes referred to as a tribe of nomadic, tent-dwelling Arabs (Ps. cxx. 5; Cant. i. 5; Jer. xlix. 28 f.); here they are villagers, what the modern Arabs call *ḥaḍarīya* (connected with the word *ḥāçēr*, used here) as opposed to the *wabarīya* or nomads (Delitzsch). In Jer. ii. 10 Kedar stands, as here, in opposition to the Mediterranean countries.

the inhabitants of the rock] (i.e. "the rock-dwellers"). R.V. has "the inhabitants of Sela," which would probably be Petra. It is difficult to say which translation is preferable. It should be mentioned that the identification of Sela, in any O.T. passage, with Petra is resisted by many scholars (see on ch. xvi. 1).

sing] Rather, **exult**,—a different word at any rate from that used in *v.* 10.

12. *glory* and *praise:* the same words as in *v.* 8.

13. The reason for the universal exultation; Jehovah takes the field against His enemies. The gracious side of His intervention is reserved for *v.* 16.

The LORD shall go forth] The technical expression for the initiation of a campaign (2 Sam. xi. 1; Am. v. 3 &c.)

as a mighty man (or, **hero**)...*a man of war*] Similar representations in ch. xxviii. 21, lix. 16 f.; Ex. xv. 3; Zech. xiv. 3, &c. *Jealousy* (better, **zeal**) means "passion" in very varied senses. Here it seems equivalent to the "battle fever." See ch. ix. 7.

He shall cry, yea, roar;
He shall prevail against his enemies.
I have long time holden my peace;   14
I have been still, *and* refrained myself:
Now will I cry like a travailing woman;
I will destroy and devour at once.
I will make waste mountains and hills,   15
And dry up all their herbs;
And I will make the rivers islands,
And I will dry up the pools.
And I will bring the blind by a way *that* they knew   16
   not;
I will lead them in paths *that* they have not known:

he shall cry, yea, roar] **He shall raise His battle cry, yea, shout aloud.**
he shall prevail] R.V. "he shall do mightily"; lit., **he shall play the hero.** The form occurs elsewhere only in Job (xv. 25, xxxvi. 9).

14—17. Jehovah rouses Himself from His inactivity. The passage, which obviously continues the figure of *v.* 13, is exceedingly bold in its anthropomorphism; it is Jehovah's battle-song.

14. *I have long time holden my peace*] Lit. "I have been silent from of old." The period of silence perhaps goes back further than the Exile; it is the time during which Jehovah has permitted the oppression of His people by the heathen.

I have been still] Lit. "been dumb"; but "still" expresses the idea better; it is abstinence from action, not from speech, that is meant.

refrained myself] Cf. Gen. xliii. 31, xlv. 1.

now will I cry **out**] The verb does not recur in the O.T. In Aramaic it is used of the bleating of sheep. Here it denotes the convulsive utterance of uncontrollable emotion, "like a travailing woman."

destroy and devour at once] Render with R.V. **gasp and pant together**; "together" uniting the *three* ideas.

15. Jehovah's breath of anger will make the fairest and best watered regions an arid waste. Cf. ch. xl. 7, 24, and note the contrasted image in xli. 18 f. For *herbs*, read **herbage.** The word *islands* is used in a peculiar sense, of dry land as opposed to water.

16. The prophet hastens on to the gracious issue of God's interposition, the homebringing of the captives through the trackless desert.

the blind here are hardly the spiritually blind, those who cannot discern God's purpose (as *v.* 18); what is meant is that the travellers cannot see their path, just as the desert is the region of "darkness" because it has no track (cf. Jer. ii. 6, 31). For *knew* and *have known*, render **know**, with R.V.

ISAIAH, XLII.

> I will make darkness light before them,
> And crooked things straight.
> These things will I do unto them, and not forsake them.
> 17 They shall be turned back, they shall be greatly ashamed, that trust in graven images,
> That say to the molten images, Ye *are* our gods.
> 18 Hear, ye deaf;
> And look, ye blind, that *ye* may see.
> 19 Who *is* blind, but my servant?
> Or deaf, as my messenger *that* I sent?

crooked things straight] crooked places a plain (cf. ch. xl. 4).
these things... forsake them] Better: These are the things I have determined to do (perf. of resolution) and not leave undone.

17. The confusion of the idolaters, through the "revelation of the glory of God" (ch. xl. 5), the Babylonians being those specially referred to (cf. ch. xlvi. 1); *they shall be* utterly *ashamed* (as ch. xli. 11).

18—25. An expostulation with Israel for its insensibility to the privileges it has enjoyed. The passage is of considerable interest for the light which it throws on the sense in which the title "Servant of the Lord" is to be understood. The discrepancy between the description in *vv*. 1—4 and that here given is at first sight perplexing. There the Servant is spoken of as the perfect and successful worker for God, here he is addressed as blind and deaf and altogether unfit for Jehovah's purpose. Yet it is extremely unnatural to suppose that the writer applies the term to two entirely different subjects. To suggest, as the prophet's meaning, that the inefficient Servant is to be replaced by another, who shall accomplish the work in which the former has failed is perhaps the least satisfactory of all explanations, and misrepresents the teaching of the prophecy. That the subject here addressed is Israel in its actual present condition is beyond dispute; hence *vv*. 1—4 must also be regarded as in some sense a description of Israel. The contrast, in short, is not between the false servant and the true,—the one a nation and the other an individual,—but between Israel as it really is and Israel according to its idea. Indeed it would seem that what the prophet wishes his people to lay to heart is just this contrast between its ideal calling and its actual accomplishments; and this is more intelligible if the ideal has been already depicted, and is still present to the writer's mind.

18. *look* and *see* are distinguished as in 2 Kings iii. 14; Job xxxv. 5, &c.; the former is to direct the gaze towards, the latter to take in the significance of an object.

19. Israel is the blind and deaf nation *par excellence*, because no other nation has been so tested by the opportunity of seeing and hearing (see on *v*. 21). *my messenger* that *I* send (R.V.)] Cf. ch. xliv. 26, where "messengers" is parallel to "servant."

Who *is* blind as he that is perfect,
And blind as the LORD's servant?
Seeing many *things*, but thou observest not;   20
Opening the ears, but he heareth not.
The LORD is well pleased for his righteousness' sake;   21
He will magnify the law, and make *it* honourable.
But this *is* a people robbed and spoiled;   22
They are all of them snared in holes,

as he that is perfect] R.V. has, "as he that is at peace with me." The meaning of the Heb. *mĕshullām* (a proper name in 2 Ki. xxii. 3; Ezra viii. 16, and often) is uncertain. Many take it as the equivalent of the Arabic "Moslim,"="the surrendered one" (Cheyne, *Comm.*). It is no objection to this that it is based on an Aramaic use of the verb; but the idea seems hardly suitable, inasmuch as it implies a state of *character* which the actual Israel does not possess. Probably a better rendering is the befriended **one** (sc. by Jehovah), after the analogy of Job v. 23. Another possible translation would be "the requited one" (see R.V. marg.), but it is difficult to attach any definite meaning to the expression in this context.

blind in the last clause should no doubt be **deaf**, as is read in some MSS.

20. *Seeing many* things] Render with R.V. in accordance with the consonantal text, **Thou hast seen many things**; the form has been quite needlessly changed by the punctuators. The idea of the verse is that the great historical facts of revelation have been within the cognisance of Israel, but it has failed to apprehend their true import. Cf. ch. vi. 9 ff.

21. The verse reads: **It was Jehovah's pleasure, for His righteousness' sake, to magnify instruction (or, Revelation) and glorify it.** (See R.V.) *Righteousness* is to be understood exactly as in *v.* 6; and the verbs "magnify" and "glorify" are subordinate to "was pleased," expressing that which Jehovah was pleased to do. (See Davidson, *Synt.* § 83, R. 1.) The only question is whether the reference is to the past revelation in law and prophecy, by which Israel has failed to profit; or to the future glorification of religion by its diffusion among the nations (*vv.* 1, 4, 6). The last is probably nearest the truth. The verse is not an explanation of the "many things" that Israel has seen and failed to see, but introduces a new thought. It expresses the great purpose which Jehovah had cherished with regard to Israel—to make it the instrument of extending the knowledge of His will to the world. This is the true "glorification" of the *Tōrāh* of Israel (*v.* 4).

22 ff. shew how this design has hitherto been frustrated by the necessity of imposing chastisement on Israel, till it should learn its true mission.

But this..] Rather, **But it.**   *snared in holes*] This is no doubt the sense, although a change of pointing seems necessary in the verb, making it a passive (read *hŭphah* for *hāphēah*). The metaphor is for

And they are hid in prison houses:
They are for a prey, and none delivereth;
For a spoil, and none saith, Restore.
23 Who among you will give ear to this?
Who will hearken and hear for the time to come?
24 Who gave Jacob for a spoil, and Israel to the robbers?
Did not the LORD, he against whom we have sinned?
For they would not walk in his ways,
Neither were they obedient unto his law.
25 Therefore he hath poured upon him the fury of his anger, and the strength of battle:
And it hath set him on fire round about, yet he knew not;
And it burned him, yet he laid *it* not to heart.

the captivity, but it is only a metaphor; the prophet does not imagine that a large proportion of the exiles were actually incarcerated in dungeons.

23. The question expresses the prophet's wish that now at last some of the people should begin to realise the significance of their relation to Jehovah, and prepare themselves for the great deliverance.

will give ear to this] i.e. to the substance of the present exhortation,—the contrast between the ideal calling of Israel and its present position, its failure to realise its mission, and (especially) the reason of that failure (*vv.* 24 f.).

for the time to come] in contrast to past disobedience. It is evident that the prophet expects the mission of Israel to be realised by a conversion of the nation. The process of that conversion is powerfully described in ch. liii.

24, 25. The enigma of Israel's history is that Jehovah its God has given it over to its enemies,—a truth which the nation as a whole has never yet laid to heart.

for a spoil] A better reading (which is probably that intended by the consonantal text) is **to the spoiler**. (Cf. ch. x. 13.)

did not the LORD] The whole of this answer is regarded by Duhm and Cheyne as spurious. Its removal gets rid of an awkward alternation of persons, and enables us to read *v.* 25 as a continuation of the question in the first part of *v.* 24. But Duhm goes too far when he objects to the *substance* of the answer, on the ground that so explicit a confession of sin is improbable before ch. xliii. 1 ff. The two last clauses are to be translated as relatives, **and in whose ways they would not walk** (so R.V.), **and whose law they would not obey**.

25. *Therefore* should be simply **and**. *the strength of battle*] **the violence of war**, which (as in ch. ix. 18 ff. etc.) is compared to a fire. *he knew not*] i.e. "understood it not;" hardly, "heeded it not." Israel felt its calamities keenly enough, but did not comprehend their significance, as a visitation from Jehovah. Note the contrast in ch. xliii. 2.

But now thus saith the LORD that created thee, O Jacob, **43**

CH. XLIII. 1.—XLIV. 5. ISRAEL, IN SPITE OF ITS SIN AND BLINDNESS, IS COMFORTED WITH GRACIOUS PROMISES OF REDEMPTION.

(i) *vv.* 1—7. This section is very closely connected in thought with *vv.* 18—25 of the previous chapter. The contrast, however, is no longer between the ideal Israel and the actual, but between Israel in the misery of exile and Israel in the glory of its coming salvation. The prophet has just reminded the captives that the author of their calamities is Jehovah, against whom they have sinned; now he assures them that in spite of these sins God has not finally cast them off, and directs their thoughts to the bright future about to dawn on them. Jehovah is about to redeem Israel, which He has formed and chosen for His own (*vv.* 1, 2); He will ransom it at the cost of powerful and wealthy nations which must take its place as servants of the world-power, because it is precious in His sight (*vv.* 3, 4); He will gather together its scattered members from the remotest quarters of the world (*vv.* 5—7).

(ii) *vv.* 8—13. The argument from prophecy is here repeated, and again in the dramatic form of a judicial process between Jehovah and the assembled nations. These are challenged to bring forward their witnesses to prove that their gods have foretold this wonderful event, or that any past prediction of theirs has been verified (*v.* 9). Jehovah on His part brings forward His servant Israel, a people blind and deaf, but able at least to bear witness to the *fact* that He has given incontestable proof of Divinity by predicting this great deliverance (*vv.* 8, 10 ff.).

(iii) *vv.* 14—21. The fall of Babylon is here for the first time explicitly announced (*vv.* 14, 15), as the preliminary to Israel's restoration. The glory of this "new thing" shall eclipse all "former things," even the wonders of the exodus from Egypt and the marching through the wilderness (*vv.* 16 ff.). The prophet's imagination again fixes on the concrete image of the miraculous way through the desert as the emblem of Jehovah's saving power (*v.* 19 ff.).

(iv) *vv.* 22—28. A renewed remonstrance with Israel, similar in tone to ch. xlii. 18—25. The general idea of the section seems to be that while Israel has been utterly careless of Jehovah (*v.* 22), burdening Him not with lavish offerings but merely with its sins and iniquities (*vv.* 23, 24), He, for His own sake, forgives its trespasses (*v.* 25), although the people have forfeited all claim on His mercy (*vv.* 26—28). (But see the Notes below, pp. 42 f.)

(v) Ch. xliv. 1—5. By the outpouring of His Spirit, Jehovah shall so bless and prosper His people, that proselytes from among the heathen shall voluntarily attach themselves to the restored nation. This promise stands in contrast to the severity of the preceding verses, exactly as *vv.* 1—7 follow upon the last strophe of ch. xlii.

1—7. Israel, though blind and deaf (ch. xlii. 18 ff.), is precious in the sight of Jehovah its Creator, who is now about to shew Himself as its Redeemer.

But now] Introducing the contrast to xlii. 25.

And he that formed thee, O Israel,
Fear not: for I have redeemed thee,
I have called *thee* by thy name; thou *art* mine.

2 When thou passest through the waters, I *will be* with thee;
And through the rivers, they shall not overflow thee:
When thou walkest through the fire, thou shalt not be burnt;
Neither shall the flame kindle upon thee.

3 For I *am* the LORD thy God,
The Holy One of Israel, thy Saviour:
I gave Egypt *for* thy ransom,
Ethiopia and Seba for thee.

4 Since thou wast precious in my sight,

that created thee...that formed thee] Three verbs which express Jehovah's creative activity are applied in this prophecy to His special relations to Israel: "create" (*vv.* 1, 7, 15); "form" (*vv.* 1, 21, xliv. 2, 21, 24, xlv. 11, xlix. 5 (lxiv. 8); "make" (xliv. 2, li. 13, liv. 5).
I have redeemed thee] Rather, **I redeem thee** (perf. of certainty). See on ch. xli. 14. *I have called* (**I call**) thee *by thy name*] i.e. I address thee as one who is familiar and dear (xlv. 3 f., cf. Ex. xxxi. 2); stronger than the simple "call" (xlii. 6, xlix. 1).

2. When Jehovah was angry the fire burned Israel (ch. xlii. 25), but now with Jehovah on its side, it is invulnerable in the severest trials. "Water" and "fire" are common images of extreme peril; the former in Ps. xxxii. 6, xlii. 7, cxxiv. 4 f.; the latter in ch. xlii. 25 (cf. Dan. iii. 17, 27); both together Ps. lxvi. 12. For *burned* render **scorched** (Prov. vi. 28).

3. *thy Saviour*] or, "Deliverer"; a favourite designation of Jehovah with this prophet; *v.* 11, ch. xlv. 15, 21, xlix. 26 (lx. 16, lxiii. 8). The second half of the verse shews on how large a scale this deliverance is to be executed.

I give Egypt as *thy ransom*...] The meaning appears to be that Cyrus will be compensated for the emancipation of Israel by the conquest of these African nations, which did not belong to the Babylonian Empire. As a matter of fact the conquest of Egypt was effected by Cambyses, the son and successor of Cyrus, although it is said to have been contemplated by Cyrus himself (Herod. I. 153) and is actually (though wrongly) attributed to him by Xenophon (*Cyrop.* VIII. 6. 20).

Seba (Gen. x. 7; Ps. lxxii. 10; ch. xlv. 14) was, according to Josephus, Meroë, the northern province of Ethiopia, lying between the Blue and the White Nile.

ransom is strictly a money payment by which a man escapes the forfeit of his life (see Ex. xxi. 30; Num. xxxv. 31 f.; Prov. vi. 35 &c.).

4. *Since thou wast...thou hast been*...] Rather, **Because thou art**

vv. 5—8.] ISAIAH, XLIII. 37

Thou hast been honourable, and I have loved thee:
Therefore will I give men for thee,
And people for thy life.
Fear not: for I *am* with thee: 5
I will bring thy seed from the east,
And gather thee from the west;
I will say to the north, Give *up;* 6
And to the south, Keep not back:
Bring my sons from far,
And my daughters from the ends of the earth;
Even every one that is called by my name: 7
For I have created him for my glory,
I have formed him; yea, I have made him.

Bring forth the blind people that have eyes, 8
And the deaf that have ears.

precious in my sight, art honourable, and I love thee (three coordinate clauses). The A.V. seems to take the conjunction in a temporal sense, a view which has been defended by some commentators on grammatical grounds, but is quite unsuitable.

men] in contrast to a money payment. For *people* read **peoples** (as R.V.).

5—7. The ingathering of the Dispersion (cf. ch. xlix. 12).

6. *my sons...my daughters*] See ch. i. 1. The individual Israelites are the children of the marriage between Jehovah and the nation (Hos. ii. 2, 5; Ez. xvi. 20, &c.).

7. *that is called by my name*] i.e. who belongs to the community in which Jehovah is worshipped.

for I have created him] Render with R.V. **and whom I have created**.

for my glory] Although it is only the restored nation that can fully manifest Jehovah's glory to the world, each of its scattered units shares the dignity which belongs to Israel as a whole.

8—13. Another imaginary judgement scene (cf. ch. xli. 1—4, 21—28), in which Israel appears as Jehovah's witness to the truth of His prophecies.

8. *Bring forth*] i.e. not "from exile," but "before the tribunal." The sense demands an imperat., and the Heb. pointing (which gives a perf.) must be altered accordingly.

a blind people that have eyes...] "a people which is blind and yet has eyes &c." This cannot mean "a people *once* blind and deaf, but *now* in possession of sight and hearing"; and it scarcely means anything so subtle as "a people which though blind and deaf yet possesses the organs of sight and hearing," and therefore can be made to see and hear (*v.* 10). The paradox is the same as in ch. xlii. 20 ("thou hast seen many things but thou observest not," &c.) and goes back to ch. vi.

9   Let all the nations be gathered together,
    And let the people be assembled:
    Who among them can declare this,
    And shew us former *things?*
    Let them bring forth their witnesses, that they may be justified:
    Or let them hear, and say, *It is* truth.
10 Ye *are* my witnesses, saith the LORD,
    And my servant whom I have chosen:

9 ff.; the sense being that while Israel lacks insight into the divine meaning of its own history, it is nevertheless a perfectly competent witness to the bare external *facts*; it has *heard* the predictions and *seen* them fulfilled.

9. *Let all the nations be gathered together*] The form of the verb in Heb. presents difficulty. By some it is treated as a rare form of imperat., on the ground of two doubtful analogies (so R.V. marg., "Gather yourselves together &c."). Others take it as a precative perf. (A.V. and R.V.) the existence of which in Heb. is also disputed (see Driver, *Tenses*, § 20). There seems, however, no reason why it should not be understood as a perf. in the ordinary sense: **All the nations are gathered together**. The assembling of the parties in the process naturally precedes the calling of witnesses; and this clause is descriptive of the scene presupposed by *v.* 8. The following verb should then be pointed as a consecutive impf.: **and the peoples are assembled**.

who among them (the heathen gods, represented by their worshippers) *can declare this*] i.e. the contents of the prophecy, *vv.* 1—7.

former things] predictions of the events that have already taken place. If they profess to do this, then *let them bring forth their witnesses*, in support of their contention.

or let them hear, and say] The subject is the witnesses, who are supposed to hear the allegations of the false deities, and corroborate them.

be justified...It is truth] See on ch. xli. 26.

10. The gods are unable to meet the challenge, and Jehovah turns to His servant Israel, whose very presence is evidence of His power both to predict and to deliver. The words *and my servant* are not a complement of the subject ("ye are my witnesses, and [so is] my Servant") but of the predicate (**ye are my witnesses and** [ye are] **my Servant**). The former view would imply some sort of distinction between the Servant and Israel, whether of an individual over against the nation, or of a part of the nation over against the whole. But whatever view may be held of the personality of the Servant, the natural construction of the sentence places it alongside of those numerous passages where the title is applied to Israel. To bear witness to Jehovah's divinity is one of the functions of Israel as the Servant of the Lord.

That ye may know and believe me,
And understand that I *am* he:
Before me there was no God formed,
Neither shall there be after me.
I, *even* I, *am* the LORD; 11
And beside me *there is* no saviour.
I have declared, and have saved, and I have shewed, 12
When *there was* no strange *god* among you:
Therefore ye *are* my witnesses, saith the LORD, that I *am* God.
Yea, before the day *was* I *am* he; 13

that ye may know...] In the very act of bearing witness, it would seem that the mind of Israel is to be awakened to the grand truth of which its own history is the evidence,—the sole divinity of Jehovah, and its own unique position as His servant.

I am *he*] See ch. xli. 4.

before me there was no god formed] Strictly, of course, the idea is, "before any god was formed I existed." The form of expression might be derived from the Babylonian cosmology, according to which the gods were the first beings to emerge from the primeval chaos. The following words occur in the Chaldæan account of creation: "When of the gods none had yet arisen, when none named a name or [determined] fate; then were the [*great*] *gods formed*" (Schrader, *Cuneiform Inscriptions on Gen.* i. 1). It is probably to this origin of the gods themselves that reference is made, rather than to the formation of their images (ch. xliv. 9).

11. *I, even I, am the* LORD] **I, I am Jehovah**; see on ch. xlii. 8. there is *no saviour*] See on *v*. 3.

12. *have declared...saved...shewed*] The arrangement of the verbs is peculiar. Some would remove the second, others the third, as dittography. But if there be any error in the text it is more likely the omission of a fourth word, which would be parallel to "saved," as "shewed" is to "declared" (so Duhm).

when there was *no strange* god] Rather as R.V. **and there was no strange** (i.e. foreign) **god**. There cannot be an allusion to an early period of the history, before idolatry had crept in; because the deliverance is conceived as having just taken place. It is true that many "strange gods" had been acknowledged in Israel; but none of them was really there, as a living active presence in their midst. The meaning is, "It was I who did this, and no god who was a stranger among you." *strange god* is strictly "stranger," as in Deut. xxxii. 16; Jer. ii. 25, iii. 13.

therefore ye are...*that I* am *God*] Render: **and ye are my witnesses, and I am God**.

13. *Yea, before the day* was] The correct translation is that of R.V. marg.: **Yea, from this day forth** (for all the future) **I am the same**

And *there is* none that can deliver out of my hand:
I will work, and who shall let it?

14 Thus saith the LORD, your redeemer, the Holy One
of Israel;
For your sake I have sent to Babylon,
And have brought down all their nobles,
And the Chaldeans, whose cry *is* in the ships.
15 I *am* the LORD, your Holy One,
The creator of Israel, your King.

(xli. 4); the deliverance marking a new era in Jehovah's manifestation of Himself as God, the only God who is a Saviour (*v.* 11).

I will work...let it?] Better: **I work, and who shall reverse it?**

14, 15. A new section (14—21) commences here with a brief but explicit announcement of the fall of Babylon.

the LORD, your redeemer] See on ch. xli. 14.

I have sent (or perhaps, **I will send**) *to Babylon*] As object of the verb we must supply, the Persian army, the "consecrated ones" of ch. xiii. 3.

and have brought...ships] This sentence is somewhat peculiar in its structure and phraseology, and many emendations have been proposed. Accepting the text as it stands, the best translation is no doubt that of R.V. **and I will bring down all of them as fugitives, even the Chaldeans in the ships of their rejoicing.** Since the verb "bring down" cannot be understood in two different senses in the two members, the idea must be that they shall all be sent down the Euphrates as fugitives in ships, which was precisely the manner in which Merodach-baladan made his escape from Sennacherib (see Schrader, *Cuneiform Inscriptions*, E.T. vol. II. p. 36). A description of the ships on the Euphrates is to be found in Herod. I. 194; they are here called "ships of rejoicing" as having formerly been used for pleasure. The rendering, however, is not altogether convincing. The "and" before "Chaldæans" seems to make a distinction between them and the fugitives, which is hardly to be explained by supposing that the latter are the foreign merchants referred to in ch. xiii. 14. The probability is that the difficulties are due to somewhat extensive omissions in the text. The word for "fugitives" might (with the change of one vowel) be read as "bolts," and this is taken by A.V., though without any justification, as a metaphor for "nobles." It might, however, be a metaphor for the defences of Babylon, or a symbol of Israel's captivity; "I will bring down the bolts" gives a good enough sense so far as it goes. Another slight emendation which naturally suggests itself is to change "ships" into "lamentations": "and the shouting of the Chaldæans into lamentations."

16—21. The sequel to the overthrow of Babylon is the deliverance of Israel, the method of which is compared with the greatest miracle in Israel's past history, the exodus from Egypt.

Thus saith the LORD, which maketh a way in the sea, 16
And a path in the mighty waters;
Which bringeth forth the chariot and horse, the army 17
and the power;
They shall lie down together, they shall not rise:
They are extinct, they are quenched as tow.
Remember ye not the former *things*, 18
Neither consider the *things* of old.
Behold, I will do a new *thing*; 19
Now it shall spring forth; shall ye not know it?

16. *Thus saith the LORD*] The oracle itself begins at *v.* 18; it is prefaced in *vv.* 16 f. by a vivid description of the mighty power of Jehovah, as illustrated once for all at the crossing of the Red Sea (Ex. xiv. f.).

in the mighty waters] Cf. Neh. ix. 11.

17. *which bringeth forth*] i.e. allows them to come forth to their destruction (cf. Ez. xxxviii. 4, where the same expression is used with regard to the expedition of Gog, king of Magog). The next words should be rendered simply **chariot and horse** (without art.).

the army and the power] Perhaps: **army and warrior**. The second word is found elsewhere only in Ps. xxiv. 8 (A.V. "mighty") in apposition with the common word for "hero." Here it may be used collectively.

they shall lie down] Better: **they lie down.**

quenched as tow] **extinguished like a wick**; the same words as in ch. xlii. 3. The alternation of tenses in the original is noteworthy and very graphic. The participial construction first gives place to the descriptive impf., and this again to two perfects of completed action.

18. Great as the wonders of the exodus were they shall be far surpassed by that which Jehovah is about to do. The verse resumes the opening clause of *v.* 16.

Remember ye not...] Cf. Jer. xvi. 14 f., xxiii. 7 f. It is not meant of course that the exodus shall be actually forgotten (see ch. xlvi. 9), but only that it shall no longer be the supreme instance of Jehovah's redeeming power.

former things...**things** *of old*] Cf. ch. xlvi. 9. Obviously the expression "former things," so often used of past events predicted, here includes the remote incidents of the deliverance from Egypt.

19. The making of the way through the desert and water for the pilgrims to drink (see on ch. xl. 3 f., xli. 18 ff.) is considered to be a miracle transcending the passage of the Red Sea, and all the miracles which attended the first exodus. This is the *new thing* on which the prophet's mind fastens as the symbol of Israel's deliverance.

now it shall &c.] Rather: **even now it is springing forth; do ye not recognise it?** In ch. xlii. 9, the new things are spoken of as announced *before* they "spring forth," while as yet there is no sign of

> I will even make a way in the wilderness,
> And rivers in the desert.
> 20 The beast of the field shall honour me,
> The dragons and the owls:
> Because I give waters in the wilderness,
> And rivers in the desert,
> To give drink to my people, my chosen.
> 21 This people have I formed for myself;
> They shall shew forth my praise.

their appearing; here to the lively imagination of the prophet they are already seen "germinating," and he calls on the people to see them as the inevitable issue of the conquests of Cyrus. But while the above seems the most effective rendering of the question, that of the E.V. is quite possible:—"shall ye not experience it."

the desert] Heb. *Jĕshîmôn*, an utterly barren and arid region (Deut. xxxii. 10; Ps. lxviii. 7, lxxviii. 40, cvii. 4 &c.) as distinguished from *midbār* ("wilderness" or "steppe"), where flocks can find a scanty sustenance. It occurs as a proper name in Num. xxi. 20 (1 Sam. xxvi. 1).

20. Even the wild beasts shall honour Jehovah, unconsciously, through their joy at the abundant supply of water.

the dragons and the owls] Render as R.V. **the jackals and the ostriches**. See on ch. xiii. 21, 22.

21. The verse supplies an apposition to "my people" of *v.* 20. It reads: **The people which I have formed for myself, they shall tell forth my praise.** As the "streams in the desert" were created for Israel and not for the "beasts of the field," so it is Israel alone that can fully celebrate the praises of the Lord, Who is its Redeemer (cf. 1 Pet. ii. 9).

22—28. Jehovah effects this deliverance for His own sake, not in return for any service He has received at the hands of Israel. The argument of the section is difficult to follow, especially in the part which speaks of sacrifice. Two questions present themselves: (*a*) does Jehovah upbraid His people with *their neglect* of ritual, or does He assert *His own indifference* to it? and (*b*), is the reference to the whole course of Israel's history or merely to the period of the Exile? The answer to (*b*) seems determined by the consideration that if understood of the history as a whole the statement is inconsistent with fact. Although the prophet undoubtedly takes a dark view of Israel's past religious condition (*v.* 27), we cannot suppose that he charges it with disregard of the externals of religion. Whatever faults Israel had been guilty of, it had not been slack in the performance of ritual (see ch. i. 10 ff.). Now if we limit the reference to the Exile, the idea of an implied reproach (*a*) must be abandoned, because the suspension of the sacrificial system was in the circumstances inevitable. In other words, the main thought here is expressed in the second half of *v.* 23

> But thou hast not called upon me, O Jacob; 22
> But thou hast been weary of me, O Israel.
> Thou hast not brought me the small cattle of thy 23
>   burnt offerings;
> Neither hast thou honoured me *with* thy sacrifices.
> I have not caused thee to serve with an offering,

more clearly than in the first halves of *vv.* 23 and 24. At the same time this hardly amounts to a repudiation of sacrifice *in principle* on the part of Jehovah. The truth appears to be that the prophet directs attention to the simple fact that during the Exile sacrifice had not been offered; whether Israel was to blame for this or not is immaterial to his argument. He has in his view the prevailing ideas of the time as to the normal attitude of a people to its God; and he shews how inadequate these are to explain Jehovah's relation to Israel. The natural and proper thing was for a nation to invoke the name of its God, and to honour Him with costly and laborious rites. Israel has done none of these things, it has only burdened Jehovah with its sins; yet Jehovah proves Himself to be its God by forgiving its iniquities and undertaking its cause against its enemies.

22. *But thou hast not called upon me*] To call upon Jehovah "in the day of trouble" was the first and most obvious duty of Israel (Ps. l. 15), but this duty Israel has neglected. The statement is of course general; it does not exclude the existence of a believing minority which poured out its heart in prayer to God. The position of the word "me" is emphatic in the original; but the emphasis on the object throws a corresponding emphasis on the subject: "But not upon *me* hast *thou* called, Jacob"; it is I who have called thee (ch. xli. 9, xlii. 6, xliii. 1 &c.). It is foreign to the context to suppose an antithesis between Jehovah and other gods.

but thou hast been weary of me] Or, perhaps: **much less hast thou wearied thyself about me** (Cheyne). The translation of E.V. is possible, although the expression is not elsewhere used of being weary of a person. The other sense, however, is much to be preferred because of *v.* 23 *b*, and is justified by the analogy of ch. xlvii. 12, 15, lxii. 8; Josh. xxiv. 13. The use of the conjunction is peculiar; the simple *kî* seems to have the same force as the fuller *'aph kî* (as in 1 Ki. viii. 27, "much less this house" &c.). The easiest solution might be to suppose that the *'aph* has been omitted, but this is not really necessary. How Israel might have "wearied itself about" Jehovah is explained in *vv.* 23 f.

23. The absence of sacrifice has not impaired the bond between Jehovah and His people. The thought presents a striking contrast to ch. i. 10 ff., a passage which was probably in the writer's mind.

the small cattle] The Heb. word serves as the noun of unity to the word for "flock" (i.e. sheep and goats). On *burnt-offerings*, *sacrifices* and *offering*, see on ch. i. 11, 13.

I have not caused thee to serve] "have not treated thee as a slave," by

>   Nor wearied thee with incense.
> 24 Thou hast bought me no sweet cane with money,
>   Neither hast thou filled me *with* the fat of thy sacrifices:
>   But thou hast made me to serve with thy sins,
>   Thou hast wearied me with thine iniquities.
> 25 I, *even* I, *am* he that blotteth out thy transgressions for mine own sake,
>   And will not remember thy sins.

exacting tribute. The statement might no doubt be understood absolutely, according to Jer. vii. 21 ff.; but it is perhaps sufficient to take it of the Exile, when the non-essential character of sacrifice was revealed by its enforced discontinuance (cf. Ps. li. 16).

incense] See ch. lx. 6; Jer. vi. 20. In both these passages incense is described as coming from Arabia, which agrees with the statement of Pliny, that it was collected in the chief city of Hadramaut and thence conveyed to Syria. The Heb. word (*lĕbônāh*), which is preserved in the Gr. λίβανος, λιβανωτός, is quite different from that found in ch. i. 13.

24. *sweet cane*] (*qāneh*) is also mentioned in Jer. vi. 20 as coming from a "far country." It is supposed to be *calamus odoratus*, a product of India, but grown also in Arabia and Syria; hence Jarchi, the Jewish commentator, explains: "because there was enough in Palestine"! It formed an ingredient in the sacred oil with which the priests, the tabernacle, &c. were anointed (Ex. xxx. 23, E.V. "sweet calamus"). One of the rare paronomasias in this prophecy is the play of words between this name and the verb for "buy" (*qānāh*).

filled me] satiated me (as R.V. marg.).

with *the fat*] cf. Jer. xxxi. 14; Ps. xxxvi. 8.

but (only) *thou hast made me to serve*...] This is the contrast which the prophet has had in view from the beginning of the section: while Jehovah has not burdened His people even with the offerings which it had been too ready to bring, it has burdened Him with its sins; and while Israel has taken its whole relation to Jehovah lightly, He has accepted the burden, and laboured in its service for the removal of its guilt.

25. Since Israel has neither brought sacrifices, nor even offered prayer acceptable to Jehovah, He himself must take the initiative in the work of redemption, blotting out its transgressions "for his own sake." In accordance with O.T. analogies, the act of forgiveness is described simply as "not remembering" sin; but the actual working out of forgiveness in history calls into exercise the resources of Omnipotence; it includes all Jehovah's dealings with His people, His handing them over to the dominion of the heathen (*v.* 28), and saving them again in His marvellous providence. The verse, moreover, contains only one half of the prophet's teaching about forgiveness; the other half is the process by which the people are brought to repentance, and this is the work of the Servant of the Lord, as described in ch. liii.

Put me in remembrance: let us plead together: 26
Declare thou, that thou mayest be justified.
Thy first father hath sinned, 27
And thy teachers have transgressed against me.
Therefore I have profaned the princes of the sanctuary, 28
And have given Jacob to the curse,
And Israel to reproaches.

Yet now hear, O Jacob my servant; 44
And Israel, whom I have chosen:
Thus saith the LORD that made thee, 2
And formed thee from the womb, *which* will help thee;

26. In order to bring home the charge of guilt (*v*. 24) Jehovah summons the people to debate their cause with Him. As *vv*. 23—25 recall ch. i. 10 ff., so this verse seems to be suggested by *v*. 18 of that chapter.

Put me in remembrance] i.e. "of any merits thou canst claim, or any plea thou canst urge, and which I have overlooked."

let us plead together] "let us implead one another," as in i. 18, though the verb is different. *declare thou*] Rather **reckon thou up** (Ps. xl. 5). *mayest be justified*] **mayest be in the right**.

27. *Thy first father*] Undoubtedly Jacob, the eponymous hero of the nation, is meant (cf. Hos. xii. 3 f.), not Abraham (who is never spoken of in the later literature as sinful), nor the earliest ancestors collectively; still less Adam.

thy teachers] Lit. as R.V. **thine interpreters** (Gen. xlii. 23), and hence "mediators" (as Job xxxiii. 23; 2 Chr. xxxii. 31); used of the prophets only here. On the idea, see Jer. xxiii. 11 ff. If the representative ancestor and the spiritual leaders of Israel were such, what must the mass of the nation have been!

28. *Therefore I have profaned*] is better than R.V. "Therefore I will profane," although it requires the change of a vowel. The verb (like the one following) is pointed as a cohortative, and as this appears sometimes to express the idea of compulsion (see Driver, *Tenses*, §§ 51—53) we may perhaps venture to render: **and so I had to profane**.

the princes of the sanctuary] Better: **consecrated princes**. The priests are so named in 1 Chr. xxiv. 5; it is doubtful whether here priests or kings or both are meant, the consecration by anointing being common to both.

and have given...curse] Render: **and had to deliver** (see on last clause) **Jacob to the ban**. R.V. changes the translation for the worse.

xliv. 1—5. Once more the gloom of the present is lighted up by the promise of a brilliant future; the Divine spirit shall be poured out on Israel, and strangers shall esteem it an honour to attach themselves to the people of Jehovah.

1. *Yet now*] **But now**; marking the contrast, exactly as in ch. xliii. 1.
2. *formed thee from the womb*] See *v*. 24, ch. xlix. 5.

> Fear not, O Jacob, my servant;
> And *thou*, Jeshurun, whom I have chosen.
> 3 For I will pour water upon *him that is* thirsty,
> And floods upon the dry *ground*:
> I will pour my spirit upon thy seed,
> And my blessing upon thine offspring:
> 4 And they shall spring up *as* among the grass,
> As willows by the water courses.

Jeshurun occurs again only in Deut. xxxii. 15, xxxiii. 5, 26; always as a synonym for Israel and a title of honour (hardly a diminutive, as the termination might suggest). It means the "Upright One," being formed from an adj. *yāshār*, which is applied to Israel in Num. xxiii. 10, and perhaps also in the phrase "book of Jashar" (see Josh. x. 13, R. V.). The history of the name is, however, altogether obscure. The opinion that it was coined in opposition to Jacob ("the supplanter") has little to recommend it; although that antithesis may have led to its *selection* by this prophet.

Should the recent supposed discovery of the name Israel on an Egyptian monument of the reign of Merenptah be confirmed, it is possible that fresh light may be thrown on the relation of the two names Israel and Jeshurun. The form in which the word there appears is said to be *Yishir'il*, the sibilant agreeing with Jeshurun but differing from the traditional pronunciation of *Yisrā'el*. *Yishir'il* and *Yeshûrûn* might be derivations from a common root, *yāshar*. (Brandt, *Theologisch Tijdschrift*, 1896, p. 511; cf. Renan, *Hist. du peuple d'Israel*, Vol. I., p. 106).

3. On the first half of the verse see ch. xli. 17 ff. Here, however, a *figurative* sense predominates, as is shewn by what follows. The "spirit" is the agent both of physical and moral regeneration, as in ch. xxxii. 15 (cf. Ez. xxxvii. 11—14); the former idea being prominent; hence the parallelism "spirit"—"blessing," the former being the cause, the latter the effect. On the figure of water for the spirit, cf. John i. 33 etc. *seed* and *offspring* are individual Israelites.

4. *spring up* as *among the grass*] R.V., more accurately, omits "as"; but the text is unquestionably corrupt. There is no doubt that the LXX. preserves the true reading: **spring up as grass among the waters**. (Instead of the impossible בְּבֵין חָצִיר, read כְּבֵין מַיִם חָצִיר.)

willows] or **poplars**; see on ch. xv. 7.

5. The result of the Divine blessing manifested in Israel's restoration will be that foreigners shall attach themselves as proselytes to the Jewish community. The promise therefore goes far beyond ch. xliii. 5—7. It is perhaps barely possible (with Dillmann) to understand this verse also of Israelites by birth, in the sense that they shall esteem it an honour to belong to their own nation; but this is certainly unnatural and scarcely to be reconciled with the second and fourth members of the verse.

One shall say, I *am* the LORD'S; 5
And another shall call *himself* by the name of Jacob;
And another shall subscribe *with* his hand unto the
  LORD,
And surname *himself* by the name of Israel.

Thus saith the LORD the King of Israel, 6

call himself *by the name of Jacob*] The words, strictly rendered, would mean "call on the name of Jacob." It simplifies the construction greatly if, with Duhm, we vocalize this verb (as well as the last verb of the verse) as a passive:—"shall be called" etc.

subscribe with *his hand unto the LORD*] Rather: **inscribe his hand 'To Jehovah.'** The allusion is to the practice of branding slaves with the name of their owner, or perhaps to the religious custom of tattooing sacred marks on the person (Lev. xix. 28). See Ezek. ix. 4; Gal. vi. 17; Rev. vii. 3, xiii. 16.

surname himself (or better **be surnamed**, see above) *by the name of Israel*] The verb is connected etymologically with an Arabic word *kunya*, although it is used here in a wider sense. The *kunya* is a sort of household name, which consists in designating a man as the father of a particular child; thus in *Nimmer ibn Kob'ân Abû Faris* (N., son of K., father of F.) the last title is the *kunya*. (Seetzen, *Reisen*, Vol. II., p. 327.) Besides this, however, the Arabs make great use of honorific titles, like *Nûr-eddîn* ("Light of the Religion") etc.; and it is in a sense corresponding to this that the Heb. verb is always used; cf. ch. xlv. 4 and esp. Job xxxii. 21 f. (A.V. "give flattering titles"). The meaning, therefore, is that in addition to their personal names the proselytes will adopt the name of Israel as a title of honour. Cf. Ps. lxxxvii. 4 f.

CH. XLIV. 6—23. THE REALITY OF JEHOVAH'S GODHEAD, EVINCED
  BY HIS PREDICTIONS, AND CONTRASTED WITH THE MANIFOLD
  ABSURDITIES OF IDOLATRY.

The passage, which is merely a restatement of ideas already expressed, consists of three divisions:
  i. *vv.* 6—8. A re-assertion and demonstration of the eternity and sole Divinity of Jehovah.
  ii. *vv.* 9—20. A fresh exposure—the most complete and remorseless that the book contains—of the irrationality of idol-worship.
  iii. *vv.* 21—23. An exhortation to the exiles to lay these truths to heart, and cleave to the God who forgives their sins and who alone can deliver. *v.* 23 is a lyrical effusion, such as the thought of the redemption frequently calls forth from the prophet.

6—8. There is no God but Jehovah and Israel is His witness: this is the substance of the verses, and the proof is the familiar one from prophecy.

the King of Israel] See on ch. xli. 21.

> And his redeemer the LORD of hosts;
> I *am* the first, and I *am* the last;
> And besides me *there is* no God.
> 7 And who, as I, shall call,
> And shall declare it, and set it in order for me,
> Since I appointed the ancient people?
> And the *things* that are coming, and shall come, let them shew unto them.

the LORD *of hosts*] this solemn appellation (see on ch. i. 9) occurs here for the first time in this prophecy (cf. ch. xlv. 13, xlvii. 4, xlviii. 2, li. 15, liv. 5).

I am *the first and I* am *the last*] So ch. xlviii. 12; see on xli. 4, and cf. Rev. i. 8, 17, xxii. 13.   *besides me* there is *no God*] a fuller expression of monotheism than ch. xliii. 10.

7. The proof of *v.* 6 is found in the incontestable fact of prophecy (as ch. xli. 22 ff., xliii. 9, 12; &c.). The verse as translated in A.V. and R.V. reads very awkwardly; it would have to be paraphrased thus: "And which of the other gods shall call etc., as I have done since I appointed the ancient people?" But the distance of the last clause from the "as I" on which it depends is so great as to make the construction unnatural. It is better, with most commentators, to suppose a parenthesis, and render thus: "And who, as I, proclaims (and let him declare it and set it in order before me) since I founded the people of antiquity?" But a parenthesis is always more or less suspicious in a Hebrew sentence, and this one is doubly so on account of the "and" which introduces it. The LXX. reads, "And who is like me? *Let him stand* and proclaim &c." The additional verb ("stand") is likely to be original, and the construction of the first part of the clause is faultless. The only difficulty is presented by the temporal clause, "since I appointed" etc., on which see below.

call] means proclaim or "prophesy," as in ch. xl. 6.

set [it] *in order*] used of the arrangement of discourse, as Job xxxii. 14; Ps. l. 21, v. 3.

since I appointed the...] Better: "since I founded the people of antiquity." The most probable meaning is that prophecy has been continuous during the long period since Israel was formed into a nation. Some take the expression to denote the earliest population of the world (cf. ch. xli. 4); but this is less likely. Ewald applies it to Israel, but in the sense "everlasting people." In Ez. xxvi. 20 the same phrase is used of the shades in the underworld.

Several difficulties in the verse are got rid of by an attractive emendation of Oort (followed by Duhm), which makes this clause read; "who hath announced from of old?" (מי השמיע מעולם) instead of משמי עם־עולם; cf. ch. xlv. 21). The whole verse would then be rendered: **And who is like me? Let him stand and proclaim, and declare it and set in order to me. Who hath announced from of old future things? and things to come let them declare.**

Fear ye not, neither be afraid: 8
Have not I told thee from that time,
And have declared *it*? ye *are* even my witnesses.
Is there a God besides me?
Yea, *there is* no God; I know not *any*.
They that make a graven image *are* all of them vanity; 9
And their delectable *things* shall not profit;
And they *are* their own witnesses;

things that are coming and *that shall come* are equivalent expressions; there is no foundation for Delitzsch's notion that the former denotes the future in general, and the latter the immediate future (see on ch. xli. 22).

8. *Fear ye not*] in the coming convulsions; the ground of confidence is that Jehovah has proved His control over these events by foretelling them. The verb for *be afraid* does not occur elsewhere.

from that time] Rather **beforehand**, or, **from of old**; as ch. xlv. 21, xlviii. 3, 5, 7.

and ye are *my witnesses* (R.V.)] Cf. ch. xliii. 10, 12.

no God] **no Rock**, as R.V. Cf. Deut. xxxii. 4, etc.

9—20. The course of thought is as follows :

(1) The makers of images are themselves frail men, and the gods they fashion cannot profit them (9—11).

(2) The process of manufacture is then described in minute detail, shewing what an expenditure of human strength and contrivance is involved in the production of these useless deities (12 f.).

(3) Nay, the very material of which they may be composed is selected at haphazard from the trees of the forest, and might just as readily have been applied to cook the idolater's food (14—17).

(4) Finally, with incisive and relentless logic, the writer exposes the strange infatuation which renders the idolater incapable of applying the most rudimentary principles of reason to his own actions (18—20).

9—11. The argument opens with the assertion of the nothingness alike of the idol and its makers. Fear on the part of Israel would be justified if other gods besides Jehovah had any power to influence the course of history.

a graven image] for "image" in general, as ch. xl. 19. The writer assumes that the god is the image and nothing more; since the image is plainly the work of human hands, the god cannot be greater than men or able to save them. This of course is directly opposed to the fundamental assumption of the idolaters themselves, who distinguished between the image and the divinity represented by it (see on *v.* 11).

vanity] lit. "chaos," as in xl. 17, xli. 29.

their delectable things] "the objects in which they delight," i.e. the idols.

and they are *their own witnesses*] R.V. "**and their** own witnesses see not," etc. Render simply : **and their witnesses**; their devotees, see ch. xliii. 9. The pronoun which suggests the "**own**" of A.V. and R.V. is marked by the so-called *puncta extraordinaria* as suspicious, and is

They see not, nor know; that they may be ashamed.
10 Who hath formed a god, or molten a graven image
 That is profitable for nothing?
11 Behold, all his fellows shall be ashamed:
 And the workmen, they *are* of men:
 Let them all be gathered together, let them stand *up*;
 Yet they shall fear, *and* they shall be ashamed together.
12 The smith *with* the tongs both worketh in the coals,
 And fashioneth it with hammers,
 And worketh it with the strength of his arms:

therefore unaccented. If it is retained in the text (as it may very well be) the better translation is, "and as for their witnesses, they see not" &c.

that they may be ashamed] The consequence of their ignorance expressed as a purpose.

10. *Who hath formed, &c.*] A rhetorical question: who has been such a fool? On *molten a graven image* see ch. xl. 19.

11. *all his fellows*] The word denotes the members of a guild, and is understood by A.V. of the gang of craftsmen employed in the making of the idol. It should rather be interpreted as the "adherents," the *clientèle* of the false god himself, as in R.V. marg., "all that join themselves thereto." Cf. Hos. iv. 17 ("associated with idols") and 1 Cor. x. 20.   *are of men*] belong to the category of men (xl. 17), and how can men produce a god? Duhm, changing the vowel-points, renders: "Behold all the spells (cf. ch. xlvii. 9, 12) are put to shame, and as for enchantments (cf. ch. iii. 3), they are of men;" an allusion to the magical process by which, in all systems of idolatry, the manufactured image is transformed into a fetish, the residence of a divinity. Similarly Cheyne (*Introd.* p. 301).

12, 13. This truth enforced by a description of the manufacture of the idols.

The smith] lit. "the workman in iron," as opposed to the "workman in wood" of the next verse. The text is corrupt at the beginning. R.V. has "the smith (maketh) an axe"; LXX. "the workman sharpeneth iron, worketh it with the adze &c.," not perceiving that the verse speaks of the *blacksmith's* labours. It is possible, no doubt, to take the word for "axe" (which is found again only in Jer. x. 3), as meaning "cutting instrument," for dividing the mass of iron on the anvil; but this is suggested by nothing in the verse; and moreover, the description is certainly not that of the manufacture of an implement, whether for the smith or the carpenter. The only feasible solution is to omit the "axe" altogether as a marginal gloss by some reader who fell into the same error as the LXX. translator. Render: **The smith works with the coals.**

fashioneth it (the iron core of the idol) *with hammers*] cf. ch. xli. 7.

and worketh it with **his strong arm**] R.V. Gesenius cites in illustration two lines of Vergil (*Georg.* IV. 174 f.),

Yea, he is hungry, and his strength faileth:
He drinketh no water, and is faint.
The carpenter stretcheth out *his* rule; he marketh it   13
out with a line;
He fitteth it with planes, and he marketh it out with
the compass,
And maketh it after the figure of a man, according to
the beauty of a man;
That it may remain *in* the house.
He heweth him down cedars, and taketh the cypress   14
and the oak,
Which he strengtheneth for himself among the trees
of the forest:
He planteth an ash, and the rain doth nourish *it*.
Then shall it be for a man to burn: 15

> "Illi inter sese magna vi brachia tollunt
> In numerum, versantque tenaci forcipe ferrum."

yea, he is hungry...] The point is that the man who makes his own gods exhausts his strength in the process; contrast ch. xl. 31.

13. *The carpenter*] lit., "the workman in wood."
stretcheth out a line, (R.V.)] to mark off the dimensions of the future image on the block of wood. For *line* in the next clause read **pencil** (as R.V.); the word, like that for "planes" (which may mean "chisels" or any cutting implement), occurs only here.
fitteth] R.V. "shapeth"; lit. **maketh**.
that it may remain in *the house*] **to dwell in a house**; either a great temple, or a private shrine.

14—17. The writer now goes back to the material of which this second kind of idol is made.
He *heweth him down*] The Heb. text, which reads "to hew down," probably contains a mistake in the first letter.
strengtheneth for himself] must mean "allows to grow strong" in its native forest. Nay, in some cases the future deity has been actually *planted* by his worshipper, and nourished by the rain from heaven! The words *tirzāh* ("cypress") and *'ōren* ("ash") occur only here in the O.T. The former, according to the Vulg. and the Greek Versions of Aquila and Theodotion, is the "holm-oak" (*ilex*); the latter may be translated "pine" (Vulg.); the corresponding word in Assyrian denotes the cedar.

15, 16. Comp. (with Lowth) Horace, *Sat.* 1. 8, 1 ff.:

> "Olim truncus eram ficulnus, inutile lignum,
> Cum faber, incertus, scamnum faceretne Priapum,
> Maluit esse Deum."

Also Wisd. Sol. xiii. 11—13.

For he will take thereof, and warm himself;
Yea, he kindleth *it*, and baketh bread;
Yea, he maketh a god, and worshippeth *it*;
He maketh it a graven image, and falleth down thereto.
16 He burneth part thereof in the fire;
With part thereof he eateth flesh;
He roasteth roast, and is satisfied:
Yea, he warmeth himself, and saith, Aha,
I am warm, I have seen the fire:
17 And the residue thereof he maketh a god, *even* his graven image:
He falleth down unto it, and worshippeth *it*, and prayeth unto it,
And saith, Deliver me; for thou *art* my god.
18 They have not known nor understood:
For he hath shut their eyes, that *they* cannot see;
And their hearts, that *they* cannot understand.
19 And none considereth in his heart,
Neither *is there* knowledge nor understanding to say,
I have burnt part of it in the fire;
Yea, also I have baked bread upon the coals thereof;
I have roasted flesh, and eaten *it*:
And shall I make the residue thereof an abomination?
Shall I fall down to the stock of a tree?
20 He feedeth on ashes:

The word rendered "falleth down (*sāgad*)" is an Aramaic verb meaning "worship," recurring in the O.T. only *vv.* 17, 19 and ch. xlvi. 6. It is the root of the Arabic word *mosque* (musǧid).

16. *part thereof*] lit. "half thereof," as opposed to "the residue thereof" in *v.* 17. Cf. *v.* 19, "upon the coals thereof."

18—20. But such is the infatuation of idolatry, that its blinded votaries never pause to reflect on their actions; the idolater has not sense enough to say to himself in plain words what he has done.

They have not...understood] Better, as R.V. **they know not, neither do they consider.** *he hath shut their eyes*] Rather: **their eyes are besmeared**, as it were plastered over, so that they cannot see (a different verb, however, from that used by Isaiah in vi. 10, &c.).

19. *considereth in his heart*] R.V. **calleth to mind**; lit. "bringeth it back to his heart," i.e. "recalls in thought," a somewhat rare expression (see ch. xlvi. 8; Deut. iv. 39, xxx. 1; 1 Ki. viii. 47).

part of it] See on *v.* 16. The word rendered *stock* occurs again only in Job xl. 20, where it seems to mean "produce."

20. *He feedeth on ashes*] lit., "a shepherd of ashes". Duhm rather

A deceived heart hath turned him aside,
That he cannot deliver his soul, nor say,
Is there not a lie in my right hand?
Remember these, O Jacob   21
And Israel; for thou *art* my servant:
I have formed thee; thou *art* my servant:
O Israel, thou shalt not be forgotten of me.
I have blotted out, as a thick cloud, thy transgressions,   22
And, as a cloud, thy sins:
Return unto me; for I have redeemed thee.

Sing, O ye heavens; for the LORD hath done *it*:   23
Shout, ye lower parts of the earth:

fancifully suggests that the image may be that of a man trying to feed his flock on a pasture that has been reduced to ashes: "A shepherd of (or on) ashes is he whom a deceived heart hath turned aside" (from the ways of reason). Another rendering might be: "One who finds satisfaction in ashes is he whom, &c." For this sense of the verb *râ‘āh* see Hos. xii. 1 (?); Ps. xxxvii. 3; Prov. xv. 14, &c. (Gesenius, *Lexicon*[12], *sub verbo*).

and *he* **shall not** *deliver his soul*] Cf. *v.* 17.

Is there *not a lie*...] Am I not cleaving to that which will disappoint my hope?

21, 22. An admonition to Israel to lay these truths to heart and realise its special relation to the one living and true God.

Remember these] i.e. **these things** (R.V.), the principles enforced in the preceding passage.

thou shalt not be forgotten of me] The Heb. construction, a passive verb with accusative suffix, is abnormal. All the ancient versions and many commentators render "thou shalt (or wilt) not forget me"; but this is hardly defensible. The suffix must denote the indirect obj. (dative) as is sometimes the case with intransitive verbs. (See Davidson, *Synt.* § 73 R. 4.) For the sense, cf. ch. xl. 27, xlix. 14 ff.

22. Cf. ch. xliii. 25. "The sense of being forgotten of God is produced by the consciousness of guilt; hence the promise of forgiveness is here repeated" (Dillmann).

as a thick cloud...as a cloud] An image of transitoriness; Hos. vi. 4, xiii. 3; Job vii. 9, xxx. 15.

23. The prophet in a transport of joy calls on heaven and earth to celebrate the wonders of Israel's redemption. Cf. ch. xlii. 10—13, xlv. 8. The poetic outburst marks the end of the section.

the LORD hath done it] The redemption is already as good as complete; see the end of the verse.

ye lower parts of the earth] or **depths of the earth**, the antithesis to "ye heavens."

Break forth *into* singing, ye mountains,
O forest, and every tree therein :
For the LORD hath redeemed Jacob,
And glorified himself in Israel.

break forth into *singing*] Cf. ch. xiv. 7.
and glorified] R.V., more correctly: **and will glorify**. Cf. ch. xlix. 3, lx. 21, lxi. 3.

CH. XLIV. 24—XLV. 25. JEHOVAH'S COMMISSION TO CYRUS, HIS ANOINTED, WHOSE VICTORIES SHALL BRING ABOUT THE UNIVERSAL RECOGNITION OF THE TRUE GOD.

The distinctive feature of this important section of the book is the prominence given to the person and work of the Persian conqueror, Cyrus. The leading idea is no longer the relation of Israel to Jehovah, but the glorious effects that are to follow its deliverance through the agency of this divinely chosen hero. In the earlier allusions to Cyrus (ch. xli. 1—4, 25—29) he is spoken of as one whose remarkable career has challenged the attention of the world and illustrated the inability of the heathen religions to deal with the great crises of history. There have been abundant intimations that he is the destined instrument of Israel's restoration, but these have hitherto occupied a secondary place in the prophet's thoughts. Here, however, the figure of Cyrus is brought prominently on the scene, he is addressed directly and by name, and the ultimate scope of his mission is clearly unfolded. He is to set the exiles free, to rebuild Jerusalem and the Temple; and the far-reaching moral result of his singular generosity to Israel will be the downfall of heathenism everywhere and the universal conviction that Jehovah is the only God who is a Deliverer. There are five divisions:

i. ch. xliv. 24—28 is an introduction to the central passage, which immediately follows. Jehovah, still addressing Israel, describes Himself by a majestic series of attributes, gradually converging from the thought of His creative power to the particular point which is the subject of the present discourse, His selection of Cyrus as the instrument of His purpose.

ii. ch. xlv. 1—8.—The Divine speaker now addresses Cyrus in person, promising to him an uninterrupted career of victory (1—3); yet it is in the interest of Israel that he, a stranger to the true God, is thus called and commissioned (4); and the final issue of his achievements will be a general recognition throughout the world of the sole Godhead of Jehovah (5—7).—The last verse (8) is a poetic interlude like ch. xlii. 10 ff., xliv. 23, &c.

iii. *vv*. 9—13.—Here the prophet turns aside to rebuke the murmurs of dissent which this novel announcement calls forth amongst his fellow countrymen (9—11). It would appear that there were some of the Israelites who rebelled against the thought of a foreign prince as the Anointed of Jehovah and the Saviour of Israel. The answer to these cavillers is an assertion of the absolute sovereignty of Jehovah, who

Thus saith the LORD, thy redeemer, 24
And he that formed thee from the womb,
I *am* the LORD that maketh all *things*;
That stretcheth forth the heavens alone;
That spreadeth abroad the earth by myself;
That frustrateth the tokens of the liars, 25
And maketh diviners mad;
That turneth wise *men* backward,
And maketh their knowledge foolish;
That confirmeth the word of his servant, 26

reaffirms His choice of Cyrus as the instrument of Israel's deliverance (12, 13).

iv. *vv.* 14—17.—Transporting himself to the time when the Divine purpose shall be realised, the writer depicts the procession of conquered nations who do homage to Israel as the people of the true God, and, renouncing idolatry, acknowledge the hand of Jehovah in Israel's everlasting salvation.

v. *vv.* 18—25.—This deliverance of Israel culminates in salvation to the world at large. The passage contains some of the most striking thoughts in the whole prophecy. The character of Jehovah, His good-will to men, is to be learned from His creation of a *habitable* world (18) and from the manner of His revelation to Israel (19). He has shewn Himself to be the only "righteous and saving God" (21); and the heathen are now invited to share in His salvation through faith in His sole divinity (20, 22). It is His irrevocable purpose thus to secure universal homage (23—25).

24—28. Jehovah, the God of creation and of prophecy, has chosen Cyrus to execute his purpose with regard to Israel.

thy redeemer] See on ch. xli. 14.   *formed thee from the womb*] as in *v.* 2.

that stretcheth...alone] Cf. ch. xl. 22; xlii. 5; Job ix. 8.

by myself] The A.V. here follows the reading presupposed by the vowel-points (*Qěrê*). The R.V. rightly goes back to the consonantal text (*Kěthîb*) which is preserved in the LXX. and Vulg. and some Hebrew MSS. Render accordingly: **who was with me?** i.e. there was none to help me.

25, 26. The overthrow of heathen soothsaying and the establishment of true prophecy as it existed in Israel.

the tokens of the liars] Or, the **signs of the praters** (cf. Jer. l. 36, and see on ch. xvi. 6 where the word means "pratings"). The "signs" (see Deut. xiii. 1 f.) referred to are the omens on which the diviners based their forecasts of the future. How much reliance was placed on these prognostications by the Babylonians will be seen from ch. xlvii.

diviners] See on ch. iii. 2.

26. *That confirmeth*] is the antithesis to "that frustrateth" in *v.* 25. (Cf. Jer. xxix. 10, xxxiii. 14).

And performeth the counsel of his messengers;
That saith to Jerusalem, Thou shalt be inhabited;
And to the cities of Judah, Ye shall be built,
And I will raise up the decayed places thereof:

27 That saith to the deep, Be dry,
And I will dry up thy rivers:

28 That saith of Cyrus, *He is* my shepherd,
And shall perform all my pleasure:

the word of his servant...the counsel of his messengers] are parallel expressions for the word of prophecy. The sing. "servant" presents some difficulty. That it is equivalent to "prophet" is clear from the context; but that a particular prophet, such as Jeremiah or the writer himself, is meant is extremely improbable. It might conceivably be used of the prophets collectively, or of Israel as the bearer of the prophetic word, but the parallelism with "messengers" in the next clause is opposed to both these interpretations. The word should probably be pointed as a plural,—**his servants**; which is the reading of the Codex Alexandrinus of the LXX.

performeth] Lit. **completeth**.

that saith &c.] **that saith of Jerusalem, Let her be inhabited; and of the cities of Judah, Let them be built.** At this point, as Delitzsch observes, the transition is made to special predictions bearing on the restoration of Israel.

decayed places] R.V. **waste places**, or ruins.

27. *the deep*] is a figure for the obstacles to the deliverance of Israel. It has been thought by some commentators (including Vitringa and Lowth) that the verse contains an allusion to the well-known stratagem by which Cyrus is said to have got possession of Babylon (Herodotus I. 185—191). The Hebrew word for "deep" might no doubt be applied to a river, as a cognate word is in Zech. x. 11. But the recently discovered Cyrus-inscriptions seem to shew that the narrative of Herodotus is legendary. See Introd. p. xviii.

28. The series of predicates here culminates in the mention by name of the conqueror of Babylon and liberator of Israel. The name Cyrus is in Persian *Kûrush*, in Babylonian *Kurash*, in Greek Kῦρος. The traditional Hebrew pronunciation is *Kôresh*, but it is probable that the original form preserved the characteristic long *u* which appears in the other languages. On the career of Cyrus see Introduction, pp. xvii ff.

He is my shepherd] Or simply, **My Shepherd.** "Shepherd" here means "ruler" as in Jer. iii. 15; Ezek. xxxiv. *pass.*; Mic. v. 5: comp. the Homeric ποιμένες λαῶν. It is one of the honorific titles alluded to in ch. xlv. 4.

perform all my pleasure] Or, **complete all my purpose**; cf. ch. xlvi. 10, xlviii. 14, liii. 10. This use of the Heb. word for "pleasure" illustrates the transition to its later sense of "business" (ch. lviii. 3, 13) or "matter" (Eccl. v. 8, viii. 6). Comp. Arab. *shay'* (= thing) from *shâ'a* (to will).

Even saying to Jerusalem, Thou shalt be built;
And *to* the temple, Thy foundation shall be laid.
Thus saith the LORD to his anointed, to Cyrus,   45
Whose right hand I have holden,

even saying] If the text be right the meaning would probably be that Cyrus would accomplish Jehovah's purpose by giving the order for the rebuilding of the Temple &c. LXX. and Vulg. read "that saith," substituting a participle for the inf. of the Heb. In this case the subject is Jehovah, as throughout the passage.

Instead of *to Jerusalem, Thou shalt be*..., the Heb. has **of Jerusalem, Let her be**.... See on *v.* 26.

According to Josephus (*Ant.* XI. i. 2) it was the reading of this verse that fired Cyrus with the ambition to restore the Jewish Temple and nationality. The statement, if true, would of course detract nothing from the significance of the prophecy. But it has no claim to be accepted, and would assuredly never have been made but for the assumption that the words were written by Isaiah "one hundred and forty years before the destruction of the Temple."

xlv. 1—7. The apostrophe to Cyrus expresses dramatically the purpose of Jehovah in raising up the Persian conqueror. The idea that the true God has made a personal revelation of Himself to the mind of Cyrus is not implied; Cyrus is to learn the religious significance of his mission from its results (*v.* 3), just as mankind at large comes to understand it (*v.* 6). The direct address to Cyrus (*vv.* 2 ff.) is prefaced in *v.* 1 by a series of clauses describing his invincible career, which has already attracted the attention of the world. There is a startling resemblance between some of the expressions here used of Jehovah's choice of Cyrus, and some of those employed by the Babylonian writer of the "Annalistic Tablet" in describing him as the favourite of Merodach. We read there that "Merodach...appointed a prince who should guide aright the wish of the heart which his hand upholds, even Cyrus..." that he "has proclaimed his title; for the sovereignty of all the world does he commemorate his name," and that he "beheld with joy the deeds of his vicegerent, who was righteous in hand and heart," and that "like a friend and comrade he went at his side." (See Introduction, p. xviii.)

to his anointed, to Cyrus] The Hebr. word for "anointed" (*māshiāh*), when used as a substantive, is almost confined to the kings of Israel; although in later times there was a tendency to employ it in a wider sense (e.g. of the Patriarchs in Ps. cv. 15, of the people in Hab. iii. 13). Unless Ps. ii. 2 be an exception it is never used in the O.T. of the future ideal king (the Messiah); hence the idea that the *rôle* of the Messianic king is by the prophet transferred to Cyrus is not to be entertained. The title simply designates him as one consecrated by Jehovah to be His agent and representative. This, however, is the only passage where the title is bestowed upon a foreign ruler; Nebuchadnezzar is called the "servant" of Jehovah (Jer. xxv. 9, xxvii. 6, xliii. 10), but the more august designation of "His Anointed" is reserved for one who as the Deliverer of Israel and the instrument of the overthrow of polytheism, stands in a

> To subdue nations before him;
> And I will loose the loins of kings,
> To open before him the two leaved gates;
> And the gates shall not be shut;
> 2 I will go before thee,
> And make the crooked places straight:
> I will break in pieces the gates of brass,
> And cut in sunder the bars of iron:
> 3 And I will give thee the treasures of darkness,
> And hidden riches of secret places,
> That thou mayest know that I, the LORD, which call
> *thee* by thy name, *am* the God of Israel.

still closer relation to Jehovah's purpose. Comp. "My Shepherd" in ch. xliv. 28; also ch. xlvi. 11, xlviii. 14.

to subdue &c.] Render: **to subdue before him nations, and to loose the loins of kings; to open before him doors, and that gates should not be shut**; the infinitive construction is resolved into the finite verb. To *loose* (lit. "open") is to ungird, or disarm; see 1 Ki. xx. 11, where the same verb forms the contrast to "gird."

2, 3. Speaking directly to His Anointed, Jehovah assures him of His continued support in the enterprise that still lies before him.

the crooked places] Lit. "protuberances" or, "swells." The original word (see on ch. lxiii. 1), which does not occur elsewhere as a noun, appears to mean "swollen" or "tumid"; and denotes "hills." Comp. Ovid *Amor.* II. 16. 51 ("tumidi subsidite montes") and Milton's

> "So high as heaved the tumid hills, so low
> Down sunk a hollow bottom broad and deep."
> (*Paradise Lost*, Bk. VII. 288.)

the gates (R.V. **doors**) *of brass*] Babylon had 100 gates "all of brass," according to the description of Herodotus (I. 179). Cf. Ps. cvii. 16.

3. *the treasures of darkness*] i.e. treasures hid in darkness. The following word rendered *hidden riches* (Heb. *maṭmôn*, held by some to be the original of the N.T. "Mammon"), means properly treasure *hidden* underground (Job iii. 21; Prov. ii. 4; Jer. xli. 8). The treasures referred to are chiefly the loot of Sardis, which Xenophon describes as "the richest city of Asia next to Babylon" (*Cyrop.* VII. 2. 11), and of Babylon itself (Jer. l. 37, li. 13). If, as is probable, the capture of the former city was past before the date of the prophecy, rumours of the fabulous wealth of Crœsus, which then found its way into the coffers of Cyrus, may have reached the prophet.

that thou mayest know &c.] Render: **that thou mayest know that I Jehovah am He that calleth thee by name** (see on ch. xliii. 1), **the God of Israel**. The prophet apparently expects that Cyrus will come to acknowledge Jehovah as the true God and the author of his success

For Jacob my servant's sake, and Israel mine elect, 4
I have even called thee by thy name:
I have surnamed thee, though thou hast not known me.
I *am* the LORD, and *there is* none else, 5
There is no God besides me:
I girded thee though thou hast not known me:
That they may know from the rising of the sun, and 6
from the west,
That *there is* none besides me.
I *am* the LORD, and *there is* none else.
I form the light, and create darkness: 7

(see ch. xli. 25). Whether this hope was actually realised is more than ever doubtful since the discovery of cuneiform inscriptions in which Cyrus uses the language of crude polytheism (*Records of the Past*, Vol. v., pp. 167 f.). [Cf. Sayce, *Higher Criticism and the Monuments*, pp. 507—511.] Many elements of the prophecy, such as the universal extinction of idolatry, remained unfulfilled, and it is possible that the anticipated conversion of Cyrus to the true faith is one of them (see Ryle's note on Ezra i. 2 in *Cambridge Bible for Schools*). The prophet nowhere explains the process by which this spiritual change is to be brought about, but he doubtless regards it as produced by the evidence of prophecy, so frequently dwelt upon in the first nine chapters of the book. The wonderful successes of Cyrus marked him out, to the mind of antiquity, as a favourite of the gods; but the further conviction that Jehovah alone is God proceeds from the knowledge that He alone has foretold his appearance.

4. The remainder of the section announces Jehovah's purpose in raising up Cyrus, which is twofold: (1) the liberation and exaltation of His Servant Israel (*v.* 4), and (2) that His Godhead may be acknowledged throughout the world (*v.* 6). These two motives are inseparable, since it is only through Israel that the character of Jehovah can be made known to the nations. Hence great as the mission of Cyrus is, he is still but the instrument, while Israel is the goal of the Divine activity (Duhm).

I have surnamed thee] i.e. bestowed on thee such honourable appellations as "My Shepherd," "My Anointed." See on ch. xliv. 5.

though thou hast not known me] Delitzsch and others somewhat strangely take this to mean "before thou hadst being." But the words present no difficulty in their natural sense, which is that Cyrus entered on his career of conquest ignorant of the true God who made his way prosperous.

5. *I gird thee*] the contrast to "loose the loins of kings" in *v.* 1.

6. The ultimate purpose of the conquest of Cyrus is the universal recognition of the truth asserted in *v.* 5, the sole divinity of Jehovah.

from the west] Lit. **from the going down thereof**. (On omission of *mappiq* see Davidson, *Grammar* § 19. R. *c*.)

> I make peace, and create evil:
> I the LORD do all these *things*.
> 8 Drop down, ye heavens, from above,
> And let the skies pour down righteousness:
> Let the earth open, and let them bring forth salvation,

7. It has been very generally supposed that the expressions of this verse cover a polemic against the Zoroastrian dualism, with its eternal antagonism between Ahuramazda, the god of light and of goodness, and Ahriman, the god of darkness and evil. The prophet's language, however, is perfectly general, and it is hardly probable that he would have contented himself with a vague allusion to so important a controversy. And apart from the question whether Cyrus was a Zoroastrian in religion, it is doubtful whether a sharply formulated dualism was a prominent feature of Persian religion in his time. It is more likely therefore that the only dualism here referred to is the dualism latent in every polytheistic system, viz., the ascription of good and evil events to different classes of deities. The context shews that the writer is thinking of the effect of Jehovah's victory, not specially on Cyrus, but upon men in general; and the truth he asserts is simply that Jehovah as the only God is the disposer of all events, good and evil alike.

and create evil] i.e. not moral evil, but physical evil, calamity. Cf. Am. iii. 6, "shall evil befall a city and Jehovah hath not done it?" The prophet's words are startlingly bold, but they do not go beyond the common O. T. doctrine on the subject, which is free from the speculative difficulties that readily suggest themselves to the mind of a modern reader. There is no thought in the O.T. of reducing all evil, moral and physical, to a single principle. Moral evil proceeds from the will of man, physical evil from the will of God, who sends it as the punishment of sin. The expression "*create* evil" implies nothing more than that. It is true (as we see from the Book of Job &c.) that the *indiscriminateness* of physical calamities had begun to cause perplexity in the age to which the prophecy belongs. But the discussion of that question never shook either of the two positions, that sin originates in man, and that God is the author of calamity.

8. A lyrical effusion, called forth by the thought of the blessings that will follow the triumph of the true religion. The heavens are represented as showering down gracious influences, which fructify the earth and cause it to bring forth the fruits of salvation. For the figure of the verse, cf. ch. lv. 10; Hos. ii. 21 f.; Ps. lxxii. 6; and esp. Ps. lxxxv. 11 ("truth springs out of the earth, and righteousness looks down from heaven").

Drop down] is a causative verb, the obj. being "righteousness" in the next line.

let them bring forth &c.] Rather: **let salvation and [...] spring forth; let her** (the earth) **cause righteousness to spring up**. The plural verb causes some difficulty. A.V. (and R.V.) appear to take heavens and earth as subj.; but this is hardly possible, first because they belong to

And let righteousness spring up together;
I the LORD have created it.
Woe unto him that striveth with his maker!
Let the potsherd *strive* with the potsherds of the earth.
Shall the clay say to him that fashioneth it,
What makest thou?
Or thy work, He hath no hands?
Woe unto him that saith unto *his* father, What begettest thou?

different distichs, and secondly, because the verb is always neuter (Deut. xxix. 17 is no exception). Perhaps a word has been omitted from the text.

Two words are here used for righteousness, that which comes down from heaven is *ҫedeq*, that which springs from the earth is *ҫĕdāqāh*. The figure might suggest that *ҫedeq* is the cause of which *ҫĕdāqāh* is the effect; the former being the divine "right" which establishes salvation &c., and the latter the human order which is an element of it. But any such distinction is precarious. *Salvation* (*yesha‘*) which ordinarily means "deliverance" appears here to be used in its wider sense of "welfare," like the kindred noun in Job xxx. 15 ("my welfare is passed away as a cloud"). See Introduction, p. xxviii *n*.

9—13. These verses are addressed to a section of the exiles who resented the idea of deliverance through a foreign conqueror. The strong word "strive" and the emphatic reassertion of the mission of Cyrus (*v.* 13), as well as the connexion with *vv.* 1—8, shew that deliberate opposition to the Divine purpose, and not mere faint-hearted unbelief (as in chs. xl. 27, li. 13), is here referred to. We know too little of the circumstances to understand the precise state of mind from which the objection proceeded. It may have arisen from reluctance to entertain the idea of deliverance through a foreign conqueror, instead of through an Israelite king, as ancient prophecies seemed to promise (e.g., Jer. xxx. 21). The same tendency of thought is probably alluded to in ch. xlvi. 12 (the "stout-hearted, that are far from righteousness").

his maker] the same word as "him that fashioned it" in the second half of the verse. It is the ordinary word for "potter."

Let *the potsherd* strive *&c.*] Render as in R.V. **a potsherd among the** potsherds **of the earth**! or, "a potsherd like (no better than) an earthen potsherd." "With" may mean "among" (as a synonymous word does in Ps. lxix. 28), or "like" (Job ix. 26), but the use of the same preposition in two different senses in one sentence is no doubt harsh.

or thy work, He hath no hands] i.e. no power. Delitzsch instances an identical Arabic phrase (*lā yadai lahu* = "it is not in his power"). The LXX. reads "Thou" instead of "He," and several commentators have suggested a transposition of the suffixes in the original: "or his work, Thou hast no hands." The emendation is plausible, though perhaps hardly necessary.

Or to the woman, What hast thou brought forth?
11 Thus saith the LORD, the Holy One of Israel, and his maker,
Ask me of *things* to come concerning my sons,
And concerning the work of my hands command ye me.
12 I have made the earth,
And created man upon it:
I, *even* my hands, have stretched out the heavens,
And all their host have I commanded.
13 I have raised him up in righteousness,
And I will direct all his ways:
He shall build my city, and he shall let go my captives,

10. The impropriety of contending with God exhibited in a still more repellent light. The words "his" and "the" are not expressed in Hebrew; simply "*a* father," "*a* woman." "The rudest and most outrageous intrusion into an unspeakably delicate and sacred relationship" (Delitzsch).

11. The last two verses were probably spoken by the prophet in his own name; here Jehovah addresses the same persons, introducing Himself as the *Holy One of Israel* (xli. 14) *and his maker* (*v.* 9). If the text be quite accurate, *ask me* must mean "ask me, but do not criticise me," and *command me* must mean "leave to my care" (as 1 Sam. xiii. 14, xxv. 30; 2 Sam. vi. 21, vii. 11). But Cheyne well observes that these parallels are not exact, the verb being used of a charge laid on an inferior by a superior; and it is doubtful if it could be suitably employed of committing anything to the charge of God. He supposes that by an easily explicable omission of a consonant an imperf. has been changed into an imper.; and his translation is perhaps more forcible than any that can be obtained from the received text: **concerning things to come** (xli. 23, xliv. 7) **will ye question** (i.e. "interrogate" in a hostile sense) **me? and concerning...the work of my hands will ye lay commands upon me?**

concerning my sons] should (according to the accents) be taken with what follows (as R.V.); but the phrase is irrelevant and should probably be omitted as a gloss based on *v.* 10.

12. Is introductory to *v.* 13; it is the Creator of all things who has destined Cyrus to be the emancipator of Israel.

I, even my hands] The "I" merely lends emphasis to the possessive: "*my* hands, and not another's."

all their host (the *stars*, not the angels, xl. 26) *have I commanded*] or, "ordained."

13. *I* (again emphatic) *have raised him* (Cyrus) *up in righteousness*] i.e. in accordance with a consistent, straightforward and right purpose (cf. ch. xlii. 6). Cf. also chs. xli. 2, 25, etc.

he (and no other) *shall build my city &c.*] See ch. xliv. 27 f.

Not for price **nor reward**,
Saith the LORD of hosts.
Thus saith the LORD,   14
The labour of Egypt, and merchandise of Ethiopia
And of the Sabeans, men of stature,
Shall come over unto thee, and they shall be thine:
They shall come after thee, in chains they shall come over,

not for price nor reward] Lit. "not for hire and not for a bribe." These words remove a difficulty which would naturally suggest itself to the exiles: viz., that there was no conceivable motive that could induce Cyrus to espouse the cause of Israel. The divine answer is that he will do so from an inward impulse (ὁρμή τις, as Josephus expresses it) inspired by Jehovah. There is an apparent but no real contradiction between this assurance and the idea of ch. xliii. 3 f. The restoration of Israel is conceived as preceding the Persian conquest of Egypt and Ethiopia (*v.* 14); that is the reward subsequently given to Cyrus, but not the inducement on which he acted.

14—17. The collapse of the heathen religions is here dramatically represented under the image of a procession of conquered nations of Africa, who pass before Israel, as tributaries and slaves, acknowledging that Israel's God is the only true divinity. This seems to be the sense, but see below on *v.* 14.

14. The peoples mentioned are the same as those named in ch. xliii. 3 (see on the passage) as the "ransom" given for Israel. They are apparently represented here as already conquered by Cyrus, the vicegerent and anointed of Jehovah. It has even been supposed that Cyrus is the person addressed in the verse, but this is impossible because of the words "Surely in thee is God," which certainly could not be addressed to Cyrus. The commonly accepted interpretation that there is no thought of conquest in the passage, but only of spontaneous homage rendered to Israel by distant nations of the earth, is less natural. The idea that the "fetters" are self-imposed is a conceit not readily to be attributed to the prophet, and the whole scene strongly suggests a submission that has been preceded by humiliation and defeat. The meaning probably is that the treasures of the nations are made over to Israel by Cyrus, while the nations themselves recognise the exaltation of Israel as the goal of the Persian victories and worship Jehovah, as the only true God.

and the *Sabæans, men of stature*] (see on ch. xviii. 2.) Omit "of" with R.V.; the Sabæans offer not tribute, but their persons (as slaves).

shall come over unto thee] Rather: **shall pass before thee** (as 1 Ki. ix. 8; 2 Ki. iv. 9).

in chains they shall come over] **in fetters** (Nah. iii. 10; Ps. cxlix. 8) **shall they pass**. The word for *make supplication* is in every other instance used of prayer to God. Israel is recognised as the mediator between the true God and mankind.

And they shall fall down unto thee, they shall make supplication unto thee, *saying*,
Surely God *is* in thee;
And *there is* none else, *there is* no God.

15 Verily thou *art* a God that hidest thyself,
O God of Israel, the saviour.

16 They shall be ashamed, and also confounded, all of them:
They shall go to confusion together *that are* makers of idols.

17 *But* Israel shall be saved in the LORD *with* an everlasting salvation:

Surely God is *in thee*] **In thee only is God.** These of course are words of the Sabæans, &c. to Israel, expressing their acceptance of the true religion. Israel's God has proved Himself to be the God of history, the only God. The expression appears to be alluded to by St Paul in 1 Cor. xiv. 25 ("declaring that God is in you indeed").

15. It is difficult to say whether this verse continues the confession of the heathen, or whether it contains the prophet's own reflexion on the marvellous issue of the deliverance.

a God that hidest thyself] The prophet would perhaps hardly have used this language in his own name (see *v.* 19). But to the nations of the world Jehovah had hitherto been a hidden deity; His power and glory had never been reflected in the fortunes of His own people. Now at length He is revealed in His true character, as a "Saviour" (or **Deliverer**) (see on ch. xliii. 3). Comp., however, ch. lv. 8 f.; Deut. xxix. 29; Prov. xxv. 2, for a sense in which Jehovah might be said to hide Himself even from Israel.

16, 17. The prophet now speaks, presenting in sharp contrast the confusion of the idolaters (*v.* 16) and the everlasting salvation enjoyed by Israel. The verbs should be rendered as presents.

They shall be ashamed &c.] Better: **they are ashamed, yea confounded all of them; they are gone away in confusion** (i.e. disgrace) etc. The perfect in Heb. depicts that which will have happened in that day.

The word for "idol" is used in the sense of "form" in Ps. xlix. 14 (R.V. marg.), only here of an idolatrous image.

17. But *Israel shall be saved in the LORD*] **Israel is saved by Jehovah.**

with *an everlasting salvation*] which shall never be turned into confusion. The state of things introduced by the deliverance is final, including the manifestation of Jehovah as He is, and such a union between Him and His people as can never be dissolved. As is usual in the prophets, the perfect dispensation, or what is called the Messianic age, is conceived as issuing immediately from the historical crisis which is the subject of the prophecy, in this case the deliverance from Babylon.

Ye shall not be ashamed nor confounded world without
end.

For thus saith the LORD that created the heavens; 18
God himself that formed the earth and made it; he
hath established it,
He created it not in vain, he formed it to be inhabited:
I am the LORD; and *there is* none else.
I have not spoken in secret, in a dark place of the 19
earth:
I said not unto the seed of Jacob, Seek ye me in
vain:

world without end] More literally: **to all eternity**. The exact
expression does not occur again.

18—25. The long passage on the mission of Cyrus closes here with
the announcement of a salvation as universal as it is eternal (*v.* 17). A
purpose of universal salvation is in harmony with the character of the
God who made the world for man to dwell in (*v.* 18) and whose
revelation of Himself to Israel bears the signature of absolute veracity
(*v.* 19).

18. The words *God himself* form a sort of parenthesis, and should
be rendered as in R.V., **he is God** (or **the God**). Cf. 1 Kings xviii. 39.

he created it not in vain] lit. **not a chaos** (*tōhû*). The significance
of the expression is seen from the contrast which immediately follows.

he formed it to be inhabited] and therefore the end of His ways cannot
be the destruction of the race for whose existence He has prepared the
earth. Jehovah's final purpose must be salvation.

19. The same character of goodwill to men is manifest in the manner
of Jehovah's revelation to Israel. It has been intelligible, explicit, and
(if the word may be used) candid.

in a dark place of the earth] R.V. **in a place of the land of darkness**.
It is doubtful if there is any direct allusion to the oracles of heathenism,
which had frequently to be sought in caves and deserts. The "land of
darkness" might be the under-world, from which dubious oracles were
obtained by necromancy and other magical arts (ch. viii. 19; 1 Sam.
xxviii. 7 ff.). But the sense is perhaps sufficiently explained (in accordance with what follows) by Jer. ii. 31: "Have I been a wilderness unto
Israel, a land of darkness?" Jehovah's revelation has not been like a
dark, trackless desert, but a light in which men might walk towards an
assured goal.

I said not...Seek ye me in vain] Lit. **in chaos** (*tōhû*, as *v.* 18), i.e.
without definite guidance and without hope of result. When Jehovah
said, "Seek me," He meant that He should be found (Jer. xxix. 13); in
other words He has dealt openly and frankly with His people. It is
this quality of revelation that is denoted by the word *righteousness* in
the last line of the verse. It is used in its ethical sense of "trust-

I the LORD speak righteousness, I declare things that are right.
20 Assemble yourselves and come;
Draw near together, ye *that are* escaped of the nations:
They have no knowledge that set up the wood of their graven image,
And pray unto a god *that* cannot save.
21 Tell ye, and bring *them* near;
Yea, let them take counsel together:
Who hath declared this from ancient time? *who* hath told it from that time?
Have not I the LORD? and *there is* no God else beside me;
A just God and a saviour; *there is* none beside me.

worthiness" or straightforwardness,—perfect correspondence between deeds and words.

things that are right] **uprightness.** The plural, as always in this word, expresses the abstract idea (see ch. xxvi. 7).

20, 21. The heathen are now summoned together that they may consider this attribute of Jehovah's character, as illustrated by the prediction of the victories of Cyrus. The question submitted to them is the same as in xli. 1—4, 21—29, xliii. 9—13 : who has foretold these events? But this scene is imagined as taking place *after* the great crisis is over; hence those addressed are the *escaped of the nations* (cf. Jer. li. 50), the survivors of a world-wide judgement, of which Cyrus is the instrument (see *v.* 14).

20. *that set up the wood*...] Render, with R.V., **that carry**, &c., in religious processions (Am. v. 26), or perhaps into battle (2 Sam. v. 21). That idols have to be carried is a sign of their powerlessness (xlvi. 1 f.; Jer. x. 5).

a god that *cannot save*] The contrast in the end of *v.* 21.

21. *Tell ye*] Better : **Declare ye,** as R.V.

bring them *near*] Some such object as "your strong arguments" (xli. 21) must be supplied, and has probably dropped out of the text.

who hath declared this...?] i.e. the rise of Cyrus and his conquests. The phrase *from that time* should be either **beforehand** or **long ago** (see on ch. xvi. 13).

a just God...beside me] Better as a single sentence : **a righteous God and a Deliverer there is not besides me.** Both attributes have been exhibited in the recent crisis; righteousness (see on *v.* 19) in the explicit predictions of Cyrus, and salvation in the deliverance of Israel.

22—25. The demonstration of Jehovah's deity is followed by the proclamation of salvation to all mankind, and the declaration of His purpose that all the world shall worship Him.

Look unto me, and be ye saved, all the ends of the 22
earth:
For I *am* God, and *there is* none else.
I have sworn by myself, 23
The word is gone out of my mouth *in* righteousness, and
shall not return,
That unto me every knee shall bow,
Every tongue shall swear.
Surely, shall *one* say, in the LORD have I righteousness 24
and strength:

22. *Look unto me*] is strictly **Turn unto me** (sc. for help), a phrase elsewhere used of the acknowledgment of false gods (Lev. xix. 4; Hos. iii. 1; Deut. xxx. 17 &c., xxxi. 18 &c.; cf. Job v. 1). The second imperative expresses the consequence of the first: "Turn to Me and ye shall be saved." "Salvation" here has still its ordinary sense of deliverance; although the great judgement is past, it is plainly assumed that only those who own Jehovah's sovereignty shall be spared (*v.* 23). But the thought that it depends on knowledge of the true God, who is the God of salvation, conveys the suggestion at least of a more positive meaning; cf. John xvii. 3.

23. By **myself** *have I sworn*] Cf. Gen. xxii. 16; Jer. xxii. 5; and see Heb. vi. 13. The form of Jehovah's oath by Himself is given in ch. xlix. 18, "as I live, saith Jehovah."

the word is gone out &c.] Or, as R.V. marg.: **righteousness is gone forth from my mouth, a word which** (lit. "and it") **shall not return** (cf. ch. lv. 10 f.).

righteousness here means that which shall be verified,—a word to which the deed will correspond.

every knee shall bow (in homage, 1 Ki. xix. 18), *every tongue shall swear* (fealty, ch. xix. 18)]. The reading "confess" is substituted for "swear" in some codices of the LXX., as in Rom. xiv. 11, Phil. ii. 10, 11.

24, 25 express the faith of the religious community of the future.

Surely, shall one say, in the LORD &c.] Better: **Only** in Jehovah, shall one say, &c. The R.V. gives a different turn to the thought by including the word for "to me" in the parenthesis ("shall one say to me" [marg. "of me"]); while the A.V. treats it as part of the main sentence ("there is to me," i.e. "I have"). On the former view *righteousness* and *strength* are divine attributes; on the latter they are blessings bestowed by Jehovah on men. The rendering of A.V. is preferable, although it is opposed to the Hebr. accents.

righteousness] lit. "righteousnesses," the idea being intensified by the plural. It is often used of the mighty acts of Jehovah, the individual instances in which His righteous character is manifested (1 Sam. xii. 7; Mi. vi. 5; Ps. lxxi. 15 ff. &c.); here in like manner it must denote the experiences through which a right relation to God is verified. The parallelism with "strength" shews that it is almost identical with salvation or victory (see on ch. xli. 2 and xlvi. 13).

Even to him shall *men* come;
And all that are incensed against him shall be ashamed.
25 In the LORD shall all the seed of Israel be justified, and shall glory.

even *to him...ashamed*] **to him shall one come** &c.; or, to him shall come with shame all that were incensed (xli. 11) against him. The verb "be ashamed" seems merely to be a qualification of "shall come."
25. *be justified*] lit. **be righteous**, i.e. "enjoy righteousness" in the same sense as *v*. 24. Comp. Jer. xxiii. 6 ("Jehovah our Righteousness").

CH. XLVI. THE DOWNFALL OF THE GODS OF BABYLON.

In this and the two following chapters the person of Cyrus is only incidentally referred to; the leading idea is now the overthrow of Babylon, and the emancipation of Israel from its tyranny. Ch. xlvi. begins with the fall of the *deities* of the city; and from their proved impotence, as contrasted with the omnipotence of Jehovah, proceeds to draw lessons for various classes among the exiles. The unity of the oracle is disputed by Duhm and Cheyne in so far as *vv*. 6—8 are concerned, and the removal of these verses would somewhat modify the reasoning of the chapter. As it stands, however, the natural divisions are the following:—

(1) *vv*. 1—4. A contrast between the Babylonian gods and the God of Israel; while these share the fate of their worshippers and *are borne* away in shameful flight, Jehovah is *the bearer* of His people, making its history and leading it to final victory.

(2) *vv*. 5—7. The scene described in *vv*. 1 f. suggests another sarcastic passage (after the manner of xl. 18—20, xliv. 9—20) on the folly of idolatry in general.

(3) *vv*. 8—11. A renewed appeal (see xli. 21—29, &c.) to the argument from prophecy, in which, with unwonted severity, the hearers are addressed as "rebels" (*v*. 8).

(4) *vv*. 12, 13. Addressing the opponents of Jehovah's purpose, the prophet announces the speedy deliverance of Israel as the goal to which events are hastening.

1, 2. The ignominious flight of the gods of Babylon.—*Bel* and *Nebo* are the Jupiter and Mercury of the Babylonian pantheon (they are represented by these planets), and were the supreme deities in Babylon at this time. Bel (*Bîlu*) is the Babylonian form of the Hebrew *Baʻal* (=lord), and like that word is a generic name applicable to any deity. When used as a proper name it usually denotes Merodach (Marduk), the tutelary divinity of the city of Babylon (so Jer. l. 2, li. 44); although there was an older Bel, who is spoken of as his father. The elevation of Bel-Merodach to the chief place among the older gods, as recorded in the mythical Chaldæan account of the Creation (Tablet IV., 1 ff.), is the legendary counterpart of the ascendency acquired by Babylon over the more ancient cities of the Euphrates Valley. Nebo (*Nabu*) was the son of Merodach; the chief seat of his worship being Borsippa, in the

Bel boweth down, Nebo stoopeth, 46
Their idols were upon the beasts, and upon the cattle:
Your carriages *were* heavy loaden;
They are a burden to the weary *beast*.
They stoop, they bow down together; 2
They could not deliver the burden,
But themselves are gone into captivity.

Hearken unto me, O house of Jacob, 3

vicinity of Babylon. His name, which is supposed to be from the same root as the Hebrew *nâbî*, "prophet," seems to mark him out as the "speaker" of the gods (another point of contact with Mercury, "the chief speaker," Acts xiv. 12). He was also regarded as the inventor of writing. The frequency with which the Chaldæan kings are named after him (Nabo-polassar, Nebu-chadnezzar, Nabo-nidus) has been thought to shew that he was the patron deity of the dynasty.

boweth down...stoopeth (better **croucheth**)] The second verb to be pointed, like the first, as perfect (prophetic pf.).

their idols (ch. x. 11) are (R.V.) *upon the beasts, and upon the cattle*] The allusion is hardly to the custom of carrying away the idols of a conquered nation (Jer. xlviii. 7, xlix. 3; Hos. x. 5 f.), but rather to an attempt of the Babylonians to carry off their images on the approach of the Persians (see *v.* 2). Similarly, Merodach-Baladan packed his idols on ships and carried them off, at the approach of Sennacherib (Schrader, *Cuneiform Inscr.*, Vol. II. p. 36.)   *Beasts* and *cattle* usually mean respectively "wild beasts" and "domestic animals"; here, however, they both denote beasts of burden simply.

your carriages were *heavy loaden*] Rather as R.V. **the things that ye carried about**, i.e. in religious processions (ch. xlv. 20), **are made** a load. "At the New Year's festival the images of Merodach and his son Nebo were carried through Babylon in solemn procession on sacred barques of great magnificence, and along a promenade prepared for this purpose since Nabopolassar" (Fried. Delitzsch, quoted by Delitzsch, *Comm.* p. 403). Such scenes must have been familiar to the prophet and his readers, and gave additional point to the contrasted picture here imagined.

2. *they could not deliver*] i.e. **cause to escape**.

themselves are gone into captivity] The distinction allowed between the gods and their images is an ironical concession to heathen modes of thought. The fact that the gods are unable to save their own images means that they have vanished. The recently discovered inscriptions have shewn, however, that the idols of Babylon had nothing to fear from Cyrus.

3, 4. In the scene which he has just described the prophet sees an emblem of the inherent weakness of heathenism. There man carries his gods, and the result is that gods and worshippers are involved in

> And all the remnant of the house of Israel,
> Which are borne *by me* from the belly,
> Which are carried from the womb:
> 4 And *even* to *your* old age I *am* he;
> And *even* to hoar hairs will I carry *you:*
> I have made, and I will bear;
> Even I will carry, and will deliver *you.*
> 5 To whom will ye liken me, and make *me* equal,
> And compare me, that we may be like?
> 6 They lavish gold out of the bag,
> And weigh silver in the balance,
> *And* hire a goldsmith; and he maketh it a god:
> They fall down, yea, they worship.

common ruin. Israel has had a far different experience of its relation to its God, having known Jehovah as One who has carried it from the beginning of its history (Ex. xix. 4; Deut. i. 31, xxxii. 11; Hos. xi. 3; cf. ch. xl. 11, lxiii. 9), and is able to bear it on to final salvation. The profound insight into the nature of religion which is characteristic of the writer is nowhere more clearly exhibited than in this striking and original contrast.

3. *all the remnant of the house of Israel*] It is doubtful whether there is a reference here to the scattered survivors of the Ten Tribes. More probably, the clause is a rhetorical variation of the previous "house of Jacob." The participles *borne* and *carried* are repeated from *v.* 1, although in inverse order ("carried things" and "made a load"). The words "by me" are better omitted.

4. *And* even *to* your *old age &c.*] Cf. Ps. lxxi. 18. What Jehovah has been to His people in the past, He will be for all the future. It is not implied that Israel is now "old and gray-headed," as an erroneous combination with ch. xlvii. 6 led Hitzig to suppose.

I am *he*] See on ch. xli. 4.

I have made] Better perhaps **I have done it.**

and will deliver] in express contrast to the false gods who "could not deliver" the dead burden of their images (*v.* 2).

5. Comp. the similar question of xl. 18, which as here introduces a sarcastic description of the manufacture of idols.

6, 7. Contemptuous description of idolatry in general. Comp. especially with ch. xliv. 9—20.

6. *They lavish gold &c.*] Better as an exclamation of contempt: **They that pour gold** etc. The *gold* and *silver* are the material out of which the images (or at least their plating) are to be made by the goldsmith (xl. 19) who is hired for the work. The word for *balance* is *qâneh* (reed), never elsewhere used in this sense. It probably denotes the beam of the balance.

they fall down] The same word (*sâgad*) in xliv. 15, 17, 19.

They bear him upon the shoulder, they carry him, 7
And set him in his place, and he standeth;
From his place shall he not remove:
Yea, *one* shall cry unto him, yet can he not answer,
Nor save him out of his trouble.
Remember this, and shew yourselves men: 8
Bring *it* again to mind, O ye transgressors.
Remember the former *things* of old: 9
For I *am* God, and *there is* none else;
I am God, and *there is* none like me,
Declaring the end from the beginning, 10
And from ancient times *the things* that are not *yet* done,
Saying, My counsel shall stand,
And I will do all my pleasure:

7. *They bear him &c.*] the newly made idol, to his appointed place, from which he is powerless to move. How vain, therefore, is it to cry to him for help! He is a "god that cannot save" (xlv. 20).

8—11. An appeal to history and prophecy in proof of Jehovah's divinity.

shew yourselves men] R.V. marg. renders "stand fast," but neither sense is suitable in an address to "rebels." The verb used (*hith'ōshāshû*) is unknown in Hebrew. The rendering of A.V. is based on a common view that it is a denominative from the word for "man" (*'îsh*), which is grammatically untenable; that of R.V. marg. connects it with a root found in Aramaic, Assyrian and Arabic, meaning to "be firm." Of proposed emendations the easiest is Lagarde's, "be ye ashamed" (*hithbōshāshû*, after Gen. ii. 25). Others, *hithbōnānû*, "consider" (ch. xliii. 18).

bring it *again to mind*] as ch. xliv. 19.

O ye transgressors] Rather **rebels** (xlviii. 8, liii. 12, lxvi. 24). From ch. xlv. 9 onwards there seems to be a growing sense of antagonism between the prophet and at least a section of his audience (see *v*. 12 and on xlviii. 1—11).

9. *former* things *of old*] See on xli. 22. The emphasis here lies less on the predictions than on the events themselves, which are of such a nature as to demonstrate that Jehovah alone is truly God.

10. *the end from the beginning*] i.e. **the issue** (of a particular series of events or period of history) from its origin.

the things *that are not* yet *done*] with closer reference to the events mentioned in *v*. 11. Cf. ch xlviii. 5 ("before it has come to pass").

My counsel shall stand] Cf. ch. xiv. 24.

my pleasure] **my purpose** (see on ch. xliv. 28).

11   Calling a ravenous bird from the east,
      The man that executeth my counsel from a far country:
      Yea, I have spoken *it*, I will also bring it to pass;
      I have purposed *it*, I will also do it.
12   Hearken unto me, ye stouthearted,
      That *are* far from righteousness:
13   I bring near my righteousness; it shall not be far off,
      And my salvation shall not tarry:
      And I will place salvation in Zion for Israel my glory.

11. The supreme illustration of the foreknowledge and power of Jehovah is the raising up of Cyrus. Cyrus is compared to a *ravenous bird* on account of the celerity of his movements (ch. xli. 3), just as Nebuchadnezzar had been likened to an eagle (Jer. xlix. 22; Ezek. xvii. 3). There can hardly be an allusion to the fact (if it be a fact) that the royal ensign of Persia was a golden eagle (Xenophon, *Cyrop.* VII. 1, 4).

from the east] xli. 2, 25.

the man that executeth my counsel] Lit. as R.V. **the man of my counsel** (the consonantal text has "his counsel"). Not of course "my counsellor" (as in xl. 13), but in the sense expressed by the A.V.

I have purposed] Lit. **I have formed**, i.e. "foreordained," as in ch. xxii. 11, xxxvii. 26.

12, 13. A call to repentance based on the nearness of deliverance.

ye stouthearted] The phrase means in Ps. lxxvi. 5 "courageous"; here it is rather akin to "stiff-hearted" in Ezek. ii. 4. The LXX. reads "ye that have lost heart" (אבדי לב for אבירי לב), and this is accepted as the true text by certain commentators. The sense is too weak in this connexion; if there are men who on the eve of deliverance are "far from righteousness" they are surely those who are in more or less conscious opposition to the divine purpose (cf. xlv. 9). "Righteousness" in *v.* 13 is parallel to "salvation," and denotes the manifestation of Jehovah's righteousness in the deliverance of Israel. In this verse it is more natural to understand it in its forensic sense, of the right relation to God, which is the condition of sharing in the outward salvation. See Appendix. Note II.

13. *for Israel my glory*] Cf. xlix. 3. But another possible translation is "I will give...my glory unto Israel" (R.V. marg.).

The two verses express a paradox which enters deeply into the thought of the prophet. While salvation is near in point of time, yet Israel is spiritually far from it. Hence the work of salvation or righteousness has two aspects; along with the providential deliverance of which the agent is Cyrus, there is an inward and spiritual salvation which consists in bringing the nation to right thoughts about itself and God. And in this spiritual transformation the instrument is the Servant of Jehovah.

Come down, and sit in the dust, O virgin daughter of 47
   Babylon,
Sit on the ground: *there is* no throne,
O daughter of the Chaldeans;
For thou shalt no more be called tender and delicate.

CH. XLVII. AN ODE ON THE FALL OF BABYLON.

The strain of prophetic exhortation is here interrupted by an ironical elegy or "taunt-song" with a strong resemblance to the ode on the king of Babylon in ch. xiv. 4—21. The humiliation of the city is represented by the graphic image of a delicate and luxurious lady of the harem, suddenly reduced to the shameful condition of a slave or a captive. This female personification of Babylon forms an effective, and no doubt intentional, contrast to the figure of Zion, the desolate and bereaved widow, who is soon to be restored to the honour and joys of motherhood (ch. xlix. 14 ff., li. 17 ff., liv.).—Although words of Jehovah occur in *vv.* 3 and 6, it is hardly natural to suppose that He is the speaker throughout. The singer is more probably either the nation of Israel (as in xiv. 4 ff.) or the prophet speaking in his own name.

The poem is usually divided into four unequal strophes, commencing with *vv.* 1, 5, 8 and 12. Dillmann finds in it a combination of several distinct poetic measures, and recognises the characteristic rhythm of the elegy only in the opening verses of the first three strophes (1, 5, 8). There is however an *approximation* to the structure of the *qînah* in many verses; and the question is suggested whether the departures from the regular form are not to be accounted for by errors in the transmission of the text. Duhm, omitting three clauses as interpolations (see below), makes out a division into five equal strophes (1—4, 5—7, 8—10 *a*, 10 *b*—12, 13—15) of seven lines each, and with a few minor alterations the elegiac cæsura (see on xiv. 4) is fairly well marked in nearly every line. The textual alterations may not commend themselves in each instance, but there is at least a presumption in favour of a stricter prosody than earlier commentators allow.

1—4. The first strophe consists of a tristich (*v.* 1) followed (on Duhm's reconstruction) by two distichs. The leading thought is the degradation of Babylon from her position of ease and luxury.

1. *virgin daughter of Babylon*] i.e. "virgin daughter, Babylon"; see on i. 8, cf. xxxvii. 22. The parallel phrase *daughter of the Chaldæans* is somewhat different. It describes Babylon as the city of (possessed by) the Chaldæans, the reigning dynasty. It *might* no doubt be a personification of the land of Chaldæa, like "daughter of Egypt" in Jer. xlvi. 11; but this is less probable.

sit on the ground] A sign not of mourning, as in iii. 26, but of abject humiliation.

there is no throne] Render: without a throne, as R.V.

thou shalt no more be called] Lit. "thou shalt no more (be one whom) they call"; the peculiar construction being partly due to the Hebrew aversion to the use of the passive.

2 Take the millstones, and grind meal:
Uncover thy locks, make bare the leg,
Uncover the thigh, pass over the rivers.
3 Thy nakedness shall be uncovered, yea, thy shame shall be seen:
I will take vengeance, and I will not meet *thee as* a man.
4 *As for* our redeemer, the LORD of hosts *is* his name,
The Holy One of Israel.

tender and delicate] See Deut. xxviii. 56, "the tender and delicate woman which would not adventure to set the sole of her foot upon the ground."

2. *Take the millstones &c.*] The luxurious lady must betake herself to the occupation of the meanest female slaves in the household; Ex. xi. 5; Job xxxi. 10.

uncover thy locks] Rather: **take off thy veil** (Cant. iv. 1, 3, vi. 7).

make bare the leg] **remove the skirt.** The last word does not occur elsewhere.   *pass over the rivers*] Render: **pass through streams,** omitting the article. The words are commonly taken to describe the hardships of a journey into exile, but they may simply refer to the degradations which she would have to undergo in performing the drudgery of a common slave (so Dillmann).

3. *Thy nakedness...seen*] These words, which undoubtedly spoil the rhythm of the verse, are deleted by Duhm as a gloss suggested by the latter part of *v.* 2.

and I will not meet thee as *a man*] The sense is very obscure. Either (*a*) "I will spare no man" (i.e. meet him with friendly intentions); the figure of the virgin being dropped: or (*b*) "I will not entreat any man (for help)": or (*c*) the vowel-points being changed, "I will let no man intercede,"—all unacceptable on one ground or another. The difficulty lies in the word for "man"; this would be got rid of by simply changing *'ādām* into *'āmar* (= "saith") read by some MSS. of the LXX. as the first word of *v.* 4. The verb then stands absolutely, and is best pointed and translated as *Niphal tolerativum*: "I will not (let myself) be entreated." (Oort and Duhm). See further on *v.* 4.

4. The verse as it stands interrupts the continuity of the poem, especially in the view of those who hold that the speaker is throughout Jehovah. Lowth and others regard it as the response of a chorus of Israelites to the words of God in *v.* 3, while Dillmann and others unhesitatingly pronounce it to be an interpolation. But all reasonable objections are removed if we supply the word "saith" as in two Greek codices. Combining this with the other suggestion of Oort mentioned above, the last distich of the strophe reads thus:—

I will take vengeance and will not be entreated,—saith our Redeemer;
Jehovah of Hosts is His name,—the Holy One of Israel.

Sit thou silent, and get thee into darkness, O daughter of 5
the Chaldeans:
For thou shalt no more be called, The lady of kingdoms.
I was wroth with my people, I have polluted mine in- 6
heritance,
And given them into thine hand:
Thou didst shew them no mercy;
Upon the ancient hast thou very heavily laid thy yoke.
And thou saidst, I shall be a lady for ever: 7

5—7. The second strophe commences anew with an apostrophe to Babylon. The keynote is struck in the words "mistress of kingdoms." She is threatened with the loss of her imperial power, because she has so grossly abused it by her cruelty to Israel.

5. *get thee into darkness*] Darkness may be a symbol either of imprisonment (ch. xlii. 7) or, more generally, of misery; Lam. iii. 2.

lady of kingdoms] Lit. "mistress" (xxiv. 2). The word is used of the queen in Jer. xiii. 18, in a connexion somewhat similar to this. Babylon is addressed as an imperial city holding the destinies of many kingdoms in her hands.

6. Jehovah speaks, charging Babylon with pitiless inhumanity towards His people when they were delivered to her for chastisement (for the thought cf. Zech. i. 15).

I was wroth with my people] Cf. liv. 9, lvii. 16 f., lxiv. 5, 9.

I have polluted (R.V. **I profaned**) *mine inheritance*] Cf. xliii. 28. "Profane" is the opposite of "holy;" as "holy to Jehovah" Israel was inviolable (Jer. ii. 3), but when this relation ceased she passed under the power of the heathen.

upon the ancient] Better, as R.V.: **upon the aged**. Although the word is sing., there can be no doubt that it is used literally of the old men on whom the hardships of captivity fell most heavily (cf. Lam. iv. 16, v. 12). The idea that Israel as a nation is meant is not to be entertained (see on ch. xlvi. 4). We have little knowledge of the circumstances of the Israelites in exile, but there is nothing improbable in the supposition that some of them were put to forced labour, and that cases of exceptional barbarity may have occurred.

7. Such inconsiderate cruelty can only be explained by the delusion that her supremacy was eternal, that no day of reckoning could ever come to her.

And thou saidst, I shall be &c.] Render (with a different division of clauses) **And thou saidst I shall be for ever—a lady eternally** (lit. "mistress of eternity"). The word here rendered "eternity" (*'ad*) is taken in the received text as a conjunction (A.V. "so *that*," strictly "until"). The rhythm requires it to be treated as a substantive in the genitive after "mistress." It is used in exactly the same way in the name "Father of eternity" (ch. ix. 6).

So that thou didst not lay these *things* to thy heart,
Neither didst remember the latter end of it.
Therefore hear now this, *thou that art* given to pleasures, that dwellest carelessly,
That sayest in thine heart, I *am*, and none else besides me;
I shall not sit *as* a widow, neither shall I know the loss of children:
But these two *things* shall come to thee *in* a moment in one day,
The loss of children, and widowhood:
They shall come upon thee in their perfection
For the multitude of thy sorceries, *and* for the great abundance of thine enchantments.
For thou hast trusted in thy wickedness: thou hast said, None seeth me.

these things] thy cruelties;—in what sense she failed to lay them to heart is explained by the following clause.

the latter end of it] or **the issue thereof,** i.e. the inevitable retribution.

8—10 *a*. The third strophe: Babylon's careless confidence in her own future shall be put to shame by the suddenness of her calamities.

thou that art *given to pleasures*] **thou voluptuous one** (Cheyne). The word does not occur again. The remaining clauses of the verse recur verbatim in Zeph. ii. 15. (of Nineveh).

that dwellest carelessly] **that sittest securely.**

I am *and none else besides me*] Rather: **I and none besides.** The words express Babylon's sense of her unique position. The vocalic ending of the word for "none" ('*aphsî* from '*ephes*=cessation, nothingness) cannot be the poss. suff. of 1st pers., which would give the sense "I am no more,"—the opposite of what is intended. It is probably an old case-termination which has ceased to have any significance in the Hebr. of the O.T. So again in *v.* 10.

9. *widowhood*] is simply a figure for desolation, which is not to be pressed by asking the question, Who was the husband? The reference could hardly be to the king (for which there are no analogies), still less to the foreign nations with whom she trafficked.

in their perfection] i.e. **in their full measure** (R.V.).

for the multitude] Better: **in spite of,** &c. (as in ch. v. 25 &c., "for all this"). Strict rhythm would here be restored by transposing the two clauses: "for the great abundance...—for the multitude..."

10. *thou hast trusted &c.*] Better perhaps: **thou hast been confident in thy wickedness**; hast perpetrated wickedness without a misgiving or a thought of retribution. "Wickedness" probably means "tyranny," as Nah. iii. 19.

Thy wisdom and thy knowledge, it hath perverted
  thee;
And thou hast said in thine heart, I *am*, and none else
  besides me.
Therefore shall evil come upon thee; thou shalt not 11
  know from whence it riseth:
And mischief shall fall upon thee; thou shalt not be able
  to put it off:
And desolation shall come upon thee suddenly, *which
  thou shalt not know.*
Stand now with thine enchantments, and with the multi- 12
  tude of thy sorceries,
Wherein thou hast laboured from thy youth;

None seeth me] No holy and righteous God takes notice. Cf. Ps.
x. 11, xciv. 7.
  10 *b*—12. The fourth strophe gives the reason for Babylon's security:
the elaborate system of magic for which she was famous, and in which
her practical religion largely consisted. For an account of Babylonian
sorcery &c., see Lenormant, *Chaldaean Magic* (transl.), esp. chs. I—IV.
  Thy wisdom and thy knowledge] The context shews that it is the
occult knowledge of sorcery, astrology &c., that is meant.
  11. *evil*] is the same word as "wickedness" in *v*. **10**; the play on
the two meanings of the word is intentional.
  from whence it riseth] The literal rendering is given in R.V. "the
dawning thereof." But the metaphor is unnatural (of calamity), and the
parallelism of the next line shews that an inf. must be read. A similar
Arabic verb means "to charm"; accordingly most commentators now
translate **which thou shalt not know (how) to charm away** (see R.V.
marg.). Some, however, prefer a slight alteration of the text, reading
"to buy off" (שחרה for שחרה; cf. the parallelism in Prov. vi. 35).
  to put off] is literally **to expiate**, i.e. avert by an offering. "They
try to avert evil and procure good, either by purifications, sacrifices,
or enchantments." (Diodorus Siculus, quoted by Lenormant, *l.c.*
p. 12.)
  which *thou shalt not know*] The parallelism with the other two lines
of the tristich suggests that an inf. should be supplied at the end: **which
thou shalt not know how to...** (so Duhm).
  12. *Stand now with &c.*] Either **Stand by thy spells**, persist in
them, stake everything upon them, as Lev. xiii. 5; Jer. xlviii. 11,
Ezek. xiii. 5 (these parallels, however, are not quite convincing); or (as
in *v*. 13) **Stand forth with thy spells.**
  wherein thou hast laboured from thy youth] Or: **with which thou
hast wearied thyself**, &c.; see on ch. xliii. 22. Duhm omits these
words entirely, for the sake of the rhythm, but they excite no suspicion
on any other ground.

If so be thou shalt be able to profit, if so be thou mayest prevail.

13 Thou art wearied in the multitude of thy counsels.
Let now the astrologers, the star-gazers, the monthly prognosticators,
Stand *up*, and save thee from *these things* that shall come upon thee.

14 Behold, they shall be as stubble; the fire shall burn them;
They shall not deliver themselves from the power of the flame:
There shall not *be* a coal to warm at, *nor* fire to sit before it.

15 Thus shall they be unto thee *with* whom thou hast laboured, *even* thy merchants, from thy youth:

if so be &c.] **perchance thou wilt be able to profit!— perchance thou wilt inspire terror!** (Cf. R.V.) keen and bitter irony.

13—15. The last strophe dwells on the futility of all the resources that the "daughter of Babel" can call to her aid.

13. *let now the astrologers &c.*] Render: **let them stand forth** (*v.* 12) **now and save thee,—they that have divided the heavens, they that gaze on the stars, that announce month by month something of what shall befall thee.**

astrologers is an apt equivalent of "they that divided the heavens" (i.e. into the constellations of the Zodiac, for astrological purposes). This at least seems the most probable meaning, although the verb for "divide" does not occur elsewhere in Hebrew (in Arab. it means to "divide into great pieces"), and the Ancient Versions render otherwise [LXX. οἱ ἀστρολόγοι τοῦ οὐρανοῦ]. So *monthly prognosticators* is a felicitous condensation of the thought of the last clause, although the E.V. (following some Jewish authorities) has mistaken the syntactical construction. The special reference here is to the preparation of monthly almanacs (based on astrological calculations) in which coming disasters were foretold, lucky and unlucky days pointed out, &c. A specimen of these almanacs is translated by Sayce in *Trans. of the Society of Bibl. Archæology*, III. 229 ff.

14. They cannot even save their own lives, much less the State. *themselves*] **their (own) life.**

there shall not be a coal &c.] Better: **It is no (glowing) coal to warm oneself withal; no fire to sit before!** i.e. no genial hearth for comfort, but an all-consuming fire! The sentence is prosaic and unnecessary, and might readily be sacrificed (with Duhm) to the exigencies of the strophe and the elegiac measure.

15. *with whom thou hast laboured*] See on *v.* 12.

They shall wander every one to his quarter; none shall save thee.

thy merchants] Cf. Nah. iii. 16 f., and see on ch. xiii. 14. The abrupt introduction of merchants here is somewhat perplexing, especially after the adverb "so"; but the word never means anything else in Hebrew; and the context requires that some new persons should be understood, since the astrologers have perished in the fire, while these make their escape. It may however be used in a wide sense, of nations that trafficked with Babylon.

every one to his quarter] Rather: **each straight before him**; cf. Ezek. i. 9 (the cherubim went "everyone straight forward.").

CH. XLVIII. EXHORTATIONS ADDRESSED TO THE EXILES IN THE NEAR PROSPECT OF DELIVERANCE.

The chapter is largely a recapitulation of certain outstanding themes of the prophecy, several of which are here touched upon for the last time. The references to the victories of Cyrus, the predictions of the fall of Babylon, the appeal to prophecy, and the distinction between "former things" and "new things" henceforth disappear from the circle of the author's thoughts, along with other familiar subjects, such as the polemic against idolatry and the impressive inculcation of the sole deity of Jehovah. This circumstance indicates that we have reached the end of the first great division of the prophecy, and the impression is confirmed by the closing hymn of praise, which carries us forward to the very eve of the departure from Babylon. On some critical difficulties of the passage see the introductory notes to *vv.* 1—11 and 17—19, below.

There are four distinct sections:

(i) *vv.* 1—11. The prophet vindicates the methods of Jehovah's revelation to Israel; predictions have been given and withheld in such a way as to remove every excuse for attributing the great events of history to any other cause than the will of God.

(ii) *vv.* 12—16. An instance of the withholding of prophecy till the eve of its accomplishment is the present announcement of the conquest of Babylon by Cyrus; it is the crowning proof of Jehovah's abiding presence with His people.

(iii) *vv.* 17—19. Jehovah's compassion finds expression in a cry of distress over the neglect of His commandments, which has stood in the way of Israel's salvation.

(iv) *vv.* 20—22. In a final jubilant outburst of praise, the exiles are summoned to flee from Babylon, whose power is already broken, and to proclaim the marvels of their redemption to the ends of the earth.

1—11. These verses present some peculiar features, both of thought and style, which have been felt by scholars representing widely diverging critical tendencies. The severe judgement on the people goes beyond anything else in the prophecy; and, as has been pointed out,

Hear ye this, O house of Jacob,
Which are called by the name of Israel,
And are come forth out of the waters of Judah,
Which swear by the name of the LORD,
And make mention of the God of Israel,
But not in truth, nor in righteousness.
For they call themselves of the holy city,
And stay themselves upon the God of Israel;
The LORD of hosts *is* his name.

seems to breathe the spirit of Ezekiel rather than of the second Isaiah. Israel is addressed as a nation of hypocrites, of apostates, and of persistent idolaters. Then the argument of the passage as a whole is very remarkable. The "former things" (i.e. the events that have just taken place) were announced long beforehand, lest Israel should be led to ascribe them to some false god (*vv*. 3—6 *a*); but the "new things" (the subject of the present prophecy) have been "hidden" till the last moment, lest the people in their perversity should say they had known of them all along (6 *b*—8). Duhm and Cheyne agree in assigning these peculiarities to an editor, who has supplied a running commentary on the words of the original author, in the shape of annotations. There is much in the section which would be more intelligible if inserted by a later writer; but the method attributed to the editor is peculiar, and no motive suggests itself for his systematic attempt to correct the tendency of this isolated passage. The difficulties are perhaps exaggerated; the stern attitude towards the nation is not without parallels (see ch. xlv. 9 ff., and on ch. xlvi. 8), and the special development of the argument from prophecy cannot be shown to involve a radical inconsistency with the prophet's general conceptions.

1. *Hear ye this*] refers to the following oracle, which commences with *v*. 3 (cf. xlvi. 3 and xlviii. 12). The rest of *vv*. 1 f. is an editorial insertion, in the view of Duhm and Cheyne (see above).

which are called] Or, **which call themselves**, as in *v*. 2 (cf. ch. xliv. 5). For the remnant of the tribe of Judah, whom the author has in his view, the name "Israel" was really a title of honour.

out of the waters of Judah] The metaphor can be explained from Ps. lxviii. 26 (R.V.), where the ancestor of the nation is compared to a fountain or cistern. It is perhaps better, however, to read (with Secker) *mimm'ê* for *mimmê*, rendering **from the bowels** (as *v*. 19) **of Judah**.

To *swear by the name of the LORD* is a profession of allegiance to Him, and as such is enjoined as a religious duty (Deut. vi. 13, x. 20).

make mention of] i.e. celebrate; Ps. xx. 7. The words *not in truth, nor in righteousness* do not refer specially to false swearing, but mean that the profession is formal and insincere.

2. *of* (or **by**) *the holy city*] The phrase is here applied to Jerusalem for the first time in the O.T. It occurs again in ch. lii. 1, elsewhere only in the books of Nehemiah and Daniel (comp. Matt. iv. 5).

I have declared the former *things* from the beginning; 3
And they went forth out of my mouth, and I shewed them;
I did *them* suddenly, and they came to pass.
Because I knew that thou *art* obstinate, 4
And thy neck *is* an iron sinew,
And thy brow brass:
I have even from the beginning declared *it* to thee; 5
Before it came to pass I shewed *it* thee:
Lest thou shouldest say, Mine idol hath done them,
And my graven image, and my molten image, hath commanded them.
Thou hast heard, see all this; 6
And will not ye declare *it*?
I have shewed thee new *things* from this time,
Even hidden *things*, and thou didst not know them.

3—6 a inculcate the lesson of the "former things," i.e. the events that have now taken place, especially the appearance of Cyrus. These were predicted in advance, that Israel might not be able to say they were done by the false gods (*v*. 5).

3. For *from the beginning*, render **beforehand**, or (as R.V.) "from of old."

they (the predictions) *went forth out of my mouth*...*I did* them] brought the events to pass; the *rê'shônôth* including both the predictions and their historical fulfilments (see on ch. xli. 22).

4. Cf. Ezek. iii. 7—9.

thy neck is *an iron sinew*] Cf. for the idea Ex. xxxii. 9; Deut. ix. 6, 13.

5. *I have even*...*thee*] And I announced it to thee beforehand (*v*. 3).

lest thou shouldest say &c.] But for the predictions the appearance of Cyrus would have been attributed to the idols rather than to the God who spoke through the prophets. The prevalence of idolatry among the exiles is abundantly proved by the book of Ezekiel.

6. *see all this*] see it all (sc. fulfilled).

and will not ye declare it?] Better (with the change of a consonant) and you, **will ye not bear witness?** (Duhm). Cf. ch. xliii. 12.

6 b—8. Jehovah has proved His power to foretell by the fulfilment of past predictions (*vv*. 3—6 a); now He announces new things.

I have shewed thee] Rather: **I shew thee** (in the act of speaking).

new things] viz. those specified in *v*. 14,—the conquest of Babylon and all that results from it, the deliverance of Israel, the overthrow of heathenism and the manifestation of the glory of Jehovah.

hidden things] Lit. "things kept" (in reserve). *and thou didst not know them*] **which thou hast not known** (R.V.). With the exception of one letter the clause coincides with one in Jer. xxxiii. 3 ("difficult things which thou knowest not").

7   They are created now, and not from the beginning;
    Even before the day when thou heardest them not;
    Lest thou shouldest say, Behold, I knew them.
8   Yea, thou heardest not; yea, thou knewest not;
    Yea, from that time *that* thine ear was not opened:
    For I knew *that* thou wouldest deal very treacherously,
    And wast called a transgressor from the womb.
9   For my name's sake will I defer mine anger,
    And *for* my praise will I refrain for thee,
    That *I* cut thee not off.

7. *They are created now*] To create is to call into being by a word; and the idea here seems to be that the prophetic word which announces, is at the same time the creative fiat of Jehovah.

not from the beginning] **not aforetime** (see *v.* 3).

even before the day when &c.] Render with R.V. and **before this day thou heardest them not.** The phrase "before the day" means "heretofore," the opposite of "from this day forth" in ch. xliii. 13.

Behold, I knew them] The events would have lost the effect of novelty if announced long before. Unbelief dies hard; when it can no longer say, "My idol did it," it is apt to take refuge in another subterfuge and say, "It is what I expected."

8. *Yea, thou heardest not &c.*] Better: **Thou hast neither heard nor known, nor was thine ear opened beforehand.** The verbal form for "was opened" is properly transitive. It is used, however, in ch. lx. 11 of gates standing open, and in Cant. vii. 13 of the opening of a flower. The LXX. reads "I opened," and this gives a better sense, the assertion being not that Israel's ear refused to open, but that Jehovah had not opened it, i.e. had not given a revelation. A similar conception of revelation, though with a different verb, in ch. xxii. 14; 1 Sam. ix. 15; with the same verb, in ch. l. 5.

that *thou wouldest deal very treacherously*] Rather: **that thou art utterly treacherous.** *a transgressor*] **a rebel.** Such has been the character of Israel as revealed in its past history; it would have abused the knowledge if the predictions had been made earlier.

9—11. A nation so sunk in unbelief must have perished, but for Jehovah's regard for His name. The thought is characteristic of Ezekiel (see esp. ch. xx.). The expression "for my name's sake" (*v.* 9) is not found elsewhere in this prophecy; "for my own sake" (*v.* 11) occurs in ch. xliii. 25.

9. The verbs should be rendered in the present tense. That for *refrain* (found only here) means literally "muzzle:" the object ("my anger") is to be supplied from the previous clause.

that I *cut thee not off*] The idea that Israel is in danger of being cut off is no doubt a surprising one in the mouth of this prophet (Duhm).

10. Instead of cutting off Israel, Jehovah has purified it in the furnace of affliction. That the process has been fruitless of beneficial

Behold, I have refined thee, but not with silver; 10
I have chosen thee in the furnace of affliction.
For mine own sake, *even* for mine own sake, will I 11
do *it:*
For how should *my name* be polluted?
And I will not give my glory unto another.

Hearken unto me, O Jacob, and Israel my called; 12
I *am* he; I *am* the first, I also *am* the last.
Mine hand also hath laid the foundation of the earth, 13
And my right hand hath spanned the heavens:
When I call unto them, they stand *up* together.
All ye, assemble yourselves, and hear; 14

result (Dillmann) is suggested only by a particular interpretation of the words.

but not with silver] The phrase is very obscure. Dillmann and others take it to mean "not with silver as a result," without obtaining any pure metal. Others render "not as silver," i.e. either "not so severely as silver is refined," or "with a refining of a different nature." None of the proposed interpretations is satisfactory.

I have chosen thee in the furnace &c.] Render: **I have tried thee** &c. (R.V. marg.). This sense of the verb is Aramaic (cf. Job xxxiv. 4?), and since the verb "choose" is a common word of the prophet, the fact of its being found here in a different sense may be an argument against his authorship.

On the figure of the verse see ch. i. 25; Jer. vi. 29, ix. 7; Zech. xiii. 9; Mal. iii. 2, 3; 1 Pet. i. 7.

11. *for how should* my name *be polluted?*] Better: **for how is it profaned!** a parenthetic ejaculation, and in all probability a marginal gloss.

I will not give my glory unto another] Cf. ch. xlii. 8. The "glory" is that of bringing to pass the marvellous "new things," the era of eternal salvation.

12—16. The substance of the "new things" (*v.* 6) is that Jehovah has called Cyrus to execute His pleasure on the Chaldæans (14 f.), and now openly announces His purpose beforehand (16).

12. *I* am *he*] See on ch. xli. 4.   *I* am *the first...the last*] xliv. 6.

13. Cf. ch. xl. 12, 22, 26; Ps. cii. 25. For *hath spanned* render **hath spread out** (as R.V.). The verb is Aramaic, and does not occur elsewhere in the O.T.

when *I call...they stand* up] Ps. xxxiii. 9.

14. *All ye*] The **summons** is addressed, **not as** in ch. xli. 1—4 &c. to the nations, but to the people of Israel; **the gods** of the heathen are referred to in the words *which among them* &c.

Which among them hath declared these *things?*
The LORD hath loved him:
He will do his pleasure on Babylon,
And his arm *shall be on* the Chaldeans.

15 I, *even* I, have spoken; yea, I have called him:
I have brought him, and he shall make his way prosperous.

16 Come ye near unto me, hear ye this;
I have not spoken in secret from the beginning;
From the time that it was, there *am* I:
And now the Lord GOD, and his Spirit, hath sent me.

The LORD *hath loved him*] is to be construed as a relative sentence: **he whom Jehovah loveth shall perform** etc. A new title, similar to those in xliv. 28, xlv. 1, xlvi. 11, is here bestowed upon Cyrus (comp. "my friend" of Abraham in xli. 8). *his pleasure*] see on xlii. 21.
and his arm shall be on *the Chaldeans*] A preposition has dropped out or must be supplied from the preceding clause; and then we may either render as E.V. (in which case "his arm" would most naturally mean the arm, i.e. the might, of Cyrus); or thus: "and (he will perform) His arm (Jehovah's mighty judgement) on the Chaldæans" (Dillmann). But although "arm" is a symbol of might, it could hardly be used alone of judgement. The LXX. ("to destroy the seed of the Chaldeans") obviously read *zera‘* instead of *zĕrô‘ô*; and this is probably the better text. Render simply **and (on) the seed of the Chaldæans**.

16. *I have not spoken in secret*] Cf. ch. xlv. 19.
from the beginning; from the time that it was] The sense is somewhat obscure. The pronoun "it" cannot refer to the world or the creation, which would require to be expressed; the implied antecedent must be the subject of which the prophet is speaking, the purpose of Jehovah against Babylon. The "beginning" will therefore be either the origin of revelation in general, or of the series of prophecies now being fulfilled. The meaning may be paraphrased thus: Jehovah has never from the beginning spoken in dark and uncertain oracles, and He does not conceal Himself now when events are already moving towards the accomplishment of His words; He is *there*, interpreting as well as guiding the course of history. That Jehovah is the speaker thus far cannot be questioned, in spite of the last clause of the verse. For the phrase "*there* am *I*," comp. Prov. viii. 27 (in the mouth of the personified Wisdom of God).
and now the Lord GOD *&c.*] Render: **and now the Lord Jehovah hath sent me and** (i.e. with) **His spirit**; "His spirit" being not a second subject along with Jehovah, but a second object. For the idea cf. ch. lxi. 1 and Zech. vii. 12. The Spirit is never spoken of in the O.T. as the sender of the prophets, or as an independent agent distinct from Jehovah. The isolation of this sentence from its context raises

Thus saith the LORD, thy redeemer, the Holy One of 17
Israel;
I *am* the LORD thy God which teacheth thee to profit,
Which leadeth thee by the way *that* thou shouldest go.
O that thou hadst hearkened to my commandments! 18

doubts as to its genuineness. The sudden change of speaker disconnects it from what precedes, and it is equally unsuitable as an introduction to *vv*. 17—19, where Jehovah Himself is again introduced by the ordinary prophetic formula. A prelude to ch. xlix. (Delitzsch) it cannot possibly be; and it is utterly arbitrary and unnatural to suppose that the words are spoken by the "Servant of Jehovah." If they are genuine they are undoubtedly words of the prophet, who here calls attention to himself and his mission, in a way which has no parallel in ch. xl.—lv. Duhm and Cheyne hold that the words are interpolated; the motive for their insertion being a misunderstanding of the first part of the verse. Taking "from the beginning" and "from the time that it was" to refer to the Creation, the editor supplied the contrast ("and now"), which he believed the author to have in his mind.

17—19. If Israel had but known Jehovah as its faithful Guide, and obeyed His commandments, how different would its present condition have been! The short passage has a striking resemblance to Ps. lxxxi. 13—16, and is of singular beauty and depth of feeling. But the disappointment expressed, that Israel has not attained to righteousness by the keeping of the Divine law, is not altogether natural in this connexion, or in the circumstances in which the prophecy was written. It breathes rather the spirit of a time of depression, when Israel seemed in danger of being "cut off," and when the faith of the Church was not sustained by the immediate prospect of deliverance. Moreover, the song of triumph in *vv*. 20 f. is the proper sequel (as in every similar instance) of the announcement of deliverance in 12—16 *a*.; and it will be felt that the obvious and natural connexion is disturbed by a sigh of regret for what might have been. It is with reluctance that one is driven to assign a thought so finely expressed to an interpolator, but a fair interpretation of the spirit of the passage points strongly to that conclusion (so again Duhm and Cheyne).

17. The introduction is in the prophet's usual manner; cf. ch. xli. 14, xliii. 14, xlix. 7.

which teacheth thee to profit] i.e. **profitably** or "for thy profit"; cf. xliv. 10 ("to no profit"), xlvii. 12.

18. *O that thou hadst hearkened &c.*] This is the strict rendering of the Hebr. idiom, which properly expresses a wish that has not been realised (see Driver, *Tenses*, § 140). It *may*, indeed (as in ch. lxiv. 1), be used in an impassioned wish for the future, and many commentators prefer that sense here,—"O that thou wouldst hearken" (see Davidson, *Syntax*, § 134). So R.V. marg. But the construction in lxiv. 1 is exceptional, and the two cases are not strictly parallel. Here the reference to the past is strengthened by the following clauses: "*then had thy*

> Then had thy peace been as a river,
> And thy righteousness as the waves of the sea:
> 19 Thy seed also had been as the sand,
> And the offspring of thy bowels like the gravel thereof;
> His name should not have been cut off nor destroyed from before me.
>
> 20 Go ye forth of Babylon, flee ye from the Chaldeans,

peace been" &c. (consec. impf.); and it is only a feeling of the unsuitability of the idea to the discourse that could ever suggest a departure from the ordinary rule of syntax. It is true that "such a retrospect here at the close would be extraordinary" (Dillmann), but in reality a hypothetical promise of future blessedness would be just as surprising. The difficulty is not grammatical but critical.

peace means national **prosperity**, "welfare," as explained in the next verse (cf. ch. lxvi. 12); *righteousness* is used in the same sense as in ch. xlv. 8.

as a river] i.e. a perennial stream, such as the Euphrates (cf. Am. v. 24). It is easy to understand the impression made on the mind of a native of Palestine, accustomed to "deceitful brooks" that run dry in the summer, by the sight of a great river, flowing on for ever in undiminished volume. The actual history of Israel had been like the *wadis* of Judæa, transient gleams of prosperity being interrupted by long intervals of misfortune; the river suggests to the writer an image of the boundless and unfailing blessedness which would have followed the keeping of the Divine commandments.

the waves of the sea] cf. ch. xi. 9.

19. *as the sand*] A common comparison; see ch. x. 22; Gen. xxii. 17; Hos. i. 10 &c.

like the gravel thereof] Lit. **the grains thereof**. The word used resembles a fem. plur. of that which immediately precedes ("bowels"); hence some commentators translate "the entrails thereof" (i.e. the fishes), taking as antecedent of the pronoun the word "sea" in the previous verse (see R.V. marg.). It would be better to explain it at once of the "entrails" of the sand (i.e. worms), for which indeed there is said to be a Syriac parallel (see Payne Smith, *Thesaurus*, col. 2185). But both comparisons alike are prosaic and unnatural. The word is no doubt identical with the Aramaic *māʻāh*, "kernel" (generally used of a small coin).

his name &c.] **its name** (that of the "seed") **should not be cut off** &c.

20, 21 (cf. ch. lii. 11, 12) form the lyrical conclusion of this division of the prophecy. In anticipation of this second exodus of Israel, the prophet puts a song of praise in the mouth of the redeemed exiles.

flee ye from the Chaldeans] or "from Chaldæa" (see on xlvii. 1). The verb *flee* probably means no more than "hasten" (see ch. lii. 12).

With a voice of singing declare ye, tell this,
Utter it *even* to the end of the earth;
Say ye, The LORD hath redeemed his servant Jacob.
And they thirsted not *when* he led them through the 21
  deserts:
He caused the waters to flow out of the rock for them:
He clave the rock also, and the waters gushed out.
There is no peace, saith the LORD, unto the wicked. 22

with a voice of singing...tell this] The exiles' shout of joy is a revelation to the world of the greatness of the God of Israel.
utter it] Lit. "send it forth," as in ch. xlii. 1.
21. These are still words of the ransomed people. The allusions are to the miracles in the wilderness of Sinai (cf. Ex. xvii. 6; Num. xx. 11) which are represented as having been repeated during the desert journey of the returning exiles.
22. The words are taken from ch. lvii. 21, where, however, they stand in their proper connexion. Here they are either a gloss or an editorial insertion intended to mark the close of a division of the prophecy. See the Introduction, p. x.

CH. XLIX. **1—13.** THE SERVANT OF JEHOVAH: HIS FIDELITY AMIDST DISCOURAGEMENTS, AND THE ULTIMATE SUCCESS OF HIS MISSION.

The beginning of ch. xlix. seems to mark a distinct advance in the development of the prophet's conceptions. "The controversial tone, the repeated comparisons between Jehovah and the idols, with the arguments based upon them, disappear; the prophet feels that, as regards these points, he has made his position sufficiently secure. For the same reason, allusions to Cyrus and his conquest of Babylon cease also; that, likewise, is now taken for granted" (Driver, *Isaiah*^{2}, pp. 148 f.). In the remaining discourses (ch. xlix.—lv.) the author concentrates his attention almost exclusively on his central message of consolation, and the glorious future in store for Israel. His treatment of this theme moves along two lines, which alternate with each other as the manner of the writer is. The first is represented by the idea of the Servant of the Lord, the second by the figure of Zion, both being personifications, although in very different senses, of the people of Israel (see on ch. xl. 1). The Servant represents the ideal Israel as Jehovah's instrument, first, in restoring the unity and prosperity of the nation, and second, in extending the knowledge of God to the nations of the world. Zion, on the other hand, is the representative of Israel in its passive aspect, as deserted and humbled in the present, but at the same time the recipient of the blessings which accrue from the work and sufferings of the Lord's Servant.

The opening section consists of:—
i. A new description of the mission and experience of the Servant of Jehovah (cf. ch. xlii. 1—4) in the form of an address by the Servant

to the nations (*vv.* 1—6). These verses form the second of the four "Servant-passages" which occur in the book.

ii. A promise of speedy restoration to Israel, obviously based on the preceding description (*vv.* 7—12).

iii. A hymn of gratitude to Jehovah, called forth as usual by the prospect of deliverance (*v.* 13).

1—6. The Servant's address to the nations. The passage forms the natural sequel to ch. xlii. 1—4, and adds some fresh features to the portrait there presented. (1) The Servant, speaking now in his own name, expresses his consciousness of the mission entrusted to him by Jehovah (*vv.* 1—3). (2) He records his failure in the past, and the sense of disappointment caused in him by the apparent fruitlessness of his labour; yet his faith in his mission remains constant (*v.* 4). (3) But now his doubts have been removed by a revelation of the great purpose for which Jehovah has raised him up; viz., to be the organ of His salvation to the ends of the earth (*vv.* 5, 6).

It still remains the most probable view that Israel is here spoken of under the name of the Servant of Jehovah; although two objections are raised in addition to those suggested by xlii. 1—4. (*a*) The Servant is described as one who has a history and an experience behind him, as well as a mission to fulfil. Now this experience is not that of the nation, which was conscious of no unique religious mission, and therefore had no such sense of defeat as is described in *v.* 4. And if we say that it is not the actual but the ideal Israel that is meant, we are asked to explain how an ideal can have a history, or when the ideal Israel was born, or before whom Jehovah mentioned its name (Duhm). (*b*) Another difficulty is created by the fact that the Servant is here expressly distinguished from Israel when it is said that the restoration of the nation is to be effected by his activity. These objections are perhaps sufficiently met by the consideration that the ideal represented by the Servant is one that has been partially realised in the experience of the best part of the nation. Since the beginning of prophecy there had been a section of the people that had laboured for the conversion of Israel, and there were doubtless many among the exiles whose feelings of disappointment are truthfully reflected by the language put into the mouth of the Servant. There is nothing unnatural in the supposition that this party should be regarded as embodying the true genius of Israel, or that their experience should be transferred to the ideal figure by which the prophet sets forth his inspired interpretation of Israel's history. Nor is there any great difficulty in the further thought that the ideal Servant, as represented by this minority, laboured for the reunion and upbuilding of the future Israel. This also corresponds to a fact of history, for nothing is more certain than that but for the influence of the prophetic teaching the Israelitish nationality would have perished during the Captivity. The prophet's conception of Israel's unique position is singularly profound as well as elevated; but it does not appear that any feature thus far introduced into the portrait of Jehovah's Servant violates the conditions of a natural personification. (See further Introduction, pp. xxxiii f.; and Appendix, Note I.)

Listen, O isles, unto me;
And hearken, ye people, from afar;
The LORD hath called me from the womb;
From the bowels of my mother hath he made mention
    of my name.
And he hath made my mouth like a sharp sword;
In the shadow of his hand hath he hid me,
And made me a polished shaft;
In his quiver hath he hid me;
And said unto me, Thou *art* my servant,
O Israel, in whom I will be glorified.

1—3. The call and equipment of the Servant by Jehovah. The nations of the world are addressed, because the great announcement that the speaker has to make (*v.* 6) concerns them. Although Jeremiah had already been conscious of being a "prophet to the nations" (Jer. i. 5), the self-consciousness here attributed to the Servant is too great to be that of any private individual, whether prophet or teacher.

O isles] see on ch. xli. 1.   For *people* render **peoples** (R.V.).

the LORD hath called me (xlii. 6 &c.) *from the womb*] Cf. ch. xliv. 2, 24, xlvi. 3, where the same metaphor is used of the beginning of the nation's history.   *made mention of my name*] Cf. xliii. 1.

2. The Servant is described as one prepared in secret for his great work. He compares himself to a weapon fashioned by Jehovah for His own use, but kept in reserve till the fulness of time. As the ideal prophet, he speaks of his *mouth*, the organ of prophetic utterance (see Jer. i. 9; Is. vi. 7), as made *like a sharp sword* in virtue of the "word" which Jehovah puts in it (ch. li. 16; cf. Heb. iv. 12).

in the shadow of his hand hath he hid me] (ch. li. 16). The metaphor perhaps denotes protection rather than secrecy.

a polished **arrow**] see Jer. li. 16.

There is nothing in the verse inconsistent with the idea that the speaker is Israel personified. The fundamental thought, translated into modern language, would be that prophecy is the highest expression of the genius of Israel; and the idealised nation is naturally identified with what is best and most characteristic in its history, and invested with the character of the ideal prophet. And again, Jehovah's hiding of His Servant may express the truth that Israel had been providentially preserved through long ages for the sake of the spiritual endowments which made it the mouthpiece of revelation. The further idea that the real mission of Israel was concealed both from the world and from the nation itself is no doubt true, but is perhaps hardly contained in the figure.

3. The word *Israel* may be read either as a vocative or as a continuation of the predicate: "(Thou art) Israel &c." (see R.V.). On either view it presents insuperable difficulties to those who hold that the Servant is an individual. To say that as the supreme personage of

4 Then I said, I have laboured in vain,
   I have spent my strength for nought, and in vain:
   Yet surely my judgment *is* with the LORD,
   And my work with my God.
5 And now, saith the LORD that formed me from the womb *to be* his servant,
   To bring Jacob again to him,
   Though Israel be not gathered,
   Yet shall I be glorious in the eyes of the LORD,
   And my God shall be my strength.
6 And he said, It is a light thing that thou shouldest be my servant

Israel's history he receives the name "Israel" is an arbitrary explanation, which is not to be justified by the observation that the name originally belonged to an individual. Since, however, the most important idea of the verse is contained in the words *my servant*, to which the clause *in whom I will be glorified* (better: **glorify myself**) naturally attaches itself, it is possible that *Israel* may be a gloss, and for that reason no great stress can be laid on the word as an argument for the national interpretation of the passage.

4. Although cast down for a moment by his want of success, he does not yield to despondency (cf. xlii. 4), but leaves his cause in the hands of God.

Then I said] R.V. **But I said** (with a certain emphasis on the "I").

my judgment] i.e. "my right," as in ch. xl. 27.   *my work* should be **my recompence** (R.V.); see ch. xl. 10.

5, 6. The Servant's faith is rewarded by the revelation of a loftier mission than he had heretofore been conscious of.

though Israel be not gathered] R.V. "and that Israel be gathered unto him." We have here the same confusion between *lō'* (not) and *lō* (to him) as in ch. ix. 3. The verb for "gather," however, is used in two senses, either "to gather in" or "to take away," "gather off" (e.g. Ezek. xxxiv. 29, R.V. marg.); by adopting the latter we might retain the negative particle as in the consonantal text: **and that Israel be not swept away**. The clause, at all events, being parallel to the preceding, must express a similar idea; the rendering of A.V. proceeds on a wrong view of the construction.

yet shall I be glorious] Rather: **and I shall be** (or am) **honourable** (a different root from that used in *v.* 3). This second half of the verse seems somewhat out of place in its present context (hence it is marked by R.V. as a parenthesis). Its original position may have been (as Duhm thinks) at the end of *v.* 3, reading: "and so I was honourable in the eyes of Jehovah, and my God was my strength."

6. *And he said*] resuming the sentence begun in *v.* 5. R.V. "Yea, he saith."

It is a light thing &c.] Better as R.V. **It is too light a thing** &c.

To raise up the tribes of Jacob,
And to restore the preserved of Israel:
I will also give thee for a light to the Gentiles,
That *thou* mayest be my salvation unto the end
of the earth.

Thus saith the LORD, the redeemer of Israel, *and* his 7
Holy One,
To him whom man despiseth, to him whom the nation
abhorreth, to a servant of rulers,

But the literal translation probably is, "It is too light for thy being a servant to me that thou shouldst raise up" &c., i.e. "To restore Israel is the least part of thy vocation as my servant." The sense is not affected, and the rendering of R.V. might be defended by the analogy of Ezek. viii. 17.   *raise up* here means "re-establish," just as "build" frequently means "rebuild" (Ps. cxxii. 3 &c.).

the preserved of Israel] those who survive the destruction of the state (Ezek. vi. 12, R.V. marg.).

I will also give thee for a light to the Gentiles] ch. xlii. 6.

that thou *mayest be my salvation &c.*] Rather: **that my salvation may be** &c. Comp. the N.T. application in Acts xiii. 47. The verse evidently describes an enlargement of the Servant's conception of his vocation. Previously, he had been conscious only of a mission to Israel, and in that mission the significance of the title "Servant of Jehovah" had seemed to be exhausted (*v.* 5). Now it is revealed to him that the name includes a higher function, that, namely, of being the mediator of salvation to all mankind. And since the greater destiny contains the less, the acceptance of this new commission delivers him from the sense of failure by which he had been oppressed (*v.* 4). Whatever view be taken of the Servant's personality, he speaks as the exponent of the religion of revelation; and the fact here represented is the expansion of that religion from being a national to be a universal religion. The ideal was realised only in the New Testament dispensation, so that in this as in many other respects the portrait of the Servant is an indirect prophecy of Christ. Cf. Luke ii. 32.

7—12. The Servant's account of his calling forms the basis of a series of promises; *v.* 7 referring to his influence on the nations, and *vv.* 8—12 to the narrower sphere of his activity, the restoration of Israel.

7. Israel shall be raised from the deepest degradation to the highest honour. The verse is remarkable as anticipating the main idea of ch. lii. 13—liii. 15.

to him whom man despiseth] Lit. **to the despised of** soul; i.e. "to one who is heartily despised," the "soul" being the seat of emotion. Comp. Ps. xvii. 9 ("my deadly enemies," = "they that hate me in the soul,"). In the parallel phrase **to the abhorred of** people, "people" seems to be used of men in general (the German *Leute*) as in Gen. xx. 4

Kings shall see and arise,
Princes also shall worship,
Because of the LORD that *is* faithful,
And the Holy One of Israel, and he shall choose thee.

8 Thus saith the LORD,
In an acceptable time have I heard thee,
And in a day of salvation have I helped thee:
And I will preserve thee, and give thee for a covenant of the people,
To establish the earth, to cause to inherit the desolate heritages;

9 That *thou* mayest say to the prisoners, Go forth;
To *them* that *are* in darkness, Shew yourselves.
They shall feed in the ways,
And their pastures *shall be* in all high places.

10 They shall not hunger nor thirst;

("righteous folk"). The words for "despised" and "abhorred" are both peculiar in form.

a servant of rulers] **of tyrants** (ch. xiv. 5).

kings shall see (the exaltation of Israel) *and arise*] in amazement and reverence (cf. ch. lii. 15). *princes also shall worship*] **princes** (sc. shall arise) **and do homage** (see R.V.).

and he shall choose thee] Better, as R.V. **who hath chosen thee** (strictly, "and he hath chosen thee"; see Driver's *Tenses*, § 76 a).

8—12. A picture of the emancipation and return of the exiles.

8. *In an acceptable time*] Better: **in a season of favour**. Cf. ch. lxi. 2, and the citation in 2 Cor. vi. 2.

for a covenant of the people] See on ch. xlii. 6.

to establish the earth &c.] Render: **to restore** (see v. 6) **the land** (of Israel), **to allot** (Deut. xxi. 16) **the desolate heritages**. It may be difficult to decide whether Jehovah Himself or His Servant is the implicit subject of these verbs, the Heb. construction being ambiguous. The latter sense is certainly the more natural; although it is only in a figure that the repeopling &c. of the land can be attributed to the agency of the ideal Israel: "what is done for the sake of the Servant, is done by him" (Dillmann).

9. That *thou mayest say*] Rather, **saying** (R.V.) or possibly (continuing the previous infs.) "To say."

the prisoners...them that are in darkness] i.e. the exiles; cf. xlii. 7. The second half of the verse introduces a new figure, that of the flock, (see ch. xl. 11) led by Jehovah, the Good Shepherd.

they shall feed in the ways] Or perhaps as LXX., **in all the ways**, wherein they go.

high places] **bare heights**; ch. xli. 18.

Neither shall the heat nor sun smite them:
For he that hath mercy on them shall lead them,
Even by the springs of water shall he guide them.
And I will make all my mountains a way,
And my highways shall be exalted.
Behold, these shall come from far:
And lo, these from the north and from the west;
And these from the land of Sinim.
Sing, O heavens; and be joyful, O earth;

10. *neither shall the heat...smite them*] The word for *heat* should probably be rendered **the hot wind** (Sirocco; LXX., καύσων). It is often taken to denote the mirage (see on ch. xxxv. 7), but that meaning is unsuitable here on account of the verb "smite."

11. The expression *my mountains* is difficult. An allusion to the mere fact of creation is not natural, and to understand it of the mountains of Palestine (as in ch. xiv. 25) would limit the image to the last stage of the return journey. Possibly the text should be amended so as to read "mountains" simply. Cf. LXX. (πᾶν ὄρος).

my highways] See on ch. xl. 4.

12. The return of exiles from the most distant parts of the earth.

these from the land of Sinim (**the Sinites**)] The last word is a hopeless enigma. As the only proper name in the verse the writer must have had some special reason for mentioning it; and the only reason that can be plausibly imagined is that *Sinim* lay on the utmost limit of his geographical horizon. This would exclude two suggested identifications: (1) the Canaanite Sinites of Gen. x. 17, and (2) Sin (Pelusium) on the nearest border of Egypt. Again, from the fact that "north" and "west" have been already mentioned we may reasonably infer that the Sinim must be looked for either in the far East or the far South. The former is the view of most commentators, who find in Sinim the name China (properly "the Chinese"). If the prophecy had been written four or five centuries later this hypothesis would be more plausible than it is. The word might be the same as the Arabic and Syriac name for China (ציני), although there is a difference in the first consonant which would excite misgivings. But it is generally considered that this name is derived from that of the Tsin-dynasty, which dates from 255 B.C.; it could not therefore have reached the West in the time of the Exile. The numerous attempts to find an older Chinese origin of the word are merely wasted ingenuity. Moreover, it is inconceivable that Jewish captives had been transported to China at so early a period; and speculations about the possibility of intercourse between the Chinese and Western Asia hardly touch the question. The Sinim are located in the *South* by the Targ. and Vulg., which render "a Southern land"; also by Cheyne, who, in his latest work, revives a suggestion of J. D. Michaelis that Syene is meant (reading סְוֵנִים for סִינִים).

And break forth *into* singing, O mountains:
For the LORD hath comforted his people,
And will have mercy upon his afflicted.

14 But Zion said, The LORD hath forsaken me,
And my Lord hath forgotten me.

13. The lyrical conclusion of the passage on the Servant, partly resembling ch. xliv. 23.

his afflicted] See on xli. 17.

CH. XLIX. 14—L. 3. THE CONSOLATION OF ZION.

(i) *vv.* 14—21. In an apostrophe to Jerusalem the prophet announces the speedy return of her population and the rebuilding of her waste places. The poetry of the passage is singularly beautiful, and charged with tender emotion. Zion, the idealised city, is the wife of Jehovah, and the mother of her inhabitants. Although she now thinks of herself as rejected and barren (*v.* 14), she is assured of the unchanging love of her God (*vv.* 15, 16) which will soon be manifested in her restoration to the joy of motherhood (17—20). The ecstasy of amazement and delight with which she recognises and welcomes her children (*v.* 21) is finely opposed to the opening picture of her desolation and despondency. Note also the contrast between the whole conception and the fate of the "virgin daughter of Babylon" (xlvii. 8, 9).

(ii) Ch. xlix. 22—l. 3. Three oracles, confirming the promise to Zion.

(1) *vv.* 22, 23. On a signal from Jehovah the nations shall bring home the scattered children of Zion; nay, their kings and queens shall esteem it an honour to foster the newly-formed community.

(2) *vv.* 24—26. No earthly power can interpose between Jehovah and the deliverance of His people; Israel is His lawful prey, and none shall pluck them from Him (see the notes below). In thus representing the deliverance as effected by force, the prophet no doubt has in view the one nation that would not obey the signal of *v.* 22.

(3) l. 1—3. Lastly, there exists no legal impediment to the redemption of Israel; Jehovah has issued no sentence of formal rejection against His people, nor has anyone acquired the rights of a creditor over them (*v.* 1). He therefore expresses surprise that there is so little response to the promise of salvation, so little faith in His almighty power.

14. *But Zion said*] Zion is the city of Jerusalem personified (cf. *v.* 16) and, by a common O.T. figure, conceived as the mother of the citizens (see further on *v.* 21). This is no doubt the primary reference of the figure, but since the city derives its religious significance from its being the centre of the national life, Zion really represents the nation of Israel, as in ch. xl. 2. Hence the complaint of this verse is the same as was previously heard from the lips of Israel (ch. xl. 27).

my Lord] Better, as R.V. **the Lord**. The word when pointed, as here (*'Adônāi*), is always equivalent to Jehovah. The suggestion that it

Can a woman forget her sucking child, 15
That *she* should not have compassion on the son of her womb?
Yea, they may forget,
Yet will I not forget thee.
Behold, I have graven thee upon the palms of *my* 16
hands;
Thy walls *are* continually before me.
Thy children shall make haste; 17
Thy destroyers and they that made thee waste shall go forth of thee.
Lift up thine eyes round about, and behold: 18
All these gather themselves together, *and* come to thee.
As I live, saith the LORD, thou shalt surely clothe thee with them all, as with an ornament,

may be used in the sense of "husband" (as Gen. xviii. 12) would demand a different vocalisation (*'Ădônî*). But although the idea of Jehovah as the husband of Zion was undoubtedly present to the prophet's mind (l. 1, liv. 6) it does not emerge in this verse.

15. Jehovah's remembrance of Zion is more enduring than the strongest human affection. Even a mother's pity for an infant may fail. *yea, they may forget*] Or, **should even these forget** (Cheyne). *yet will I not forget thee*] See on ch. xliv. 21.

16. *I have graven thee*] Not the name merely but the picture of the city, as the next clause shews. *Thy walls* may refer to the ruined walls with their mute appeal to Jehovah's compassion, or to the plan of the new walls, which reminds Him of His purpose to rebuild them. The latter is more likely.

upon the palms of my hands] **upon both hands**.

17, 18. Already in vision the prophet sees the return of the exiles and calls on Zion to welcome her sons.

Instead of *Thy children* the chief ancient Versions, and the important Babylonian Codex have "Thy builders" (בָּנַיִךְ for בָּנָיִךְ), a sense which is recommended both by the antithesis to "thy destroyers" &c., and the connexion with the previous verse. Yet it is doubtful if the reading on the whole is preferable to that of the received text. The latter at least is true to the fundamental image of the passage, which appears again in *vv.* 20 f.

For *shall make haste* read in the present tense (as R.V.) **make haste**.

thy destroyers &c.] The expressions almost suggest that Jerusalem was still occupied by Chaldæan troops.

18. *As I live, saith the LORD*] Jehovah's oath by Himself, ch. xlv. 23. It introduces a new, though closely related, conception; the inhabitants being compared to the bridal attire with which Zion replaces the signs of her widowhood.

And bind them *on thee*, as a bride *doth*.

19 For thy waste and thy desolate places, and the land of thy destruction,
Shall even now be too narrow by reason of the inhabitants,
And they that swallowed thee up shall be far away.

20 The children which thou shalt have, after thou hast lost the other, shall say again in thine ears,
The place *is* too strait for me:
Give place to me that I may dwell.

21 Then shalt thou say in thine heart, Who hath begotten me these,

bind them on thee] Strictly **gird them on**. The verb is connected with the word for "girdle" in ch. iii. 20 (*gishshûrîm*, A.V. "headbands"). It was evidently an ornamental girdle, possibly a part of the bridal costume (cf. Jer. ii. 32, "can...a bride forget her girdle").

19, 20. In place of her present solitude, the ideal Zion shall yet look down on a densely peopled city, whose inhabitants are embarrassed for want of room.

19. *For as for thy waste and thy desolate places and thy land that hath been destroyed, surely now shalt thou be too strait for the inhabitants, &c.*] So R.V. But there appears to be some textual disorder, the subjects in the first half of the verse having no predicate. The R.V. gets over the difficulty by taking "thy waste places" &c. as a sort of *casus pendens*, resumed in the "thou" of the last clause; but this is a forced construction. The most probable solution is that the original conclusion of the first clause has been lost in copying (Duhm); the second would then commence with the words **For now**.

the land of thy destruction] lit. "thy land of destruction," i.e., as R.V., **thy land that hath been destroyed**.

20. *The children...other*] Lit. **the sons of thy bereavement**, i.e. those born to thee in the time of thy bereavement (see v. 21).

shall yet say *in thine ears*] The mother overhears the talk of her vigorous and enterprising offspring.

the place is *too strait for me*] Cf. 2 Ki. vi. 1.

Give place to me] This peculiar sense of the verb (usually "draw near") finds an exact parallel in Gen. xix. 9. Comp. lxv. 5, "draw near to thyself" = "stand off,"—a different, but synonymous verb.

21. Zion is bewildered at finding herself once more "a joyful mother of children" (Ps. cxiii. 9).

Who hath begotten] Rather, **Who hath borne** (in spite of the masculine gender of the verb). The peculiar figure is probably to be explained by the custom illustrated in Gen. xvi. 1 ff., xxx. 1 ff., &c. The exile was the time of Zion's barrenness; the generation of Israelites that had grown up in a foreign land are regarded as not her natural

Seeing I have lost my children, and *am* desolate,
A captive, and removing to and fro?
And who hath brought up these?
Behold, I was left alone;
These, where *had* they *been?*
Thus saith the Lord God,   22
Behold, I will lift up mine hand to the Gentiles,
And set up my standard to the people:
And they shall bring thy sons in *their* arms,
And thy daughters shall be carried upon *their* shoulders.
And kings shall be thy nursing fathers,   23
And their queens thy nursing mothers:
They shall bow down to thee *with their* face *toward* the earth,
And lick up the dust of thy feet;

children, although legally they belong to her, having been borne *for* her by a stranger.

seeing I have lost &c.] **seeing I am childless and unfruitful.** The clause immediately following (which must be rendered **exiled and put away**) introduces a conception alien to the image of the verse. Zion herself was not "exiled" but "left alone," when her children were taken from her. The words are wanting in the LXX. and may be a gloss.

these, where had *they* been?] If this were the sense intended, the verb "had been" (or "were") would probably require to have been expressed. But the question that Zion broods over is not *where* her children had been, but *how* she comes to have children at all, who are strangers to her. Render, therefore (with Dillmann), **these,** how (is it) with them? of what description are they? (cf. Jud. viii. 18).

22, 23. The first of the three short oracles describes the restoration of the exiles as a spontaneous act of homage on the part of the Gentiles. The conception is intermediate between that of ch. xlv. 14 ff., where the nations acknowledge the divinity of Jehovah and the religious supremacy of Israel, and that of ch. lx. 4, 8, lxvi. 20; cf. ch. xi. 11, 12. For *Gentiles* read **nations,** and for *people,* **peoples,** as R.V.

set up my standard] as a signal; see on ch. v. 26.

they shall bring thy sons **in the bosom**] of the garment (*sinus*) where little children were carried (Num. xi. 12). The word belongs to late Hebrew (Neh. v. 13 [E.V. lap]; Ps. cxxix. 7).

23. *thy nursing fathers*] **thy guardians**; i.e. of course, the guardians of her children (in spite of ch. lx. 16); see Num. xi. 12; 2 Ki. x. 1; Esth. ii. 7 &c. The figure appears to express the permanent relation of the kingdoms of the world to the glorified people of God.

lick up the dust of thy feet] An extravagant, but thoroughly Oriental, metaphor for abject self-humiliation (cf. Mic. vii. 17; Ps. lxxii. 9).

And thou shalt know that I *am* the LORD:
For they shall not be ashamed that wait for me.
24 Shall the prey be taken from the mighty,
Or the lawful captive delivered?

Gesenius quotes from a Persian poem the following sentiment of a prince to his conqueror: "When I shall have the good fortune to kiss the dust of thy feet, then I shall believe that fortune flatters me," &c. Comp. ch. xlv. 14, lx. 14.

for they shall not be ashamed &c.] Strictly a relative sentence, "they that wait on Whom shall not be ashamed"; which is perhaps hardly English. Render as R.V. **and they that wait for me shall not be ashamed.**

24—26. The emancipation of Israel is here regarded as having to be effected by force, and Jehovah pledges His omnipotence to the task. The bright picture of *v.* 22 does not touch the gravest difficulty of the situation, the formidable power and settled hostility of Babylon.

24. *from the mighty*] **from a hero.** *the lawful captive*] lit. **the captivity** (=captives) **of a righteous one.** This is the only sense that the phrase will properly bear; all the attempts to construe it otherwise are futile. Many authorities, however, adopt the reading of the Pesh. and Vulg. (עריץ instead of צדיק, as *v.* 25), and render: "captives of a terrible one." (1) The verse has generally been considered to be a new utterance of despair on the part of the Israelites, "Can the tyrant be made to disgorge his prey?" (Cheyne),—to which *v.* 25 gives an affirmative answer. On this view (which is certainly the one that first suggests itself) the substitution of '*ārîç* (terrible) for *çaddîq* (righteous) seems imperative, since the latter expression could not possibly be applied to the Chaldæans. To suppose that by the "hero" and the "righteous one" Cyrus is meant is at variance with the whole tenor of the prophecy (xli. 25, xliv. 28, xlv. 1 ff.). (2) Dillmann on the other hand holds that the reference in *v.* 24 is to Jehovah, who Himself asks if any power can deprive Him of His lawful captives, the Israelites. The answer to be supplied is, "No"; and this is confirmed by *v.* 25: "*For* even the captives of a (human) hero *may* be delivered, yet will I (the Almighty) contend with" &c. This is not altogether natural; the antithesis of the *divine* hero in *v.* 24 and a *human* hero in *v.* 25 being indicated by nothing in the words. (3) A simpler view is that question and answer are related as in *v.* 14; the question stating a supposition in the highest degree improbable (though still conceivable), and the answer conceding the possibility in order the more strongly to assert that the idea cannot be entertained with regard to Jehovah. The sense might be paraphrased as follows: "Can the captives of a mighty man be rescued from his grasp? Yes, the captives of the mighty *may* be delivered, but *I* will (victoriously) maintain thy cause against thy enemies" &c. (so, apparently, Duhm). In this case also it is better to read '*ārîç*, which may be used in a neutral sense as in Jer. xx. 11 (of Jehovah). The image of Israel as the prey of Jehovah has a certain resemblance to that of the lion and his prey in ch. xxxi. 4.

But thus saith the LORD, 25
Even the captives of the mighty shall be taken away,
And the prey of the terrible shall be delivered:
For I will contend with him that contendeth with thee,
And I will save thy children.
And I will feed them that oppress thee with their own 26
flesh;
And they shall be drunken with their own blood, as with sweet wine:
And all flesh shall know that I the LORD *am* thy Saviour
And thy redeemer, the mighty One of Jacob.

Thus saith the LORD, 50
Where *is* the bill of your mother's divorcement, whom I have put away?

25. Read **For** instead of *But*, and later in the verse **but** instead of *for*.
26. *I will feed them that? &c.*] Better: **I will cause thine oppressors** (the Chaldæans) **to eat their own flesh** (cf. ch. ix. 20; Zech. xi. 9). The enemies of Zion shall be consumed by internecine war—a common eschatological representation (Ezek. xxxviii. 21; Hag. ii. 22; Zech. xiv. 13).
and all flesh shall know] Comp. "And thou shalt know" at the end of the previous oracle (*v.* 23).
the mighty One of Jacob] See on ch. i. 24, and cf. lx. 16.
L. 1—3. The third oracle meets another doubt which must have occurred to the exiles, viz., that the covenant relation between Jehovah and Israel has been broken beyond possibility of renewal. In *v.* 1 this fear is dispelled by the help of two analogies from common life.
Where is the bill...whom I have put away?] (better, as R.V., **wherewith I have put her away**). No such document exists. Although Jehovah has had good reason to adopt this extreme measure (Jer. iii. 8), He has not done it, but has left the way open for a reconciliation. The effect of the "bill of divorcement" was to make the separation absolute and final; the woman was free to marry another, but could not after that be received back by her former husband (Deut. xxiv. 1—4). (A specimen of the form of words used by later Jews is given in Dalman's *Aramäische Dialektproben*, p. 5.) In Mohammedan law a man may divorce his wife twice and take her back without any ceremony, but a third divorce (or a triple divorce conveyed in one sentence) is final, *unless* the woman have contracted a fresh marriage in the interval and been released from it either by divorce or the death of the husband (*Koran*, Sura ii. 229 f.; see Lane, *Modern Egyptians*, chap. III.). Both the Mosaic and the Mohammedan laws accord to a

Or which of my creditors *is it* to whom I have sold you?
Behold, for your iniquities have you sold yourselves,
And for your transgressions is your mother put away.
2 Wherefore, when I came, *was there* no man?
When I called, *was there* none to answer?
Is my hand shortened at all, that *it* cannot redeem?
Or have I no power to deliver?
Behold, at my rebuke I dry up the sea,
I make the rivers a wilderness:
Their fish stinketh, because *there is* no water, and dieth for thirst.

husband the unrestricted right of divorce, and for this reason the Jewish custom was pronounced by our Lord to be inconsistent with the true idea of marriage and a concession to the weakness of human nature (Matt. xix. 3 ff.; Mark x. 2 ff.).

which of my creditors is it &c.] i.e. "what creditor of mine is there to whom" &c.? The selling of children into slavery in payment of a debt is another practice tolerated, though hardly approved, by the Law (Ex. xxi. 7; cf. 2 Ki. iv. 1; Neh. v. 5). Since it is inconceivable that Jehovah should have a creditor, so it is impossible that He should have surrendered His rights over His own children.

Behold, for your iniquities &c.] This is the true explanation of the slavery of the children and the divorce of the mother, and this cause is removed by the offer of forgiveness (xl. 2). It is remarkable that the prophet does not, like Hosea and Ezekiel, directly attribute sin to the ideal mother of the nation, but only to the individual Israelites, to whom this whole expostulation is addressed (cf. Hos. ii. 2).

For *have you sold yourselves* render with R.V. **were ye sold** (so again ch. lii. 3). The phrase is frequently used in the Book of Judges of the delivering of Israel into the power of its enemies (Jud. ii. 14 &c.).

2. Jehovah expresses surprise that His message of redemption (delivered through the prophet) has been received with so little enthusiasm by the people.

was there *no man?*] The expression occurs again in lix. 16; in both places the indefinite "man" is explained by the second member of the parallelism; here, therefore, it means "no man to answer."

Is my hand shortened at all &c.] **Is it the case that my hand is too short to redeem?** (cf. lix. 1). And the unreasonableness of such doubts as to Jehovah's power is then proved by an appeal to His mighty works in the natural sphere, probably with a special allusion to the miracles of the Exodus period.

at (by) *my rebuke*] Cf. ch. xvii. 13; esp. Ps. civ. 7, cvi. 9.
I make [*the*] *rivers a wilderness*] Ps. cvii. 33.
their fish stinketh &c.] Ex. vii. 18.

I clothe the heavens with blackness,
And I make sackcloth their covering.

3. Comp. Ex. x. 21   *with blackness*] with murky storm-clouds. The word, which occurs only here, denotes (like sackcloth in the next clause) the garb of mourning. Cf. Rev. vi. 12.

The strophe ends somewhat abruptly, and the thought is perhaps incomplete.

CH. L. 4—11. THE LORD'S SERVANT MADE PERFECT THROUGH SUFFERINGS.

In *vv.* 4—9 the Servant is again introduced, speaking of himself and his work, as in xlix. 1—6. He describes in the first place the close and intimate and continuous communion with God through which he has learned the ministry of comfort by the Divine word, and his own complete self-surrender to the voice that guides him (*vv.* 4, 5); next, his acceptance of the persecution and obloquy which he had to encounter in the discharge of his commission (6); and lastly he expresses his unwavering confidence in the help of Jehovah and the victory of his righteous cause and the discomfiture of all his enemies (7—9).

vv. 10, 11 are an appendix to the preceding description, drawing lessons for the encouragement of believers (*v.* 10) and the warning of unbelievers (*v.* 11). They contain expressions and even thoughts which are unlike those of the second Isaiah; and are possibly (with Duhm and Cheyne) to be regarded as a later insertion in the prophecy.

Although the word "Servant" never occurs in this passage, its resemblance to the three other "servant-passages" makes it certain that the speaker is none other than the ideal character who comes before us in xlii. 1—4, xlix. 1—6, and lii. 13—liii. 15. The passage, indeed, forms an almost indispensable link of connexion between the first two and the last of these. Whilst it takes up and developes certain ideas thrown out in the earlier sections, and in its dramatic form most resembles the second of them, its closest affinities are with lii. 13 ff. Common to both is the new conception of the Servant as a *sufferer*, here at the hands of men, there at the hands of men and God alike. In the present passage we have the Servant's own consciousness with regard to his sufferings, these being regarded from an ethical point of view as brought on him by fidelity to his Divine mission. In ch. lii. 13 ff. it is the religious aspect of them that is mainly dwelt upon: their value in the sight of God, and their efficacy for the salvation of men.—The view, therefore, that the prophet here speaks in his own name cannot be maintained, although it is no doubt the one that would be most readily suggested if the verses stood alone. So also the further question whether the Servant be the ideal Israel must be considered with due regard to the other places where the same idea is presented (see Appendix, Note I). Here it is only necessary to observe that the conception cannot in any case be applied to Israel as a whole and its sufferings from other nations. We have seen from ch. xlix. 6, 7 that the Servant has two spheres of activity, one within Israel, and the other

4   The Lord God hath given me the tongue of the learned,
    That *I* should know how to speak a word in season to *him that is* weary:
    He wakeneth morning by morning,
    He wakeneth mine ear to hear as the learned.
5   The Lord God hath opened mine ear,

directed to the world at large; and there can be no reasonable doubt that the persecutions referred to belong to the narrower sphere, representing the experience of the godly minority in whom the true ideal of Israel was partly realised, in conflict with their unregenerate fellow-countrymen.

4, 5. The relation of the Servant to Jehovah is that of a favourite disciple to his master; from Him he had learned the art of persuasive and consoling speech, and to Him he daily looks for the substance of his message. Comp. xlix. 2 (the Servant's endowment with prophetic eloquence), and xlii. 3 (the gentleness of his ministry).

the tongue of the learned] **a disciples' tongue** (see ch. viii. 16), i.e. a disciplined tongue (R.V. "of them that are taught"). The stress laid on the Divine education of the Servant is connected with the fact that his ministry of consolation was almost a new departure in prophecy. In the hands of the earlier prophets the word of Jehovah had been like a hammer breaking the rock in pieces (Jer. xxiii. 29) rather than a dew reviving the spirit of the humble.

that I should know...weary] A difficult clause. The verb rendered "speak in season" (*ûth*) is unknown in Hebrew. The A.V., following the Jewish interpreters, takes it to be a denominative from the word for "time" (*ēth*), but that is an impossible etymology. The LXX. gives a similar sense (τοῦ γνῶναι ἡνίκα δεῖ εἰπεῖν λόγον) but based on a different text. Of the traditional interpretations the most suitable is perhaps that of the Vulg. and Aquila (which is followed by the R.V.): **that I should know how to sustain the weary with a word.** Modern authorities who adopt this rendering support it by an Arabic verb meaning "to help," which however is not an exact philological equivalent. Another Arabic analogy has suggested the translation "water" (i.e. "refresh"). It is impossible to get beyond conjecture, although the general sense is clear.

he wakeneth (sc. my ear) *morning by morning*] (cf. xxviii. 19). A far simpler sentence results if we omit with Cheyne the first word of the Heb. (or with Duhm the first two words) as an uncorrected slip of a copyist, reading the adverbial expression with the following verb; thus: "morning by morning (or "in the morning") he wakeneth my ear to hear" &c.

as the learned] **after the manner of disciples.**

5. *hath opened mine ear*] The phrase used of the imparting of a prophetic communication in 1 Sam. ix. 15 (cf. Ps. xl. 6, different verbs).

And I was not rebellious,
Neither turned away back.
I gave my back to the smiters,   6
And my cheeks to them that plucked off the hair:
I hid not my face from shame and spitting.
For the Lord GOD will help me;   7
Therefore shall I not be confounded:
Therefore have I set my face like a flint,
And I know that I shall not be ashamed.
He is near that justifieth me;   8
Who will contend with me? let us stand together:
Who *is* mine adversary? let him come near to me.
Behold, the Lord GOD will help me;   9
Who *is* he *that* shall condemn me?

and I was not rebellious &c.] a circumstantial clause ("I being not rebellious" &c.). Comp. Jonah i. 3 and Jer. xx. 9. The character and history of Jeremiah seem to have contributed many traits to the portrait of the "Servant of Jehovah."

6. That persecutions were to be incurred in the performance of his work is already indicated in the last words of *v.* 5; now the speaker declares his voluntary acquiescence in the hardships of his appointed lot.

I gave my back to the smiters] In Ps. cxxix. 3 the same figure is applied to the sufferings of Israel as a nation.

to them that plucked off the hair] of the beard (cf. Ezra ix. 3; Neh. xiii. 25); an extreme insult to an Oriental, to whom the beard is the symbol of dignity (see on ch. vii. 20).

from shame and spitting] Num. xii. 14; Deut. xxv. 9; Matt. xxvi. 67, xxvii. 30.

7. The verse is better rendered thus: **But the Lord Jehovah helps me, therefore I was not ashamed** (i.e. felt no shame); **therefore I made my face like flint** (figure for determination, cf. Ez. iii. 9), **and knew that I should not be put to shame**. For the thought cf. ch. xlii. 4.

8, 9. The consciousness of innocence is expressed (as often in the Book of Job) under the conception of a legal process.

8. He is *near that justifieth me*] Cf. ch. xlix. 4 ("my judgement is with Jehovah"); li. 5. To "justify" is, as nearly always, to declare in the right; so "condemn" in *v.* 9 is to pronounce in the wrong.

who will contend with me?] cf. Job xiii. 19.

stand together] **stand forth together** (as xlviii. 12, 13).

who is *mine adversary?*] lit. "the master of my cause" (dominus litis). A similar expression is used in Ex. xxiv. 14.

9. *who* is *he* that *shall condemn me?*] Comp. Rom. viii. 33 f.

Lo, they all shall wax old as a garment; the moth
shall eat them up.

10 Who *is* among you that feareth the Lord,
That obeyeth the voice of his servant,
That walketh *in* darkness, and hath no light?
Let him trust in the name of the Lord,
And stay upon his God.
11 Behold, all ye that kindle a fire, that compass *your-
selves* about with sparks:

wax old (better, **be worn out**) *as a garment; the moth &c.*] Common images of gradual but inevitable destruction (cf. ch. li. 6, 8; Ps. xxxix. 11, cii. 26; Job xiii. 28 &c.).

Two striking parallels to the latter part of this discourse occur in the Book of Jeremiah. See ch. xvii. 17 f.; "Thou art my refuge in the day of evil. Let them be ashamed that persecute me, but let not me be ashamed...bring upon them the day of evil, and destroy them with double destruction": and xx. 7, 11 ff.: "I am become a laughing-stock all the day, every one mocketh me...." "But the Lord is with me as a mighty one and a terrible; therefore my persecutors shall stumble, and they shall not prevail; they shall be greatly ashamed" &c. Cf. also Ps. xxii. 6—21.

10, 11. A double message of encouragement and warning based on the preceding soliloquy of the Servant. It seems evident that the Servant here is regarded as the nucleus of the godly party who are addressed in *v.* 10; in other words, as a personification of the true Israel which is in process of being separated from the unbelieving part of the nation. These last are addressed in *v.* 11 as opponents and persecutors of the faithful Israelites.

10. Those who fear the Lord are exhorted to imitate the Servant's trust in God.

that obeyeth the voice of his servant] (lit. "that hearkeneth to" &c.). The LXX. reads "let him hearken," which certainly gives a better balanced verse: "Whoso among you feareth Jehovah, let him hearken" &c. The reference is not merely to the words just spoken (*vv.* 4—9), but to the whole revelation of which the Servant is the organ.

that walketh] Better, as R.V., **he that walketh**—commencing a new sentence.

in *darkness*] lit. "in dark places"; i.e. in trouble.

let him trust &c.] Cf. ch xxvi. 4; Hab. ii. 4.

11. *that compass* yourselves *about with sparks*] Lit. as R.V., that **gird yourselves about with firebrands** (cf. Prov. xxvi. 18). The verb "gird" hardly suits the metaphor; hence it is better with many authorities to change מאזרי into מאירי ("that kindle"). "Fire" and "firebrands" are both images for the machinations of the ungodly party against the true servants of Jehovah (cf. Ps. vii. 13; Eph. vi. 16).

Walk in the light of your fire, and in the sparks *that*
ye have kindled.
This shall ye have of mine hand;
Ye shall lie down in sorrow.

walk in the light &c.] Rather: **walk into the flame of your fire** &c. Their mischievous designs shall recoil on themselves (Ps. vii. 15 f.).

this shall ye have of mine hand] Better: **from my hand is this** (appointed) **for you.**

ye shall lie down in sorrow] perhaps: **in the place of torment**; see on ch. lxvi. 24.

CH. LI. 1—16. ENCOURAGEMENTS ADDRESSED TO TRUE ISRAELITES.

The strain of consolation, which was interrupted by the soliloquy of the Servant at ch. l. 4, is now resumed, and is continued till we reach the fourth and last of the Servant-passages, lii. 13—liii. 12. Throughout this long passage (li. 1—lii. 12) the prophet's thoughts are occupied with the near prospect of deliverance, and his high-strung emotion finds vent in a series of short impassioned oracles, mostly of a lyrical character. These may be divided into two groups, each consisting of three oracles. While those of the second group (li. 17—lii. 12) are addressed to the prostrate and desolate Zion, the first (li. 1—16) contains words of cheer to the faithful but timid hearts in whom the prophet's message had found an entrance. This section shews some points of contact with the preceding descriptions of the Servant, and the line of thought was probably influenced by the last of these, in l. 4—9. The contents of the section are as follows:—

i. *vv.* 1—8. A glowing and animated appeal to the believing exiles to put away the fears and misgivings which hinder their full acceptance of the promise of salvation. The thrice-repeated "Hearken to me" (see, however, on *v.* 4) indicates a division into three strophes. (1) The first draws a lesson of encouragement from the example of the solitary patriarch Abraham, who by the blessing of Jehovah became the progenitor of a great nation. Let the true-hearted believers, therefore, take courage, in spite of the fewness of their number, for the same blessing rests on them, and will transform the waste places of Zion into a scene of joy and gladness (*vv.* 1—3). (2) The next strophe directs the hope of the loyal Israelites to the glorious future that belongs to those who wait for Jehovah's salvation; though heaven and earth pass away that world-wide salvation is imperishable and eternal (*vv.* 4—6). (3) The last strophe, re-echoing one of the voices of the Prologue (xl. 6—8), reminds the exiles that the reproach they fear is that of frail and short-lived mortals, while the salvation they hope for endures for ever.

ii. *vv.* 9, 10. Here for a moment the prophetic discourse is interrupted by a magnificent apostrophe to the "arm" of Jehovah. The speakers are most probably those to whom the previous words were

51 Hearken to me, ye that follow after righteousness, ye
that seek the LORD:
Look unto the rock *whence* ye are hewn,
And to the hole of the pit *whence* ye are digged.
2 Look unto Abraham your father,
And unto Sarah *that* bare you:
For I called him alone,
And blessed him, and increased him.
3 For the LORD shall comfort Zion:

addressed. As if all their doubts had been swept away by the impressive appeals to which they have listened, their impatience breaks forth in this impetuous challenge to Jehovah to reveal His power as in the days of old. (*v.* 11 has been inserted from ch. xxxv. 10.)

iii. *vv.* 12—16. The Divine voice is again heard (in answer to the people's prayer). Since their comforter is Jehovah Himself, the Creator of heaven and earth, how unreasonable is their craven fear of their cruel oppressors! (*vv.* 12, 13). Towards the close, however, the connexion becomes very obscure (see the notes).

1—3. The opening exhortation alludes to a difficulty naturally arising in the minds of believing exiles, viz., that they were too few in number to inherit the glorious promises made to them. This is removed by pointing to the marvellous increase of the nation from a single patriarchal family. There is a curious coincidence between this passage and Ezek. xxxiii. 24, where a parallel line of reasoning, on the part of the ungodly remnant left in the land of Canaan, is denounced by the prophet as impious. The history of Abraham and the religious lessons to be drawn from it must have been familiar in the age of the Captivity.

1. *ye that follow after* (lit. "pursue") *righteousness*] "Righteousness" here means, not "salvation" (as in *vv.* 5, 6, 8), but righteousness in conduct, a way of life in accordance with the will of God (as *v.* 7); cf. Prov. xv. 9; Rom. ix. 30 f.

look unto the rock &c.] The ancestors of the nation are compared to a quarry, the Israelites to the stones hewn from it,—a peculiar image found nowhere else. The word for *hole* does not occur again in the O.T.; but a noun from the same root is found in the first line of the Siloam Inscription with the sense of "perforation" or "excavation."

2. The explanation of the figure.

I called him alone] lit. "as one," i.e. a single individual.

blessed him, and increased him] Cf. Gen. xii. 2, 3, xxii. 17. The strict rendering of the Massoretic text would be "that I might bless" &c.; but the verbs should no doubt be pointed as consec. impfs. Without completing the analogy, the prophet proceeds at once in the next verse to comfort the spiritual children of Abraham with the assurance of the restoration of Zion.

3. *shall comfort...will comfort...will make*] lit. as R.V. **hath comforted...hath made** (perf. of certainty).

He will comfort all her waste places;
And he will make her wilderness like Eden,
And her desert like the garden of the LORD;
Joy and gladness shall be found therein,
Thanksgiving, and the voice of melody.
Hearken unto me, my people;   4
And give ear unto me, O my nation:
For a law shall proceed from me,
And I will make my judgment to rest for a light of
    the people.
My righteousness *is* near; my salvation is gone forth,   5
And mine arms shall judge the people;

like the garden of the LORD] Gen. xiii. 10; cf. Ezek. xxviii. 13, xxxi. 8 f.

joy and gladness &c.] Cf. Jer. xxxiii. 11.

4—6. The universal extension of the true religion is the second ground of comfort which the prophet is commissioned to offer to his fellow believers. The language of *vv.* 4, 5 is obviously moulded on that of ch. xlii. 1—4; the functions there assigned to the Servant of the Lord are here assumed by Jehovah Himself. At the same time the thought is implied that the restored Israel is to be the bearer of salvation to the world at large, and thus the further idea is suggested that the ideal represented by the Servant will be realised by the people of Israel when it emerges purified from the discipline of the Captivity.

4. *Hearken unto me*] Better as R.V. **Attend unto me**, the verb being different from that used in *vv.* 1 and 7.

a law shall proceed from me] See ch. ii. 3 ("for out of Zion shall go forth *Tôrāh*"). For *a law (tôrāh)* read. as usual, **instruction**. The word *judgment* in the next line is probably to be rendered "religion" as in xlii. 1, 3, 4 (see on xlii. 1).

The verb rendered "make to rest" has three meanings in the O.T. (*a*) to "cause to rest" (Jer. xxxi. 2) or "be at rest" (ch. xxxiv. 14), (*b*) to "set in commotion" (Jer. l. 34, see on *v.* 15 below), and (*c*) to "do a thing in the twinkling of an eye" (Jer. xlix. 19). Of these (*a*) is alone possible in the present connexion, though hardly quite suitable; the sense "establish," given by some critics, seems to have no sufficient support. By the LXX. the word is taken with *v.* 5, and in the sense (*c*), and this suggests the true reading, although it requires a slight modification of the following word. The construction would be the same as in Jer. xlix. 19, and the rendering perhaps, "Suddenly I bring near my righteousness." The word is at all events superfluous in *v.* 4, the last clause of which reads simply: **and my judgment for a light of the peoples** (cf. xlix. 6).

5. *My righteousness* is *near*] See the last note and cf. ch. xlvi. 13. For *people* read **peoples** (as R.V.).

The isles shall wait upon me,
And on mine arm shall they trust.
6 Lift up your eyes to the heavens,
And look upon the earth beneath:
For the heavens shall vanish away like smoke,
And the earth shall wax old like a garment,
And they that dwell therein shall die in like manner:
But my salvation shall be for ever,
And my righteousness shall not be abolished.
7 Hearken unto me, ye that know righteousness,
The people in whose heart *is* my law;
Fear ye not the reproach of men,
Neither be ye afraid of their revilings.

the isles shall wait upon me] Cf. xlii. 4.
on mine arm] i.e. "on my strength," my protection (xxxiii. 2).
6. From the thought of the universality of religion the prophet rises to that of its eternity, which is here expressed by a contrast of surprising boldness between the "things which are seen" and the "things which are not seen." The whole visible creation, the heavens above and the earth beneath, are transitory, but Jehovah's salvation endures for ever.

the heavens shall vanish away (or "be dissolved") *like smoke*] To feel the force of the metaphor we must bear in mind the ancient conception of the "firmament" as a solid vault overarching the earth. The word for "vanish away" is connected with noun rendered "rotten rags" in Jer. xxxviii. 11 f.

wax old like a garment] See on ch. 1 9, from which the expression is taken. Cf. also Ps. cii. 26.

shall die in like manner] Rather, as R.V. marg., **shall die like gnats.** The word *kēn* does not occur elsewhere in this sense, unless Num. xiii. 33 be an instance, which is doubtful. It might be a collective noun corresponding to the fem. *kinnāh* (noun of unity = a single gnat), found in Talmudic Hebrew. Several commentators, however, think it necessary to read *kinnīm* (also a collective), a word used in Ex. viii. 16—18 of the "lice" of Egypt. The Ancient Versions and the Jewish interpreters explain as E.V., taking *kēn* to be the common particle "so."

salvation and *righteousness* are practically synonymous, as often. See Appendix, Note II.

7, 8. In the hope of this everlasting salvation the true Israelites may well endure for a season the reproach of men.

7. To *know righteousness* does not differ in meaning from "follow after righteousness" in *v.* 1. Both expressions refer to righteousness in the ethical sense; there it is represented as an ideal steadily pursued, here as a rule of life apprehended by the heart and conscience. This inward possession of righteousness is the earnest of the external righteousness, the vindication of right, spoken of in *vv.* 6 and 8.

the people in whose heart is *my* **instruction**] Cf. Jer. xxxi. 33.

For the moth shall eat them up like a garment, 8
And the worm shall eat them like wool:
But my righteousness shall be for ever,
And my salvation from generation to generation.

Awake, awake, put on strength, O arm of the LORD; 9
Awake, as *in* the ancient days, *in* the generations of old.
Art thou not it that hath cut Rahab, *and* wounded
the dragon?

8. *For the moth &c.*] See again ch. l. 9; another indication that the Servant is the type of the true Israel, and hence an example to individual Israelites.

The word rendered "worm" (*sās*, cf. the Greek σής) means strictly "moth." Although common in Semitic, it is found only here in Hebr.

9, 10. These verses are addressed to Jehovah, either by the prophet himself, or by the community of true Israelites. It is difficult to decide between these two views, but the dramatic unity of the passage is best preserved if we adopt the latter, taking *vv.* 9, 10 as a prayer called forth by the previous exhortation, and *vv.* 12 ff. as the Divine answer to this prayer.

The imagery of the verses is obviously mythological. It rests on the conception of a conflict in days long past between Jehovah and the monsters called Rahab and the Dragon. Now both these names came to be used as symbols of Egypt (see on ch. xxx. 7, and xxvii. 1); and most commentators have thought that this is the case here, the historic reference being to the humiliation of Egypt, and the dividing of the Red Sea in the days of Moses. But it is doubtful if this interpretation *exhausts* the significance of the passage. The prophet seems to make direct use of current mythological representations, as is frequently done by the author of the Book of Job (see the notes on iii. 8, ix. 13, xxvi. 13 in Davidson's *Book of Job*). And if this be so there cannot be much doubt as to the nature of the myth in question. It is most probably a Hebrew variation of the Babylonian creation-hymn, according to which the creation of the world was preceded by a conflict between the God of light and order and the monsters that symbolise the dark powers of Chaos (so Duhm; see also Gunkel, *Schöpfung und Chaos*, pp. 30 ff.). The fundamental idea of the verses would therefore seem to lie in the analogy between the original creation of the material world, and the restoration of the moral order of the universe, which has been disturbed by the reign of brute force in the Babylonian empire (cf. *v.* 16). At the same time, the undoubted allusion to the Exodus in 10 *b*, shows that the historical application of the imagery was present to the mind of the prophet (see below).

9. *put on strength*] Lit. "clothe thyself with strength," as Ps. xciii. 1.
The *arm of the LORD* is apostrophised, as the symbol of His might, possibly with a reference back to *v.* 5.

that hath cut Rahab &c.] R.V. that cut **Rahab in pieces, that**

10 *Art* thou not it which hath dried the sea, the waters of the great deep;
That hath made the depths of the sea a way for the ransomed to pass over?

11 Therefore the redeemed of the Lord shall return,
And come with singing *unto* Zion;
And everlasting joy *shall be* upon their head:
They shall obtain gladness and joy;
And sorrow and mourning shall flee away.

pierced the dragon. The verb "cut" is strictly "hewed" or "split." *Rahab* is the sea-monster (ch. xxx. 7); and the "dragon" (*tannín*) probably one of the "helpers of Rahab" (Job ix. 13); both together represent the chaotic elements from whose dominion the habitable world had to be recovered; hence the line expresses poetically the same thought as the following "Art thou not it which dried up the sea" &c.? The original mythical emblem survives in one of the most beautiful personifications of O.T. poetry, the comparison of the sea to a restless, unruly creature, waging impotent war with heaven, and seeking to devour the land, but a creature whom Jehovah holds completely in His power, now stirring it to fury (see *v.* 15) by His rebuke, and again stilling its commotions.

10. *the great deep*] (Gen. vii. 11; Am. vii. 4; Ps. xxxvi. 6) is the primeval ocean of Gen. i. 2, out of which the dry land appeared. The Hebrew (*tĕhôm*) is connected etymologically with *Tiâmat*, the name of the Chaos-monster in the Babylonian creation tablets.

a way for the ransomed to pass over] The reference to the Exodus is here unmistakeable. The transition is explained by the fact that every exhibition of Jehovah's power over the sea was regarded as a repetition on a smaller scale of the original miracle of creation. Both alike are illustrations of what the "arm of the Lord" can do, and of the great miracle of redemption to which the prophet looks forward.

11. For *Therefore* render as R.V. **And.** The verse is almost verbally identical with xxxv. 10, which is clearly its original setting. Here its connexion with what precedes is somewhat loose, and since ch. xxxv. is of more recent date than this prophecy, the verse must have been transferred by a copyist.

12—16. Jehovah again speaks as the comforter of His people. That the passage is a direct answer to the importunate appeal of *vv.* 9 f., seems probable, although it cannot be confidently affirmed; it is at all events virtually an answer. A point of contact might be found in Jehovah's assertion of His power over the sea in *v.* 15; but the connexion of ideas in the last three verses is difficult to make out, and the text itself probably confused.

12, 13. An expostulation with the exiles, who having the Almighty Creator for their God, live in constant terror of being destroyed by their oppressors.

I, *even* I, *am* he that comforteth you: 12
Who *art* thou, that thou shouldest be afraid of a man *that* shall die,
And of the son of man *which* shall be made *as* grass;
And forgettest the LORD thy Maker, 13
That hath stretched forth the heavens, and laid the foundations of the earth;
And hast feared continually every day because of the fury of the oppressor,
As if he were ready to destroy?
And where *is* the fury of the oppressor?
The captive exile hasteneth that *he* may be loosed, 14
And that he should not die in the pit,

12. *I* am *he that comforteth you*] Cf. xl. 1, xlix. 13. The Israelites are here addressed as individuals; this gives place immediately to the feminine collective, *Who art thou &c.?* and this again in *v.* 13 to the masc. sing. The rhetorical question means simply "How is it that thou fearest" &c.? (on the use of the consec. impf. see Davidson's *Syntax* § 51. R. 3). For *made* as *grass* we may translate "given up (to destruction) as grass" (cf. ch. xl. 6).

13. *And forgettest the* LORD] Not in the sense of apostatising from Him (as ch. xvii. 10 and often), but of failing to realise His omnipotence as the Creator of all things (see ch. xlix. 14).

that hath stretched forth the heavens &c.] Cf. xl. 22, xlii. 5, xliv. 24, xlv. 12.

and hast feared...day] Better as R.V. **and fearest continually all the day.** The *oppressor* is of course the Chaldæan Empire (see ch. xlvii. 6), a proof that this part of the book was not written after the fall of Babylon.

as if he were ready to destroy] R.V. **when he maketh ready to destroy**; lit. "aims (his arrow) to destroy," the verb being used technically of an archer directing his arrow; so Ps. xxi. 13, cf. Ps. vii. 13, xi. 2.

and where is *the fury of the oppressor?*] Cf. ch. xxxiii. 18. The question gives a weak ending to the verse, and indeed both in this clause and the preceding the soundness of the text is doubtful.

14. The received text is probably best rendered as follows: **Speedily shall the crouching** (prisoner) **be set free, and he shall not die** (and go down) **to the pit, nor shall his bread fail** (see R.V.); Israel in exile being compared to a prisoner in danger of death through starvation. The image reminds us of Jeremiah in the dungeon (xxxviii. 9, 10). The verse is full of obscurities, and its connexion with what precedes is of the loosest kind. The LXX. gives what is obviously a conjectural rendering, and it is not unlikely that the Hebr. represents another attempt to restore an illegible text.

Nor that his bread should fail.
15 But I *am* the LORD thy God,
That divided the sea, whose waves roared:
The LORD of hosts *is* his name.
16 And I have put my words in thy mouth,
And have covered thee in the shadow of mine hand,
That I may plant the heavens, and lay the foundations of the earth,
And say unto Zion, Thou *art* my people.

15, 16. These verses contain a remarkable number of resemblances to other passages (see below). *v.* 15, apart from the introductory words, occurs in Jer. xxxi. 35, though it is doubtful to which passage it originally belongs. Giesebrecht (on Jeremiah) unhesitatingly pronounces it a citation from this verse.

15. *that divided the sea &c.*] Render with R.V. **which stirreth up** (see on *v.* 4) **the sea so that the waves thereof roar** (cf. Job xxvi. 12).

The idea is parallel with that of *vv.* 9 f., being an illustration of Jehovah's power over the elements. He can, as it were, play with the sea, for His stirring it up to fury implies that He is able to restrain it, and at the right time to still it again.

the LORD of hosts is his name] Chs. xlvii. 4, xlviii. 2, liv. 5.

16. *I have put my words in thy mouth*] recurring in ch. lix. 21.

covered thee in the shadow of mine hand] Taken almost exactly from xlix. 2.

that I may plant &c.] This is no doubt the right translation, not "that thou mayest plant" (lit. "to plant"). The metaphor of "planting" the heavens is strange; some critics substitute "to stretch forth" (changing a letter), as in *v.* 13, with which likewise the following words correspond.

The verse is remarkable in two respects. (1) It throws an important light on the idea of the Servant of the Lord. Language which is elsewhere used of the Servant is here applied to Israel, to whom the verse is undoubtedly addressed. This would be a strong confirmation of the theory that the Servant is in some sense a personification of Israel. (2) The conception of a new moral universe about to be created is partly anticipated both in *v.* 6 (where the transitoriness of the present world is asserted), and in *vv.* 9 f. (see the notes above). This verse, however, adds the further idea that the new creation is the ultimate goal of God's dealings with Israel, whose religious mission culminates in a universal and everlasting salvation.

CH. LI. 17—LII. 12. THE LORD WILL TURN THE CAPTIVITY OF ZION.

The three oracles into which this passage naturally falls are these:—
(1) *vv.* 17—23. The prophet, returning to the thought with which the book opens (ch. xl. 2), announces that the period of Jerusalem's

Awake, awake, stand up, O Jerusalem, 17
Which hast drunk at the hand of the LORD the cup
of his fury;
Thou hast drunken the dregs of the cup of trembling,
and wrung *them* out.
There is none to guide her among all the sons *whom* 18
she hath brought forth;

degradation has expired. The city is figured as a woman lying prostrate and senseless, intoxicated with the cup of the Lord's indignation which she has drunk to the dregs, her sons unable to help her (17—20). But the cup is now taken from her and passed to the enemies who had oppressed and insulted her (21—23).

(2) lii. 1—6. In a new apostrophe, the image is carried on; let Zion lay aside her soiled raiment, and the emblems of her slavery, and put on her holiday attire (1, 2). Jehovah will no longer endure that His name should be blasphemed through the banishment of His people (3—6).

(3) *vv.* 7—12. A description of the triumphal return of Jehovah to Zion, obviously based on the last section of the Prologue (ch. xl. 9—11). The writer pictures the scene of joy within the city when the heralds of the King arrive (7, 8); he calls on the waste places of Jerusalem to break forth into singing (9, 10); and finally, turning to the exiles (as in xlviii. 20 f.) he summons them to hasten their escape from the land of their captivity (11, 12).

17—20. The description of Jerusalem's degradation. The rhythm is that of the *qînah*, and the resemblances to the book of Lamentations are so striking that Ewald has conjectured that the passage is taken from one of the elegies composed during the Exile.

Awake] Better **Arouse thee** (Cheyne); the verb being a reflexive as distinct from the simple "Awake" of lii. 1 (and li. 9).

which hast drunk...the cup of his fury] The image of the cup of the Divine wrath originated in Jeremiah's great vision of judgement (ch. xxv. 15 ff.), where the prophet hands the cup to all nations, beginning with Jerusalem. Cf. also Jer. xlix. 12; Hab. ii. 16; Ezek. xxiii. 31—34; Lam. iv. 21; Obad. 16; Rev. xiv. 10.

the dregs of the cup of trembling] R.V. **the bowl of the cup of staggering.** "Dregs" is a mistaken Jewish rendering of a word (*qubba'ath*), found only here and in *v.* 22. It means undoubtedly a "bowl" or "chalice," and the pleonasm "bowl of the cup" has probably arisen through the common word for cup being added as an explanatory gloss.

of trembling] **of intoxication.** Ps. lx. 3 (A.V. "wine of astonishment").

and *wrung* them *out*] **drained** (cf. Ezek. xxiii. 34)—an asyndetic construction in the Hebr.—"hast drunk, hast drained," i.e. "hast drunk to the dregs." The whole clause reads:—

Thou who hast drunk from Jehovah's hand—the cup of His wrath,
The chalice of intoxication—hast thou drunk to the dregs.

Neither *is there any* that taketh her by the hand of all the sons *that* she hath brought up.

19 These two *things* are come unto thee; who shall be sorry for thee?
Desolation, and destruction, and the famine, and the sword:
By whom shall I comfort thee?

20 Thy sons have fainted, they lie at the head of all the streets, as a wild bull *in* a net:
They are full *of* the fury of the LORD, the rebuke of thy God.

21 Therefore hear now this, thou afflicted,
And drunken, but not with wine:

22 Thus saith thy Lord the LORD,
And thy God *that* pleadeth the cause of his people,

19. *These two* things] (ch. xlvii. 9), i.e. two kinds of calamities; namely, **devastation and destruction** on land and city; **famine and sword** on the inhabitants.

who shall be sorry for thee] Better **who condoles with thee** (Jer. xv. 5; Nah. iii. 7), i.e. "thou hast no sympathizers." To "condole" is in Hebr. to shake the head (cf. Jer. xvi. 5; Job ii. 11, xlii. 11 &c.), a similar gesture, expressed by a different verb, denotes contempt (see on ch. xxxvii. 22).

by whom shall I comfort thee?] Rather: **how** (lit. who) **shall I comfort thee?** The idiom cannot be reproduced exactly; see Am. vii. 2, 5 and comp. Davidson's *Synt.* § 8 R. 1 (where it is suggested that the peculiar use of the pronoun may be provincial or colloquial). The Ancient Versions, however, read the third person, which is far easier; "who comforts thee?"

20. *Thy sons have* **swooned**] lit. "were shrouded,"—a usual oriental metaphor (Am. viii. 13; Jon. iv. 8; Nah. iii. 11). For the idea cf. Lam. ii. 11, 19, 21. *at the head of all the streets*] Lam. ii. 19, iv. 1.

as a wild bull in a net] R.V., rightly, **as an antelope** (Deut. xiv. 5) **in a net**, exhausted by its vain struggles to get free.

they are full of the fury &c.] The children have drunk of the same cup as their mother.

21—23. The message of comfort.

21. *hear now this*] See ch. xlvii. 8.

drunken, but not with wine] Cf. ch. xxix. 9.

22. *thy Lord the LORD*] **thy Lord Jehovah.** It is in cases like this that we are made to feel the inconvenience arising from the Jewish reluctance to pronounce the sacred Name Yahveh.

I have taken] Better **I take** (a perf. of instant action, as 1 Sam. ii. 16).

Behold, I have taken out of thine hand the cup of trembling,
Even the dregs of the cup of my fury;
Thou shalt no more drink it again:
But I will put it into the hand of them that afflict 23 thee;
Which have said to thy soul, Bow down, that we may go over:
And thou hast laid thy body as the ground,
And as the street, to them that went over.

Awake, awake; put on thy strength, O Zion; 52
Put on thy beautiful garments, O Jerusalem, the holy city:
For henceforth there shall no more come into thee the uncircumcised and the unclean.

the cup of trembling...fury] **the cup of intoxication, the chalice of mine indignation** (see on *v.* 17).

23. *them that afflict thee*] **thy tormentors.** The word occurs three times in the Lamentations (i. 5, 12, iii. 32).

to thy soul] i.e. "to thyself," although without special emphasis (cf. Ps. iii. 2, xi. 1).

Bow down, that we may go over] The figure is taken from the Eastern custom of treading or even riding on the backs of conquered enemies. Comp. Lane's account of the Mohammedan ceremony of the *Dooseh* or "Treading," as he witnessed it at Cairo in 1834; when the Sheikh of the Saadiyeh dervishes, mounted on horseback, rode over the prostrate bodies of a large number of dervishes. (See *Manners and Customs of the Modern Egyptians*, pp. 417 f., 432 f. [Ed. 1890].)

and thou hast laid &c.] **so that thou madest thy back as the earth.** Gesenius cites in illustration an Arabic proverb: "To him who pleases me, I will be earth."

Ch. lii. **1, 2.** Here the prophet's imagination takes a higher flight. The cup of indignation having finally passed from her hands, Jerusalem is summoned to shake off her stupor, and array herself in garments befitting her dignity as the bride of Jehovah. The description is influenced by the contrast (evidently intentional) to the taunt-song on the "daughter of Babylon" (ch. xlvii. 1 ff.).

put on thy strength] Cf. ch. li. 9.

the holy city] as ch. xlviii. 2.

for...there shall no more come &c.] Note the correspondence with xlvii. 1, 5.

the uncircumcised and the unclean] i.e. not foreigners generally (as Joel iii. 17), as if the passage expressed the exclusiveness of later

2 Shake thyself from the dust; arise, *and* sit down, O Jerusalem:
Loose thyself from the bands of thy neck, O captive daughter of Zion.
3 For thus saith the LORD,
Ye have sold yourselves for nought;
And ye shall be redeemed without money.
4 For thus saith the Lord GOD,
My people went down aforetime *into* Egypt to sojourn there;
And the Assyrian oppressed them without cause.
5 Now therefore, what have I here, saith the LORD,

Judaism, but the "destroyers" and "wasters" who at present desecrate her soil; see on xlix. 17. Cf. Nah. i. 15; Zech. ix. 8.

2. *arise* and *sit down*] The meaning might be, "arise from the dust, and sit on thy throne,"—a contrast to xlvii. 1.

loose thyself...neck] Better perhaps **loose for thee the bonds** &c.; the reflexive verb having the same force as an ethical dative. The alternative rendering of R.V. marg. "the bands of thy neck are loosed" represents the Hebrew consonantal text. The Qerê, however, is here supported by the Ancient Versions, and is undoubtedly to be preferred.

3—6. There is here a sudden change both in form and subject. The rhythmic structure of the preceding verses gives place to prose, and the figure of Jerusalem arising from the dust is altogether abandoned. Jehovah is represented as deliberating with Himself on the religious situation, so injurious to His honour, brought about by the unprecedented calamities of His people (*vv*. 4, 5), and as resolving to end it by their deliverance (6). It is doubtful if the passage was the original sequel to *vv*. 1, 2.

3. *Ye have sold yourselves*] R.V. **Ye were sold**; see on ch. l. 1; cf. Ps. xliv. 12.

redeemed without money] Cf. ch. xlv. 13. Jehovah *gained* nothing by delivering Israel into the hand of its enemies, and He *asks* nothing as the price of its redemption.

4. For *aforetime* render with R.V. **at the first**, at the outset of its history.

without cause] i.e. probably, "for nought," without having acquired any right over Israel by services rendered to Jehovah. The meaning can hardly be that Israel suffered innocently.

5. *Now therefore*] Rather, **But now**, accentuating the gravity of the present situation. Exile and oppression were indeed no new experiences for Israel (*v*. 4), but no such overwhelming disaster as this had ever befallen it hitherto.

what have I here &c.] The sentence may be variously understood. The main idea obviously is that the state of things described in what follows is not to be endured, being inconsistent with the honour of

That my people is taken away for nought?
They that rule over them make *them* to howl, saith the
   LORD;
And my name continually every day *is* blasphemed.
Therefore my people shall know my name: 6
Therefore *they shall know* in that day that I *am* he that
   doth speak : behold, *it is* I.

Jehovah. The formula "What is there to me?" expresses a strong sense of incongruity between what is and what ought to be (see iii. 15, xxii. 1, 16), and we may render either, "What am I about (xxii. 1) here (in Babylonia)?" or, more generally, "What do I find here?" i.e. in the existing position of affairs, as contrasted with the historic parallels in *v*. 4. The last is perhaps to be preferred. The meaning can hardly be, "What have I to do here (ch. xxii. 16) now that my people is taken away?"

that (better **for**) *my people is taken away*] destroyed outright (ch. liii. 8).

they that rule over them (the Chaldæans) *make* them *to howl* (R.V. **do howl**)] The R.V. rightly avoids the causative sense of the verb, which has no support in usage. On the other hand, it is nowhere else used of a shout of exultation, as it must be here; comp. with Gesenius and others, "laetis *ululare* triumphis" (Lucan, 6, 261). In Syriac also the word appears occasionally to undergo a similar modification.

my name...is blasphemed] lit. **despised**. (The form should probably be pointed as part. Pual.) The meaning is that the calamities of Israel were attributed by the heathen to the impotence of their God, and thus the majesty of Jehovah was impaired,—a thought frequently expressed by Ezekiel (see Ezek. xxxvi. 20 &c.). The words are cited in Rom. ii. 24.

continually **all the** *day*] (R.V.), as ch. li. 13.

6. The contempt thus brought on His name is the crowning motive of Jehovah's interposition,—another point of affinity with Ezekiel (see xxxvi. 21).

my people shall know my name] i.e. shall know by experience what My name imports; comp. "shall know that I am Jehovah," in Ezekiel (xx. 42, 44 and often). The second *therefore*, followed by no new verb, is both superfluous and difficult and should probably be omitted, with LXX.

that I am *he that doth speak: behold*, it is *I*] The last words "behold me" are hardly to be taken as obj. of the verb "speak"; they simply repeat the sense of the preceding clause: "They shall know that it is I who speak; here am I" (cf. Ezek. v. 13).

7—12. The return of Jehovah to Zion.

7 Describes, in vivid pictorial imagery taken from ch. xl. 9, the arrival in Jerusalem of the first tidings of the deliverance from Babylon and the establishment of the kingdom of God. Part of the verse occurs in Nah. i. 15.

How beautiful upon the mountains are the feet of him that bringeth good tidings, that publisheth peace;
That bringeth good tidings of good, that publisheth salvation;
That saith unto Zion, Thy God reigneth!
Thy watchmen shall lift up the voice;
With the voice together shall they sing:
For they shall see eye to eye,
When the LORD shall bring again Zion.
Break forth into joy, sing together, ye waste places of Jerusalem:

of him that bringeth good tidings] The *měbassēr* (see on xl. 9 and cf. xli. 27) is one of the prophet's *dramatis personæ*, occupying a position somewhat analogous to that of "the fugitive" in the Book of Ezekiel (xxiv. 26 f., xxxiii. 21 f.). He is the "evangelist," the herald of salvation whose single function is to announce to Zion the speedy advent of her God. He is an ideal creation of the writer's mind, and the conception fluctuates between that of an individual (as here and xli. 27) and of a company (in xl. 9). In St Paul's application of the figure (Rom. x. 15) it becomes a type of the gospel ministry.

Thy God reigneth] Rather, **thy God hath become king**, has established His everlasting kingdom (cf. ch. xxiv. 23; Ps. xciii. 1, xcvii. 1).

8. *Thy watchmen...sing*] Render, **Hark, thy watchmen! they lift up the voice, together do they sing** (see R.V.). Although the prophets are often called "watchmen" (ch. lvi. 10; Hab. ii. 1; Jer. vi. 17; Ezek. xxxiii. 2 ff.) there is no reason to suppose that they are referred to here. Prophets are no longer required after the herald of salvation has arrived and Jehovah Himself is at hand. The word is used in its ordinary sense of the watchmen posted on the city walls, who are naturally represented as the first to see and announce the actual approach of the King.

for they shall see &c.] Rather, **for eye to eye do they look upon Jehovah's return to Zion.** The expression *eye to eye* occurs only once again, in Num. xiv. 14, where Jehovah is said to be "seen eye to eye" in Israel; i.e. He is visibly present there (cf. Jer. xxxii. 4, "his eyes shall look on the eyes of Nebuchadnezzar"). The idea here must be similar; Jehovah shall be seen in person when He comes to Zion, as closely and clearly as when two men look one another in the face. The phrase certainly has not in Hebr. the sense of harmony and unity which it has come to bear in English. But it can hardly mean merely that the watchmen shall form a dense throng, looking *each other* in the face! That is a thought quite irrelevant in the context.

9. *Break forth into joy, sing...*] Render, **Break forth into singing** (lit. "Break forth, sing"). Cf. xliv. 23.

For the LORD hath comforted his people, he hath redeemed Jerusalem.
The LORD hath made bare his holy arm in the eyes of all 10 the nations;
And all the ends of the earth shall see the salvation of our God.
Depart ye, depart ye, go ye out from thence, 11 touch no unclean *thing*;
Go ye out of the midst of her; be ye clean, that bear the vessels of the LORD.
For ye shall not go out with haste, 12
Nor go by flight:
For the LORD will go before you;
And the God of Israel *will be* your rereward.

the LORD *hath comforted his people*] li. 3.

10. Here (if not already in *v.* 9) the prophet withdraws his gaze from the future, and describes Jehovah as preparing Himself for the conflict which leads to the joyous scene of *vv.* 7 f.

hath made bare his holy arm] throwing back the sleeveless upper garment from the right shoulder, in readiness for action: δεξιὸν ὦμον γυμνὸν ἔχων ἐν τῇ μάχῃ (Arrian, *Alex.* 5. 18, quoted by Dillmann). See the contrasted metaphor in Ps. lxxiv. 11. *his holy arm* means "His divine arm" (Ps. xcviii. 1). The "arm" of Jehovah, as ch. li. 9 (cf. also liii. 1).

shall see the salvation (i.e. **the deliverance** or "victory") *of our God*] a different idea from that of xlv. 22.

11, 12. A summons to the exiles to prepare for their departure from Babylon (cf. xlviii. 20, 21). These are to accompany Jehovah in his triumphal "return to Zion" (see on ch. xl. 10, 11).

go ye out from thence] from Babylon; "in this section (*vv.* 7—12) the prophet places himself in spirit at Jerusalem" (Cheyne).

touch no unclean thing] They are to "purify themselves" (see below) as those who take part in a religious procession. The stress laid on ceremonial purity in this verse is an exceptional feature in the prophecy.

be ye clean (**cleanse yourselves ye**) *that bear the vessels of the* LORD] As in the exodus from Egypt, the priests bearing the sacred utensils march at the head of the procession. Some have rendered "ye that are Jehovah's armour-bearers" (so Cheyne, formerly), a military figure suggested by the Hebrew phrase, but perhaps a little far-fetched in the context.

12. Unlike the former exodus, the departure is to take place deliberately and in perfect security, without *haste* (Ex. xii. 11; Deut. xvi. 3), a representation differing somewhat from xlviii. 20.

the LORD *will go before you*] Ex. xiii. 21 f., &c.

will be your rereward] **your rear guard**; see Ex. xiv. 19.

13 Behold, my servant shall deal prudently,

CH. LII. 13—LIII. 12. THE SERVANT'S SACRIFICE
AND HIS REWARD.

This is the last and greatest, as well as the most difficult, of the four delineations of the Servant of Jehovah, and in several respects occupies a place apart. In the previous passages the Servant has been described as the ideal prophet or teacher, conscious of a world-wide mission in the service of God, which he prosecutes amid discouragement and persecution with inflexible purpose and the unfaltering assurance of ultimate success. There has been no hint that his activity was interrupted by death. Here the presentation is quite different. The conception of the Prophet is all but displaced by that of the Man of Sorrows, the meek and patient martyr, the sin-bearer. The passage is partly retrospective and partly prophetic. In so far as it is a retrospect there is no allusion to the prophetic activity of the servant; it is only after he has been raised from the dead that he is to assume the function of the great religious guide and authority of the world. But the most striking feature of the passage is the unparalleled sufferings of the Servant, and the effect they produce on the minds of his contemporaries. The tragedy of which they have been spectators makes an impression far more profound and convincing than any direct teaching could have done, compelling them to recognise the mission of the Servant, and at the same time producing penitence and confession of their own sin. The whole conception here given of the Servant of the Lord makes the prophecy the most remarkable anticipation in the Old Testament of the "sufferings of Christ, and the glory that should follow."

The passage may be divided into three parts:—

(1) An introduction, briefly stating the import of all that follows,— the coming exaltation of the Servant in contrast to his past abasement (lii. 13—15).

(2) A historical review of the Servant's career, as he had appeared to his contemporaries in the days of his humiliation (liii. 1—9).

(3) An announcement of the glorious future and the astonishing success in store for him as the reward of his obedience unto death (*vv*. 10—12).

The middle section may be further subdivided into three strophes, yielding an arrangement (recognised by most commentators) of the whole in five strophes of three verses each.

13—15. Jehovah utters a brief but pregnant announcement of the brilliant destiny in store for His Servant. Known to many in his misfortunes as an object of aversion and contempt, he shall suddenly be revealed in his true dignity; and the unexpected transformation will startle the whole world into astonishment and reverence. The verses form a prelude to ch. liii., being a summary of what is there described in detail; and they indicate what is the main idea of the whole passage, viz. the unexampled contrast between the present (and past) degradation and the future glory of Jehovah's Servant.

13. *my servant shall deal prudently*] A more appropriate rendering

He shall be exalted and extolled, and be very high.
As many were astonied at thee;
His visage *was* so marred more than *any* man,
And his form more than the sons of men:

is that of R.V. marg. **my servant shall prosper**, i.e. his career shall be crowned with complete success. The primary idea of the verb used is no doubt "wisdom" (not mere shrewdness, however, rather "insight," see Gen. iii. 6; Isa. xliv. 18), but it also includes the success which is the normal result of wise action, and sometimes this secondary idea almost supplants the original meaning (Josh. i. 7 f.; 1 Sam. xviii. 5, 14 f. etc.). This sense seems to be required here by the parallelism with the next line, for there is nothing in the whole prophecy to justify us in regarding the Servant's elevation as the *effect* of his wisdom. The verse is "a simple prediction of the exaltation awaiting the Servant, in contrast with his past sorrows and abasement" (Davidson).

he shall be exalted and extolled] or "high and lifted up." The same combination used of Jehovah in ch. lvii. 15; of His throne in vi. 1.

14, 15 must be read as a single compound sentence. The protasis is the first line of *v.* 14 ("According as many were astonied at thee"); the corresponding apodosis follows in *v.* 15 ("so shall he sprinkle &c."), the intervening clauses being a parenthesis suggested by the word "astonied."

as many were astonied at thee] The word "astonied" expresses the blank amazement, mingled with horror, excited in the minds of beholders by the spectacle of the Servant's unparalleled sufferings (cf. 1 Ki. ix. 8; Jer. ii. 12, xviii. 16). It is natural to suppose that the "many" here referred to are the same as the "many nations" who witness the Servant's subsequent exaltation (*v.* 15), but the point is not to be pressed, and on the hypothesis that the Servant is an individual Israelite, the spectators of the Servant's abasement could hardly be the nations of the world. Instead of "thee" the Targ. and Pesh. seem to have read "him," thus avoiding an embarrassing change of person. The LXX., on the other hand, preserve the 2nd pers. throughout *v.* 14. The change of person may no doubt be explained as caused by the parenthesis, but it is awkward nevertheless, and almost misleading, and many commentators prefer to alter the text in accordance with the Targ.

his visage was *so marred, &c.*] Render:

—so marred from that of man was his aspect,
and his form from that of the sons of men—

The sentence is inserted parenthetically to explain the repugnance felt by all who beheld the Servant in his former abject condition. The meaning is that he was so disfigured by disease (see ch. liii. 3) as to be no longer human in appearance. The word for "marred" is pointed as a noun (not found elsewhere): "a marred object." A participle (*moshḥāth*) would read more naturally after the adverb "so," although the punctuators must have had some reason for avoiding the more obvious form.

15   So shall he sprinkle many nations;
    The kings shall shut their mouths at him:
    For *that* which had not been told them shall they
      see;
    And *that* which they had not heard shall they
      consider.

15. *so shall he sprinkle many nations*] The verb rendered "sprinkle" means elsewhere to "scatter (a liquid) in small drops," and its usage is confined to the ceremonial act illustrated by Lev. iv. 6; Num. xix. 18 f. etc. This is the sense intended by the A.V. and the ancient authorities (Aquila, Theodotion, Vulg.) which it follows; the antithesis suggested being that as the Servant had been shunned by many as unclean, so he shall (metaphorically) "sprinkle" them, i.e. make them clean. But this interpretation imports into the passage ideas which are not expressed, and is besides inadmissible on grammatical grounds; i.e. the verb always means to *sprinkle* (a liquid), not to *besprinkle* (a person or thing). The only rendering at all compatible with the ceremonial use of the word would be that of the Targ.: "so shall he scatter many nations," where the nations are actually, by a most unnatural metaphor, compared to spirting drops of water. To reach a satisfactory sense it is only necessary to assume that the Hebrew verb had a wider range of meaning than is represented in the O.T. It might be causative of a verb (found in Arabic) meaning to "spring" or "leap," just as the English "sprinkle" is perhaps etymologically the causative of "spring." We may thus render with R.V. marg. **so will he startle many nations**, i.e. "cause them to spring" in surprise, or (better) "cause them to rise up suddenly" in reverential admiration. Cf. ch. xlix. 7 and Job xxix. 8 ("The aged arose and stood up"). Most modern writers agree in this explanation, although some have recourse to emendation of the text. The LXX. expresses the same general idea (θαυμάσονται ἔθνη πολλά, "many nations shall marvel").

kings shall shut their mouths **because of** *him* (R.V. marg.)] Comp. again Job's touching description of the respect paid to him in the days of his prosperity: "The princes refrained talking, and laid their hand on their mouth. The nobles held their peace, and their tongue cleaved to the roof of their mouth" (xxix. 9 f.). The art. before "kings" should be omitted (as in R.V.).

for that *which had not been told them &c.*] The meaning is either that the exaltation of the Servant is an event of which they had received no announcement beforehand, or that it is one the like of which had never been known. If the reference be to the coming elevation of Israel, either sense would be suitable; if on the other hand the resurrection of an individual be predicted, the second would be more appropriate.

ch. liii. 1—9. Having thus indicated the subject of his discourse, the prophet now proceeds to describe the career of the Servant, and the impression he had made on his contemporaries. This is prefaced in

> Who hath believed our report? 53
> And to whom is the arm of the LORD revealed?

v. 1 by a confession or complaint of the universal unbelief which had led to his being so grievously misunderstood.

The speakers in this section are certainly not the heathen mentioned in lii. 15, but either all Israel or one Israelite in the name of all. The "nations" and "kings" are surprised by the Servant's exaltation because they had not previously heard of it; those who now speak confess a deeper fault, they have heard but did not believe. It is generally assumed that there is a change of speaker in *vv.* 7—9, where the use of the 1st pers. plu. is discontinued, and where (*v.* 8) we come across the expression "*my* people." This assumption is to be avoided if possible, because *vv.* 7 ff. continue the narrative of the Servant's sufferings, and it is unnatural to think that the story begun by one speaker should be completed by another unless there were some clear indication that this is the case. There appears to be no difficulty in the supposition that the prophet himself speaks throughout; although in *vv.* 2—6 he associates himself with his generation, the contemporaries of the Servant. There must be some reason for his thus merging his individual consciousness in that of the community; and the obvious reason is that in depicting the Servant as he appeared to men, he writes as a spectator along with others, and realises his solidarity with his nation. In *vv.* 7—9 the description simply becomes less subjective; the emphasis lies less on what men thought of the Servant, and more on what he was and endured; and when the prophet again has occasion to refer to Israel it is natural that he should do so as "my people."—Another thing to be noted is that the language is consistently retrospective. Historic tenses are employed throughout, the speaker looks back on the completed tragedy of the Servant's career, and on the people's former thoughts of him as things that belong to the past. On the other hand, the exaltation of the Servant is always spoken of (both in lii. 13—15, and in liii. 10—12) as something still future. The standpoint assumed here seems therefore to be intermediate between the death of the Servant and his exaltation; and the great moral change which is described as taking place in the mind of the people is not the result of the revelation of his glory, but is brought about by reflection on his unparalleled sufferings, and his patient demeanour under them, preparing the people to believe the prophecies which had hitherto seemed incredible.

1. The verse should probably be rendered,

Who believed **that which was revealed to us**,

And the arm **of Jehovah**—to (lit. "on") **whom was it disclosed?**

The word which E.V. renders "report" is passive in form (lit. "a thing heard"); *our report*, therefore, is not "that which we reported" but either "the report concerning us" (2 Sam. iv. 4) or "that which was reported to us." The last sense is alone admissible in this connexion, and the only question that remains is, What kind of report is referred to? Usually the word denotes a rumour circulated by the ordinary channels of intelligence (ch. xxxvii. 7 &c.), and this meaning might be

124   ISAIAH, LIII.   [v. 2.

For he shall grow up before him as a tender plant,

thought of here if we could suppose the words spoken *after* the elevation of the Servant. But this is objectionable, (*a*) because the standpoint of the speakers is not subsequent to the glorification of the Servant, but prior to it (see above), (*b*) the speakers, being Israelites, cannot readily be supposed to learn the Servant's exaltation from rumour, and (*c*) it would be necessary to render the verb "Who *could have* believed?" which although possible is not natural. The question implies a negative answer: "No one believed it." It is better therefore to take the word in its religious sense of a Divine revelation (see on ch. xxviii. 9), a "thing heard" from Jehovah. "Our revelation" might of course be said by the prophet of a communication made directly to himself; but it might also be said by the people of a revelation which had reached them through the medium of the prophets. The reference will be to the prophecies bearing on the Servant's glorious destiny, especially ch. xlii. 1—4, xlix. 1—6, l. 4—9, and perhaps lii. 13—15.

The *arm of the* LORD is, as in ch. li. 9, lii. 10 &c., a metaphor for Jehovah's operation in history. It was He who raised up the Servant, and all through his tragic history God was working by him for the redemption of His people and the inbringing of eternal salvation. But this Divine power behind the Servant had not been "disclosed" to any of his contemporaries; they had neither perceived it for themselves nor believed it when declared to them, and so in the blindness and deafness of their unbelief they had misconceived him in the manner exhibited in *vv.* 2 ff.

The verse is cited, with reference to the rejection of the Gospel by the Jews, in John xii. 38 and (in part) Rom. x. 16.

2. The verse seems to take us back to the origin of the Servant's career, in order to account for the powerful prejudices with which his contemporaries regarded him. From the first he had been mean and unprepossessing in appearance, like a stunted shrub struggling for existence in an arid soil. To this corresponded the first impressions of the people, which were mainly of a negative kind; they found in him nothing that was attractive or desirable. Beyond this the verse does not go.

For he shall grow up] Lit. **And he grew up**. It is not easy to make out such a connexion between this sentence and the last as would naturally be expressed by "and." If what is here stated were the explanation of the unbelief confessed in *v.* 1, the proper conjunction would be "for," and so the word is by many rendered. Others take it as the "and" of consequence (= and so), but the clause is not a statement of what the people thought of the Servant in consequence of their unbelief, but of what he actually was. The phrase "before him" seems decisive on that point, unless with Ewald and others we change the reading to "before us." With that alteration the whole verse speaks of the impressions men formed of the Servant, and these impressions might readily be regarded as the result of their want of spiritual insight. But if the received text be retained (and there is no sufficient reason for departing from it) the description begins with a

And as a root out of a dry ground:
He hath no form nor comeliness;
And when we shall see him, *there is* no beauty that we
should desire him.
He is despised and rejected of men; 3
A man of sorrows, and acquainted with grief:
And we hid as it were *our* faces from him;

statement of fact and then proceeds to the effect on the mind of the people. It is probable that no logical connexion with the preceding is intended. The conjunction may mark the commencement of the narrative, in accordance with a tendency to begin a speech with "and" (Josh. xxii. 28; Jer. ix. 21; cf. ch. ii. 2).

as a tender plant] **a sapling**. Cf. Ez. xvii. 22; Job xiv. 7.

a root (cf. ch. xi. 10) *out of a dry ground*] The "dry ground" might, on some theories of what is meant by the Servant, symbolise the Exile with its political hardships and lack of religious advantages, but it is doubtful if the figure should be pressed so far. The Servant is compared to a plant springing up in such a soil, but whether the prophet thought of his lowly growth as due in any degree to unfavourable circumstances is uncertain.

In what follows *hath* should be **had**, and *comeliness*, **majesty**. The words for *form* and *beauty* are the same as those rendered "form" and "aspect" in lii. 14. Both are here used in the sense of "pleasing form" &c.; comp. "a man of form" in 1 Sam. xvi. 18, and the Latin *formosus* from *forma*, or "shapely" from "shape."

and when we shall see him] Rather, **when we saw him**. The clause, however, might (disregarding the accents) be read with what precedes: "...and no majesty, that we should look upon him—and no aspect that we should desire him" (see R.V. marg.). This at least yields a more perfect parallelism in the last two lines.

3. Not only did the Servant fail to attract his contemporaries (*v.* 2); there was that in his appearance which excited positive aversion. He is represented as one stricken with loathsome and disfiguring disease, probably leprosy (see on *v.* 4), so that men instinctively recoiled from him in horror and disgust.

He is despised and rejected of men] Better, **Despised and man-forsaken**, i.e. one with whom men refuse to associate, or, perhaps, one who renounces the hope of human fellowship. The corresponding verb is used by Job when he complains of the estrangement of his friends: "my kinsfolk have failed" (ch. xix. 14).

For *sorrows...grief*, read **pains...sickness**. Although both words may be used tropically of mental suffering, it is plain that *in the figure* of this verse and the following they are to be taken in their literal sense.

and we hid &c.] More literally, and as one from whom there is a hiding of the face; his appearance was such as to cause men involuntarily to cover their face from the sight of him. The expression

He was despised, and we esteemed him not.
Surely he hath borne our griefs,
And carried our sorrows:
Yet we did esteem him stricken,
Smitten of God, and afflicted.

is similar to another phrase of Job's: "I am a spitting in the face" (xvii. 6). For the idea cf. Job xix. 19, xxx. 10. Leprosy is again suggested. The rendering of LXX. and Vulg. "and as one who hid his face from us" is grammatically defensible, but conveys a wrong idea; the Servant "hid not his face from shame and spitting" (ch. l. 6).

esteemed him not] (lit. "reckoned him not"), held him of no account.

4—6. While *vv.* 2, 3 describe the natural instinctive impressions produced by the Servant's appearance, *vv.* 4—6 reveal incidentally the moral judgement which the people were led to form regarding him. His unparalleled sufferings had seemed to them to mark him out as a special object of Jehovah's anger (*v.* 4), just as Job's calamities were believed by his friends to be the evidence of great, though secret, sins. But it is the reversal of this judgement, and the perception thereby gained of the true nature of the Servant's mission, that is the chief theme of this section. The people now see that although he suffered greatly he was himself innocent, and from this they have advanced to the conclusion that he suffered vicariously, bearing the penalty due to the sin of his nation. This change of attitude towards the Servant marks the beginning of repentance in the people; the consciousness of their own guilt takes possession of their minds when they read God's judgement upon it in the chastisement borne by their substitute.

4. *Surely he hath borne &c.*] Render:
> Surely it was our sicknesses that he bore
> and our pains that he carried.

The emphasis of contrast lies on the words *our* and *he* in both lines. To "bear" sickness is not to take it away (although that will be the effect of vicarious bearing of it) but simply to endure it (as Jer. x. 19). In Matt. viii. 17 the words are applied to our Lord's miracles of healing, but the prophet's meaning plainly is that the Servant endured in his own person the penal consequences of the people's guilt.

yet we did esteem &c.] Rather, **while we accounted him stricken** &c. The subject "we" is strongly emphasised, and the clause is circumstantial, introducing the people's false estimate of the Servant as a concomitant of the main statement of the verse. "Stricken" is the expression used when God visits a man with severe and sudden sickness (Gen. xii. 17; 1 Sam. vi. 9), especially leprosy, which was regarded as preeminently the "stroke" of God's hand (Job xix. 21; 2 Ki. xv. 5; Lev. xiii. 3, 9, 20) and the direct consequence of sin. That the Servant is pictured as a leper is suggested by several particulars in the description, such as his marred and disfigured form, and his isolation from human society, as well as the universal conviction of his contemporaries that he

> But he *was* wounded for our transgressions, 5
> *He was* bruised for our iniquities:
> The chastisement of our peace *was* upon him;
> And with his stripes we are healed.
> All we like sheep have gone astray; 6
> We have turned every one to his own way;
> And the LORD hath laid on him the iniquity of us all.

was a special object of the divine wrath; and the impression is confirmed by the parallel case of Job, the typical righteous sufferer, whose disease was elephantiasis, the most hideous form of leprosy. It has to be borne in mind, of course, that the figure of the Servant is in some sense an ideal creation of the prophet's mind, so that the leprosy is only a strong image for such sufferings as are the evidence of God's wrath against sin.

5. In *v*. 4 the people confess that the Servant was their substitute in his endurance of pains and sicknesses; here they penetrate more deeply into the meaning of his sufferings, perceiving the connexion between his passion and their own sin. The connexion is twofold; in the first place the Servant's suffering was the penalty due to the people's transgressions, and in the second place it was the remedy by which they were restored to spiritual health.

But he was pierced because of our rebellions,
Crushed because of our iniquities.

The strong verbs "pierced" (see ch. li. 9) and "crushed" (Job vi. 9) are probably metaphors expressing the fatal ravages of leprosy.

the chastisement of our peace] i.e. the chastisement needful to procure peace or well-being for us. "Chastisement" is pain inflicted for moral ends and with remedial intent (Prov. iii. 11 f. &c.). Cheyne's assertion that the notion of punishment is the primary one in this word is not borne out by O.T. usage.

with his stripes] lit. **weals** (see ch. i. 6).

That the people themselves had suffered for their sins is not excluded, but is apparently implied in the last words ("we are healed"), and is expressly said in other parts of the book (ch. xl. 2, xlii. 24 f. &c.). What the verse teaches is that the people could not be healed by their own suffering; it was only through the Servant's voluntary submission to the divine chastisement (*v*. 7), and his bearing it in an extraordinary degree, that an atonement was effected between Jehovah and Israel (see on ch. xl. 2).

6. Looking back on their former irreligious condition the people see that their rejection of the Servant was the natural outcome of the heedless and inconsiderate selfishness in which they were living. For the figure of the strayed sheep, cf. Ps. cxix. 176; Matt. ix. 36, x. 6; Luke xv. 4.

For *have gone...have turned*, read **had gone...had** turned.

every one to his own way] selfishly following his individual impulses and interests; cf. lvi. 11.

hath laid on him the iniquity] **made to light on** him the guilt.

7 He was oppressed, and he was afflicted,
Yet he opened not his mouth:
He is brought as a lamb to the slaughter,
And as a sheep before her shearers is dumb,
So he openeth not his mouth.
8 He was taken from prison and from judgment:

7—9. The narrative of the Servant's sufferings is in these verses brought to its conclusion: after enduring violence and injustice at the hands of men, his life was cut short and he was laid in a dishonoured grave. The passage presents many difficulties, and the details of the picture are somewhat uncertain. Thus it is doubtful whether the Servant be represented as put to death by men, or as carried off by the disease with which Jehovah had smitten him. With perhaps less reason it has been questioned whether there is any reference to human cruelty in the verses at all, whether the strong expressions "oppressed," "oppression," "judgement" are not to be understood figuratively of the hard fate which relentlessly pursued the sufferer to his death (so Duhm). These matters, however, are of subordinate interest; the prominent feature of the description is the meek and submissive demeanour of the Servant under his undeserved sufferings.

7. *He was oppressed and he was afflicted*] The first verb ("oppressed") may summarize the preceding account of the Servant's afflictions (Dillmann), but more probably it introduces a feature not previously adverted to, namely, the outrages inflicted on the Servant by his contemporaries, in consequence of their false judgement of him. It denotes harsh, cruel and arbitrary treatment, such as that of a slave-driver towards those who are under him (Ex. iii. 7; Job iii. 18), and is nowhere employed of God's action towards men. The second verb is shewn by the form of sentence to be a contrast to the first, and must therefore be rendered as in R.V.: **yet he humbled himself** (cf. Ex. x. 3, "How long dost thou refuse to *humble thyself*...?"). And as this is the main idea of the verse, the meaning may best be brought out if we translate the first two lines thus:

> Though oppressed, he was submissive
> and opened not his mouth.

Cf. Ps. xxxviii. 13, 14, xxxix. 9.

he is brought...dumb] Two relative sentences, to be rendered with R.V.

> **as a lamb** (lit. "sheep") **that is led to the** slaughter,
> **and a sheep** (lit. "ewe") **that before her shearers** is dumb.

Comp. Jer. xi. 19: "I was like a gentle lamb that is led to the slaughter."

so (R.V. "yea") *he openeth not his mouth*] in the Hebr. an exact repetition of the second line. Since the tetrastich is complete without it, the clause may possibly have been inserted through an error in transcription.

8. *He was taken from prison and from judgment*] Every word here

And who shall declare his generation?
is ambiguous. The principal interpretations are as follows: (1) "Without hindrance and without right he was taken away," i.e. he was put to death without opposition from any quarter, and in defiance of justice. The only exception that can fairly be taken to this view is the translation "hindrance," a sense of the noun for which there are no parallels. Yet the verb from which the noun is derived occurs in the sense of "detain" (1 Ki. xviii. 44, &c.), and as the noun is very uncommon, the rendering cannot be pronounced impossible. (2) "Through oppression and through judgement he was taken away" (so virtually R.V.). "Judgement" here means "judicial procedure," and the rendering "oppression" is guaranteed by Ps. cvii. 39. "Oppression and judgement" may mean (as explained by Cheyne) an oppressive judgement ("through distressful doom," see his *Introduction*, p. 428), the idea being that the Servant's death, like that of our Lord, was a judicial murder. For "taken away" in the sense of "put to death" see on ch. lii. 5, and cf. Ezek. xxxiii. 4 (where, however, a different part of the verb is used). (3) "From oppression and from judgement he was taken away," i.e. released by death, or taken by God to Himself (2 Ki. ii. 10). Here the sense of "oppression and judgement" is indeterminate; the meaning might either be simply that by death he was finally released from his troubles, or that God took him away from the malice of his persecutors. The rendering "imprisonment" instead of "oppression" could be justified from the usage of the verb (2 Ki. xvii. 4 &c.), although not of the noun itself; only in this case we must not read, "From imprisonment...he was led away (to execution)," for that is an idea which could hardly have suggested itself apart from the fulfilment of the prophecy in the crucifixion of Christ. Of the three interpretations the last seems the most natural, although everything turns on the question whether the death of the Servant is conceived as caused directly by men or by God through sickness. (See below on the last clause of this verse.)

And who shall declare his generation?] A still more difficult clause. The Hebr. word for "generation" (*dôr*) may mean (*a*) the time in which he lived, (*b*) the circle of his contemporaries, (*c*) those like-minded with him (Ps. xii. 7, xiv. 5; Prov. xxx. 11 ff.); but is never used with any such significance as "length of life," or "life-history," or "posterity." In neither of its three senses does it supply a suitable object to the verb *declare* or rather **consider** (Ps. cxliii. 5 "meditate"). We may, however, take it in the sense (*b*), and render with R.V. and **as for his generation who (among them) considered** &c. (On this construction see Davidson, *Synt.* § 72, Rem. 4). Yet the construction as direct obj. of the verb is so much the more natural that any suggestion would be acceptable which might enable us to retain it. Duhm (following Knobel) takes the word in its Aramaic sense of "dwelling-place" (see on ch. xxxviii. 12) and translates "who enquires after his dwelling-place" (with God)? It would be better, perhaps, to understand "dwelling-place" exactly as in xxxviii. 12, of the earthly dwelling-place, the place that once knew him but knows him no more: "Who enquires

> For he was cut off out of the land of the living:
> For the transgression of my people was he stricken.
> 9 ⋆ And he made his grave with the wicked,
> † And with the rich in his death;

after it, or thinks about it?" he has vanished from the thoughts of men.

for he was cut off (Ps. lxxxviii. 5; Ezek. xxxvii. 11) *out of the land of the living*] Comp. again Jer. xi. 19. The R.V. makes this clause an object sentence governed by the verb "considered" (reading *that* instead of *for*). This is perhaps necessary if the R.V. rendering of the previous line be adopted.

for the **rebellion** *of my people was he stricken* (lit. "(was) a stroke upon him")] The last word in the Hebr. (לָמוֹ) would be translated most naturally "upon them" (but see Davidson, *Gram.* § 19 R. *c.*); hence some render "because of the rebellion of my people, *the stroke (due) to them*." A far more satisfactory sense is obtained by the help of the LXX. Read לְמוּת and change the preceding noun into a passive verb (*nugga'* for *nega'*) and render **was he stricken** unto death. The expression "stricken" is from the same verb which in *v.* 4 suggested leprosy as the cause of the Servant's disfigurement; and its use here in connexion with his death is in favour of the view that he died of his sickness and not by the hands of his persecutors. If this conclusion be sound it confirms the view expressed above as to the sense of the first clause of this verse.

9. The unrelenting antipathy which the Servant experienced through life is continued even after his death, and expresses itself in the manner of his burial.

And **they** (R.V.) *made his grave with the wicked*] The subject is indefinite, the construction being equivalent to a passive: "And his grave was made" &c. "With the wicked" need not imply that a special burial-ground was set apart for them as a class, but only that such persons were buried ignominiously and away from the family sepulchre, like Absalom (2 Sam. xviii. 17). From Jer. xxvi. 23 (cf. 2 Ki. xxiii. 6) it appears that it was a disgrace to be buried among the "common people." In this case the "wicked" probably means the notoriously wicked, criminals, apostates, and such like. With these the Servant was numbered because his calamities had seemed to mark him out as a heinous sinner in the sight of God.

and with the rich in his death] This clause must express the same idea as the preceding. To take the two antithetically: "they meant his grave to be with the wicked, but he was with the rich in his death" (Delitzsch) is utterly unwarrantable. It is, no doubt, somewhat difficult to justify this sense of "rich" as synonymous with "wicked" from O.T. usage, although it might perhaps be suggested by the common identification of poverty with piety. This explanation, however, is not

v. 10.]   ISAIAH, LIII.   131

>   Because he had done no violence,
>   Neither *was any* deceit in his mouth.
>   Yet it pleased the LORD to bruise him; he hath put   10
>   *him* to grief:

quite satisfactory, and several emendations have been proposed, such as "the oppressor" (עָשׁוֹק for עָשִׁיר), "the defrauder" (עָשִׁיק, Aramaic), "evil-doers" (עֹשֵׂי רָע).

in his death] lit. "in his deaths." The use of the plural is variously explained. Some find in it an intimation of the collective character of the subject spoken of under the name of the Servant; but even if the Servant be a collective idea, it is inconceivable that the writer should have here abandoned the personification which he has so strictly maintained throughout. Nor is it any relief to say that it means "in his state of death." It is better to read the singular with the LXX. There is, however, another reading found in a few MSS. and adopted by many commentators, according to which the clause would form a perfect parallelism with the first line:

"And with the rich (or oppressor, &c.) *his sepulchral mound*."
But the word *bāmāh* (=high-place) is not elsewhere used in this sense.

because he had done no violence &c.] Render with R.V. **although** ("in spite of the fact that") &c. as in Job xvi. 17. With this assertion of his innocence the narrative of the Servant's career reaches its conclusion. While absolute sinlessness is not explicitly predicated of him, but only freedom from "violence" and "deceit," yet the image of the lamb led to the slaughter, and his patient resignation to the will of God, strongly suggest that the prophet had in his mind the conception of a perfectly sinless character.

10—12. These difficult verses describe, partly in the prophet's own words and partly in those of Jehovah, the Divine purpose which is realised through the sufferings of the Servant. In *vv.* 10, 11 it is impossible to trace a clear connexion of ideas; the grammar also is peculiar, and in all probability there is considerable textual disorder. The main thought, however, is that the Servant is to be the instrument in establishing the true religion, by removing the burden of guilt and bringing many to righteousness. As the reward of his sufferings he will enjoy a brilliant future and have a numerous spiritual offspring. He will become a great power in the world, attaining a position like that of a mighty conqueror. The idea of a resurrection from the dead appears to be necessarily implied. If the Servant be a personification of Israel, this is merely a figure for national restoration from exile; but if he be an individual, then his resurrection must be accepted as a literal fact, just as his death must be literally understood.

10. *Yet it pleased...grief*] The sentence must be a restatement of the fact that the Servant has suffered by the will of Jehovah, this being repeated in order to introduce the explanation of Jehovah's purpose in imposing chastisement upon him. The second clause, *he hath put him to grief*, represents a single Hebrew word, which is

When thou shalt make his soul an offering for sin,
He shall see *his* seed, he shall prolong *his* days,
And the pleasure of the LORD shall prosper in his hand.

11 He shall see of the travail of his soul, *and* shall be satisfied :

vocalised and translated by the LXX. as the noun for "sickness" (*v.* 3). The meaning intended by the punctuators is probably "he hath made him sick" (R.V. marg.), although the form is anomalous and the syntax uncertain. Since it is too short to form an independent line, it must be closely attached to what precedes: hence the rendering of Dillmann and others, "It pleased Jehovah to crush him incurably," i.e. grievously (cf. Mic. vi. 13; Nah. iii. 19). This is perhaps the best that can be made of the received reading, but it is most probable that the textual derangement which prevails in these verses begins here.

when thou shalt make his soul an offering for sin] Rather "if (or when) his soul should present a guilt-offering." The difficulty here does not lie in the analogy of the guilt-offering, for this probably signifies nothing more than has been already expressed in plain words, that the Servant's death is the means of removing guilt (*vv.* 4, 5, 6). It does not appear that the distinctive ritual and function of the guilt-offering ('*āshām*, see Lev. v. 14 ff., &c.) throws any light on this passage. The chief difficulty is the hypothetical character of the sentence, of which no satisfactory explanation has been given. No doubt the atoning effect of the sufferings is the condition of Jehovah's great purpose being attained, but the condition has been already fulfilled, whereas it is here spoken of as an event which is, if not problematic, at least future.—The subject is ambiguous, but on every ground it is better to suppose that "his soul" is subject than that Jehovah is addressed. Ewald and Cheyne, however, prefer to read (with the change of a consonant) "when he shall make his soul a guilt-offering."

he shall see a seed (cf. Gen. l. 23) *he shall prolong* his *days*] i.e. shall enjoy long life. His "seed" are the true spiritual Israel of the future, those who by his means are converted to the knowledge of Jehovah.

the pleasure (i.e. **the purpose**, see on xliv. 28) *of the* LORD] the establishment of the universal religion, the eternal salvation. The verse returns on itself by repetition of the opening idea (as *vv.* 3, 6, 7)— "palindromically," as Delitzsch would say.

11. An amplification of the meaning of *v.* 10.   *He shall see &c.*] Lit. **Of the travail of his soul he shall see, shall be** satisfied. It is doubtful if the preposition "of" can express *result*, as the E.V. suggests, or can introduce the object of the verb "he shall see." It may be used in its local sense ("away from," or "free from") or causally ("in consequence of"), hardly in a temporal sense ("after"). The asyndetic construction of the two verbs probably indicates that one is to be subordinated to the other: **he shall see with** satisfaction, sc. the cause of Jehovah prospering in his hand (as *v.* 10). The LXX. deserves

By his knowledge shall my righteous servant justify
 many;
For he shall bear their iniquities.
Therefore will I divide him *a portion* with the great,   12
And he shall divide the spoil with the strong;
Because he hath poured out his soul unto death:
And he was numbered with the transgressors;

attention: "And it pleased the Lord to deliver (a variant reading of the last clause of *v.* 10) (him) from the trouble of his soul: to cause him to see light" &c.

by his knowledge] The gen. is not that of the obj. ("by the knowledge of him") but of the subj.; the knowledge of God and salvation which he possesses, and which he communicates to others. The reference is to the prophetic activity of the Servant (see xlii. 1 ff., xlix. 2, l. 4 f.) which had seemed to be cut short by his death, but will be resumed and crowned with success in his exalted state.

shall my righteous servant justify many] Rather: **shall a righteous one, my servant, make the many righteous**; but the Hebr. is very peculiar. The ordinary sense of the word for "justify" ("declare righteous") is here unsuitable, and the only other passage where it bears the ethical sense of "making righteous" is probably based on this verse (Dan. xii. 3, "they that turn the many to righteousness"). The *many* contains a reference to lii. 14 f. The clause would read more smoothly if we could suppose that the word rendered "a righteous one" has arisen through dittography; but the source of the difficulty probably lies deeper.

he shall bear their iniquities] Cf. *v.* 4.

12. As the reward of his unmerited sufferings and his mediatorial work, the Servant shall attain an influence equal to that of the great potentates of the world. To "divide spoil" is a figurative and proverbial expression for victory or success; Prov. xvi. 19 ("It is better to be of lowly spirit with the meek than to divide spoil with the proud"). It is therefore not necessarily implied that the Servant's future greatness will be political, although that is certainly suggested.

Instead of *will I divide*, the LXX. reads "he shall inherit" (which is perhaps preferable as avoiding the recurrence of the same verb in two consecutive lines), but it is a mistake of some authorities to follow this version in treating the "many" as direct obj. of the verb; the sense must be either "he shall inherit," or "I will give him a share" **amongst the many**.

The latter part of the verse returns to the great contrast that runs through the passage, between the true meaning of the Servant's afflictions and the false construction put on them.

because he poured out (omit "hath" with R.V.) *his soul*] his blood, which is the seat of life; Lev. xvii. 11. For the expression cf. Ps. cxli. 8.

was numbered with the **rebels**] See *v.* 9. Cited Mark xv. 28; Luke xxii. 37.

And he bare the sin of many,
And made intercession for the transgressors.

and he bare &c.] **whereas he bare**, the true view of his death as opposed to the false judgement of men,—a circumstantial clause.

for the transgressors] **for the rebellious**, the class to which he was himself reckoned.

Although several things in this marvellous description of the innocent suffering for the guilty be obscure, the salient features of the picture stand out with great clearness. Whether the portrait be that of an individual or of a personified community is a question that need not here be discussed (see Appendix, Note I.). If there be personification it is as consistently maintained as it is vividly conceived, and we are hardly entitled to assume that the writer has anywhere allowed the collective reality to peer through the veil of allegory. The figure brought on the scene is that of a man, so marred and deformed by revolting sickness as to be universally shunned and despised and maltreated as one bearing the manifest tokens of the divine displeasure; yet the dignity and patience of his demeanour profoundly impresses his contemporaries, so that after his death their thoughts are irresistibly drawn back to the tragedy of his fate, and they come to the conviction that he was indeed what he professed to be, the Servant of Jehovah, that he was the one innocent person in his generation, and that his sufferings were due not to his personal guilt, but to the guilt of a whole nation, which is by them atoned for and taken away. And finally it is prophesied concerning him that he shall rise again, to the astonishment of the whole world, and that his career shall be crowned with success even more conspicuous than his humiliation had been.—It has already been pointed out that this conception of the Servant has certain affinities with the figure of Job, and it may be partly moulded on the story of that patriarch's trial. But the religious teaching of this passage moves on a different plane from that of the Book of Job. The problem of individual retribution, of how it can be that the righteous suffer, does not seem to have been present to the mind of the writer, although he no doubt furnishes an important contribution to the solution of that mystery. This is found in the idea of vicarious suffering, which is so emphatically expressed throughout the passage. Now the principle that the individual bears the guilt of the community to which he belongs was perfectly familiar to the ancient world, and many startling applications of it occur in the O.T. (Josh. vii. 24; 2 Sam. xxi. 6 &c.). It is true that it had begun to excite protest towards the time of the Exile (Deut. xxiv. 16; 2 Ki. xiv. 6; Jer. xxxi. 29; Ez. xviii. 20); but this prophet accepts the principle and discerns in it a moral significance by which it is deprived of the appearance of arbitrariness or injustice. The essence of the Servant's sacrifice lies in the fact that whilst himself innocent he acquiesces in the divine judgement on sin, and willingly endures it for the sake of his people. And it is the perception of this truth on the part of the people that brings home to them the sense of their own guilt, and removes the obstacle which their impenitence had interposed to Jehovah's

Sing, O barren, thou *that* didst not bear;   54
Break forth *into* singing, and cry aloud, thou
that didst not travail with child:

purpose of salvation. The suffering of the innocent on behalf of the guilty is thus seen to be a moral necessity, since it was only through such sufferings as the sinless Servant of the Lord was alone capable of, that punishment could reach its end in the taking away of sin and the bringing in of everlasting righteousness.

CH. LIV. THE FUTURE FELICITY OF ZION, REUNITED TO JEHOVAH IN AN EVERLASTING COVENANT.

The chapter continues the series of oracles of consolation which commences at xlix. 14, and is broken by the two passages on the Servant of the Lord in l. 4—11 and lii. 13—liii. 12. The direct influence of the latter passage on ch. liv. is less obvious than might have been expected from the singularly profound conceptions there unfolded of the work of Jehovah's Servant. The points of contact adduced by some commentators are few and unessential, and they fall into insignificance by the side of the fact that "it cannot be shown that any of the characteristic ideas of ch. liii. are clearly referred to in ch. liv." (Cheyne.) Yet the supposition that this chapter was originally the sequel to lii. 12 and that the intervening prophecy was inserted by an afterthought is neither necessary nor altogether natural. The summons to depart from Babylon (lii. 11, 12) marks a pause in the development of the prophet's thought, and (just as after the similar apostrophe in xlviii. 20—22) a fresh point of departure is found in the idea of the Servant of the Lord. Moreover, although it may not be possible to trace the direct dependence of ch. liv. on ch. liii., we may nevertheless suppose a real connexion between the two in the prophet's mind. The two chapters deal with the same subject from two distinct standpoints. Whatever view be held as to the Servant's personality, there is no doubt that his exaltation implies the restoration of Israel, and that his work is the indispensable condition of that restoration being accomplished. Thus while ch. liii. describes the inward process of conversion by which the nation is made righteous, ch. liv. describes the outward deliverance which is the result; and the impression is probably correct that the glowing hopes here uttered are sustained in the last resort by the contemplation of the Servant's mission as described in ch. liii.

The chapter consists of two sections:—
i. *vv.* 1—10. (1) Zion, addressed as a barren and desolate woman, is comforted with the assurance that her children are more numerous than those she formerly had as the "married wife" of Jehovah. She is bidden to extend her tent so as to receive them, for they shall spread abroad on every side, peopling the deserted cities and taking possession of the territory of the Gentiles (*vv.* 1—3). (2) The shame of her youth and the reproach of widowhood are wiped out by her reconciliation to Jehovah, her Husband and her Maker (*vv.* 4—6). (3) It will be seen

For more *are* the children of the desolate than the children of the married wife, saith the LORD.

2 Enlarge the place of thy tent,
And let them stretch forth the curtains of thine habitations:
Spare not, lengthen thy cords, and strengthen thy stakes;

3 For thou shalt break forth *on* the right hand and *on* the left;
And thy seed shall inherit the Gentiles,
And make the desolate cities to be inhabited.

4 Fear not; for thou shalt not be ashamed:

that her rejection was but a brief withdrawal of Jehovah's favour for her; her restoration now is final, resting on a covenant as unchangeable as the oath to Noah, or the everlasting mountains (*vv*. 7—10).

ii. *vv*. 11—17. Jerusalem shall be rebuilt in lavish magnificence (*vv*. 11, 12); her citizens, being all disciples of Jehovah, shall enjoy perfect peace, undisturbed by the thought of oppression (13,); her enemies shall be confounded, and no weapon forged against shall prosper (15—17).

1—3. The ideal Zion is called upon to rejoice in the multitude of her children. As in ch. xlix. 21, the children are conceived as already born, and waiting to be acknowledged by their mother.

more are the children of the desolate (2 Sam. xiii. 20) *&c.*] The contrast is not between Zion and other cities, but between Zion's present and her past: even now in her widowhood and barrenness she has more children than she had before her separation from her Husband.

the married wife] Cf. ch. lxii. 4; Gen. xx. 3; Deut. xxii. 22. The image of the verse is applied by St Paul to the contrast between the spiritual and the earthly Jerusalem; i.e. the church of Christ and the Jewish community (Gal. iv. 27).

2. The idea of the verse is expressed in xlix. 20, 21; for the figure of the tent (in an opposite sense) cf. Jer. x. 20.

The *curtains* are the tent-hangings (Jer. xlix. 29; Hab. iii. 7), the *stakes*, the tent-pegs (ch. xxxiii. 20).

The words *spare not* should, according to the accents, be joined to the preceding clause.

3. The tent must be larger than of old, for the new community shall **spread abroad** (cf. Gen. xxviii. 14, xxx. 30, 43) on *the right hand and* on *the left*, i.e. in all directions.

inherit the Gentiles] **take possession of nations** (cf. Gen. xxii. 17, xxiv. 60). The reference is not to be limited to the heathen who had occupied the soil of Palestine; although the *desolate cities* in the parallel clause are no doubt primarily those of the holy land.

4—6. Zion shall forget her former shame in the joy of reconciliation to her God.

Neither be thou confounded; for thou shalt not be put
  to shame:
For thou shalt forget the shame of thy youth,
And shalt not remember the reproach of thy widowhood
  any more.
For thy Maker *is* thine husband; 5
The LORD of hosts *is* his name;
And thy redeemer the Holy One of Israel;
The God of the whole earth shall he be called.
For the LORD hath called thee as a woman forsaken and 6
  grieved in spirit,
And a wife of youth, when thou wast refused, saith thy
  God.

4. *the reproach of thy widowhood* clearly refers to the period of the Exile when Zion regarded herself as cast off by Jehovah. The sense of *the shame of thy youth* is less obvious. Since the conception has some affinity with the striking allegory in Ezek. xvi. it is probable that the reference goes back to the origin of the nation (cf. Ezek. xvi. 4—8); the reference being to the Egyptian oppression.

5. *thy Maker* is *thine husband*] Rather, **thy husband is thy Maker**: He who has entered into this closest and tenderest of relations is none other than He who made thee. "Husband" in the original is a partic.; lit. "he who marries thee"; and both nouns are in the plural after the analogy of words like *ădōnîm* (= lord, the so-called plural of majesty).

thy redeemer] See on xli. 14.

shall he be called] Perhaps, **is he called**, parallel to "is his name." The ground of comfort lies in the thought that He who acknowledges Zion as His wife is the God of the whole earth, the ruler of all the forces of the universe.

6. Although Zion is temporarily estranged from Jehovah, she is yet a "wife of youth" holding a permanent place in her husband's affections.

For the LORD hath called thee] i.e. "calls thee" now (Cheyne, "hath recalled thee"). The reference is not to the first espousals of the nation at the exodus, but to the renewal of conjugal intercourse in the restoration from exile.

as **a wife** (R.V.) *forsaken and grieved in spirit*] neglected by her husband, and left to her own bitter reflexions, but not cast off. Cf. Hos. iii. 3.

and a wife of youth, when thou wast refused] R.V. "even a wife of youth, when she is cast off." The clause is difficult. Probably it is an exclamation: **and a wife of youth—can she be rejected?** (so Cheyne, after Ewald); it is impossible that she should be finally disowned.

a wife of youth] one who has been wooed and won in youth; Prov. v. 18; Mal. ii. 14 f.

7 For a small moment have I forsaken thee;
But with great mercies will I gather thee.
8 In a little wrath I hid my face from thee for a moment;
But with everlasting kindness will I have mercy on thee,
Saith the LORD thy redeemer.
9 For this *is as* the waters of Noah unto me:
For *as* I have sworn that the waters of Noah should no more go over the earth;
So have I sworn that *I* would not be wroth with thee, nor rebuke thee.
10 For the mountains shall depart,
And the hills be removed;
But my kindness shall not depart from thee,
Neither shall the covenant of my peace be removed,
Saith the LORD that hath mercy on thee.
11 O thou afflicted, tossed with tempest, *and* not comforted,

7, 8. Jehovah's anger was but a momentary interruption of His kindness to Israel; His mercy is everlasting. Comp. Ps. xxx. 5.
will I gather thee] can hardly mean "draw thee to myself"; it denotes the gathering together of the scattered children of Zion.

8. *In a little wrath*] **In an outbreak of wrath** (Heb. *shéçeph qéçeph*). The word *shéçeph* is probably another form (chosen for the sake of assonance) of *shéṭeph* which occurs in Prov. xxvii. 4.

9, 10. The permanence of the new covenant relation is illustrated first by the promise made to Noah, of which the rainbow is the perpetual token, and then by the steadfastness of the unchanging hills.
For this is as *the waters of Noah unto me*] Or, according to the reading of several MSS. and the ancient versions (though not the LXX.), **As the days of Noah is this** (i.e. the present juncture) **to me** (see R.V. marg.). The difference of reading is very slight, consisting merely in the conjunction of two words which the received text separates (כימי for כי מי). The second alternative is better.
for as *I have sworn &c.*] **as I have sworn** &c. (omitting "for"). Comp. Gen. viii. 21 f., ix. 11—17. The absence of any mention of an oath in the narrative is immaterial.

10. Comp. Ps. xlvi. 2 f.; Hab. iii. 6.
The first sentence may be rendered concessively: **Though the mountains should remove and the hills be shaken, yet** &c.
my *covenant of peace*] (R.V.) Ezek. xxxiv. 25, xxxvii. 26; Mal. ii. 5.
that hath **compassion**] as xlix. 10.

11, 12. The outward splendour of the new Jerusalem described in highly figurative language; comp. Tob. xiii. 16, 17; Rev. xxi. 18—21.

Behold, I will lay thy stones with fair colours,
And lay thy foundations with sapphires.
And I will make thy windows *of* agates,   12
And thy gates of carbuncles,
And all thy borders of pleasant stones.
And all thy children *shall be* taught of the LORD;   13
And great *shall be* the peace of thy children.
In righteousness shalt thou be established: 14
Thou shalt be far from oppression; for thou shalt not
    fear:

I will lay thy stones with fair colours] lit. **in antimony** (R.V. marg.). Antimony (*pûkh*) was used by Oriental females as an eye-powder to blacken the edges of the eyelids and enhance the lustre of the eyes (2 Ki. ix. 30; Jer. iv. 30; comp. the name of Job's third daughter, Keren-hap-pukh, 'horn of eye-powder,' Job xlii. 14. See further Lane, *Manners and Customs*, &c. ed. 1890, pp. 29 ff.). In the figure the antimony would represent the costly mortar used to set off the brilliancy of the still more costly stones. The ἄνθραξ of the LXX. seems to stand for נֶפֶךְ (instead of פּוּךְ), a kind of precious stone; see Ex. xxviii. 18 &c. In 1 Chron. xxix. 2, where we read of "stones of *pûkh*" (R.V. "stones for inlaid work") prepared for the Temple, the idea must be different; but whether that passage has any connexion with the present image is doubtful.

I will lay thy foundations (lit. "I will found thee") *with sapphires*] Ex. xxiv. 10; Ezek. i. 26.

12. *thy windows*] Rather as R.V. **pinnacles**. The word is derived from that for "sun," and appears to denote those parts of the building which glitter in the sun's rays. (Comp. the Arab. "minaret," used primarily of a lantern or a lighthouse.)

agates] (Ezek. xxvii. 16) "sparkling" stone, perhaps **rubies** (so R.V.).

carbuncles] (only here) "fiery" stones; although the LXX. renders "stones of crystal."

all thy borders] R.V. **border**, perhaps the outer wall (the περίτειχος, see on ch. xxvi. 1).

13, 14. The righteousness, peace and security of the inhabitants.

taught of the LORD] lit. **disciples of Jehovah**, initiated in the true knowledge of God, and obedient to His will. Cf. Jer. xxxi. 34; John vi. 45. The expression is probably suggested by what the Servant of Jehovah says of himself in ch. l. 4; the idea being that the citizens of the new Jerusalem shall be the spiritual seed of the servant.

14. *In righteousness shalt thou be established*] (lit. **shalt thou establish thyself**) cf. Prov. xxiv. 3. "Righteousness" may describe the character of the citizens, but more probably it means that the position of the commonwealth is unassailable because based on *right* —on conformity to the divine order (see *v*. 17).

thou shalt be far from oppression] lit. **be thou far** from oppression

And from terror; for it shall not come near thee.
15 Behold, they shall surely gather together, *but* not by me:
Whosoever shall gather together against thee shall fall for thy sake.
16 Behold, I have created the smith
That bloweth the coals in the fire,
And that bringeth forth an instrument for his work;
And I have created the waster to destroy.
17 No weapon *that* is formed against thee shall prosper;
And every tongue *that* shall rise against thee in judgment thou shalt condemn.

(R.V. marg.), i.e. let it be far from thy thoughts. Here it is obvious from the context that "oppression" is not wrong perpetrated within the city, but external oppression which might be inflicted by its enemies.

thou shalt not fear] i.e. hast no cause to fear.

terror] or **destruction**.

15. The verse is somewhat difficult. The rendering "gather together" can hardly be defended, and moreover it does not suit the construction ("against," in the second line, is really "with"). The verb is perhaps best explained as a by-form of a root meaning to "stir up" (strife) or pick a quarrel (Prov. xv. 18). The sense would be: **If (any) should stir up strife (it is) not of me; whosoever stirs up strife with thee shall fall**, &c. (See R.V. and marg.)

fall **because of thee**] or perhaps "fall upon thee" to his own ruin (cf. ch. viii. 14 f.). R.V. marg. suggests "fall away to thee," i.e. go over to thy side, which is the sense given by some of the ancient versions. The phrase has this meaning in Jer. xxi. 9, xxxvii. 14 ("fall away to the Chaldæans"), but it is little appropriate in this verse.

16, 17. No weapon formed against Zion shall prosper, because both the makers of weapons and those who use them are alike created by Jehovah, and all their activity is under His control.

the smith that bloweth **the fire of coals** (R.V.)] Cf. ch. xliv. 12.

an instrument for his work] rather **for its work**, or perhaps "according to its work," adapted to the particular work for which it is intended,—a scythe for reaping, a sword for slaughter, and so on. The smith will turn out anything, amongst other things deadly weapons, but all by the permission of Jehovah who has made *him*.

the waster to destroy] Not "to destroy the weapon that the smith has made"; the "waster" is the one for whose use the weapon is made; he also is the creature of Jehovah.

17. Israel therefore has no cause to fear any material weapon, and even the Satanic weapon of false accusations, which assail her righteous standing before God, she shall be able to foil.

every tongue...thou shalt condemn] i.e. shew to be in the wrong (cf. ch. l. 8 f.).

This *is* the heritage of the servants of the LORD,
And their righteousness *is* of me, saith the LORD.

This is *the heritage &c.*] A concluding summary. "This," viz., all the blessings just enumerated, peace, righteousness, security, triumph over opposition.

of the servants of the LORD] The title "servants of Jehovah" (in the plural) has not hitherto been used in the prophecy (with the doubtful exception of ch. xliv. 26, where it denotes the prophets). It is possible that its occurrence here forms a link of connexion between this chapter and the last. The ideal represented by *the* Servant of Jehovah is now reproduced in each individual member of the new Israel; they are all of the spiritual seed which was promised to him, and the salvation they enjoy is the fruit of the travail of his soul (liii. 10, 11). It is noteworthy, at all events, that while from this point the Israelites are spoken of as servants of Jehovah, the ideal Servant is never again mentioned.

and their righteousness is *of me*] Rather, **and** (this is) **their righteousness from me.** The righteousness, or justification, bestowed on them by Jehovah (cf. Ps. xxiv. 5) is manifested in such blessedness as has just been spoken of.

CH. LV. A CALL TO INDIVIDUALS TO EMBRACE THE COMING SALVATION.

(i) *vv.* 1—5. A gracious invitation to the blessings of the new Covenant.

(1) Salvation freely offered to the thirsty. Addressing those who are engaged in the pursuit of earthly good, the prophet, in the name of Jehovah, promises them the complete satisfaction of their wants by accepting a share in the kingdom of God (*vv.* 1, 2).

(2) On the condition of obedience Jehovah will make an everlasting Covenant with them, incorporating them in the Messianic community, in which the promises made to the house of David shall be realised (*vv.* 3—5).

(ii) *vv.* 6—13. This kingdom is at hand.

(1) The summons (*vv.* 1 ff.) is urgent, for Jehovah is near; now is the day of grace when He may be sought and found, and when even the wicked may obtain pardon through repentance (*vv.* 6, 7).

(2) Jehovah is in truth near, although His thoughts and purposes are too exalted to be apprehended by the narrow and earth-bound vision of selfish men (*vv.* 8, 9).

(3) Already the word has gone forth which is to renew the world and bring in the eternal redemption; it shall no more return empty than the rain and the snow return to heaven without having fertilized the earth (*vv.* 10, 11).

(4) The prophet here reverts to an image frequent in the earlier discourses. The great deliverance is on the eve of being accomplished; the exiles shall go out (from Babylon) with joy, and the noble trees

> 55 'Ho, every one that thirsteth, come ye to the waters,
> And he that hath no money;
> Come ye, buy, and eat;
> Yea, come, buy wine and milk without money and without price.

which spring up along their desert journey shall remain as an everlasting memorial of Jehovah's power (*vv.* 12, 13).

1, 2. The invitation. The message of the Gospel—its freeness, its appeal to the individual, its answer to the cravings of the heart—is nowhere in the O.T. more clearly foreshadowed than in this truly evangelical passage (cf. John iv. 10 ff., vi. 35 ff., vii. 37 f.; Rev. xxi. 6, xxii. 17; also Prov. ix. 1 ff.; Ecclus. xv. 3). The promises are of course not to be materialised, as if water, bread, wine, milk were meant literally, or merely as symbols of comfortable earthly existence in Palestine. At the same time when we seek to recover the original historical sense of the words, there is a possibility of spiritualising overmuch. The images used do, indeed, typify the blessings of salvation; but salvation itself in the O.T. is never without a national and therefore earthly element. Those here addressed are exiles (see *v.* 12), many of whom had doubtless carried out only too thoroughly the injunction of Jeremiah to "build houses and dwell in them; to plant gardens and eat the fruit of them; to take wives &c." in Babylon (Jer. xxix. 6). They were in danger of losing their nationality, and with it their religion and their own souls through devotion to selfish and material aims. This is the fate against which the prophet warns them in *v.* 2; and the salvation he offers is a personal interest in the new covenant, or membership in the kingdom of God. To this they are freely invited, with the assurance that there they shall find the satisfaction and blessedness that a life of worldliness can never yield.

1. *every one that thirsteth*] in a figurative sense, primarily of the weariness and discontent of exile (cf. xli. 17, xliv. 3), but also of conscious need in general.

come (lit. "go" and so throughout) *ye to the waters*] The image is probably connected with xli. 18, the miraculous fountain opened by Jehovah for the relief of His people ("wells of salvation," ch. xii. 3). A reference to the cry of the water-sellers in the streets of an Oriental city is less natural.

and he that hath no money] In the East access to a well has often to be paid for. According to the Heb. accents this clause should be joined to the preceding,—"even he that hath no money"—in apposition with "thirsty." The word for *buy* is connected with a noun meaning "grain" and is only used of buying corn. It should probably be so understood in both cases here, although in the second its government extends over two similar objects. The last clause must then be rendered, **buy corn without money, and without price wine and milk.**

2. Whilst the religious life is a receiving without spending, the worldly life is a continual spending without lasting profit or satisfaction.

Wherefore do ye spend money for *that which is* not bread?
And your labour for *that which* satisfieth not?
Hearken diligently unto me, and eat ye *that which is* good,
And let your soul delight itself in fatness.
Incline your ear, and come unto me:
Hear, and your soul shall live;
And I will make an everlasting covenant with you,
Even the sure mercies of David.

spend money] lit. "weigh silver." *your labour*] your **earnings** (as ch. xlv. 14).

hearken diligently &c.] Or, **if ye but hearken to me ye shall eat good**, and your soul shall &c. (See Davidson's *Syntax*, § 86 *c*; and § 132 *b*).

delight itself (ch. lviii. 14, lxvi. 11) *in fatness*] the choicest and most nourishing food (cf. ch. xxv. 6).

3—5. The offer of *vv.* 1, 2 is summed up in the promise of an everlasting covenant. See ch. xlii. 6, xlix. 8; and cf. lxi. 8; Jer. xxxii. 40, xxxi. 31—33.

Incline your ear &c.] The condition imposed is simply the consent and submission of the heart to the divine will.

an everlasting covenant...the sure mercies of David] i.e. the mercies (lovingkindnesses) irrevocably promised to David and his house. Comp. the "Last Words of David," 2 Sam. xxiii. 5 ("an everlasting covenant ordered in all things and secured"), Ps. xviii. 50 ("shewing lovingkindness...to David and to his seed for ever"), lxxxix. 28 ("for ever will I keep my lovingkindness to him, and my covenant is sure to him"), and *v.* 49; and the great promise to which all these passages point, 2 Sam. vii. 8—16. The comparison of the everlasting covenant to these Davidic "mercies" cannot mean simply that the one is as sure as the other. It is identity rather than comparison that is implied, the idea being that the contents of the covenant are the same as the mercies promised to David, and that it will be the fulfilment of the hopes that clustered round the Davidic dynasty. But an intricate question arises with respect to the sense in which this fulfilment is to be understood in the next two verses.

4, 5. (*a*) Most modern authorities hold that the person spoken of in *v.* 4 is the historical David, and that *vv.* 4 and 5 institute a parallel between the position he occupied in the heathen world of his time and that which Israel shall occupy in the future; the thought expressed, therefore, is that the Messianic hope is transferred from the dynasty to the nation. The view is thus succinctly stated by Driver; "as David became ruler of subject nations (2 Sam. viii.), a knowledge of his religion, however imperfect, spread among them; thus he was a 'witness' to them. This position of David is idealised in Ps. xviii. 43

4 Behold, I have given him *for* a witness to the people,
A leader and commander to the people.

('Thou makest me a *head of nations*; a people *whom I have not known shall serve me*'); and the position, as thus idealised, is here enlarged, and extended in a *spiritual* sense to Israel (v. 5)." (*Isaiah*², p. 156.) (*b*) Others think that the reference in v. 4 is to the future Messianic king (who is called David in Jer. xxx. 9; Ezek. xxxiv. 23 f.), so that the two verses represent under two aspects the future greatness of Israel. (*c*) An intermediate position is taken by some, viz., that v. 4 goes back to the promise made to David, but regards it as one destined to be fulfilled in the person of his son the Messiah. It is very difficult to decide between these conflicting explanations. Against (*b*) and (*c*) it is urged (1) that the tenses in v. 4 are perfects and are naturally understood of the historic past, since those of v. 5 are futures. (2) The idea of a personal Messiah appears nowhere else in the prophecy. (3) A further objection, which however savours of fastidiousness, is that the Messiah is never named David *absolutely*, even in Jer. xxx. and Ezek. xxxiv. On the other side it may be said, (1) that the distinction of tense is accounted for by the fact that v. 4 speaks of what is really past (viz. Jehovah's decree concerning the Messiah), whereas v. 5 refers to a consequence still to be manifested. (2) Although the idea of the Messiah is not found elsewhere in the book, there is nothing in the prophet's conceptions inconsistent with it; where he thinks of Israel as a restored nation he will naturally think of it as represented by a Davidic king. (3) Neither in the fundamental passage (2 Sam. vii.) nor in any of those which point back to it (2 Sam. xxiii.; Ps. xviii., lxxxix.) is anything said of David being a "witness" to the true religion; and it could hardly occur to anyone to think of him as in the *first* instance a witness and in the *second* a prince. The third view (*c*) seems on the whole the best; the original covenant guarantees an endless dominion to the family of David, and after the restoration this will assume a spiritual character and expand into universal empire in the reign of the Messiah. This interpretation, however, is complicated by the further question as to the relation of the Messiah to the Servant of the Lord. If the Servant be the ideal Israel there is of course no difficulty; the two conceptions stand side by side and are independent. But if he be an individual, he is almost necessarily to be identified with the ideal king, although features are thus introduced into the portrait of the Messiah of which hardly a trace is found in the subsequent literature, until the conception of Messiahship through suffering and death was realised in Christ.

4. *Behold, I have given him*] Better, **I have appointed him**; or, if we adopt the view (*a*) above, "I set him" (aorist).

for *a witness*] of Jehovah's power and faithfulness (cf. xliii. 10, xliv. 8).

to the people] **peoples** (as R.V.).

a leader] The word *nāgîd* (ruler or prince) is used in 2 Sam. vii. 8 of David's kingship over Israel.

Behold, thou shalt call a nation *that* thou knowest not, 5
And nations *that* knew not thee shall run unto thee
Because of the LORD thy God,
And for the Holy One of Israel; for he hath glorified thee.

Seek ye the LORD while he may be found, 6
Call ye upon him while he is near:
Let the wicked forsake his way, 7
And the unrighteous man his thoughts:
And let him return unto the LORD, and he will have mercy upon him;
And to our God, for he will abundantly pardon.
For my thoughts *are* not your thoughts, 8
Neither *are* your ways my ways, saith the LORD.
For *as* the heavens are higher than the earth, 9
So are my ways higher than your ways,
And my thoughts than your thoughts.
For as the rain cometh down, 10

5. *thou* (Israel) *shalt call a nation &c.*] i.e. many a nation (see on ch. xxv. 3) hitherto unknown to thee.

because of the LORD &c.] Cf. ch. xlix. 7.

glorified thee] Cf. xliv. 23, xlix. 3.

6, 7. The call to repentance, because of the nearness of the kingdom of God.

while he may be found...while he is near] in the "acceptable time" the "day of salvation" (ch. xlix. 8). Comp. further Jer. xxix. 12—14.

7. *the unrighteous man*] lit., "the man of evil" or falsehood.

8, 9. Jehovah's thoughts transcend those of man as much as the heaven is higher than the earth. The point of the contrast is not the moral quality of the Divine thoughts as opposed to those of the "wicked"; the thoughts and ways of Jehovah are His purposes of redemption, which are too vast and sublime to be measured by the narrow conceptions of despairing minds (xl. 27 f.). Comp. Jer. xxix. 11 ("I know the thoughts that I entertain towards you, thoughts of peace and not of evil, to give you a future and a hope"), Mic. iv. 12. The verses, therefore, furnish a motive not merely for repentance but also for eager and expectant hope.

10, 11. This purpose of salvation is embodied in the word which goes forth from Jehovah's mouth. The "word" is conceived as endowed with a self-fulfilling energy (see on ch. ix. 8); and its silent but irresistible efficacy is set forth by a beautiful comparison from nature. The same idea was expressed in ch. xl. 8.

as the rain cometh down &c.] The image is suggested by "the heavens" in *v.* 9.

>   And the snow from heaven,
>   And returneth not thither,
>   But watereth the earth,
>   And maketh it bring forth and bud,
>   That it may give seed to the sower, and bread to the eater:
> 11 So shall my word be that goeth forth out of my mouth:
>   It shall not return unto me void,
>   But it shall accomplish that which I please,
>   And it shall prosper *in the thing* whereto I sent it.
> 12 For ye shall go out with joy,
>   And be led forth with peace:
>   The mountains and the hills shall break forth before you *into* singing,
>   And all the trees of the field shall clap *their* hands.
> 13 Instead of the thorn shall come up the fir tree,
>   And instead of the brier shall come up the myrtle tree:
>   And it shall be to the LORD for a name,
>   For an everlasting sign *that* shall not be cut off.

> 56 Thus saith the LORD,
>   Keep ye judgment, and do justice:
>   For my salvation *is* near to come,

but watereth] Rather, **without having watered** &c.
seed to the sower and bread to the eater] Cf. 2 Cor. ix. 10.
11. *return...void*] **empty**, having achieved nothing, as 2 Sam. i. 21.
but it shall accomplish] **without having** accomplished, as in *v.* 10.
12, 13. The joyful exodus from Babylon; this is the "thing whereto Jehovah has sent" His word.
and be led forth] by Jehovah in person, ch. xl. 10, lii. 12. Cf. Mic. ii. 13.
shall clap their *hands*] Ps. xcviii. 8; Ezek. xxv. 6.
13. The word for *thorn* occurs again only in ch. vii. 19. That for *brier* (*sirpād*) is unknown. LXX. renders κόνυζα (fleabane). All that can be said is that some desert plant is meant. On *fir-tree* (**cypress**) and *myrtle tree*, see on ch. xli. 19.
for a name...for a sign] i.e. a memorial to His praise. The meaning appears to be that the marvellous vegetation so often alluded to as springing up in the desert as the procession of the redeemed passes through, shall remain throughout the future ages as a monument to Jehovah. It shews at least (Dillmann, etc.) that the conception is not to be regarded as a mere poetical figure.

And my righteousness to be revealed.
Blessed *is* the man *that* doeth this, 2

CH. LVI. 1—8. REMOVAL OF THE RELIGIOUS DISABILITIES OF EUNUCHS AND PROSELYTES.

(1) The passage opens with a general exhortation to righteous conduct and a correct religious attitude, to be manifested by a strict regard for the sanctity of the Sabbath (*vv.* 1, 2). (2) The main subject of the oracle is then introduced, viz., the fears entertained by foreigners and eunuchs that they would be excluded from participation in the blessings of the covenant (*v.* 3). (3) To the latter class is promised the signal honour of a monument in the Temple and a name "better than sons and daughters," i.e. more than compensating for the loss of that perpetuation through posterity of which a cruel fate had deprived them (*vv.* 4, 5). (4) In like manner the "sons of the stranger" are reassured by the confirmation of their right to a full share in the worship of the new Temple (*vv.* 6, 7 *a*). (5) The principle on which this privilege rests is stated in all its breadth and spirituality, viz., the destiny of the religion of Israel to supersede distinctions of race and to unite men of all nations in the common worship of the true God (7 *b*, 8).

The short oracle stands in no very close connexion either with what precedes or with what follows. Although it has often been treated as an appendix to ch. lv., its real affinities seem rather to be with the group of prophecies which follow. Like them it presents features which are thought by some recent critics to point to a period subsequent to the return of the first exiles from Babylon (see Introduction, pp. lv—lx). It is urged that the religious status of the two classes referred to would hardly become a practical question until the new community was formed; that the adhesion of proselytes is spoken of by the second Isaiah as a natural consequence of Israel's exaltation (xliv. 5), and that nothing that happened prior to the release of the Jews is likely to have given rise to such misgivings as are expressed in *v.* 3. Further, that the most obvious inference from *vv.* 7 *b*, 8 is that the Temple is already in existence, and that *part* of Israel has already been gathered. These indications, taken in conjunction with many references in chs. lvii. ff., render it probable that we are here face to face with the problems raised by the situation of the new Jewish community in Palestine.

1, 2. The exhortation to righteousness is based on the nearness of Jehovah's salvation (cf. xlvi. 13, lv. 6). *justice* should be **righteousness** (as in R.V.), the same word as in the last line of the verse, but in a different sense. In the first case righteousness means conformity to the law of God (cf. lviii. 2), in the second it is, as often, equivalent to salvation. The thought that salvation is near is as characteristic of the later chapters of this book as of chs. xl.—lv. (see lvii. 14, lviii. 8 ff., lix. 15 ff., lx. 1 ff., lxii. 6 &c.), but it is equally prominent in the post-Exilic prophecies of Haggai, Zechariah, and Malachi. The establishment of the Jews in their own land had not realised the glorious predictions connected with it in xl.—lv.; yet the conviction remained

> And the son of man *that* layeth hold on it;
> That keepeth the sabbath from polluting it,
> And keepeth his hand from doing any evil.
> 3 Neither let the son of the stranger, that hath joined
>   himself to the LORD, speak, saying,
> The LORD hath utterly separated me from his people:
> Neither let the eunuch say, Behold, I *am* a dry tree.

immoveable that the final act of redemption was at hand, and was retarded only by the sin of the people.

2. The blessing attached to *v.* 1 extends to mankind in general (note the expressions *man* and *son of man*), i.e. to all who comply with the conditions of membership in the Jewish community.

that *layeth hold on it*] Better as R.V. **that holdeth fast by it** (and so *v.* 4 and *v.* 6).

that *keepeth the sabbath from* **profaning** *it* (R.V.)] (i.e. "so as not to profane it," so *v.* 6). The same emphasis on Sabbath observance appears in ch. lviii. 13, and so in Ezek. xx. 12 ff., xxii. 8, 26 (cf. Jer. xvii. 19 ff.). Although one of the most ancient of Israel's religious institutions (Ex. xx. 8; Deut. v. 15; Am. viii. 5) the Sabbath acquired peculiar significance during the Exile, when the ordinances of public worship were suspended and the Sabbath and circumcision became the chief external badges of fidelity to the covenant of which it was the sign (Ex. xxxi. 13, 14; Ezek. xx. 12).

from doing any evil] such offences as are specified in lviii. 4 ff., lix. 3 f.

3. *the son of the stranger* means simply the individual foreigner (R.V. **the stranger**), not one whose father was a foreigner.

The LORD hath utterly separated] Render with R.V., **will surely separate**. The case supposed is that of a foreigner who has *joined himself to the LORD*, i.e. has become a proselyte by accepting the symbols of Jewish nationality (circumcision, &c.), but now has reason to fear that his qualifications will be disallowed. This anxiety is hardly to be explained by the law of Deut. xxiii. 3—8; for the regulations there laid down apply only to Moabites, Ammonites, Egyptians and Edomites; and the general tendency of the legislation is in favour of the religious rights of proselytes. (See the exhaustive monograph of Bertholet, *Die Stellung der Israeliten und der Juden zu den Fremden*, 1896.) It is more likely that the immediate cause of apprehension was some manifestation of an exclusive and intolerant spirit amongst the leaders of the new Jerusalem. Against this spirit (if it existed) the prophet's words enter a strong protest (see *vv.* 6, 7).

the eunuch] Such persons are excluded from the congregation by Deut. xxiii. 1. On that passage Prof. W. R. Smith remarks that "Presumably the original sense of this rule was directed not against the unfortunate victims of Oriental tyranny and the harem system, but against the religious mutilation of the Galli" &c. (Driver's *Deuteronomy*, p. 259). If this be so, the present passage need not be regarded as

> For thus saith the Lord unto the eunuchs that keep 4
>   my sabbaths,
> And choose *the things* that please me,
> And take hold of my covenant;
> Even unto them will I give in mine house and within my 5
>   walls
> A place and a name better than *of* sons and *of* daughters:
> I will give them an everlasting name, that shall not be
>   cut off.
> Also the sons of the stranger, that join themselves to 6
>   the Lord,
> To serve him, and to love the name of the Lord,
> To be his servants,
> Every one that keepeth the sabbath from polluting it,

superseding the Deuteronomic law; it may be only a protest against its extension to cases which it did not contemplate; for it is certain that those here referred to *were* "the unfortunate victims of Oriental tyranny."

I am *a dry tree*] He could not become the head of a family in Israel, and therefore felt that he had no real and permanent share in the hopes of the nation.

4, 5. In spite of his disability the God-fearing eunuch shall be recognised as a worthy member of the congregation of Jehovah, and his name shall be had in everlasting honour in the new Israel.

that keep my sabbaths] For the expression, cf. Lev. xix. 3, 30, xxvi. 2, &c.

hold fast (as *v.* 2) *my covenant*] by conscientious obedience.

5. *a place*] **a monument**; lit., "a hand." There seems no reason to doubt that the promise is to be understood literally. An illustration of what is meant is found in 2 Sam. xviii. 18, where we read that Absalom, in the prospect of dying childless, erected the pillar to his own memory which was known as "Absalom's *hand*" (cf. also 1 Sam. xv. 12, R.V. marg.). The case of those here spoken of is precisely similar. They have "no son to keep their name in remembrance," but their memory shall be perpetuated by a monument erected within the Temple-walls; and such a memorial, testifying to the esteem of the whole community, is **better** (and more enduring) **than sons and daughters**.

6, 7. The answer to the misgivings of proselytes (*v.* 3).

to serve him] Better as R.V. **to minister unto him**. The verb is used of honourable personal service (Gen. xxxix. 4, xl. 4), and especially of the priestly service of God at the sanctuary. It is found again in ch. lx. 7, 10, lxi. 6.

to love the name of the Lord] Cf. Deut. vi. 5, xi. 1, &c.

to be his servants] i.e. worshippers (a different word from that used above).

And taketh hold of my covenant;
7 Even them will I bring to my holy mountain,
And make them joyful in my house of prayer:
Their burnt offerings and their sacrifices *shall be* accepted upon mine altar;
For mine house shall be called a house of prayer for all people.
8 The Lord God which gathereth the outcasts of Israel saith,
Yet will I gather *others* to him, besides those that are gathered unto him.

7. Foreigners who fulfil these conditions have full access to the sanctuary.

make them joyful] "cause them to rejoice." The phrase is formed from a common Deuteronomic expression for taking part in the Temple ritual: to "rejoice before Jehovah" (Deut. xii. 7, 12, 18, &c.).

my house of prayer] The Temple is the place where prayer is answered; see 1 Kings viii. *passim*, esp. *vv.* 29 f., and 41—43.

The *sacrifices* of proselytes are referred to in the Law: Num. xv. 14 ff.; Lev. xxii. 18 ff., xvii. 8 ff.

for mine house...people] (R.V., rightly, **for all peoples**) Cited by our Lord, Matt. xxi. 13; Mark xi. 17; Luke xix. 46. The emphasis lies on the last words; that the Temple is a house of prayer has been already said, what is now added is that it shall be so to men of all nationalities.

8. *The Lord God...saith*] **Saith the Lord Jehovah** &c. The formula usually *follows* the sentence to which it refers; here it introduces it, as ch. i. 24; Zech. xii. 1; Ps. cx. 1.

which gathereth the **dispersed** *of Israel*] Cf. ch. xi. 12; Ps. cxlvii. 2.

Yet will I gather others &c.] Lit. "I will yet further gather to him, to his gathered ones." "His gathered ones" is the antithesis to the "dispersed" above. The language certainly suggests (though it may not absolutely *prove*) that a partial gathering has taken place: the promise is that yet more shall be gathered, and, amongst these, men from "all peoples."

CH. LVI. 9—LVII. 21. A PROTEST AGAINST THE UNWORTHY SHEPHERDS OF GOD'S FLOCK, AND THE ARROGANT HEATHENISM BY WHICH IT IS THREATENED; FOLLOWED BY A MESSAGE OF CONSOLATION TO TRUE ISRAELITES.

This sombre and impassioned discourse is composed of three parts:
i. ch. lvi. 9—lvii. 2.—The defenceless condition of the community, due to the incompetence of its spiritual leaders.
(1) All the wild beasts of the field and the forest are invited to come and devour the unprotected flock (*v.* 9). (2) For its rulers neglect their duty; they are inefficient as dumb dogs, they are slothful, greedy and

All ye beasts of the field, come to devour,   9
Yea, all ye beasts in the forest.

sensual (*vv.* 10—12). (3) In consequence of their incapacity the righteous perish, none regarding their fate (lvii. 1, 2).

ii. lvii. 3—13 *a*. A bitter tirade against an insolent and aggressive paganising party, animated by a contemptuous hostility towards the true religion.

(1) This party, which is characterised as a bastard and hybrid race, the illegitimate offspring of an adulterer and a harlot, is summoned to the bar to hear the Divine sentence on their career of flagrant idolatry (*vv.* 3, 4). (2) The indictment follows, in the form of a recital of the varied heathen rites to which they were addicted (*vv.* 5—9), and in which with infatuated perversity they still persist in spite of all the teachings of experience (*vv.* 10, 11). (3) Judgement is then pronounced; Jehovah will unmask the hypocrisy of their pretended righteousness, and leave them to the protection of the false deities whom they have so diligently served, but who shall be unable to save them (*vv.* 12, 13).

iii. *vv.* 14—21. The prophet now turns with a message of comfort to the depressed and contrite people of God. The obstacles in the way of their salvation shall be removed (*v.* 14); Jehovah, whose condescension brings Him near to the lowly in heart, will at length avert His anger, and bring healing and peace (*vv.* 15—19); only the wicked who persist in their impenitence are excluded from the promised blessing (*vv.* 20, 21).

lvi. 9—lvii. 2. Denunciation of the worthless rulers of the Jewish community.—The difficulty of supposing that this passage refers to the state of things in the Exile is obvious. Israel is compared to a flock in charge of its own shepherds; and these shepherds are responsible both for the internal disorders from which it suffers, and the outward dangers which threaten it. An invitation to the wild beasts (the heathen nations) to come and devour a people already "robbed and spoiled" (xlii. 22) by foreign conquest, is almost inconceivable. It is of course possible, as many scholars hold, that the verses are extracted from a pre-exilic prophecy; but the description is at least as applicable to the conditions which existed after the return from Babylon. The books of Malachi and Nehemiah reveal incidentally a state of affairs which would go far to account for the dark picture here presented of the ruling classes in the restored community.

9. The apostrophe to the wild beasts is suggested by the following comparison of the people to an ill-guarded and therefore defenceless flock. That a new chastisement at the hands of the heathen is actually contemplated need not be assumed. A close parallel is found in Jer. xii. 9; cf. Ezek. xxxiv. 5, 8.

10—12. The delinquencies of the rulers. The *watchmen* are the spiritual leaders of the community, who in the earlier post-exilic period were the priests and the prophets (see Neh. vi. 10—14). Elsewhere the word is used metaphorically only of the prophets (Jer. vi. 17; Ezek. iii. 17, xxxiii. 2 ff.) and to them the description here chiefly applies, although there may be no reason for excluding the priests, with whom the higher

10 His watchmen *are* blind: they are all ignorant,
They *are* all dumb dogs, they cannot bark;
Sleeping, lying down, loving to slumber.
11 Yea, *they are* greedy dogs *which* can never have enough,
And they *are* shepherds *that* cannot understand:
They all look to their own way,
Every one for his gain, from his quarter.
12 Come ye, *say they*, I will fetch wine,

authority lay, and who shared in the vices here specified. These guides are *blind*, not discerning the evils of the time, and *dumb*, afraid to speak out against them.

they are all ignorant] Lit. "they all of them know not." Several codices of the LXX. supply an infinitive (φρονῆσαι), by which the sense and parallelism are improved (cf. the similar phrase in *v.* 11 "they know not how to observe": E.V. "cannot understand").

dumb dogs, they cannot bark] in contrast to the true prophet, who "cries aloud and spares not," shewing the people their transgressions (see ch. lviii. 1; cf. Ezek. xxxiii. 1 ff.), and specially gives warning of the approach of an enemy; Ezek. xxxiii. 6. Sheep-dogs are mentioned in Job xxx. 1.

sleeping] R.V. "dreaming," better **raving**. The word, which occurs only here, means in Arabic to talk deliriously in sickness. Cheyne suggests that it contains a play on the word for "seers," from which it differs in a single letter (*hōzim* and *hōzîm*).

loving to slumber] The laziness of the dog was proverbial amongst the Arabs: "he delays like a sleepy hound" (Gesenius).

11. The first line reads, **And the dogs are greedy** (lit. "strong of soul," i.e. appetite), **they know not how to be satisfied.** The charge of cupidity and of selling oracles for gain is one frequently brought against the false prophets (Mic. iii. 5, 11; Jer. vi. 13; Ezek. xiii. 19, xxii. 25); a contemporary instance may be the incident of Shemaiah (Neh. vi. 10 ff.). That the priesthood was infected with the same vice of covetousness is shown by Mal. i. 12; on the upper classes generally see Neh. v. 7 ff.

and they are *shepherds &c.*] The meaning can hardly be that those who have been called dogs are really the shepherds of the flock; but it is not easy to obtain a satisfactory sense. Cheyne renders "and these, pastors as they are," taking "pastors" in the figurative sense of rulers. Dillmann with a slight change of the text reads "and even these, the shepherds," supposing that a class of persons different from the "watchmen" (prophets) are now spoken of, viz., the nobles and elders. On any view the sentence is awkward; it adds nothing to the thought, and may originally have been a marginal gloss.

they all look to their own way] R.V. **they have all turned to their own way**; all pursue their selfish interests (cf. liii. 6).

from his quarter] Render, **without exception**, as Ezek. xxv. 9; Gen. xix. 4.

12. As an illustration of their highest idea of enjoyment, one of these

And we will fill ourselves with strong drink;
And to morrow shall be as this day, *and* much more abundant.
The righteous perisheth, and no man layeth *it* to heart: 57
And merciful men *are* taken away, none considering
That the righteous is taken away from the evil *to come*.
He shall enter *into* peace: 2
They shall rest in their beds,

watchmen is introduced inviting his fellows to a prolonged carousal. Cf. ch. v. 11 f., 22, xxviii. 1, 7 f.; Mic. ii. 11.

we will fill ourselves &c.] a coarse bacchanalian expression: "we will swill strong drink."

and *much more abundant*] Rather, as R.V. (a day) great beyond measure!

lvii. 1, **2**. The most alarming feature of the situation, though the least noticed, is the gradual removal of the righteous members of the community. Comp. Ps. xii. 1.

merciful men] lit., men of piety (cf. ch. lv. 7, xxviii. 14).

none considering that the righteous is taken away from the evil to come] The idea conveyed by this rendering is that the natural death of many good men was a divine intimation, little heeded by the community, that some great calamity was impending. The translation is perfectly admissible, and the thought is in accordance with the religious sentiment of the O.T. (cf. 2 Ki. xxii. 20); yet it is doubtful if we are entitled to read so much into the prophet's language. There is nothing to indicate that "the evil" is future, nor is it likely that the prophet has in view a future of terror for the righteous. The clause may be equally well rendered that (or for) the righteous is swept away before the evil; and this is probably all that is meant. The "evil" is the prevailing wickedness and oppression caused by the misgovernment described in lvi. 10—12. The words "none considering" are parallel to "no man layeth it to heart," and mean that the community takes no note of the fact that its best members are disappearing from its midst.

2. Render with R.V. (and marg.) He entereth into peace; they rest in their beds, each one that walked straight before him. The "peace" and "rest" spoken of are those of the grave (Job iii. 13 ff.), the "bed" is the bier or coffin; cf. 2 Chron. xvi. 14; Ezek. xxxii. 25. The same word is used of the sarcophagus in the Phœnician inscription of Eshmunazar ("the lid of this bed").

"After life's fitful fever he sleeps well."

The same feeling is expressed with great pathos in an eloquent passage of the book of Job (iii. 13 ff.). It is a sentiment that has appealed to the human mind in all ages; but to the O.T. believers it brought no relief from the shuddering recoil from death expressed in other passages, nowhere more forcibly than in the words of Job himself.

Each one walking *in* his uprightness.

3 But draw near hither, ye sons of the sorceress,
The seed of the adulterer and the whore.

each one **that walked**, &c.] i.e. every one who led a simple, straightforward, upright life; cf. Prov. iv. 25—27. The clause is an extension of the subject of the sentence.

3—13. Invective against an idolatrous party.—With regard to the reference of this obscure and difficult passage the following points have to be noticed: (1) The scenery of *vv.* 5, 6 is unmistakeably Palestinian (wadis, clefts of the rock, terebinths). (2) Several of the rites specified bear the complexion of Canaanitish heathenism, and could not have been performed in Babylonia. (3) The opening words ("But ye") seem to imply that the people addressed are distinct from those whose leaders are denounced in lvi. 10—12. (4) Those spoken of are animated by contempt and hatred of the cause and people of Jehovah (*v.* 4), while at the same time they advance pretensions to "righteousness" or correctness of religious standing (*v.* 12). (5) They have persisted in their abominations down to the time of the prophecy (*vv.* 10—13).

On the supposition that the prophecy was written after the return from Babylon, there is much plausibility in the view that the party here addressed is the Samaritan community. This theory is at all events simpler than that advocated by the majority of critics, who have felt the force of the objections against exilic authorship, and have accordingly supposed that the passage (or its original) was written at some time previous to the Captivity and borrowed by the great prophet of the Exile as a warning against idolatrous tendencies which still manifested themselves in Babylon. (See further Introduction, pp. lvii, lix). The connexion between this section and the preceding would be explained by the fact that the Jewish aristocracy cultivated friendly relations with the Samaritans; there was a serious danger that the struggling Jewish community should by these alliances be dragged down to the level of their semi-pagan neighbours.

3, 4. Indignant summons to the apostate community.

But draw near hither] Better, **But as for you, draw near hither** &c. to hear your doom (cf. xli. 1, xlv. 20, xlviii. 16).

ye sons of a sorceress] The most galling insult to an Oriental is to revile his mother (see 1 Sam. xx. 30). By the use of the phrase here the persons addressed are described as nursed in witchcraft and superstition.

seed of an adulterer and a whore] Cf. Ezek. xvi. 3, 45 ("thy father an Amorite, thy mother a Hittite"). It is not improbable that the words contain a specific allusion to the mixed origin of the Samaritans (2 Ki. xvii. 24 ff.); the "adulterer" may be the remains of the old Israelitish population (who had been untrue to the marriage bond with Jehovah), and the "harlot" the heathen element which had been imported by successive kings of Assyria.

Against whom do ye sport yourselves? 4
Against whom make ye a wide mouth, *and* draw out
the tongue?
Are ye not children of transgression, a seed of false-
hood,
Inflaming yourselves with idols under every green tree, 5
Slaying the children in the valleys under the clifts of
the rocks?

4. On the contemptuous attitude of the Samaritans towards the
Jews, see Neh. iv. 1—4, and comp. ch. lxvi. 5.
sport yourselves] Lit. "take your delight" (ch. lv. 2, lviii. 14, lxvi.
11); only here used of malevolent satisfaction.
make a wide mouth] Ps. xxxv. 21.
are ye not &c.] Are you not yourselves the proper objects of derision
and abhorrence?
5 ff. Description of the varied idolatries to which they were
devoted.
Inflaming yourselves with idols] Rather, as R.V., **Ye that inflame
yourselves among the oaks** (or "terebinths," the same word in ch. i. 29,
lxi. 3). The A.V. follows the chief ancient Versions in taking the last
word to be the plural of that for "god"; but it is never used expressly
of an idol or false god (not even in Ex. xv. 11 or Dan. xi. 36). The
reference is, if not to the actual primitive tree-worship (traces of which
are still found in Palestine), at least to that modification of it in which
the sacred tree became a place of sacrifice and the scene of the licentious
rites indicated by the expression "inflame yourselves." Comp. Hos.
iv. 13.
under every green (i.e. evergreen) *tree*] Cf. Deut. xii. 2; Jer. ii. 20,
iii. 6; Ezek. vi. 13; 1 Ki. xiv. 23; 2 Ki. xvii. 10 &c.
slaying the children (Ezek. xvi. 21)] i.e. sacrificing them either to
Jehovah or some false deity (Baal or Molech). On the subject of
human sacrifice in Israel consult the notes in Davidson's *Ezekiel*
(*Camb. Bible for Schools*, &c.), pp. 107 f., 143. Cf. Jer. vii. 31, xix. 5;
Ezek. xx. 25, xxiii. 39; 2 Ki. iii. 27, xvi. 3, xxi. 6; Mic. vi. 7; Lev.
xviii. 21; Deut. xii. 31, &c., and 2 Ki. xvii. 31.
in the valleys (or wadis, dry watercourses) *under the clifts of the rocks*]
Probably weird and desolate places were chosen by preference for these
revolting rites, although this is the only passage where such a thing is
suggested.
6. As commonly explained, the verse refers to the worship of stone
fetishes; but this is very doubtful. It is obvious, indeed, that by the
smooth (ones) of the wadi some objects of worship are denoted, but is
it necessary to suppose that they were smooth *stones*? The expression
"smooth ones" (*ḥalqê*) is chosen for the sake of a play of words between
it and "portion" (*ḥēleq*). If we take it literally it is of course natural
to think of stones worn smooth by the winter torrents (cf. 1 Sam.
xvii. 40), although even then there is force in Duhm's observation that

6 Among the smooth *stones* of the stream *is* thy portion;
They, they *are* thy lot:
Even to them hast thou poured a drink offering.
Thou hast offered a meat offering.
Should I receive comfort in these?
7 Upon a lofty and high mountain hast thou set thy bed:
Even thither wentest thou up to offer sacrifice.
8 Behind the doors also and the posts hast thou set up thy remembrance:

such featureless objects were least of all likely to be chosen as fetishes. (See Tylor, *Primitive Culture*³, Vol. II. p. 144 f.) But the word occurs in the metaphorical sense of "slippery," flattering, deceitful (Ezek. xii. 24; cf. Prov. vii. 5, 21, xxix. 5; Ps. v. 9, &c.); and such a term might readily be applied to false gods of any kind (cf. e.g. "lies" in Am. ii. 4). We may therefore render (following Duhm), "In the deceivers of the wadi is thy portion"; although the special connexion of the deities with the wadi remains obscure.

thy portion] As Jehovah is said to be the portion of His people (Deut. iv. 19; Jer. x. 16; Ps. xvi. 5, cxlii. 6) so these deceitful beings are the portion of those who do homage to them in the manner described in the second half of the verse.

thou hast offered a meat-offering] or, more generally, **an** oblation, as R.V. (see on ch. i. 13).

should I receive comfort in these?] Better, as R.V., **shall I be appeased for these things?** i.e. "leave them unpunished." Cf. Jer. v. 9.

Note that from this verse onwards the female personification is employed, indicating that a definite community is addressed.

7. As in the valleys, so on the hill-tops, the people had sacrificed to strange gods. Cf. Hos. iv. 13; Jer. ii. 20; Ezek. vi. 13.

hast thou set thy bed] The image is suggested by the frequent comparison of idolatry (in Israel) to adultery. Cf. Hos. iv. 12; Jer. ii. 20, iii. 2; Ezek. xvi. 25.

8. The first part of the verse seems to allude to some form of household idolatry. Many commentators explain the expression as a violation of the command in Deut. vi. 9, xi. 20. In these passages the Israelites are directed to write certain sentences of Scripture on the doorposts of their houses, and it is supposed that the practice here denounced is placing the texts at the *back* of the door so as to be out of sight! This is an utterly improbable interpretation. The thing called "remembrance" (*zikkarôn*, better **memorial**, as R.V.) must be some heathen emblem, whose exact nature cannot be determined; and from the fact that it stood at the entrance of the house, it may be presumed to have represented the patron deity of the family.

For thou hast discovered *thyself to another* than me,
and art gone up;
Thou hast enlarged thy bed, and made thee *a covenant*
with them;
Thou lovedst their bed where thou sawest *it*.
And thou wentest to the king with ointment, 9
And didst increase thy perfumes,
And didst send thy messengers far off,

for thou hast discovered...bed] The last word appears to be the object to each of the three verbs: **for away from me thou hast uncovered and ascended and enlarged** thy **bed**. The connexion ("for") may lie in the thought that they sought every possible opportunity of being unfaithful to Jehovah, their household cults being an expression of their irresistible inclination to idolatry.

and made thee a **covenant** *with them &c.*] The sense is uncertain: either, "and thou hast made a contract with them" &c. (?); or, substituting a verb meaning "purchase" (in Deut. ii. 6; Hos. iii. 2), "and thou didst procure for thee (some) of those whose bed thou lovest." For the idea, cf. Ezek. xvi. 16 ff., 32 ff.

where thou sawest it] Lit. "thou hast seen a hand." The rendering of E.V. cannot be maintained, but the real meaning of the expression is altogether obscure.

9. Pilgrimages and deputations to the shrines of foreign deities form a fitting conclusion to the enumeration of their idolatries. Another view taken of the verse is that it refers to political embassies sent to court the favour of some great heathen power. This idea derives support from the resemblance of the passage to Ezek. xxiii. 16, 40, but it is out of keeping with the other allusions of the verse. Oil and ointment have nothing to do with politics; on the other hand unguents of various kinds played a great part in the cultus of the Semites. (See W. R. Smith, *Religion of the Semites*², pp. 232 f., 382 f.) And the last line of the verse is most naturally explained as an allusion to infernal deities.

And thou wentest to the king, &c.] Rather, **And thou hast journeyed to Melek with** oil. "Melek" means king, and is here understood by many of the **Great King of Assyria or** Babylon. But for the reasons given above it is necessary to explain it as the name of a deity. It is, in fact, the word which has come to us in the Hebrew Bible under the form Molech, its proper vowels having been replaced in Jewish tradition by those of *bōsheth*, "shameful thing." (See W. R. Smith, *l.c.* p. 372.) It was a title applied by the Northern Semites to many gods, and even (among the Israelites) to Jehovah, as "king." Here it seems to be used as a proper name, and the verb "journey" shows that a foreign god is meant; possibly, as Duhm thinks, Milkom, the chief god of the Ammonites, with whom the Samaritans seem to have been in close alliance (Neh. ii. 10, iv. 7, vi. 1 ff.).

thy perfumes] or ointments.

and didst send thy messengers far off] Where they could not go in person they sent messengers with offerings.

And didst debase *thyself even* unto hell.
10 Thou art wearied in the greatness of thy way;
Yet saidst thou not, There is no hope:
Thou hast found the life of thine hand;
Therefore thou wast not grieved.
11 And of whom hast thou been afraid or feared, that thou hast lied,
And hast not remembered me, nor laid *it* to thy heart?
Have not I held my peace even of old,
And thou fearest me not?

and didst debase thyself even *unto hell*] Rather, **and hast sent deep to Sheol** (lit. "hast deepened [sc. thy sending] to Sheol"), i.e. they sought the favour of the deities of the underworld, by consulting their oracles etc.

10, 11. Although wearied by these idolatries they have persisted in them with an infatuation which has blinded them to their desperate situation, and rendered them indifferent to the fear of Jehovah.

in the greatness of thy way] i.e. "through thy much wandering," thy multifarious religious observances.

There is no hope] Lit. "*desperatum est*"; cf. Jer. ii. 25, xviii. 12 (with a somewhat different shade of meaning).

thou didst find the life of thine hand] A very obscure and variously explained phrase. R.V. **a quickening** (i.e. renewal) **of thy strength** is perhaps the most feasible interpretation, but the peculiar expression is hardly accounted for, unless it be a current proverb.

thou wast not grieved] lit. **sick**, weak and faint. Comp. Jer. v. 3, "Thou hast smitten them and they did not become sick," i.e. did not feel weak.

11. Most critics detect in this verse a milder tone on the part of the Divine speaker, as if He would find a partial excuse for the apostasies of the people in their undue fear of other gods, and distrust of Jehovah, who had so long time kept silence (cf. ch. li. 12 f., xlii. 14). If this impression be right, the theory that the Samaritans are the persons addressed at once falls to the ground. Another view is, however, possible. The question *of whom hast thou been afraid and feared?* may imply a simple negative answer,—"thou hast been absolutely fearless." The language of the verse yields itself to either interpretation.

that thou hast lied] Or, "for thou art treacherous."

have not I held my peace, &c.] Or "Is it not so? I have been silent" etc.: "It was because I held my peace that thou didst not fear me, but other gods." Cf. Ps. l. 21 ("These things thou didst and I kept silence" etc.).

even of old] (xlii. 14). The LXX. and Vulg. evidently vocalised the word differently (מֵעֹלָם for מֵעֹלָם), so as to read "and covered (sc. my eyes)"; (cf. Ps. x. 1; Isa. i. 15).

I will declare thy righteousness, 12
And thy works; for they shall not profit thee.
When thou criest, let thy companies deliver thee; 13
But the wind shall carry them all away; vanity shall take *them*:
But he that putteth his trust in me shall possess the land,
And shall inherit my holy mountain;
And shall say, Cast ye up, cast ye up, prepare the 14
way,

12, 13. But Jehovah will no longer be silent; He will proceed to judgement (cf. again Ps. l. 21).

I will declare thy righteousness] must be spoken ironically: "I will expose thy (pretended) righteousness." This might be said of the Samaritans, who claimed to be true worshippers of Jehovah just as ancient Israel had always done (Ezra iv. 2).

and thy works, &c.] Render with R.V. **and as for thy works, they shall not profit thee.**

13. *When thou criest, let thy companies deliver thee*] Cf. Jer. ii. 28. The word for "companies" does not occur elsewhere; it means **them which thou hast gathered** (R.V.): **thy rabble** of idols (R.V. marg.) (see Mic. i. 7).

vanity] R.V. **a breath.**

The second half of the verse forms a transition to the next section, which is a promise of salvation to the true Israel.

14—21. In striking contrast to the menacing tone of *vv.* 3 ff. is the impressive and elevated language in which the prophet now sets forth the gracious thoughts of Jehovah towards His erring but repentant people.

14. *And shall say*] or, **And it shall be said** (R.V. marg.). The speaker is Jehovah ("my people"), not one of the angelic beings of the Prologue. The expression means simply "the word shall go forth."

The image of the highway of salvation is taken from ch. xl. 3 (see also lxii. 10), but seems to be applied somewhat differently. There it meant an actual highway for the return of the exiles through the desert; here, as the context shews, it is only a figure for the removal of spiritual obstacles to the redemption of Israel (*v.* 17). Such a modification of the conception, although of course no proof of post-exilic authorship, is certainly very intelligible on that hypothesis. After the return of the first band of exiles it became apparent that the inauguration of the Messianic age was not to take the form of a triumphal march of Jehovah and His people across the desert to Canaan. The prophet's bold image of the miraculous highway necessarily lost its primary physical significance, and could be retained only as an emblem of the preparation for that larger deliverance to which the hopes of the post-exilic community were eagerly directed. It is applied, in short, in precisely the same way as at a later time to the preparatory mission of the Baptist (Mark i. 3; John i. 23).

Take up the stumblingblock out of the way of my people.
15 For thus saith the high and lofty One
That inhabiteth eternity, whose name *is* Holy;
I dwell *in* the high and holy *place*,
With him also *that is* of a contrite and humble spirit,
To revive the spirit of the humble,
And to revive the heart of the contrite ones.
16 For I will not contend for ever,
Neither will I be always wroth:

15. *high and lofty*] An Isaianic phrase, ch. ii. 12 ff., vi. 1 (cf. lii. 13).

that inhabiteth eternity] Rather, "that sitteth (enthroned) for ever."

I dwell in *the high and holy* place] The strict rendering perhaps is "on high and Holy (as a holy One) I dwell." Cf. lxvi. 1.

of a contrite and humble spirit] **crushed and of a lowly** spirit. The expressions do not necessarily imply what we mean by contrition—the crushing effect of remorse for sin—but only the subdued, self-distrusting spirit which is produced by affliction. Comp. ch. lxvi. 2; Ps. li. 17.

The word "holy" (here used as a proper name, see on ch. xl. 25) and the expressions "high and lofty" seem to shew the influence of Isaiah's vision (ch. vi.). The thought of the verse is very striking. It is the paradox of religion that Jehovah's holiness, which places Him at an infinite distance from human pride and greatness, brings Him near to the humble in spirit (comp. Ps. cxiii. 5, 6, cxxxviii. 6). No contrast is indicated: Jehovah dwells on high *and* (not *but yet*) with the lowly. It would be a mistake, however, to infer that holiness means or even includes gracious condescension. The two attributes are not mutually exclusive, but still less are they identical. The holiness of God is expressed by saying that He dwells on high; His dwelling with the contrite is another fact which manifests a different aspect of His character. Through the discipline of the Exile Israel had come to know God in both characters—as infinitely exalted and infinitely condescending; it had learned that peace with God, the high and lofty One, is reached through humility, which is the recognition of His holiness and majesty.

16. Hardly less remarkable is the motive here assigned for the Divine clemency,—Jehovah's compassion for the frailty of His creatures (Ps. ciii. 9, 13 f., lxxviii. 39). The argument somewhat resembles that of ch. xlv. 18 ff.: it cannot be Jehovah's purpose to undo His own creation. The continuance of His anger would annihilate the souls which He Himself has made; therefore when chastisement has produced the contrite and humble spirit, He relents and shews mercy.

The word for *souls* is that which in Gen. ii. 7 means "breath (of life)," the principle of life in virtue of which man becomes "a living person" (cf. ch. xlii. 5). The parallel *spirit* has the same sense; it is the Divine power by which human life is sustained.

For the spirit should fail before me,
And the souls *which* I have made.
For the iniquity of his covetousness was I wroth, and 17
smote him:
I hid me, and was wroth,
And he went on frowardly in the way of his heart.
I have seen his ways, and will heal him: 18
I will lead him also, and restore comforts unto him
and to his mourners.
I create the fruit of the lips; 19
Peace, peace to *him that is* far off, and to *him
that is* near, saith the LORD;

17. *For the iniquity of his covetousness*] The mention of "covetousness" as the typical sin of the community here addressed affords some support to the theory that the post-exilic Jews are referred to. See Hag. i. 2, 9; Mal. i. 8, 13, 14, iii. 8; Neh. v. These passages shew that a sordid, avaricious spirit was characteristic of the returned exiles, although on the other hand Jer. vi. 13 shews that it was prevalent before the Captivity (cf. Ezek. xxxiii. 31). The same feature is touched on in ch. lvi. 11 and in ch. lviii. The significant thing is that it is specified as the besetting sin of the time, and this again appears to indicate that the people spoken of are distinct from those who were guilty of the more heinous offences enumerated in *vv.* 5—9.

covetousness is strictly "gain"; (Gen. xxxvii. 26) then **unjust gain**.

I hid me, and was wroth] **hiding myself in my wrath** (lit. "hiding and being wroth"; see Davidson's *Syntax*, § 87 R. 1).

and he went on frowardly] (cf. Jer. iii. 14, 22, xxxi. 22, xlix. 4) lit. "turning away" (R.V. marg.). The meaning can hardly be that the effect of punishment was to harden the people in sin, and that *therefore* Jehovah desists from it. The clause does not give the consequence of the chastisement, but continues the description of the sinful life of the people which had drawn forth the Divine anger.

18. *I have seen his ways*] Either "his sinful ways" or "the amendment of his ways." The first view is perhaps more probable, in which case the words would be better joined to the preceding verse (so Duhm).

and will heal him] Or, "And I will heal him,"—beginning a new sentence. Cf. Hos. vi. 1, xiv. 4; Jer. iii. 22.

For *comforts* read **comfort**.

his mourners] ch. lxi. 2, lxvi. 10.

19. *I create the fruit of the lips*] Better, **creating fruit of the lips**, continuing *v.* 18. "Fruit of the lips" means praise and thanksgiving, as Hos. xiv. 2 (R.V. marg.); Heb. xiii. 15. Jehovah will create this, cause it to spring forth spontaneously, from those who experience His lovingkindness.

Peace, peace &c.] **Peace, peace to the far off and to the near!** an exclamation, like *v.* 21. The contrast of the "far off" and the "near"

And I will heal him.
20 But the wicked *are* like the troubled sea,
When it cannot rest,
Whose waters cast up mire and dirt.
21 *There is* no peace, saith my God, to the wicked.

is probably that between the Jews still in exile, and those who have returned and are "near" to Jerusalem (cf. ch. lvi. 8).

20, 21. Their peace is contrasted with the eternal unrest of the wicked. For the image cf. Jude 13.

when (for) *it cannot rest*] as Jer. xlix. 23.

21. There is *no peace &c.*] See on ch. xlviii. 22.

CH. LVIII. AN ORACLE ON FASTING AND THE OBSERVANCE OF THE SABBATH.

(1) The prophet announces his commission to expose the sin of his people, especially the formal and perfunctory character of their religious service (*vv.* 1, 2). (2) He then takes up the question of fasting, which is the immediate occasion of the discourse; in answer to the complaint that their fasts are disregarded by Jehovah (*v.* 3 *a*), he asks his hearers if they suppose that the kind of fasting practised by them can possibly be acceptable to God (*vv.* 3 *b*—5). (3) In contrast to such unspiritual and hypocritical fasting as theirs, he indicates the nature of the fast required by Jehovah, which consists in justice to the oppressed and kindness to the destitute (*vv.* 6, 7). (4) When they understand what true religion is and comply with its requirements, their salvation shall no longer tarry, their prayers shall be answered, their darkness turned to light, and the waste places of the land restored (*vv.* 8—12). (5) A similar promise is attached to the hallowing of the Sabbath-day (*vv.* 13, 14).

Although only one statutory fast is known to the Law—that of the great Day of Atonement (Lev. xvi. 29)—the practice was readily and spontaneously resorted to in ancient Israel as a means of propitiating the Deity (cf. e.g. Jud. xx. 26; 1 Sam. vii. 6; 1 Ki. xxi. 12; Jer. xxxvi. 9). During the Exile four regular fast-days came to be observed; and it is all but certain that these commemorated special incidents of the fall of Jerusalem (see the Commentaries on Zech. viii. 19). It is probable that such fasts as these, rather than the fast of the Day of Atonement (which may not have been instituted at this time), gave rise to the complaint dealt with in this prophecy. That the mind of the post-exilic community was exercised about these fasts appears from Zech. vii. 1 ff., a passage which presents an instructive parallel to that now before us. The question was put to the priests and prophets in Jerusalem whether the fast-days should not after seventy years' observance be discontinued (vii. 3, 5); and Zechariah replies that if the people will give heed to the divine admonitions through the "former prophets" and practise righteousness and mercy, the Messianic promises shall be fulfilled, and then the fasts shall be turned into days of rejoicing (viii. 19). The

Cry aloud, spare not, 58
Lift up thy voice like a trumpet,
And shew my people their transgression,
And the house of Jacob their sins.
Yet they seek me daily, 2
And delight to know my ways,
As a nation that did righteousness,
And forsook not the ordinance of their God:
They ask of me the ordinances of justice;
They take delight in approaching to God.
Wherefore have we fasted, *say they*, and thou seest 3
not?

answer, in short, is practically identical with the teaching of this chapter. It is of course not impossible that the question of fasting might have been raised during the Exile and answered as it is answered here; but there is nothing in the chapter that can be appealed to in favour of this view.

1. *Cry aloud*] lit. **Cry with the throat**, with the full power of the voice.

shew my people their transgression &c.] The function of the true prophet as distinguished from the false; see Mic. iii. 8, a verse which seems to have been in the prophet's mind.

2. The people indeed are zealous in the performance of their external religious duties, and imagine that this suffices to put them in a right relation to God. They are ostensibly as eager to know the divine will as if they were in reality, and not merely in profession, a people that practised righteousness. A somewhat strained interpretation has been put upon the verse by many modern commentators, who suppose that it refers to the people's desire for a speedy manifestation of Jehovah's righteousness in their favour. This feeling was no doubt in their minds, but it is not expressed here (see below).

they seek me] i.e. **enquire of me**,—the word used of consulting an oracle.

ordinances of justice] not "righteous judgements" on the enemies and oppressors of Israel, but **ordinances of righteousness**, i.e. directions as to how righteousness is to be achieved.

they take delight in approaching to God] R.V. **they delight to draw near to God.** Cf. ch. xxix. 13; Ps. lxxiii. 28. To render "in the approach of God (to judgement)" is arbitrary, and unsuited to the verb "delight."

3. The first half of the verse expresses the people's sense of disappointment at the failure of their efforts to win the favour of Jehovah; the second half begins the prophet's exposure of their hypocrisy. There is an incipient Pharisaism in their evident expectation that by external works of righteousness they would hasten the coming of the Messianic salvation. The prophet also maintains that salvation is conditioned by righteousness on the part of the people; but he insists that the

Wherefore have we afflicted our soul, and thou takest no knowledge?
Behold, in the day of your fast you find pleasure,
And exact all your labours.

4 Behold, ye fast for strife and debate,
And to smite with the fist of wickedness:
Ye shall not fast as *ye do this* day,
To make your voice to be heard on high.

5 Is it such a fast that I have chosen?
A day for a man to afflict his soul?
Is it to bow down his head as a bulrush,

righteousness which secures the fulfilment of the promises is ethical righteousness, not the mechanical observance of ceremonial forms.

have we afflicted our soul] See below on *v*. 5.

you find pleasure] Rather **business** (see on ch. xliv. 28), i.e. "you find opportunity to do a profitable stroke of business." Cf. *v*. 13.

and exact all your labours] Or, as R.V. marg., **and oppress all your labourers**. According to the law of Lev. xvi. 29 a fast implied universal cessation of work, but these men while fasting themselves, extorted from their slaves and hired servants their full tale of work. On slavery in the post-exilic community see Neh. v. 5. The translation "labourers" is somewhat uncertain; the word does not occur elsewhere in this sense.

4. *ye fast for strife and* **contention** (R.V.)] The fasting made them as irritable as Arabs in the month of Ramadan; it produced a quarrelsome temper which even led to open violence,—"smiting with godless fist."

ye shall not fast &c.] Render: **ye do not fast at present so as to make** &c., i.e. "with your present mode of fasting, your prayers can never reach the ear of Jehovah."

"My words fly up, my thoughts remain below:
Words without thoughts never to heaven go."
Hamlet, Act III. Scene iii. 97; f.

5. Should such be the fast that I choose? Can mere gestures and symbols of humiliation avail anything, along with such evidences of an unspiritual frame of mind?

to afflict his soul] Both here and in *v*. 3 the phrase expresses what is of moral value in the act of fasting, the repression of sensual impulses through abstinence, &c. It is so used also in Ps. xxxv. 13 ("I humbled my soul through fasting"), and in the laws about fasting it becomes almost a technical expression (Lev. xvi. 29, 31, xxiii. 27, 32; Num. xxix. 7). From it comes the noun *ta'anîth* (humiliation), the common term for fasting in late Hebrew (found Ezra ix. 5). How little the true end of fasting was attained in the case of those here addressed has been shewn in *v*. 4.

And to spread sackcloth and ashes *under him*?
Wilt thou call this a fast,
And an acceptable day to the Lord?
Is not this the fast that I have chosen? 6
To loose the bands of wickedness,
To undo the heavy burdens,
And to let the oppressed go free,
And *that* ye break every yoke?
Is *it* not to deal thy bread to the hungry, 7
And that thou bring the poor that are cast out *to thy house*?
When thou seest the naked, that thou cover him;
And that thou hide not thyself from thine own flesh?
Then shall thy light break forth as the morning, 8

6, 7. Description of the true fast in which Jehovah delights. The duties enjoined fall under two heads: (1) abstinence from every form of oppression (*v.* 6), and (2) the exercise of positive beneficence towards the destitute (*v.* 7). In naming these things as the moral essence of fasting, the prophet may be guided by the principle so often inculcated by our Lord, that he who would obtain mercy from God must shew a merciful disposition towards his fellow-men (Matt. v. 7, vi. 12, xviii. 35 &c.). Or the idea may be that the spirit of self-denial possesses no value before God unless it be carried into the sphere of social duty.

the bands (R.V. **bonds**) *of wickedness*] i.e. unjust and oppressive obligations.

to undo the heavy burdens] Lit. **to untie the bands of the yoke.**

the oppressed is literally the "broken" (Deut. xxviii. 33; ch. xlii. 3), —bankrupts, whose liberty had been forfeited to their creditors (cf. Neh. v. 5).

7. Comp. Ezek. xviii. 7 f., 16 f.; Job xxxi. 13 ff.

the poor that are cast out] **the vagrant** (homeless) **poor**. The word rendered "vagrant" is peculiar, but is supposed to come from a verb meaning "wander." It occurs with an abstract sense, and along with the abstract noun corresponding to the word here rendered "poor," in Lam. i. 7, iii. 19.

hide not thyself (Deut. xxii. 1, 3, 4) *from thine own flesh*] from thy fellow Israelites (as in Neh. v. 5).

8 ff. When these conditions are complied with, the glory of the latter days shall break on the regenerated community.

thy light] (ch. lx. 1, 3), the emblem of salvation; cf. ch. ix. 2.

break forth as the **dawn**] "Break forth" is the verb used in ch. xxxv. 6; Gen. vii. 11; Ps. lxxiv. 15, of the bursting of waters through a fissure in the earth's surface; by a vivid metaphor the dawn was conceived as "splitting" the heavens and flooding the world with light. The same word occurs on the Moabite Stone (l. 15) in the phrase "from the splitting of the dawn."

And thine health shall spring forth speedily:
And thy righteousness shall go before thee;
The glory of the Lord shall be thy rereward.
9 Then shalt thou call, and the Lord shall answer;
Thou shalt cry, and he shall say, Here I *am*.
If thou take away from the midst of thee the yoke,
The putting forth of the finger, and speaking vanity;
10 And *if* thou draw out thy soul to the hungry,
And satisfy the afflicted soul;
Then shall thy light rise in obscurity,

thine health] **thy healing** (as R.V.), or **thy recovery**. The word (Heb. *ărûkah*, Arab. *'aríka*) seems to mean literally the new flesh which is formed when a wound is healing (see Delitzsch's *Commentary* on the verse); it is used three times by Jeremiah with the sense of recovered health or prosperity; in Neh. iv. 7 (iv. 1 Heb.) and 2 Chr. xxiv. 13 the metaphor is applied to the repairing of damages (in the walls or the Temple). Since *v.* 12 shews that the prophet has the restoration of ruins in his mind, the coincidence with Neh. iv. 7 is certainly suggestive; but the figure here does not go beyond the general idea of recovered prosperity.

shall go before thee...shall be thy rereward] Comp. ch. lii. 12. It is difficult to say whether *righteousness* means in this case "right vindicated" by outward tokens of Jehovah's favour, or ethical righteousness as described in *vv.* 6, 7.

9 a. The immediate answer to prayer, in contrast to the complaint of *v.* 3, is the evidence of harmony re-established between Jehovah and His worshippers; comp. ch. lxv. 24, xxx. 19.

9 b should be joined to *v.* 10. The conditions of acceptance with God are recapitulated in terms differing slightly from those of *vv.* 6, 7.

the putting forth of the finger] a gesture of contempt (Prov. vi. 13) towards the oppressed mentioned in *vv.* 6, 7. Compare (with Gesenius) the *infamis digitus* (*Pers.* II. 33).

10. *draw out thy soul to the hungry*] A very peculiar expression. The most natural sense would be "let thy desire go out" &c.; but most commentators rightly feel that the object ("the hungry") demands some more specific definition of duty than this. Hence they take "thy soul" to mean "that in which thy soul delights" (see R.V. marg.), i.e. "thy sustenance" (Cheyne), which is hardly an improvement, and is moreover a rendering not easily to be justified. The Peshitto reads "bread" instead of "soul"; the LXX. has both words (τὸν ἄρτον ἐκ ψυχῆς σου). Since the word "soul" immediately follows (in the original) it is not improbable that there is an error in the text, and that what the prophet wrote was "thy bread." Render therefore **and bestow** thy **bread on the hungry**. This sense of the verb is guaranteed by a very similar use in Ps. cxliv. 13 (E.V. "afford").

then shall thy light rise &c.] See *v.* 8.

vv. 11, 12.]   ISAIAH, LVIII.   167

And thy darkness *be* as the noonday:
And the LORD shall guide thee continually,   11
And satisfy thy soul in drought,
And make fat thy bones:
And thou shalt be like a watered garden,
And like a spring of water, whose waters fail not.
And *they that shall be* of thee shall build the old   12
   waste places:
Thou shalt raise up the foundations of many generations;
And thou shalt be called, The repairer of the breach,
The restorer of paths to dwell in.

11. *the LORD shall guide thee*] Cf. ch. lvii. 18 "I will lead him,"— the same verb in Hebr.
   satisfy thy soul (cf. v. 10) *in drought*] R.V. "dry places".
   make fat thy bones] So the LXX. The verb (which does not elsewhere occur in this form) may mean "make strong" (thy bones). But it is best to accept an old emendation of Secker and Lowth, and read **renew thy strength** (see ch. xl. 29, 31).
   like a watered (**well-watered**, cf. xvi. 9) *garden*] Jer. xxxi. 12.
   whose waters fail not] Lit. **deceive not**. From this root comes the technical word *'akzāb*, the "deceitful brook" (Jer. xv. 18; Mic. i. 14, R.V.). Comp. John iv. 14.
   12. Comp. ch. lxi. 4, xlix. 8. The importance attached to the restoration of the ruined places shews that what the prophet has in view is chiefly the recovery of temporal and political prosperity. It may also throw some light on the date of the prophecy. The description of the ruins as "ancient" suggests a period considerably later than the Exile (which only lasted half a century), although the argument is not one that can be rigorously pressed.
   they that shall be of thee] Strictly "some of thee." Weir and Cheyne emend the text and read "thy children" (בָּנַיִךְ for מִמֵּךְ). König on the other hand (*Syntax*, p. 37) suggests a change of the verb (reading וְנִבְנוּ): "and the wastes shall be built by thee."
   the old waste places] Better, **the ancient ruins** (xliv. 26).
   the foundations of many generations] might mean places which had been *founded* many generations back, but the correspondence with ch. lxi. 4 seems to shew that foundations which have *lain waste* for many generations are referred to.
   The repairer of the breach &c.] The restoration of the walls and highways will be an achievement by which the community is remembered.
   paths to dwell in] Cf. Job xxiv. 13.
   13, 14. A promise attached to the strict and cheerful observation of the Sabbath. See on ch. lvi. 2.

13 If thou turn away thy foot from the sabbath,
From doing thy pleasure on my holy day;
And call the sabbath a delight,
The holy of the LORD, honourable;
And shalt honour him, not doing thine own ways,
Nor finding thine own pleasure, nor speaking *thine own* words:
14 Then shalt thou delight thyself in the LORD;
And I will cause thee to ride upon the high places of the earth,
And feed thee with the heritage of Jacob thy father:
For the mouth of the LORD hath spoken *it*.

If thou turn away thy foot from the sabbath] treating it as "holy ground" (ἄβατος). The metaphor is translated into literal terms in the following clause.

from *doing thy pleasure*] **so as not to do thy business** (as *v.* 3).

call the sabbath a delight] Great stress is laid on heartiness in the observance of this command; for a contrast see Am. viii. 5. The next clause must be translated as in R.V. **and** [sc. call] **the holy of the LORD honourable, and shalt honour it**. "The holy of Jehovah" is a remarkable designation for the Sabbath, and all the expressions of the clause are peculiar.

not doing thine own ways] **so as not to do after thy wont** (Cheyne). For *pleasure* render, as before, **business**.

nor speaking thine own *words*] Lit. **a word**, i.e. "idle words"; cf. Hos. x. 4.

14. *Then shalt thou delight thyself*] Better: **Then shalt thou have thy delight**; Job xxii. 26. The same verb as in ch. lvii. 4.

and I will cause thee to ride **over the heights** *of* **the earth**] Apparently a quotation from Deut. xxxii. 13. The meaning is "I will carry thee triumphantly over all obstacles" (cf. Deut. xxxii. 11).

and feed thee with] **and make thee to eat**, i.e. enjoy; cf. ch. i. 19.

CH. LIX. THE HINDRANCES TO ISRAEL'S SALVATION AND THEIR REMOVAL THROUGH THE INTERPOSITION OF JEHOVAH.

The chapter is closely connected in thought with the preceding, and may perhaps be regarded as a continuation of the same discourse. The first verse justifies the utterance of such promises as are contained in the latter part of ch. lviii., and the second explains why they remain as yet unfulfilled. The range of the prophecy is wider than in the former chapter, but the central theme and the historical situation are the same, and, as in the case of chs. lvi.—lviii., the phenomena of the chapter are most naturally accounted for on the assumption of a post-exilic date. In particular the prominence given to abuses of public justice (*vv.* 4, 14) in the catalogue of social crimes, implies a degree of independence and

vv. 1, 2.] ISAIAH, LIX. 169

Behold, the LORD's hand is not shortened, that *it* 59
cannot save;
Neither his ear heavy, that *it* cannot hear:
But your iniquities have separated between you and 2
your God,
And your sins have hid *his* face from you, that *he* will
not hear.

political responsibility which can hardly be attributed to the Jews in exile.

The chapter falls obviously into three sections:

i. *vv.* 1—8.—In opposition to the thought naturally arising in the mind of the people, that the obstacle to their deliverance must be impotence or indifference on the part of Jehovah (*v.* 1), the prophet asserts that the true reason of His inactivity is the sin that has come between Him and them (*v.* 2). He points to the flagrant breaches of the moral law of which the community as a whole is guilty (*vv.* 3, 4): and draws an appalling picture of the hopelessly corrupt character and conduct of many of his contemporaries (*vv.* 5—8).

ii. *vv.* 9—15 *a*.—A pathetic description of the people's vain longing for deliverance and peace (*vv.* 9—11), followed by a confession of the sins which are the cause of their misery (*vv.* 12—15 *a*). The prophet here identifies himself with the nation and speaks in its name.

iii. *vv.* 15 *b*—21.—At the middle of *v.* 15 the tone of the discourse suddenly alters; the language of complaint and prayer gives place to that of prophetic anticipation. Since the people is hopelessly entangled in its own sins, and no human champion appears on the scene, Jehovah Himself, represented as a warrior arming for the conflict, undertakes the work of salvation (*vv.* 15 *b*—17). The world-wide consequences of His interposition are then described: destruction to His enemies, manifestation of His divinity to all mankind, and redemption to Zion (*vv.* 18—20). The chapter closes with a promise confirming the gift of the divine spirit and word to the true Israel in perpetuity (*v.* 21).

1, 2. These verses state briefly and forcibly the argument of which the whole chapter is the expansion: not the powerlessness or the indifference of Jehovah, but the sin of the people, is the hindrance to the promised redemption.

1. Behold the hand of Jehovah is not too short (cf. ch. l. 2) **to save,**
   Nor His ear too heavy (ch. vi. 10) **to hear.**

2. *your iniquities have separated*] Lit. "have been separating." The expression is that used of the firmament in Gen. i. 6; it implies that guilt has been a permanent cause of alienation between Israel and its God.

have hid his *face*] i.e. caused Him to withdraw His favour (cf. ch. viii. 17). Instead of "his face," the Hebr. has simply "face" as in Job xxxiv. 29. Various explanations are offered of this peculiar expression; perhaps the easiest is that "the Face" had come to be used absolutely of the face of God.

3 For your hands are defiled with blood,
And your fingers with iniquity;
Your lips have spoken lies,
Your tongue hath uttered perverseness.
4 None calleth for justice, nor any pleadeth for truth:
They trust in vanity, and speak lies;
They conceive mischief, and bring forth iniquity.
5 They hatch cockatrice' eggs,

    3. *your hands are defiled with blood*] Cf. ch. i. 15.
hath uttered] Better **muttereth** (as R.V.).
    4. The first half of the verse should be rendered as R.V.
        None sueth in righteousness,
        And none pleadeth in truth.
The reference is to the abuse of legal procedure: lawsuits instituted and conducted with absolute disregard of righteousness and truth. Cf. ch. xxix. 21.
    calleth] with the sense of "summon" (in jus vocare), as in Job ix. 16, xiii. 22.
    pleadeth] i.e. "pleadeth a cause", litigates; the same word as in xliii. 26.
    The rest of the verse probably continues the same subject, describing the sophistical and mischievous arguments employed by the litigants to make the worse appear the better reason, and subvert the ends of justice. The verbs are infinitives (as in *v.* 13 and Hos. iv. 2) and should be translated thus:
        Trusting in emptiness (lit. "chaos" as xl. 17) **and speaking vanity!**
        Conceiving mischief and bringing forth evil!
The last line occurs almost verbatim in Job xv. 35.
    5—8. These verses differ somewhat in character from *vv.* 3 f., and are regarded by Duhm and Cheyne as a quotation from some Psalm or collection of proverbs. In point of fact the first part of *v.* 7 appears in Prov. i. 16, but probably as an interpolation, since the verse is wanting in the LXX. On the other hand, *vv.* 7, 8 are partly reproduced in the LXX. recension of Ps. xiv. 3, as in Rom. iii. 10 ff. These facts do not by themselves raise any presumption against the genuineness of the passage in this discourse; and the first image of *v.* 5 connects itself naturally enough with the conclusion of *v.* 4. It must be admitted, however, that the description can only apply to a limited class of utter reprobates, and there is some difficulty in conceiving that it can be the continuation of *vv.* 3, 4, which contain perfectly definite and intelligible accusations against a whole community.
    5. *cockatrice' eggs*] or **basilisks'** eggs. See on ch. xi. 8. The figure is expanded in the latter part of the verse, and the meaning seems to be that the persons spoken of brood over and bring to maturity projects of wickedness, whose effects are almost equally fatal to those who acquiesce in them and to those who oppose them.

vv. 6—8.]   ISAIAH, LIX.   171

And weave the spider's web:
He that eateth of their eggs dieth,
And that which is crushed breaketh out *into* a viper.
Their webs shall not become garments,
Neither shall they cover themselves with their works:
Their works *are* works of iniquity,
And the act of violence *is* in their hands.
Their feet run to evil,
And they make haste to shed innocent blood:
Their thoughts *are* thoughts of iniquity;
Wasting and destruction are in their paths.
The way of peace they know not;
And *there is* no judgment in their goings:
They have made them crooked paths:
Whosoever goeth therein shall not know peace.

he that eateth of their eggs] (cf. Deut. xxxii. 33) i.e. either he who enters into their schemes, or he who is their victim.

that which is crushed...viper] Should one try to stamp out one of their diabolical plots, its deadly nature will only be the more clearly manifested.

6. Development of the second image of *v.* 5, the point of comparison being the uselessness for any good social end of the schemes devised by the ungodly.

shall not become garments] i.e. "shall not serve for a garment."

neither shall they cover themselves &c.] Better, **neither shall men cover themselves** &c. (indefinite subj.).

7, 8. Cf. Prov. i. 16; Rom. iii. 15—17.

7. *their thoughts* are *thoughts of iniquity* (or **evil**)] corresponding to their deeds, *v.* 6.

wasting and destruction] as ch. li. 19, lx. 18; an alliteration in the Hebr.

in their paths] Lit. **in their highways**, cf. Prov. xvi. 17.

8. *judgment* here means **right** (R.V. marg.).

goings] tracks, a common word in the Book of Proverbs.

they have made them &c.] **they have made their paths crooked.** Cf. Prov. ii. 15, x. 9, xxviii. 18.

whosoever goeth therein] i.e. makes common cause with them.

9—11. The sorrow and dejection of the people is depicted in striking and pathetic images. It is the better mind of the community which is here expressed,—its intense desire for the fulfilment of the divine promises, its weariness through hope deferred making the heart sick. The contrast to the buoyant enthusiasm of the second Isaiah is very great, and it is hardly credible that the state of feeling here described should have arisen in the short interval which elapsed between the announcement of deliverance and the actual release from captivity.

9   Therefore is judgment far from us,
    Neither doth justice overtake us:
    We wait for light, but behold obscurity;
    For brightness, *but* we walk in darkness.
10 We grope for the wall like the blind,
    And we grope as if *we had* no eyes:
    We stumble at noonday as *in* the night;
    We are in desolate places as dead *men*.
11 We roar all like bears,
    And mourn sore like doves:
    We look for judgment, but *there is* none;
    For salvation, *but* it is far off from us.
12 For our transgressions are multiplied before thee,
    And our sins testify against us:
    For our transgressions *are* with us;

9. *Therefore*] on account of these sins and disorders, and not on account of Jehovah's remissness (*vv.* 1, 2).

judgment...justice (R.V. **righteousness**) are here again synonyms for salvation, right manifested by a judicial interposition of Jehovah, as in *v.* 11 and the latter part of ch. lvi. 1.

overtake us] The nation has struggled on its dreary and difficult way in the confident expectation that salvation would not tarry long behind, but hitherto this hope has been disappointed.

10. *We grope for the wall, &c.*] Rather, **along the wall** seeking an outlet. Comp. the very similar passage Deut. xxviii. 29.

we are *in desolate places as dead* men] R.V. **among them that are lusty we are as dead men**. The A.V. follows the Vulgate, but the rendering "desolate places" seems destitute of any etymological basis. The word, which occurs only here, comes apparently from a root denoting "fatness"; hence the translation of the R.V., which gives a more effective turn to the figure than any other that has been proposed. The soundness of the text, however, is open to suspicion.

11. *We roar* (better **groan**) *all like bears*] Comp. (with Gesenius) Horace, *Epod.* 16. 51:

"Nec vespertinus circumgemit ursus ovile."

The comparison would no doubt gain in force if we could suppose, as Duhm hesitatingly suggests, that captive animals, pining for liberty, are meant. But this is not indicated.

On the "mourning" of the dove, cf. ch. xxxviii. 14; Ezek. vii. 16; Nah. ii. 7; and see Davidson's *Ezekiel* (Cambridge Bible), p. 49.

we look for judgment, &c.] returning to the thought of *v.* 9.

12—15 a. Confession of the sins previously denounced, the prophet speaking in the name of the people.

12. *our sins testify against us*] So Jer. xiv. 7.

our transgressions are *with us*] present to our conscience, Job xii. 3,

And *as for* our iniquities, we know them;
In transgressing and lying against the LORD,   13
And departing away from our God,
Speaking oppression and revolt,
Conceiving and uttering from the heart words of falsehood.
And judgment is turned away backward,   14
And justice standeth afar off:
For truth is fallen in the street,
And equity cannot enter.
Yea, truth faileth;   15
And he *that* departeth from evil maketh himself a prey:

xiv. 5 &c.; comp. also Ps. li. 3 ("my transgressions I know, and my sin is before me continually").

13. The sins referred to in *v.* 12 are enumerated in a series of infinitives (cf. *v.* 4), which should be construed as in apposition to the terms "sin," "iniquities," &c. employed in the general confession of *v.* 12.

Rebellion and denial of Jehovah, and turning back from after our God, etc.
It is doubtful if there is any reference here to the sin of idolatry; the charge of apostasy is perhaps rather to be understood of offences against social morality, which amounted to a renunciation of the authority of Jehovah.

The last two lines deal with sins of speech, committed against men.
revolt is literally "defection," and appears to be used in the same general sense as Deut. xix. 16 of declension from truth and right.

uttering from the heart] The verb here is identical in form with that rendered "mutter" in *v.* 3 and "mourn" in *v.* 11. The vocalisation of both the verbs in this clause is anomalous, and should probably be changed (read *hārô, hāgô*).

14. The confession, following the same order as the indictment in *vv.* 3, 4, proceeds from personal sins to public injustice.

judgment and *justice* (**righteousness**) are not the divine vindication of Israel's right (as in *v.* 9), but the fundamental civic virtues. These, by a bold personification, are conceived as eager to take their rightful place in the administration of justice, but as kept at a distance by the prevailing social corruption. For **truth** (the essential basis of righteousness) **stumbleth in the broad place, and** uprightness (R.V.) **cannot enter**. The "broad place" is probably the open space at the city gate where cases were decided by the judges (Jer. v. 1 &c.).

15. *Yea, truth faileth*] Lit. **And truth is missing**,—conspicuous by its absence.

maketh himself a prey] i.e. must submit to extortion (Ps. lxxvi. 6). Another, and possibly a better rendering is, "withdraws himself"; compare the peculiar use of the simple verb in Ruth ii. 16 (="draw out" corn from the sheaf).

And the LORD saw *it*, and it displeased him
That *there was* no judgment.
16 And he saw that *there was* no man,
And wondered that *there was* no intercessor:
Therefore his arm brought salvation unto him;
And his righteousness, it sustained him.
17 For he put on righteousness as a breastplate,
And a helmet of salvation upon his head;
And he put on the garments of vengeance *for* clothing,
And was clad with zeal as a cloke.

15 b introduces the peroration of the discourse, in which the prophet describes the manner in which salvation shall at last "overtake" the sinful and misgoverned community. The logical development of the argument seems to be arrested by the conviction that the existing situation is hopeless, and only to be terminated through the personal intervention of Jehovah. This conviction clothes itself first of all in a prophetic vision of Jehovah as He appears to judgement; which is followed by an announcement of the consequences of His interposition for the two classes within Israel and for mankind at large. Although the transition in the middle of this verse is abrupt and unexpected there is no sufficient reason to doubt the unity of the discourse.

16. Comp. the closely parallel passage, ch. lxiii. 5.
there was *no man*] See on ch. l. 2.
no intercessor] Better **none to interpose**, i.e. on behalf of truth and right (cf. Ezek. xxii. 30). Duhm finds in these expressions an allusion to the absence of any human hero to play the *rôle* assigned to Cyrus in the earlier part of the book. This is perhaps to strain the prophet's language unduly; but see on lxiii. 5.
therefore his arm &c.] Jehovah's only allies in this conflict with wickedness are His own attributes.
brought salvation unto him] "wrought deliverance for Him." Cf. Jud. vii. 2.

That the whole description refers to a future event can hardly be questioned. The perfects in this verse and the next are those of prophetic certainty.

17. The idea of Jehovah as a warrior occurs several times in this book (ch. xlii. 13, xlix. 24 f., lii. 10); but the fully developed image of His arming Himself with His own attributes has no exact parallel in the O.T. (cf. however, ch. xi. 5). It is reproduced and further elaborated in Wisd. v. 17 ff.; and in the N.T. it suggests the figure of the Christian armour (Eph. vi. 14 ff.; 1 Thess. v. 8).
And he put on righteousness as a coat of mail (R.V. marg.). "Righteousness," as in v. 16, is a divine attribute,—zeal for the right, the stedfast purpose to establish righteousness (and its correlate, salvation) on the earth.
zeal] Cf. ch. xlii. 13, ix. 7.

vv. 18, 19.]   ISAIAH, LIX.   175

According to *their* deeds, accordingly he will repay,   18
Fury to his adversaries, recompence to his enemies;
To the islands he will repay recompence.
So shall they fear the name of the LORD from the west,   19
And his glory from the rising of the sun.
When the enemy shall come in like a flood,

18—20. The consequences of Jehovah's interposition.
18. *According to* their *deeds*] Or **deserts**. The word means simply an accomplished deed, either in a good or bad sense; but it is chiefly used in expressions which imply a reference to reward or retribution. In the next line it denotes the recompence itself (cf. ch. xxxv. 4).

According to...accordingly] The form of the comparative sentence is hardly grammatical. The compound preposition which introduces both protasis and apodosis has in the second case no noun to govern, and it cannot be treated either as a conjunction or as an adverb. We must either (with Dillmann) omit "accordingly" as dittography, or (with Duhm) change "he will repay" into a noun; rendering, "as the deserts so the retribution." The sentence, however, would read awkwardly without a verb.

to the islands he will repay recompence] The clause seems to identify the "adversaries" and "enemies" of Jehovah with the "islands" (cf. xli. 1), i.e. the heathen world; but that is almost certainly a misinterpretation of the sense of the passage. If there is any connexion with the earlier part of the discourse, the "adversaries" spoken of must be the apostate Jews,—those who by their sins hindered the coming of salvation. The prophet cannot mean that because Israel's sin has separated it from Jehovah, *therefore* judgement will descend on the heathen. Apart from this clause, indeed, there is nothing in the context to suggest the thought of a world-judgement, although of course the conception of a judgement beginning with Israel and extending to the nations is possible (see on ch. iii. 13). The words, however, are wanting in the LXX., and the verse would be greatly simplified by their removal. Their insertion is easily accounted for through a misunderstanding of *v.* 19.

19. The effect of the judgement, as a manifestation of Jehovah's glory, will be coextensive with humanity. The verse gives no hint that the judgement itself will be universal; the nations are affected by it only in so far as it reveals the character and deity of the God of Israel. Comp. ch. xviii. 3.

fear the name of the LORD] Cf. Ps. cii. 15.

When the enemy shall come in, &c.] R.V. reads: **for he shall come as** a **rushing stream** (marg. **a stream pent in**), **which the breath of the LORD driveth**. The rendering of A.V. is based on the Targ., Pesh., and Jewish commentators, and is followed by a few in recent times; that of R.V. has the authority of the LXX. (in part) and Vulg., and is adopted by nearly all the best modern authorities. The chief points of difference are (1) the construction of the word which A.V. translates by *enemy* (Heb. *çār*). According to the Massoretic pointing and accentua-

The spirit of the LORD shall lift up a standard against him.
20 And the redeemer shall come to Zion,
And unto them that turn from transgression in Jacob, saith the LORD.
21 As for me, this *is* my covenant with them, saith the LORD;
My spirit that *is* upon thee,
And my words which I have put in thy mouth,
Shall not depart out of thy mouth,
Nor out of the mouth of thy seed,
Nor out of the mouth of thy seed's seed, saith the LORD,
From henceforth and for ever.

tion it is the subject of the sentence, and may be rendered indifferently "adversary" or "adversity." On the other view it is an adjective qualifying "stream," and may mean either as an act. part. "rushing," or (less probably) "straitened," "pent up." (2) The verb for *lift up a standard* (R.V. "driveth," Heb. *nôsēs*). The A.V. understands it as a denominative from the common word for "standard" (see on ch. x. 18), while the R.V. derives it from the verb for "flee" (Pil'el = "drive forward"). The other differences need no elucidation. The second interpretation is alone suitable to the connexion, which "requires a continuous description of the theophany" (Cheyne). For the image in the last clause cf. ch. xxx. 28 ("His breath is as an overflowing stream").

20. The consequences for Israel.

And the redeemer shall come] Rather **And he shall come as a redeemer** (ch. xli. 14).

and unto them that turn from transgression in Jacob] LXX. has "and shall turn away ungodliness from Jacob,"—a different and more expressive text. So also in the quotation, Rom. xi. 26, where the words are applied in a Messianic sense.

21. Confirmation of the covenant to the true Israel. The verse, on account of its apparent want of connexion with what precedes, and its change of person and number, is regarded by some as an insertion.

My spirit that is *upon thee*] The change of pronouns (*with them*... *upon thee*) presents little difficulty here. It is caused by the transition from indirect to direct address; what follows being the substance of an oracle that was already gone forth. Comp. the similar promise in ch. xliv. 3. The person addressed is the spiritual Israel, which is even now endowed with the divine spirit and word. Whether Israel is conceived as "the bearer of the idea of the Servant of Jehovah" (Dillmann) is doubtful in view of the possible post-exilic origin of the prophecy. Against the view that the prophet himself is addressed, Dillmann pertinently remarks that the O.T. knows nothing of a hereditary transmission of the prophetic gift.

Ch. LX. The Glory of the New Jerusalem.

At length the dark clouds of sin and impending judgement roll away before the prophet's vision, and in three magnificent chapters (lx.—lxii.) he hails the rising sun of Jerusalem's prosperity. Ch. lx., a prophecy complete in itself, is a continuous apostrophe to the ideal Zion, describing her future splendour, the restoration of her children, the submission of the nations, the influx of costly tribute from all parts of the earth, &c. All the main features can be paralleled from ch. xl.—lv., and the strong resemblance to ch. xlix. 14 ff., li. 17 ff., liv. would naturally lead to its being assigned to the same author. Had the chapter occupied a different position doubt on this point would hardly arise; it would be accepted without difficulty as a prophecy of return from Exile, written in Babylon. But the fact that it follows a series of chapters which there are strong reasons to regard as post-exilic, raises the question whether it be a misplaced discourse of the second Isaiah, or whether it may not have been composed in the same circumstances as the gloomy oracles with which it is immediately connected. A closer examination of the passage reveals little that is decisive on either side, but apparently nothing inconsistent with the latter hypothesis. The promise of the return of the exiles (*vv.* 4, 9) obviously refers to the Jews dispersed throughout the world, whose ingathering remained an object of prophetic anticipation long after the restoration of the Jewish community in Palestine. Equally indeterminate are the allusions to the sanctuary in *vv.* 7, 13; it does not appear whether the Temple has yet to be rebuilt or only to be beautified. That the walls are still unbuilt (*v.* 10) only proves that the date is earlier than the governorship of Nehemiah. In the absence of definite indications, all that can safely be said is that the theory of post-exilic authorship is perfectly admissible, and is probably to be preferred in the interests of critical simplicity. The prophecy at all events loses none of its significance if it is regarded as a message of consolation to the depressed and misgoverned and poverty stricken community depicted in the foregoing chapters.

The poem, according to Duhm and Cheyne, consists of ten strophes. The order of ideas may be thus exhibited:—

i. *vv.* 1—3. An introductory strophe. While the rest of the world is shrouded in darkness, the light of Jehovah's glory breaks on Zion, and the nations are attracted to it.

ii. *vv.* 4—9. The main subject of the next three strophes is the return of the exiled children of Zion from East and West. As in ch. xlix. 22, they are represented as brought home by the nations among whom they have sojourned; the resources of the world are placed at their disposal, and they bring with them the wealth of distant countries as tribute to the God of Israel.

iii. *vv.* 10—16. The relation of the new Israel to the outer world (again three strophes). Zion becomes the mistress of the nations; her walls are built by strangers, and kings are her servants (*v.* 10); through her open gates a constant stream of treasure flows to beautify the sanctuary (*vv.* 11—13); she is the joy and praise of the whole earth, and is nourished by the "milk of the Gentiles" (*vv.* 14—16).

60 Arise, shine; for thy light is come,
And the glory of the LORD is risen upon thee.
2 For behold, the darkness shall cover the earth,
And gross darkness the people:
But the LORD shall arise upon thee,
And his glory shall be seen upon thee.
3 And the Gentiles shall come to thy light,
And kings to the brightness of thy rising.
4 Lift up thine eyes round about, and see:
All they gather themselves together, they come to thee:
Thy sons shall come from far,
And thy daughters shall be nursed at *thy* side.

iv. *vv.* 17—22. The last three strophes describe the internal prosperity, both material and moral, of the future community. Peace and righteousness are the ruling powers within its borders; perfect order and security prevail (*vv.* 17 f.); instead of the natural luminaries of heaven, Jehovah Himself is its "everlasting light" (*vv.* 19 f.); the inhabitants are all righteous, possessing the land for ever, as the branch of the Lord's planting (*vv.* 21 f.).

1—3. The image in these strikingly beautiful verses is that of a city glittering in the first rays of the morning sun. Zion is no doubt addressed in the feminine gender, but the personification is much less complete than in ch. xlix. 18 ff., li. 17 ff., lii. 1 ff., liv. 1 ff. The name "Jerusalem" is inserted by the LXX., Targ. and Vulg., but the addition is unnecessary (cf. liv. 1).

1. *for thy light is come*] Cf. ch. lviii. 8, 10, lix. 9. It is the light of the promised salvation, so long looked for in vain. The perfect tenses are used from the ideal standpoint of the future.

2, 3. While Zion is thus illuminated by the presence of Jehovah the heathen world still lies in darkness. Jerusalem is the one point of light on the earth's surface, to which the nations and their kings are attracted. For *people* read with R.V. **peoples.**

but the LORD *&c.*] Better: **but upon thee** (emphatic) **shall Jehovah arise.**

3. *And the Gentiles*] **And nations** (R.V.).

4, 5. In this and the two following strophes two things are closely associated: the restoration of Zion's banished children, and the influx of wealth from all parts of the world. The first half of *v.* 4 is repeated literally from ch. xlix. 18.

4. *shall be nursed at* thy *side*] Rather, **shall be nursed on the side,** i.e. carried on the hip, the Eastern mode of carrying young children. Cf. ch. lxvi. 12, xlix. 22. The idea, therefore, is the same as in ch. xlix. 22 f.; the nurses who bring back the children representing the heathen nations. See Muir, *Life of Mahomet*, p. 8 (abridged Ed.): 'Thou gavest me this bite upon my back, when I carried thee on my hip'.

Then thou shalt see, and flow *together*, 5
And thine heart shall fear, and be enlarged;
Because the abundance of the sea shall be converted
  unto thee,
The forces of the Gentiles shall come unto thee.
The multitude of camels shall cover thee, 6
The dromedaries of Midian and Ephah;
All they from Sheba shall come:

5. *and flow* together] See ch. ii. 2. But the right translation is that of R.V. **and be lightened** (cf. Ps. xxxiv. 5). The two verbs are identical in form but belong to distinct roots.

thine heart shall fear] Lit., **shall throb**, obviously from joy, as in Jer. xxxiii. 9. These are perhaps the only two instances where the word is so used. Usually it means to tremble from fear.

and be enlarged] Ps. cxix. 32.

the abundance of the sea] "Abundance" is lit. "tumult"; it often means "multitude" (see ch. v. 13 f., xiii. 4, xxxiii. 3), but in late usage it acquires the sense of "wealth" (Eccl. v. 9; Ps. xxxvii. 16). The wealth of the sea is not the produce of the sea, but seaborne wealth, the wealth of maritime nations.

shall be converted unto thee] **shall be turned to thee** (R.V.). The stream of commerce shall be diverted from its old channels and flow to Zion.

the forces of the Gentiles] **the riches of nations**. Cf. Hag. ii. 7 (R.V. "the desirable things of all nations").

6, 7. The promise of *v.* 5 is expanded in two pictures, seen from Jerusalem's commanding position between the desert and the sea. The first is a procession of camels and flocks representing the tribute of the East.

6. A *multitude of camels*] Cf. Ezek. xxvi. 10; Job xxii. 11. The word for "multitude" is used of Jehu's small escort in 2 Ki. ix. 17. Perhaps "train of camels."

dromedaries] properly "young camels." The word does not occur in the O.T. elsewhere; amongst the Arabs it denotes, according to some of the native lexicographers, a camel less than nine years old (Lane's *Lexicon*).

Ephah] a Midianite tribe (Gen. xxv. 4). The Midianites are often mentioned in the O.T., although nearly always (except Hab. iii. 7) in connexion with the early history. In Gen. xxxvii. 28, 36 they appear as traders between the desert and Egypt (in another source—*vv.* 25, 28 —they are called Ishmaelites); in Ex. ii. and xviii. we find them occupying the Sinaitic peninsula; in Num. xxii., xxv., xxxi. on the east of the Jordan; in Jud. vi.—viii. their hordes invade Palestine. Their proper territory is said to have been east of the Gulf of Akaba, where Ptolemy and the Arabian geographers mention a city of Madian.

all they from Sheba] i.e. (probably) **all those of Sheba**; although the Hebrew accentuation implies that the subject is the "dromedaries of

They shall bring gold and incense;
And they shall shew forth the praises of the LORD.
7 All the flocks of Kedar shall be gathered together unto thee,
The rams of Nebajoth shall minister unto thee:
They shall come up with acceptance on mine altar,
And I will glorify the house of my glory.
8 Who *are* these *that* fly as a cloud,
And as the doves to their windows?
9 Surely the isles shall wait for me,
And the ships of Tarshish first,

Midian"; hence R.V. "they all shall come from Sheba." The meaning would then be that the produce of Sheba was conveyed by Midianite caravans. *Sheba* (Gen. x. 7 &c.) is a people and country in Arabia Felix (Yemen).

gold and incense] See 1 Ki. x. 2; Ezek. xxvii. 22; Ps. lxxii. 15; Jer. vi. 20.

shew forth the praises of the LORD] Lit. "proclaim the glad tidings of" His praiseworthy deeds; cf. ch. lxiii. 7.

7. *Kedar* (see on ch. xxi. 16)...*Nebajoth*] Cf. Gen. xxv. 13 &c. The identification of the latter tribe with the Nabatæans of the classical writers is disputed by some eminent authorities, but it is at least a significant circumstance that "Nabataei et Cedrei" are bracketed together by Pliny, as Nabaitai and Kidrai are associated in Assyrian inscriptions (Schrader, *Cuneiform Inscriptions*, on Gen. xxv. 13 f.). The Nabatæans were as powerful in the last three centuries B.C. as the Midianites appear to have been in the days of Moses and the Judges (see on ch. xxxiv. Introd. Note).

shall minister unto thee] serve thee for sacrificial victims. The verb has a liturgical sense (see ch. lvi. 6) and the somewhat peculiar expression is explained by the following clause.

I will glorify &c.] **my beautiful house I will beautify** (*v.* 13). It is difficult to say whether these words imply that the Temple was already in existence.

8, 9. From the East the prophet turns to the West, and describes the ships of the Mediterranean "like white doves upon the wing" converging on Jerusalem. These also bring from afar the exiled sons of Zion, as well as rich treasures from the nations.

8. *as doves to their windows*] Gen. viii. 9. The point of comparison is rather the swiftness of the flight, than the whiteness of the wings and sails.

9. *Surely the isles shall wait for me*] ch. xlii. 4, li. 5. Duhm proposes to read "For to me shall the seafarers be gathered" (substituting ציים [see on ch. xxiii. 13] for איים, and slightly changing the verb). Some such sense would better explain the word "first" in the following line.

To bring thy sons from far,
Their silver and their gold with them,
Unto the name of the LORD thy God,
And to the Holy One of Israel, because he hath glorified thee.
And the sons of strangers shall build up thy walls, 10
And their kings shall minister unto thee:
For in my wrath I smote thee,
But in my favour have I had mercy on thee.
Therefore thy gates shall be open continually; 11
They shall not be shut day nor night;
That *men* may bring unto thee the forces of the Gentiles,
And *that* their kings *may be* brought.
For the nation and kingdom that will not serve thee 12
shall perish;
Yea, *those* nations shall be utterly wasted.
The glory of Lebanon shall come unto thee, 13

ships of Tarshish] See on ch. ii. 16.
glorified thee] beautified thee (as *v.* 7).
10 ff. The restoration of Zion's material prosperity through the labour and gifts of foreign peoples.
10. *the sons of strangers*] strangers (R.V.), as in ch. lvi. 3; although the reference here is not to individual proselytes, but to foreigners in general. It is not even certain that the verse implies a willing cooperation of heathen converted to the religion of Israel, although this is to be presumed. In either case the rebuilding of the walls by the heathen who had destroyed them is the sign of the complete removal of the divine anger against Israel.
for in my wrath &c.] Cf. ch. liv. 7, 8.
11. For *Therefore* read And (R.V. "also").
the riches *of* nations] as *v.* 5.
and that their kings may be *brought*] R.V. and their kings led with them;—a circumstantial clause. Some commentators would change the passive participle into an active: "their kings being the leaders." The alteration seems unnecessary.
12. Comp. Zech. xiv. 17, 18. The verse is objected to by Duhm and Cheyne on account of its prosaic character and unrhythmical structure, and also because it violates the strophic arrangement which these writers find in the chapter. It certainly seems to intrude awkwardly between *v.* 11 and *v.* 13.
shall be utterly wasted] The verb applies strictly to the lands rather than to the peoples (see the notes on ch. xxxvii. 18).
13. Forest trees from Lebanon shall be brought for the adornment of the Temple. It is difficult to say whether the reference be to building materials for the sacred edifice, or to ornamental trees planted in the

> The fir tree, the pine tree, and the box together,
> To beautify the place of my sanctuary;
> And I will make the place of my feet glorious.
> 14 The sons also of them that afflicted thee shall come bending unto thee;
> And all they that despised thee shall bow themselves down at the soles of thy feet;
> And they shall call thee, The city of the LORD,
> The Zion of the Holy One of Israel.
> 15 Whereas thou hast been forsaken and hated,
> So that no man went through *thee*,
> I will make thee an eternal excellency,
> A joy of many generations.
> 16 Thou shalt also suck the milk of the Gentiles,
> And shalt suck the breast of kings:
> And thou shalt know that I the LORD *am* thy Saviour
> And thy redeemer, the mighty One of Jacob.

Temple-courts. The former view, though less poetic, is more probable; and it is certainly unfair to cite the proverbial expressions of *v.* 17 as an argument against it.

the fir tree, the pine tree, and the box together] See ch. xli. 19.

the place of my sanctuary] is the Temple (Jer. xvii. 12), not the city of Jerusalem, as the place where the Temple is situated.

the place of my feet] Cf. Ezek. xliii. 7 ("the place of the soles of my feet").

14. The homage done to Zion by her former oppressors is probably to be regarded as the consequence of the new glory which accrues to the Sanctuary (*v.* 13).

The sons also...feet] The LXX. reads simply: "And there shall come crouching unto thee the sons of thine afflicters and despisers." The words omitted ("*all*" and "*shall bow...feet*") are probably a gloss.

The Zion of the Holy One of Israel] On the construction of the proper name followed by a genitive see Davidson, *Syntax*, § 24, R. 6.

15, 16. Instead of being shunned and hated by all nations, Zion shall become the joy of the whole earth, her wants being abundantly supplied from the best that the nations can bestow.

15. Instead of thy being *forsaken and hated*] Cf. ch. xlix. 14, 21; liv. 6, 11.

so that no man went through thee] **with none passing by** (or **through**).

16. For the figure in the first half of the verse, cf. ch. xlix. 23; the second half is repeated from xlix. 26.

17, 18. The inner order and security of the commonwealth shall correspond to its material splendour,—a double contrast to its present (or past) condition.

For brass I will bring gold, 17
And for iron I will bring silver,
And for wood brass,
And for stones iron:
I will also make thy officers peace,
And thine exactors righteousness.
Violence shall no more be heard in thy land, 18
Wasting nor destruction within thy borders;
But thou shalt call thy walls Salvation,
And thy gates Praise.
The sun shall be no more thy light by day; 19
Neither for brightness shall the moon give light unto
    thee:
But the LORD shall be unto thee an everlasting light,
And thy God thy glory.

17. *For brass...gold &c.*] Cf. ch. ix. 10; 1 Ki. x. 21, 27, and the opposite experience, 1 Ki. xiv. 26 f.
I will also make, &c.] Render: **and I will appoint Peace as thy government, and Righteousness as thy ruler.** The word for *officers* is an abstract noun (like "management" or "magistracy") used in a concrete sense; *exactors* is a plural of majesty, precisely as in ch. iii. 12. Its use here is an *oxymoron;* it denotes a tyrannous, arbitrary ruler (see on ch. liii. 7), the idea conveyed being that the tyranny of the present shall be replaced by the genial rule of Righteousness. In other words, Peace and Righteousness (personified qualities, as ch. lix. 14) shall be the governing powers in the new Jerusalem. The other rendering, "I will make thy governors peaceful" &c. (so virtually the LXX.) is grammatically possible, but yields a sense feeble and unsatisfying.

18. *wasting nor destruction*] ch. lix. 7, li. 19.
thou shalt call thy walls Salvation, &c.] This rendering is decidedly preferable to that of most recent commentators: "thou shalt call Salvation thy walls, &c." Moreover the *rule* in such cases (although v. 17 furnishes an exception) is that "the nearer obj. is usually def. and the more remote indef." (Davidson, *Syntax*, § 76). See also on ch. xxvi. 1.

19, 20. Comp. Rev. xxi. 23: "And the city had no need of the sun, neither of the moon, to shine in it; for the glory of God did lighten it, and the Lamb is the light thereof"; and xxii. 5. It is not implied that the sun and moon shall cease to exist; all that is said is that the new Jerusalem shall not be dependent on these natural luminaries. But that an actual physical illumination of the city by the glory of Jehovah is contemplated by the prophet can hardly be doubted. The basis of the conception is perhaps to be found in Ezek. xliii. 2.

19. *thy glory*] thy beauty; *vv.* 7, 9. 13.

20 Thy sun shall no more go down;
  Neither shall thy moon withdraw itself:
  For the LORD shall be thine everlasting light,
  And the days of thy mourning shall be ended.
21 Thy people also *shall be* all righteous:
  They shall inherit the land for ever,
  The branch of my planting, the work of my hands,
    that *I* may be glorified.
22 A little one shall become a thousand,
  And a small one a strong nation:
  I the LORD will hasten it in his time.

20. *the days of thy mourning*] Cf. ch. lvii. 18, lxi. 2.

21, 22. The community, composed exclusively of righteous persons, shall possess the land for ever; and Jehovah shall be glorified in them.

inherit] Better: **possess**.

the branch of my planting] i.e. "which I have planted." Cf. ch. lxi. 3. The word for *branch* denotes strictly a "shoot"; so also in ch. xi. 1, xiv. 19. For the figure cf. ch. v. 7.

22. *A little one...a small one*] Better perhaps: **The least...the smallest**. The word for "thousand" (*ĕleph*) means also a larger or smaller group of families,—"clan" or **tribe**. This is doubtless the sense in which it is employed here: comp. the parallel "nation" in the next line.

will hasten it in his time] The fulfilment shall be instantaneous when once the appointed time has arrived. The reference is to the whole of the preceding prophecy.

CH. LXI. THE PROCLAMATION OF GLAD TIDINGS TO ZION.

i. *vv.* 1—3. The speaker (see below) introduces himself as the herald of the coming salvation. Anointed with the spirit of the Lord, he is commissioned to cheer and comfort the distressed people of God by the announcement of a day of spiritual emancipation and privilege which issues in eternal splendour.

ii. *vv.* 4—9. In the end of *v.* 3 the soliloquy has passed insensibly into objective description of the glorious future of Israel; and this is the subject of the remainder of the prophecy. The old waste places shall be rebuilt (*v.* 4); Israel shall be recognised as the priestly people among the nations, while strangers feed its flocks and till its fields (*vv.* 5, 6); the people shall receive double compensation for their past sufferings, and the blessing of Jehovah shall visibly rest on them (*vv.* 7—9).

iii. *vv.* 10—11. The prophet, speaking as it would appear in the name of the community, exults in the glorious prospect thus disclosed of a spiritual spring-time when Jehovah shall cause righteousness and praise to sprout before all the nations.

It will be seen that in substance the passage deals with the same theme as ch. lx., the future blessedness of Zion. The important difference is

61 The Spirit of the Lord GOD *is* upon me;

the prominence given in the opening **monologue** (*vv.* 1—3) to the personality and mission of the speaker. The question necessarily arises, Who is this speaker? Whilst the **Targum** and perhaps a majority of well-known commentators assign **the speech** to the prophet himself, a number of the best authorities regard it as a self-delineation of the ideal Servant of Jehovah such as we have found in ch. xlix. 1—6 and l. 4—9. The question is one of much difficulty, and the chief points involved are the following: (1) The name "Servant of the Lord" does not here occur. But this really counts for nothing, since the same is true of ch. l. 4—9, where it cannot be doubted that it is the Servant who speaks. (2) It is said that the prophet invariably keeps his own personality in the background and that where any other than Jehovah speaks of Himself at length, it is always the Servant. This is true of the author of ch. xl.—lv., but is much less obvious if the present passage has to be assigned to a later writer. The prophet's consciousness of his own mission is strongly expressed in ch. lviii. 1, probably also in ch. lxii. 1, and it is unsafe to assert that he might not have expanded it in such terms as are here used. Another exception to the rule is found in the earlier part of the book in ch. xlviii. 16 (which may however be an interpolation. See on the verse). (3) There are undoubtedly affinities between the conception here and the portrait of the Servant; e.g. the gift of the spirit (xlii. 1), the helpful and consoling ministry (l. 4, xlii. 3), the message of emancipation (xlii. 7, xlix. 9). On the other hand the function claimed by the speaker cannot be said to transcend that of a prophet, and seems to fall below the level of the Servant's great work. He is only the herald of salvation, whereas the Servant is its mediator; there is nothing here to suggest the profound moral influence which is the characteristic of the Servant's ministry to Israel, for it does not appear that the mission of consolation here described consists in anything else than the proclamation of the coming glory. We miss also the element of universalism which is so conspicuous in the Servant's work; and the allusion to a "day of vengeance" strikes a note which is never found in the undoubted utterances of the Servant. (4) Although it is a begging of the question to assert that the personification of the Servant ceases with ch. liii., it is certainly difficult to find a place for this portrait in the cycle of Servant-passages. These passages shew a well-marked progression and connexion of thought, and one must hesitate to believe that after the climax in ch. liii. the same personage should again appear in what must be considered a subordinate character. On the whole the objections to taking the words as those of the prophet appear less cogent than those against attributing them to the Servant, but it is probable that the writer was familiar with the earlier portraits of the Servant and that his conception of his prophetic office was influenced by them. That our Lord quotes the passage as descriptive of Himself and His message (Luke iv. 18 f.) does not decide the question, for the ideal prophet is as truly a type of Christ as the Servant himself.

1—3. The prophet as Evangelist.

1. *The Spirit...upon me*] Cf. xlii. 1, xlviii. 16 (lix. 21).

Because the LORD hath anointed me to preach
  good tidings unto the meek;
He hath sent me to bind up the broken-hearted,
To proclaim liberty to the captives,
And the opening of the prison to *them that are* bound;
2 To proclaim the acceptable year of the LORD,
And the day of vengeance of our God;
To comfort all that mourn;
3 To appoint unto them that mourn in Zion,
To give unto them beauty for ashes,

because the LORD hath anointed me] The abiding possession of the spirit is the consequence of this consecrating act of Jehovah. "Anoint" is used, as often, in a metaphorical sense. The idea that prophets were actually anointed with oil is supported only by 1 Ki. xix. 16, and even there the sense may be metaphorical since (as Cheyne observes) we do not read that the act was performed.

to preach good tidings] The verb is *bassēr* (εὐαγγελίσασθαι), on which see the notes to xl. 9 and lii. 7. It is to be remarked that in ch. xl.—lv. the *mĕbassēr* (or *mebasséreth*) is an ideal personage or company, whose function is quite distinct from that of the prophet or the Servant.

to bind up (i.e. **heal**) *the broken-hearted*] Cf. Ps. cxlvii. 3, xxxiv. 18, li. 17.

The terms "meek" and "broken-hearted" denote the *religious* qualities which characterise the recipients of the prophet's Evangel. How far the following designations, "captives," "bound," "mourners," are to be understood in a spiritual sense is doubtful. It is not unlikely that the immediate reference is to the social evils whose redress is already demanded in ch. lviii. 6, 9.

to proclaim liberty] a suggestive expression, shewing that the idea of the year of salvation is based on the institution of the Jubilee; see Lev. xxv. 10; and cf. Jer. xxxiv. 8, 15, 17; Ezek. xlvi. 17. These, indeed, are the only occurrences of the word for "liberty," which is thus seen to denote always a universal emancipation by public decree.

the opening of the prison] The rendering "opening of the eyes" (R.V. marg.) does not suit the context, though it is true that the word is generally used of the opening of eyes (once of ears). [In the Heb. read *pĕqahqôah* as a single word, = "opening."]

2. *the acceptable year of the LORD*] Rather, **a year** of Jehovah's **favour** (ch. xlix. 8); and so in the next line, **a day** of our God's **vengeance** (cf. lxiii. 4, ch. xxxiv. 8).   *vengeance*] i.e. on the oppressors of Israel, perhaps also on the sinful members of the nation (lix. 16 ff.).

to comfort all that mourn] Cf. ch. lvii. 18. The clause belongs properly to the next verse.

3. *them that mourn in Zion*] Lit. "the mourners of Zion," which may mean either "those that mourn *for* Zion" (as lxvi. 10) or those who mourn in her.

beauty for ashes] R.V. **a garland** (but it. "a turban") **for ashes**.

The oil of joy for mourning,
The garment of praise for the spirit of heaviness;
That they might be called trees of righteousness,
The planting of the LORD, that *he* might be glorified.
And they shall build the old wastes, 4
They shall raise up the former desolations,
And they shall repair the waste cities,
The desolations of many generations.
And strangers shall stand and feed your flocks, 5
And the sons of the alien *shall be* your plowmen and your vinedressers.
But ye shall be named the Priests of the LORD: 6
Men shall call you the Ministers of our God:
Ye shall eat the riches of the Gentiles,

Ashes sprinkled on the head were a sign of mourning (2 Sam. xiii. 19); these shall be replaced by the headdress which betokened dignity or festivity (see on *v.* 10). There is a paronomasia in the Hebrew which cannot be imitated in English; Germans render "Putz statt Schmutz."

oil of joy for mourning] (Omit the art.) As anointing with oil was a mark of joy or honour (Ps. xlv. 7, xxiii. 5; Luke vii. 46) so its omission was one of the tokens of mourning (2 Sam. xiv. 2).

the spirit of heaviness] **a failing spirit**; the same word as "dimly burning" in ch. xlii. 3.

that they might be called] Strictly: **and they shall be called**.

trees of righteousness] lit. "oaks" or "terebinths." The evergreen tree is a favourite emblem of the life of the righteous: Jer. xvii. 8; Ps. i. 3, xcii. 14.

the planting...glorified] see ch. lx. 21.

4. Comp. ch. xlix. 8, lviii. 12, lx. 10.

5, 6. Israel's priesthood among the nations, and the services rendered to it by the latter. The meaning of course is not that all Israelites shall minister in the Temple or that a separate sacerdotal order shall not exist (see on the contrary ch. lxvi. 21) but simply that in relation to the Gentiles, Israel shall enjoy a position of privilege analogous to the relation between priests and laymen. The fundamental idea of priesthood in the O.T. being the right of approach to God, this idea is conceived as realised in a system which may be likened to a series of concentric circles,—priests, Levites, ordinary Israelites, Gentiles,—each grade standing nearer to God than the next. It was Israel's calling to be a "kingdom of priests" (Ex. xix. 6), and in the latter days this destiny will be fulfilled in their mediatorial relation to the outer world. Although prophecy in general accords a position of supremacy to Israelites in the future kingdom of God, the distinction is perhaps nowhere so definitely formulated as here.

5. *the sons of the alien*] Render with R.V. **aliens** (as ch. lvi. 3).

6. *the riches of the Gentiles*] **the wealth of nations**, as ch. lx. 5, 11.

188   ISAIAH, LXI.   [vv. 7—10.

And in their glory shall you boast yourselves.
7 For your shame *you shall have* double;
And *for* confusion they shall rejoice in their portion:
Therefore in their land they shall possess the double:
Everlasting joy shall be unto them.
8 For I the LORD love judgment,
I hate robbery for burnt offering;
And I will direct their work in truth,
And I will make an everlasting covenant with them.
9 And their seed shall be known among the Gentiles,
And their offspring among the people:
All that see them shall acknowledge them,
That they *are* the seed *which* the LORD hath blessed.
10 I will greatly rejoice in the LORD,
My soul shall be joyful in my God;

in their glory shall you boast yourselves] So the chief Ancient Versions. Another rendering is **to their glory shall ye succeed** (R.V. marg.); the exact idea being that Israel and the heathen shall "exchange places," the glory that now belongs to the latter being transferred to the former.

7. The first half of the verse is harsh in construction; and the text as it stands is corrupt. The general sense, however, is sufficiently established by the second half: the prosperity of the future shall be a twofold recompense for the miseries of the past and the present.
the double] in the same sense (*mutatis mutandis*) as ch. xl. 2.
everlasting joy] ch. xxxv. 10 (=li. 11).

8. Jehovah's righteousness demands this reversal of the present relations of Israel and the heathen.
I hate robbery &c.] Render with R.V. **I hate robbery with iniquity, and I will give them their recompense in truth** (i.e. faithfully). Instead of עוֹלָה (=burnt-offering) we must point עַוְלָה (=iniquity). The translation of the A.V. would shut us up to a wrong interpretation of the prophet's thought. The robbery to which he refers is not that practised by Israelites on God (Mal. iii. 8, 9), but the iniquitous treatment of Israel by its foes.
an everlasting covenant] Cf. ch. lv. 3.

9. In virtue of this everlasting covenant the blessing of Jehovah descends on their offspring (cf. ch. lxv. 23), compelling the admiration of the world.
For *Gentiles...people* render with R.V., **nations...peoples.**

10. According to the Targum and some critics the speaker here is the Zion of the future; while Delitzsch and others, who assign the preceding words to the Servant of Jehovah, suppose that he is still the speaker. If the prophet is the speaker he transports himself to a future standpoint, and there is no reason why he should not at the same time become the

For he hath clothed me with the garments of salvation,
He hath covered me with the robe of righteousness,
As a bridegroom decketh *himself* with ornaments,
And as a bride adorneth *herself* with her jewels.
For as the earth bringeth forth her bud, 11
And as the garden causeth the things that are sown in it to spring forth;
So the Lord GOD will cause righteousness and praise to spring forth
Before all the nations.

For Zion's sake will I not hold my peace, 62
And for Jerusalem's sake I will not rest,

mouthpiece of the redeemed community. Duhm and Cheyne agree in thinking that the verse stands out of its proper position and interrupts the connexion of *v.* 9 with *v.* 11.

garments of salvation &c.] Cf. ch. lix. 17; Ps. cxxxii. 9, 16. *salvation* and *righteousness* are, as often, synonymous.

as a bridegroom decketh himself *with ornaments*] R.V. "with a garland" (as *v.* 3). The last word denotes a headdress worn by priests (Ex. xxxix. 28; Ezek. xxiv. 17, xliv. 18), by fashionable ladies (ch. iii. 20), and (according to this passage) by a bridegroom. The verb for "decketh himself" means to officiate as a priest (Hos. iv. 6, &c.), and its use here, ("maketh his headdress priestly,") is so peculiar as to be suspicious.

and as a bride &c.] Better, **and like a bride that putteth on her jewels** (as Gen. xxiv. 53) or **her attire** (as Deut. xxii. 5).

11. *as the earth &c.*] i.e. as surely as the seed germinates in the earth, so surely will Jehovah bring to pass the great redemption here promised through the self-fulfilling power of His word. Cf. ch. lv. 10, xlii. 9, xliii. 19, lviii. 8.

CH. LXII. INTERCESSION FOR THE SALVATION OF ZION, WITH FURTHER PREDICTIONS OF HER GLORY.

Although the chapter is commonly treated as forming along with ch. lxi. a single discourse, it has a distinct character of its own, and is perhaps better regarded as the last member of the Trilogy commencing with ch. lx. There are three clearly marked sections:

i. *vv.* 1—5.—The prophet announces his purpose to labour unremittingly on behalf of Zion (*v.* 1), assured that the time is at hand when her righteousness shall be manifested to all the world, and a new name shall symbolize her new relation to Jehovah (*vv.* 2, 3). Instead of being forsaken and desolate she shall be reunited to her Husband and her children, and her God shall rejoice over her as a bridegroom over his bride (*vv.* 4, 5).

Until the righteousness thereof go forth as brightness,
And the salvation thereof as a lamp *that* burneth.
2 And the Gentiles shall see thy righteousness,
And all kings thy glory:
And thou shalt be called by a new name,
Which the mouth of the LORD shall name.
3 Thou shalt also be a crown of glory in the hand of the LORD,

ii. *vv*. 6—9.—Even now the prophet sees in vision the walls of the city crowned with faithful "watchers," whose function is to remind Jehovah unceasingly of His promises to Jerusalem (*vv*. 6, 7). For the encouragement of the "remembrancers" these promises are supplemented by the oath of Jehovah, that strangers shall no longer be permitted to rob the community of the fruit of its labours (*vv*. 8, 9).

iii. *vv*. 10—12.—A last summons to "prepare the way of the people," i.e. the returning exiles (*v*. 10). The proclamation has gone forth to the end of the world; Zion's salvation draws near and her sentence of rejection is finally reversed (*vv*. 11, 12). This last section is almost wholly made up of reminiscences of earlier passages.

1. The speaker here is most naturally to be supposed the prophet, although the words are often explained as those of Jehovah Himself. This, however, is less probable, in spite of the fact that the verb for "hold my peace" is always in these chapters, except here and *v*. 6, used by or of Jehovah (ch. xlii. 14, lvii. 11, lxiv. 12, lxv. 6); for when Jehovah breaks His silence salvation has come. The thought of the verse is entirely appropriate on the lips of the prophet who wrote ch. lxi. 1 ff.; he declares that he will persevere in the course of action there described until the year of Jehovah's favour has actually come.

until the righteousness...brightness] i.e. until her right, at present obscured, becomes brilliantly manifest (Ps. xxxvii. 6). Comp. ch. lx. 2, 3, lviii. 8.

a lamp that burneth] **a burning torch.**

2. *And the Gentiles &c.*] Rather, **And nations.** Cf. ch. lx. 3.

a new name] the symbol both of a new character and a new relation to God. Cf. Rev. ii. 17, iii. 12, ch. lxv. 15.

which the mouth of the LORD shall name] Rather, shall determine (as Gen. xxx. 28). This new name is a mystery (see Rev. ii. 17) yet to be disclosed, and is not to be brought into connexion with the names of *v*. 4 and *v*. 12.

3. *a crown of glory*] R.V. **of beauty.** There is probably an allusion to the mural crown which tutelary deities of cities are sometimes represented as wearing, on ancient coins &c. The prophet for some reason hesitates to adopt the heathen image in its completeness; and pictures Jehovah as holding the crown in His hand.

4, 5. The reunion of Zion with her Husband and her children. Cf. ch. xlix. 14 ff., liv. 1 f., 4 ff.

And a royal diadem in the hand of thy God.
Thou shalt no more be termed Forsaken;   4
Neither shall thy land any more be termed Desolate:
But thou shalt be called Hephzi-bah,
And thy land Beulah:
For the LORD delighteth in thee,
And thy land shall be married.
For *as* a young man marrieth a virgin,   5
So shall thy sons marry thee:
And *as* the bridegroom rejoiceth over the bride,
So shall thy God rejoice over thee.

Forsaken] Hebr. *'ăzûbāh*; found as a proper name in 1 Ki. xxii. 42. Similarly *Hephzi-bah* (= "delight in her") is the actual name of the mother of Manasseh (2 Ki. xxi. 1).
Beulah] (*bĕ'ûlāh*) i.e. "married," see ch. liv. 1.
5. so *shall thy sons marry thee*] The harshness of the conception is obvious; and it is hardly relieved by pointing to the double meaning of the verb *bā'al* ("marry" and "possess"). Lowth and others, by a slight emendation of the text, read "so shall thy Builder (Jehovah) marry thee." (So Cheyne, who refers to Ps. cxlvii. 2: "Jehovah is the builder up of Jerusalem.") See on xlix. 17.
6, 7. Jehovah hears perpetually the voice of importunate intercession ascending for the ruined walls of Jerusalem. This is the thought poetically expressed in the two verses, but the details of the conception present several difficult questions. In the first place, Who are meant by the *watchmen*, or rather **watchers**? [The word differs from that used in lvi. 10, lii. 8 (= "lookers out") and means literally "keepers" or "guards" (Cant. iii. 3, v. 7; Ps. cxxvii. 1)]. (*a*) Some hold that it is here a name for the company of prophets, but this view has really little in its favour. The function ascribed to the watchers is not strictly prophetic, and the word is nowhere else used of a prophet except in ch. xxi. 11 f., where there is obviously a *comparison* of the prophet to a city watchman. (*b*) Another, but less probable, opinion is that pious Israelites are meant. (*c*) The best interpretation seems to be that of the Jewish exegetes, that the "watchers" are angelic beings, forming the invisible guard of the city. The representation, therefore, is purely ideal, and this fact has to be borne in mind in considering the second question, Who is the speaker in the first half of *v*. 6? The prophet could not strictly be said to appoint either angelic or prophetic watchers; hence the prevalent opinion is that Jehovah is the speaker. On the other hand it seems to some unnatural that Jehovah should appoint those who are to remind Himself of His own promises, and it is certainly the prophet who speaks in the latter part of the verse. It might be held that the language is not too bold for the prophet to use of himself in describing a scene which belongs to the region of the spiritual imagination, just as other prophets do things in vision which exceed human

6 I have set watchmen upon thy walls, O Jerusalem,
Which shall never hold their peace day nor night:
Ye that make mention of the LORD,
7 Keep not silence, and give him no rest,
Till he establish, and till he make Jerusalem a praise in the earth.
8 The LORD hath sworn by his right hand, and by the arm of his strength,
Surely I will no more give thy corn *to be* meat for thine enemies;
And the sons of the stranger shall not drink thy wine, for the which thou hast laboured:
9 But they that have gathered it shall eat it, and praise the LORD;
And they that have brought it together shall drink it in the courts of my holiness.

authority (cf. Zech. xi. 7 ff.). Cheyne alone regards the three passages lxi. 1 ff., lxii. 1 ff., and 6 f., as soliloquies of the ideal Servant of Jehovah, or rather of that ideal as reflected in the mind of a later disciple of the second Isaiah.

6. *I have set...walls*] Another translation might be: "I have appointed guardians of thy walls." The verb for "set" means strictly "commission," and the thing put in commission is expressed by the prep. rendered "upon." On either view, the "walls" are the ruined walls of the actual city, rather than those of the ideal Zion of the future (cf. ch. xlix. 16).

ye that make mention of the LORD] Render with R.V. **ye that are the LORD'S remembrancers**. The words are to be joined with *v.* 7.

7. *Keep not silence*] Lit. "No silence to you!" The word *rest* in the next clause is the same as "silence."

8, 9. Jehovah has sworn that the Israelites shall no longer be spoiled by their enemies, but shall be secured in the peaceful enjoyment of the fruits of the ground. The phrase "no longer" seems to imply that at the time of writing the community was exposed to the depredations of its hostile neighbours. This would be an additional indication of post-exilic authorship, which is confirmed by the mention of the Temple courts in the end of *v.* 9.

8. *The LORD hath sworn by his right hand &c.*] i.e. so surely as He has the power to help. Cf. ch. xlv. 23, liv. 9.

the sons of the stranger] R.V. **strangers**.

thy wine] Lit. "new wine," must.

9. Cf. ch. lxv. 21, 22.

in the courts of my holiness] Render, **in my holy courts**; not as R.V., "in the courts of my sanctuary." The allusion is to the festivals

Go through, go through the gates; prepare you the way 10
   of the people;
Cast up, cast up the highway; gather out the stones;
Lift up a standard for the people.
Behold, the LORD hath proclaimed unto the end of 11
   the world,
Say ye to the daughter of Zion, Behold, thy salvation
   cometh;
Behold, his reward *is* with him,

in the Temple, where the first-fruits were eaten with rejoicing before Jehovah (Deut. xii. 17 f., xiv. 23 ff., xvi. 9—17).

10—12. Announcement of the return of the exiles. The passage resembles ch. xlviii. 20 ff., lii. 11 f.; and at first sight it seems to imply that no exodus from Babylon has as yet taken place. This indeed has been the prevalent view of commentators, based on the assumption that the writer is the same as in the two parallels. But the secondary character of the passage, betrayed by the accumulated citations, is somewhat adverse to this hypothesis, and it will be seen that the language itself is susceptible of a different construction. It is certain that a return of exiled Israelites is announced, but there is nothing to exclude the supposition that (as in ch. lx. 4, 9) the return of those who took advantage of the edict of Cyrus lies behind the prophet's standpoint.

10. *Go through, go through the gates*] To whom are these words addressed? The gates might be those of Babylon, in which case the passage is the exact counterpart of ch. xlviii. 20 ("Go ye forth of Babylon") and lii. 11 ("go ye out from thence"). It is possible, on the other hand, that those addressed are the present inhabitants of Jerusalem, who are invited to prepare for the final restoration of the Dispersion. The gates must then be those of Jerusalem or of the Temple (so Duhm).

prepare you the way of the people] In ch. xl. 3 a similar command is addressed to angelic beings, and the "way" is that by which Jehovah Himself is to return, at the head of His people. Here the persons addressed must be the same as in the first clause of the verse; and throughout this section the prophet appears studiously to avoid the idea, so prominent in the earlier part of the book, of a triumphal march of Jehovah in person through the desert to Jerusalem.

cast up the highway] ch. lvii. 14.
lift up an ensign for the **peoples** (R.V.)] Cf. ch. xlix. 22.
11. *Behold, the* **LORD** *hath proclaimed unto the end of the world*] Cf. ch. xlviii. 20. There redeemed Israel is enjoined to declare to all the world the great salvation it has experienced; here Jehovah Himself makes it known.

thy salvation cometh] Instead of "the Lord GOD shall come" in ch. xl. 10.

Behold his reward is *with* **him** *&c.*] Repeated from xl. 10 (see on the

And his work before him.

12 And they shall call them, The holy people, The redeemed of the LORD:
And thou shalt be called, Sought out, A city not forsaken.

63 Who *is* this *that* cometh from Edom,

passage). The chief Ancient Versions seem to have felt the want of a personal antecedent to the pronouns; hence they render in the previous clause "thy Saviour" for "thy salvation."

12. Zion and its people shall then be recognised in their true character by all.

The holy people] The priesthood of humanity; ch. lxi. 6.
The redeemed of the LORD] ch. xxxv. 10 [li. 10]; cf. xlviii. 20.
Sought out] i.e. "much sought after." Cf. Jer. xxx. 17, "This is Zion whom no man seeketh after."
A city not forsaken] See v. 4.

CH. LXIII. 1—6. THE DAY OF VENGEANCE IN EDOM.

These verses form a detached oracle, representing the final triumph of Jehovah over the enemies of His people. The image presented is one of the most impressive and awe-inspiring in the O.T., and it is difficult to say which is most to be admired, the dramatic vividness of the vision, or the reticence which conceals the actual work of slaughter and concentrates the attention on the Divine Hero as he emerges victorious from the conflict.—A solitary and majestic figure, in blood-red vesture, is seen approaching from the direction of Edom. A question of surprise escapes the prophet's lips as he contemplates the singular and startling apparition; and a brief reply comes from afar, indicating that the Hero is Jehovah, the Saviour-God of Israel (*v.* 1). The prophet then ventures to address himself directly to the advancing figure, inquiring the meaning of His crimson-stained raiment (*v.* 2). What follows (*vv.* 3—6) contains Jehovah's answer to the prophet's challenge, and the explanation of His strange appearance. The day of vengeance, the necessary preliminary to redemption, has come and passed (*v.* 4); the foes of Israel have been annihilated, as in some vast winepress (*vv.* 3, 6); and this great act of judgement has been accomplished by Jehovah alone, no human helper having been found to execute His will (*v.* 5).

It was a serious misapprehension of the spirit of the prophecy which led many of the Fathers to apply it to the passion and death of Christ. Although certain phrases, detached from their context, may suggest that interpretation to a Christian reader, there can be no doubt that the scene depicted is a "drama of Divine Vengeance" (G. A. Smith), into which the idea of propitiation does not enter. The solitary figure who

With dyed garments from Bozrah?
This *that is* glorious in his apparel,
Travelling in the greatness of his strength?
I that speak in righteousness, mighty to save.

speaks in *vv.* 3 ff. is not the Servant of the Lord, or the Messiah, but Jehovah Himself (comp. the parallel ch. lix. 16); the blood which reddens His garments is expressly said to be that of His enemies; and the "winepress" is no emblem of the spiritual sufferings endured by our Lord, but of the "fierceness and wrath of Almighty God" (Rev. xix. 15) towards the adversaries of His kingdom. While it is true that the judgement is the prelude to the redemption of Israel, the passage before us exhibits only the judicial aspect of the Divine dealings, and it is not permissible to soften the terrors of the picture by introducing soteriological conceptions which lie beyond its scope.

1. On *Bozrah*, a city of Edom, see on ch. xxxiv. 6.

with dyed garments] Better, **with bright coloured garments**. The word for "dyed" means literally "sharp," "piercing."

The mention of Edom as the scene of a judgement which is obviously universal (see *vv.* 3, 6), including all the enemies of Jehovah and Israel, is a feature common to this prophecy and that of ch. xxxiv. It is partly accounted for by the embittered relations between the two peoples, of which traces are found in post-exilic writings (see the note on ch. xxxiv.); and partly perhaps by the ancient conception that Jehovah marches from Edom to the succour of His people (Jud. v. 4). There can hardly be a reference to anticipated resistance on the part of the Edomites to the re-establishment of the Jewish State, for the judgement is not on Edom alone but on all nations; and moreover the prophecy in all probability belongs to a date subsequent to the first return of the exiles from Babylon.

glorious in his apparel] The word for *glorious* is lit. "swelling," being identical with that which is wrongly rendered "crooked" in ch. xlv. 2 (see the note). It is doubtful what is the exact sense of the expression "swelling in his raiment." Duhm's suggestion of loose robes inflated by the wind seems a little fanciful. On the other hand "glorious" or "splendid" (LXX. ὡραῖος) conveys an impression hardly consistent with the image, since the garments of the divine champion are said to be "defiled" by the blood of His enemies (*v.* 3).

travelling] R.V. **marching**; Vulg. *gradiens*. This however may represent a variant reading (*çô'ēd*, cf. Jud. v. 4) which is perhaps preferable to the Massoretic text (*çô'eh*). The Hebr. word occurs in the difficult passage li. 14 with the sense of "crouching." Those who retain it here explain it in various ways with the help of the Arabic as a "gesture of proud self-consciousness" (Del.); "swaying to and fro"; "with head thrown back," &c.

I that speak in righteousness &c.] i.e. "speak righteously" (cf. xlv. 19). Jehovah declares Himself to be true in speech, faithfully fulfilling His prophecies, and powerful in deed (*mighty to save*).

13—2

2 Wherefore *art thou* red in thine apparel,
   And thy garments like him that treadeth in the winefat?
3 I have trodden the winepress alone;
   And of the people *there was* none with me:
   For I will tread them in mine anger,
   And trample them in my fury;
   And their blood shall be sprinkled upon my garments,
   And I will stain all my raiment.
4 For the day of vengeance *is* in mine heart,
   And the year of my redeemed is come.

2. The meaning of Jehovah's appearing is not yet explained, and so the dialogue proceeds.

Wherefore art thou *red in thine apparel*] Better, **Wherefore is there red on thine apparel**; the form of the question indicating that the red colour is not that of the vesture itself but is something adventitious. "Red" (*'ādōm*) is suggested by *Edom*, just as the figure of the winepress may be suggested by the resemblance of *Boçrāh* (*v.* 1) to *bāçir* (vintage). The figure, however, is in itself an appropriate one; the winepress appearing "as an emblem on the coins of Bostra during the Roman rule" (Cheyne, *Comm.*).

3 ff. Jehovah's answer, disclosing the reason of His appearing.

I have trodden the winepress] or **winetrough**. The word (*pûrāh*), from a root meaning to "foam," seems to be poetic, although the only other instance of its use is prosaic enough (Hag. ii. 16). For the image of the winepress cf. Lam. i. 15; Joel iii. 13.

and of the **peoples** (R.V.) there was *none* (**no man**) *with me*] See *v.* 5.

for I will tread them &c.] Render **and I trod them** &c. The substitution of past tenses for futures throughout the verse is imperatively demanded by the sense, although it requires a series of changes in the vowel-points (*Vav* consec. for simple *Vav*). The reason of the Massoretic punctuation was the desire to make it plain that the prophecy relates to the future. This of course is true; but though the event be in itself future, it is represented in the vision as past, from the standpoint of the Divine speaker. Otherwise, the verse would contain no answer to the question of *v.* 2.

their blood] R.V. their **lifeblood**; lit., "their juice." The word occurs only here and in *v.* 6. *shall be sprinkled*] **was sprinkled** (2 Ki. ix. 33; see on ch. lii. 15).

I will stain] Rather, **I have defiled**. (The form in the original is Aramaic.)

4. *the day of vengeance*] announced in ch. lxi. 2.

is *in mine heart*] i.e. in my purpose.

the year of my redeemed] Another rendering, preferred by many authorities, is **the year of my redemption**: the plural being taken as

And I looked, and *there was* none to help; 5
And I wondered that *there was* none to uphold:
Therefore mine own arm brought salvation unto me;
And my fury, it upheld me.
And I will tread down the people in mine anger, 6
And make them drunk in my fury,
And I will bring down their strength to the earth.

expressing the abstract idea, in accordance with a common Hebr. usage. The year of redemption is the same as the year of Jehovah's favour in ch. lxi. 2; it is the time of Israel's victory and salvation, a year that has no end.

5. Comp. ch. lix. 16. The verse explains why it is that Jehovah treads the winepress "*alone*" (*v.* 3). The expectation that some human helper would appear on the side of Jehovah is more remarkable here than in ch. lix. 16, where the judgement was on Israel itself, and the complaint might be that even within the chosen nation no champion of righteousness could be found. The idea that such a champion might have been found amongst heathen nations is of course much less easily explained; unless, with Duhm, we suppose that the prophet is sadly contrasting his own age with the more hopeful time of the Second Isaiah, when the faith of Israel was directed to Cyrus as the agent of Jehovah's purposes on earth.

6. Repetition of the thought of *v.* 3.

And I will tread down the people] R.V. rightly, **And I trod down the peoples**, though the verb differs from either of those in *v.* 3. Past tenses are to be restored throughout.

make (**made**) *them drunk*] Some MSS., as well as the first printed edition of the Hebrew Bible (Soncino, 1488) read "broke them in pieces." The Targ. likewise supports this reading, which is more suitable to the context than that of the received text. The orthographic difference is minute (substitution of ב for כ).

and I will...strength] R.V. **and I poured out their lifeblood**,—as in *v.* 3. The A.V. thinks of another noun, similar in form, but from a different root, meaning "glory" (cf. 1 Sam. xv. 29).

Ch. LXIII. 7—LXIV. 12. A Prayer of the People for the Renewal of Jehovah's former Lovingkindness.

(1) *vv.* 7—9. The prayer begins with thankful commemoration of Jehovah's goodness to the nation in the days of old (*v.* 7). The reference is to the time of Moses and Joshua, when Jehovah's loving confidence in His children had not yet been betrayed (*v.* 8), and when He continuously manifested Himself as their Saviour, bearing them safely through all dangers (*v.* 9).

(2) *vv.* 10—14. This ideal relation between Israel and its God has indeed long since been broken, through the rebellion and ingratitude of the people (*v.* 10). But in seasons of distress the better mind of the

nation dwells wistfully on those ancient wonders of grace, and longs that Jehovah may again put forth His strength and vindicate His glorious name (*vv.* 11—14).

(3) *vv.* 15, 16. From the past the writer turns to the gloomy present, beseeching Jehovah to take notice of and have compassion on the affliction of His people. For He alone, and not Abraham or Israel, is the Father of the nation, and its Redeemer from of old.

(4) *vv.* 17—19. From this point the increasing impetuosity of the language reveals for the first time the extremity of the Church's anguish. The prophet remonstrates with God for so withdrawing Himself from the people as to harden them in sin (*v.* 17) and cause them to be as if He had never ruled over them (*v.* 19).

(5) lxiv. 1—3. A passionate wish that Jehovah might now rend asunder the solid firmament, and melt the mountains, and make Himself known to the nation by terrible acts, surpassing the expectations of His people.

(6) *vv.* 4—7. In a more reflective strain the writer appears to seek for a reconciliation of Jehovah's attitude to Israel with His eternally righteous character. He, the only God known who meets the righteous man, is yet wroth with His people so that they fall into sin (*vv.* 4, 5). The lamentable consequences of this hiding of God's face on the religious condition of the people are described in *vv.* 6, 7.

(7) *vv.* 8—12. Final appeal to the Fatherhood of God, and His consideration for the work of His hands (*v.* 8). Let Him moderate His wrath and remember that we are His people (*v.* 9). For surely the punishment of sin has been sufficient,—the holy cities ruined, Jerusalem a desolation, the Temple burned with fire (*vv.* 10, 11). Can Jehovah look on these things and yet restrain His compassion (*v.* 12)?

The passage is one of the most instructive of O.T. prayers, and deserves careful study as an expression of the chastened and tremulous type of piety begotten in the sorrows of the Exile. Along with much that is of the permanent essence of prayer,—thanksgiving, confession of sin, and supplication,—it contains utterances which may cause surprise to a Christian reader, although they are paralleled in some of the Psalms, and in other portions of the literature. Very singular is the plea that the sinfulness of the people is due to the excessive and protracted anger of Jehovah, who "causes them to err from His ways" (lxiii. 17; cf. lxiv. 5, 7). This feeling appears to proceed from two sources; on the one hand the ancient idea that national calamity is the proof of Jehovah's anger, and on the other the lesson taught by all the prophets, that the sole cause of Jehovah's anger is the people's sins. The writer seems unable perfectly to harmonize these principles. He accepts the verdict of Providence on the sins of the nation, but he feels also a disproportion between the offence and the punishment, which neutralises all efforts after righteousness, unless Jehovah will relent from the fierceness of His wrath. The higher truth that the Divine chastisement aims at the purification of the people, and is therefore a mark of love, is not yet grasped, and for this reason the O.T. believers fall short of the liberty of the sons of God. Yet amid all these perplexities the faith of the Church holds fast to the truth of the Fatherhood of God,

I will mention the lovingkindnesses of the LORD, *and* 7
the praises of the LORD,
According to all that the LORD hath bestowed on us,
And the great goodness towards the house of Israel,
Which he hath bestowed on them according to his
  mercies,
And according to the multitude of his lovingkindnesses.
For he said, Surely they *are* my people, 8

and appeals to the love which must be in His heart, although it be not manifest in His providential dealings.

So far as the *ideas* of the passage are concerned, it might have been composed at any time from the Exile downwards. Nor are the historical allusions so clear as could be desired. From lxiii. 18, lxiv. 11 f. we learn that the Temple has been burned, and the land laid waste. It is natural to understand this of the destruction of the city and Temple by the Chaldæans in 586, and to conclude that the prayer was written during the Exile or at least before the rebuilding of the Temple in 520. In lxiii. 18 it is said that the Holy Land has been possessed "but a little while." If the prayer was written in exile this must refer to the whole period from Joshua to the Captivity, which is not an interpretation that commends itself at first sight. It would no doubt be more intelligible if written not long after the restoration under Zerubbabel (cf. Ezra ix. 8). But then we are confronted with the difficulty of the destruction of the Temple, for Duhm's explanation that the writer ignores the second Temple because of its inferiority to the first can hardly be regarded as satisfactory; and to assume (with Kuenen and others) a destruction of the Temple by the Samaritans (see Ryle's note on Neh. i. 3) is hazardous in face of the silence of history. Partly for these reasons, and partly because of affinities to ch. xxiv.—xxvii., and some Psalms which he assigns to the same period, Cheyne brings down the date of composition to the time of Artaxerxes Ochus (cf. Vol. I. of this commentary, p. 204). Apart from lxiii. 18, the hypothesis of exilic authorship presents no serious difficulty, for although the surrounding discourses are probably post-exilic, it is quite conceivable that an earlier writing might have been incorporated with them as sufficiently expressive of the mind of the nation at the later period.

7—9. Celebration of Jehovah's past mercies to Israel,—a frequent feature of O.T. prayers (Ps. lxxvii. 10—15, lxxviii. 1—4, lxxxix. 1 f., cv. 1 f., cvi. 2; Neh. ix. 5 ff., &c.).

7. *I will mention*] lit. "commemorate," but with the implied idea of praise, as 1 Chr. xvi. 4; Ps. xlv. 17, lxxi. 16; Isa. xxvi. 13, &c.

the praises of the LORD] the **praiseworthy deeds**, as ch. lx. 6.

and the great goodness] Cf. Ps. cxlv. 7, where the expression occurs.

according to his mercies &c.] Cf. Ps. li. 1,—one of several points of resemblance,—also Ps. cvi. 45.

8. The retrospect goes back to the beginning of the nation's history,

Children *that* will not lie:
So he was their Saviour.
9 In all their affliction he was afflicted,
And the angel of his presence saved them:
In his love and in his pity he redeemed them;
And he bare them, and carried them all the days of old.

when Jehovah's affection for His people was still unimpaired. Cf. Hos. xi. 1, "When Israel was a child then I loved him."

children (**sons**) that *will not lie*] Contrast ch. i. 2, xxx. 9.

so he was their Saviour] **and he became to them a saviour.** LXX. adds from the following verse: **in all their distress.** On metrical grounds the addition is an obvious improvement; and it leads to an interesting explanation of the first part of *v.* 9 (see below).

9. *In all their affliction he was afflicted*] (lit. "there was affliction to Him"). This is the sense of the *Qĕrê*, which substitutes *lô* (to him) for the *lō'* (not) of the *Kĕthîb* (see on ch. ix. 3). It is impossible to obtain a good sense from the consonantal text; and it is accordingly rejected in favour of the *Qĕrê* by nearly all commentators. There is, however, no equally strong expression of Jehovah's sympathy with His people in the O.T.; both Jud. x. 16, and Ps. cvi. 44 fall far short of it. The LXX. (joining "in all their affliction" to the previous verse) continues: οὐ πρέσβυς οὐδὲ ἄγγελος, ἀλλ' αὐτὸς ἔσωσεν αὐτούς; i.e. **Not a messenger or an angel (but) His Presence saved them.** The only textual difference here is that צִיר ("messenger" or "ambassador") is read instead of צָר ("affliction"). It is true that צִיר is not elsewhere used of an angelic representative of Jehovah; but the metaphor is a natural one, and otherwise the translation has much to recommend it. (*a*) The "Presence" (lit. "Face") of Jehovah is used elsewhere of His self-manifestation. The fundamental passage is Ex. xxxiii. 14, 15: "My presence shall go... If thy presence go not, &c." But comp. also Deut. iv. 37; Lam. iv. 16, and see on ch. lix. 2. (*b*) An "angel of the Presence" on the other hand is a figure elsewhere unknown to the O.T.; the phrase would seem to be "a confusion of two forms of expression, incident to a midway stage of revelation" (Cheyne). (*c*) The "Face" of Jehovah, however, is not (as the LXX. inferred) just the same as Jehovah Himself in person. It is rather a name for His highest sensible manifestation, and hardly differs from what is in other places called the *Mal'ak Yahveh* (Angel of Jehovah). This is shewn by a comparison of Ex. xxxiii. 14 f., with xxiii. 20—23. The verse therefore means that it was no ordinary angelic messenger, but the supreme embodiment of Jehovah's presence that accompanied Israel in the early days. The idea has its analogies in Semitic heathenism, as when at Carthage the goddess Tanit was worshipped as the "Face of Baal," although this has been otherwise explained (Euting, *Punische Steine*, p. 8).

and he bare them] Better, **took them up**, as in ch. xl. 15. Cf. Deut. xxxii. 11.

But they rebelled, and vexed his **holy Spirit**: 10
Therefore he was turned to be their enemy, *and* he fought against them.
Then he remembered the days of old, Moses, *and* his 11 people, *saying*,
Where *is* he that **brought them up out of the sea with the** shepherd of his flock?
Where *is* he that put his holy Spirit within him?

10—14. The rebellion of the people, by which Jehovah is made to be their enemy, and their vain regrets. Comp. Deut. xxxii. 15 ff.

10. *and vexed his holy Spirit*] Comp. Acts vii. 51; Eph. iv. 30. Except here and in *v.* 11 and Ps. li. 11 the predicate "holy" is never in the O.T. used of the spirit of Jehovah. It is perhaps impossible to determine the exact connotation of the word in this connexion. It cannot be accidental that in all three cases the holy spirit is a principle of religious life; hence the phrase hardly signifies so little as merely "His divine **spirit**"; as Jehovah's "holy arm" may mean no more than His divine **arm**. Nor is it likely that it describes the spirit as the influence that imparts to Israel the quality of holiness, i.e. separateness from other nations, and consecration to Jehovah. The idea rather is that the spirit is holy in the same sense as Jehovah Himself is holy,—a principle which is both pure and inviolable, which resents and draws back from the contact of human impurity and especially of wilful opposition. This spirit is a national endowment, residing in the community (see *v.* 11); it is the spirit of prophecy, resting on Moses, but manifesting its presence also through other organs of revelation (see Deut. xxxiv. 9; Num. xi. 25 ff.). Hence it is said to have led the people (*v.* 14), and to "**vex**" the spirit is to resist his guidance, by disobeying the divine word which he inspires. The use of this verb marks the highest degree of personification of the Spirit attained in the O.T., preparing the way for the N.T. doctrine concerning Him.

11. In adversity the people realised the privilege they had forfeited by their rebellion, and longed for a return of the days of Moses.

Then he (i.e. Israel) *remembered &c.*]. Since the second half of the verse contains obviously words of the people, the subject of "remembered" must be Israel, not Jehovah. In the view of many commentators this subj. is expressed in the following phrase "his people" ("Then his people remembered the days of old"). But this order of words would be unnatural. The two expressions "Moses" and "**his people**" probably represent separate marginal glosses which have crept into the text, the first explanatory of "shepherd" and the second perhaps of "his flock." Neither is found in the LXX.

Where is he &c.] Or, **Where is He that brought up from** the sea the shepherd of His flock (i.e. Moses)? This reading is easier than that of the Massoretic text; it is supported by Hebr. MSS., and is followed by the LXX. The plural "shepherds" of R.V. represents the received Hebrew text; but the singular is the older and better reading.

12   That led *them* by the right hand of Moses *with* his glorious arm,
     Dividing the water before them, to make himself an everlasting name?
13   That led them through the deep,
     As a horse in the wilderness, *that* they should not stumble?
14   As a beast goeth down into the valley,
     The Spirit of the LORD caused him to rest:
     So didst thou lead thy people,
     To make thyself a glorious name.

15   Look down from heaven, and behold

The plural was no doubt substituted in order to include Aaron (cf. Ps. lxxvii. 20).

This turning back of the people's mind to the wonders of the Exodus is a hopeful sign of penitence which Jeremiah did not discover in the men of his day: "neither said they, Where is the Lord that brought us up out of the land of Egypt?" (Jer. ii. 6).

that put his holy Spirit within him] Rather, **within it**, i.e. His flock, the community; see on *v.* 10. Cf. Hag. ii. 5; Neh. ix. 20; Num. xi. 17, 25.

12. Render with R.V. **That caused his glorious arm to go at the right hand of Moses** &c.; accompanying him with its wonder-working power symbolized by the "rod of God" (Ex. xvii. 9). The reference in the latter part of the verse is not, as some have thought, to the bringing forth of water from the rock (ch. xlviii. 21; Ex. xvii. 1—7) but to the passage of the Red Sea.

13. *the deep*] R.V. **the depths**; Hebr. *tĕhômôth*, see on ch. li. 10.

as a horse in the wilderness] treading as firmly and securely as the horse on the open pasture. Comp. the parallelism Ps. cvi. 9: "He led them through the depths as through a pasture-land."

14. **As the cattle that go down into the valley** (R.V.). It is doubtful whether this clause does not continue *v.* 13, adding a second image of the security with which Israel went down into the depths of the sea. It has certainly a more forcible sense in that connexion than if taken as an illustration of the words which follow. The only difficulty is that these words may seem too short to stand alone.

caused him to rest] i.e. brought him (the nation) to the resting-place, the Promised Land (Ex. xxxiii. 14; Deut. xii. 9; Josh. i. 13 &c.). The ancient versions read, less suitably, "led him."

so didst thou lead &c.] Summarising the previous description and concluding the retrospect.

15, 16. A piteous appeal to the Divine clemency, based on Israel's filial relation to Jehovah.

Look down from heaven, and behold] (Ps. lxxx. 14). By a natural

From the habitation of thy holiness and of thy glory:
Where *is* thy zeal and thy strength,
The sounding of thy bowels and of thy mercies towards
 me? are they restrained?
Doubtless thou *art* our father, 16
Though Abraham be ignorant of us,
And Israel acknowledge us not:
Thou, O LORD, *art* our father, our redeemer;
Thy name *is* from everlasting.
O LORD, why hast thou made us to err from thy ways, 17
And hardened our heart from thy fear?

anthropomorphism the O.T. attributes the prevalence of evil on earth to a suspension of Jehovah's watchfulness; hence He is said to come down from heaven to enquire (Gen. xviii. 21), or, as here, to look down (cf. Ps. xiv. 2, cii. 19, &c.). To this writer it seems as if He had for the present withdrawn into His palace, and did not fully realise the sufferings of His people.

where is thy zeal (or **jealousy**)] Cf. ch. lix. 17. For *strength* read with R.V. **mighty acts**.

the sounding of thy bowels] i.e. the yearning of thy compassion. See ch. xvi. 11.

towards me? are they restrained] Rather, as R.V., **are restrained towards me** (LXX. "towards us"). Cf. ch. xlii. 14.

16. The verse reads: **For thou art our Father; for Abraham knoweth us not and Israel doth not recognise us; Thou Jehovah art our Father; our Redeemer from of old is Thy Name.** Jehovah is the Father of Israel, i.e. the Creator and founder of the nation (Deut. xxxii. 6; Mal. ii. 10; cf. Ex. iv. 22; Hos. xi. 1; Isa. i. 2; Jer. iii. 4, 19; Mal. i. 6). The idea of the divine Fatherhood is not yet extended in the O.T. to the individual believer, although a remarkable anticipation of the N.T. doctrine is found in Ecclus. xxiii. 1, 4: "O Lord, Father and Master of my life,...O Lord, Father and God of my life." (Cheyne.)

17—19. Expostulation with Jehovah for the hard treatment which makes righteousness and true religion impossible to the nation.

17. Render: **Why shouldest Thou leave us to wander, O Jehovah,** from Thy ways; and harden **our heart so that we fear Thee not?** etc. Israel had rejected God's guidance, and He had given them up to their sins; how long was this to last? The idea underlying this plea seems to be that the people's faint aspirations Godward were checked and baffled by the continued evidence of Jehovah's displeasure. Some measure of outward success was needed to guide them into the path of obedience, and no such token was vouchsafed.

hardened our heart from thy fear] so that we cannot attain to the true fear of God, i.e. true religion or piety. "Harden" in the original is a strong word, recurring only in Job xxxix. 16.

> Return for thy servants' sake,
> The tribes of thine inheritance.
> 18 The people of thy holiness have possessed *it* but a little while:
> Our adversaries have trodden down thy sanctuary.
> 19 We are *thine:* thou never barest rule over them;
> They were not called by thy name.
>
> 64 O that thou wouldest rend the heavens, that thou wouldest come down,
> That the mountains might flow down at thy presence,

Return for thy servants' sake] Cf. Ps. xc. 13.

18. *The people...while*] The want of an acc. to the verb excites suspicion, for it is hardly possible to take "thy sanctuary" as the obj. common to the two clauses. The text of the LXX., which reads "mountain" instead of "people" and has the verb in the first pers. plu., is perhaps to be preferred: **For a little while have we possessed Thy holy mountain.** Comp. ch. lvii. 13.

The second part of the verse speaks of a desecration of the Temple, which apparently *followed* the possession of the land. The difficulty of reconciling these two facts has been pointed out in the Introductory Note above. If any destruction of the second Temple were known to have taken place about the time of Ezra, the circumstances would be explained. But the stronger statements in lxiv. 10, 11 make it unlikely that if such a calamity had really happened it should not have been expressly mentioned, even in the meagre historical records which have been preserved of that period.

19. Render: **We are become (as those) over whom from of old Thou hast not borne rule, over whom Thy name has not been called.** The visible splendours of Jehovah's kingship have been absent throughout the later period of the nation's history. Comp. ch. xxvi. 13, and (for the second part of the verse) Deut. xxviii. 10; Jer. xiv. 9.

lxiv. 1—3. The language of complaint again gives place (as in lxiii. 15) to impatient prayer for a Theophany,—an imposing manifestation of Jehovah in His might. It is the great "day of the Lord" towards which the desire of the people reaches forward. In the Hebr., ch. lxiv. begins with *v.* 2 of our version, *v.* 1 forming the conclusion of lxiii. 19.

1. *O that thou wouldest rend &c.*] Lit. "hadst rent." So "hadst come down," "had quaked." This use of the perf. in the expression of a real wish, whose realisation is contemplated, is unusual, and is only to be explained by the urgency of the speaker's feeling. Driver, *Tenses*, § 140. See on ch. xlviii. 18.

rend the heavens] Cf. ch. li. 6; Ps. xviii. 9, cxliv. 5.

might flow down] Rather, **might quake**; cf. Jud. v. 5. For the general conception of the Theophany cf. Ps. l. 1—6; Hab. iii. 3 ff.

As *when* the melting fire burneth, the fire causeth the 2
waters to boil,
To make thy name known to thine adversaries,
That the nations may tremble at thy presence.
When thou didst terrible things *which* we looked not 3
for,
Thou camest down, the mountains flowed down at thy
presence.
For since the beginning of the world *men* have not 4
heard, nor perceived by the ear,
Neither hath the eye seen, O God, besides thee,
What he hath prepared for him that waiteth for
him.

2. Render: **As fire kindleth brushwood, as fire maketh water boil**, &c.

to make thy name known to thine adversaries &c.]—the purpose of the Theophany. Cf. ch. lix. 18, 19.

3. The second part of the verse, being (in the original) verbally repeated from *v.* 1, ought probably to be omitted as a copyist's error. The passage gains in compactness by its excision. *Vv.* 1—3 will then form a single sentence, the last clause of which runs: **while thou doest terrible things which we hoped not for**; i.e. surpassing all our expectations.

terrible things] A standing phrase, as Cheyne remarks, for the marvels of the Exodus, the type of the great final deliverance. Cf. Deut. x. 21; 2 Sam. vii. 23; Ps. cvi. 22.

4—7. This difficult passage contains (1) an appeal to that which distinguishes Jehovah from all other deities: He is the only God who works for them that wait for Him in the way of righteousness; (2) a confession of the people's sinful condition due to the persistency of the divine wrath. A contrast between these thoughts is probably intended; the severity of Jehovah's dealings with Israel seems at variance with His known character. But the text is in some places hopelessly corrupt, and the exact sense is somewhat uncertain.

For since the beginning...heard] Lit. "And from of old they have not heard." It is tempting (with Duhm) to take this as a relative clause parallel to and continuing *v.* 3 ("...terrible things which we hoped not for, and which from of old men have not heard"). There is an awkwardness, however, in commencing a new sentence with the next clause, and still greater difficulty in carrying on the sentence of *v.* 3 to the word "seen" (Hitzig). Accepting the traditional division, *v.* 4 will read nearly as in R.V., **And from of old men have not heard, have not perceived by the ear, no eye hath seen a God beside Thee, Who worketh for him that waiteth for Him**. The rendering of A.V. is partly accommodated to St Paul's language in 1 Cor. ii. 9, where, however, a different text (not the LXX.) seems to be followed. Jerome

206   ISAIAH, LXIV.   [vv. 5—7.

5   Thou meetest him that rejoiceth and worketh righteousness,
    Those that remember thee in thy ways:
    Behold, thou art wroth; for we have sinned:
    In those is continuance, and we shall be saved.
6   But we are all as an unclean *thing*,
    And all our righteousnesses *are* as filthy rags;
    And we all do fade as a leaf;
    And our iniquities, like the wind, have taken us away.
7   And *there is* none that calleth upon thy name,
    That stirreth up himself to take hold of thee:

says that the Apostle's words are found in certain Apocalyptic books, although he will not admit that they are quoted from them.

"Worketh for"="sheweth Himself active on behalf of"; without obj., as Gen. xxx. 30; Ps. xxxvii. 5.

5. *Thou meetest*] (a perf. of experience). The verb is obviously used here in a good sense, as Gen. xxxii. 1.

that rejoiceth and worketh righteousness] i.e. **that joyfully worketh righteousness.** The words *rejoiceth and* are not in the LXX.

those that remember thee in thy ways] Cf. ch. xxvi. 8.

thou art wroth &c.] R.V. **thou wast wroth and we sinned.** Cf. ch. lvii. 17.

in those is continuance and we shall be saved] R.V. "in them have we been of long time, and shall we be saved?" The text is quite unintelligible. LXX. has simply διὰ τοῦτο ἐπλανήθημεν. The last word suggests a satisfactory emendation (perhaps ונשע for ונושע). Of further conjectural restorations one may be mentioned, due to Lowth. Instead of בהם עולם he reads בְּהֵמְעוֹלָם = "against the evil-doers"; thus obtaining a parallelism with the preceding line.

"Behold Thou wast wroth and we sinned,
Against the evildoers, and we fell away."

This is at least a meaning, though not one that is altogether convincing.

6, 7. A pathetic description of the degeneracy and spiritual lethargy of the people, caused by the divine wrath.

6. And we are all become as one unclean— in a ceremonial sense, like the leper.

and all our righteousnesses &c.] our righteous deeds,—our best efforts after the fulfilment of the divine will, are stained and rendered ineffective by our general sinful condition.

as filthy rags] **as a polluted garment.**

our iniquities, like the wind, &c.] cf. ch. lvii. 13; Job xxvii. 21, xxx. 22. The image is here that of the leaf, already sere and faded, swept from the tree by the winter blast: so our iniquities hurry us away to destruction.

7. *And* there is *none that calleth, &c.*] an easily intelligible hyperbole.

stirreth himself up] "arouseth himself," the same verb as in li. 17.

consumed us, because of our iniquities] lit. "melted us by the hand of

For thou hast hid thy face from us,
And hast consumed us, because of our iniquities.
But now, O LORD, thou *art* our father;   8
We *are* the clay, and thou our potter;
And we all *are* the work of thine hand.
Be not wroth very sore, O LORD,   9
Neither remember iniquity for ever:
Behold, see, we beseech thee, we *are* all thy people.
Thy holy cities are a wilderness,   10
Zion is a wilderness, Jerusalem a desolation.
Our holy and our beautiful house,   11

our iniquities." Cf. Ezek. xxxiii. 10, "Our transgressions and our sins are upon us, and we waste away in them, how should we then live?" A better reading, supported by LXX., Pesh. and Targ., is **delivered us into the hand** (i.e. the power) **of our iniquities**. Cf. Job viii. 4.

8—12. The prayer now ends in a direct and touching supplication, supported by various pleas, that Jehovah will at last cause His wrath against His people to cease.

8. *thou art our father*] See on lxiii. 16.

we are *the clay, and thou our potter*] The nearest parallel to this application of the common image of clay and potter is perhaps Job x. 9. It is the plea of the creature against seeming unreasonableness on the part of the Creator. Can the potter allow the work on which he has lavished his utmost skill and care to be broken in pieces?

9. *neither remember iniquity for ever*] Ps. lxxix. 8. The nation feels that it is bearing the inexhaustible penalty of past sins. Such a thought was specially natural after the Restoration, when it appeared as if even the immeasurable calamity of the Exile had not wiped out the arrears of hereditary guilt (cf. Zech. i. 12).

10, 11. The evidences of Jehovah's displeasure are to be seen on every hand, in the desolation and ruin of the sacred places.

10. *Thy holy cities*] is a phrase which does not occur elsewhere, and both LXX. and Vulg. substitute the sing. for the plur. It is not necessary, however, to follow them. If the land is holy (Zech. ii. 12) there is no reason why the epithet should not be applied to all its cities.

11. The reference must apparently be to the first Temple and its destruction by the Chaldæans. The expression, and indeed the whole tone of the passage, suggest an event not quite recent; it is not the present generation, but their fathers who praised God in the "holy and beautiful house." The question then comes to be whether this could have been said after the erection of Zerubbabel's Temple. In spite of the tendency to hyperbolical language which marks the prayer, and the painful contrast between the magnificence of the first Temple and the poverty of the second, it is difficult to think that the author should absolutely ignore the existence of the sanctuary if it had been restored. See Introductory note.

Where our fathers praised thee,
Is burnt up with fire:
And all our pleasant things are laid waste.
12 Wilt thou refrain thyself for these *things*, O LORD?
Wilt thou hold thy peace, and afflict us very sore?

is burned with fire] Lit. "has become a burning of fire"; cf. ch. ix. 5.
our pleasant things] Rather, our desirable places; cf. 2 Chr. xxxvi. 19; Lam. i. 10; Ezek. xxiv. 21, 25.
12. *refrain thyself*] See ch. lxiii. 15.

CH. LXV. THREATS AND PROMISES, ADDRESSED TO TWO DISTINCT PARTIES.

The chapter may be divided into two nearly equal portions:—
i. *vv.* 1—12. A contrast is drawn between the servants of Jehovah and a party who have apostatised from the true religion.
(1) *vv.* 1—7. The divine speaker complains that His gracious invitations have been scorned by an "obdurate people" (*vv.* 1, 2), who have provoked Him continually by scandalous and abominable superstitions (*vv.* 3—5), and against whom He now pronounces a final sentence of rejection (*vv.* 6, 7).
(2) *vv.* 8—10. The method of Jehovah's dealings with Israel illustrated by a figure from the vintage. As the grape cluster is spared for the sake of the new wine that is in it, so for the sake of the spiritual principle embodied in Israel, Jehovah will "not destroy the whole" (*v.* 8). On the contrary a seed shall be brought forth from Jacob to inherit the Holy Land from the west to the east (*vv.* 9, 10).
(3) *vv.* 11, 12. The schismatics, here directly addressed as they that "forsake the Lord" and repudiate the Temple worship in their service of strange gods, are threatened with extinction. The first section ends, as it began, by reminding the apostates of the overtures of Divine love and condescension which they had so wantonly spurned.
ii. *vv.* 13—25. The final separation of the two classes.
(1) *vv.* 13—16. The future of the idolaters is more explicitly contrasted with that of the "servants" of Jehovah (*vv.* 13 f.). The former shall be annihilated, leaving behind them nothing but a name for a formula of imprecation (*v.* 15); while Jehovah's true servants remain in the land to "bless themselves in the God of truth" (*v.* 16).
(2) *vv.* 17—25. The blessings reserved for the people of God in the Messianic age: an entire transformation of the conditions of human existence, compared to the creation of "new heavens and a new earth" (*v.* 17); Jehovah's delight in His handiwork dissipating the sorrows of earth (18, 19); patriarchal longevity (20); undisturbed possession of the land (21—23); immediate answer to prayer (24); and harmony in the animal world (25) are the features of this captivating picture of the latter days.

In the view of most expositors ch. lxv. is Jehovah's answer to the preceding intercession (lxiii. 7—lxiv. 12). But this connexion, as Cheyne

I am sought of *them that* asked not *for me:* **65**
I am found of *them that* sought me not:

has long insisted, is far from obvious and probably does violence to the natural interpretation of *vv.* 1, 2. The persons there referred to are sharply and explicitly distinguished from those in whose name the prayer is uttered. The community which in lxiv. 9 says, "We are *all* thy people" cannot surely have included amongst its members the openly pagan party described in lxv. 3 ff., 8 ff. And to suppose the meaning to be that Jehovah has always been ready to answer prayer, but must first effect a separation between the two classes, is very like an attempt to force a connexion where none exists. The theory becomes still more untenable when we take into account the extremely close resemblance between ch. lxv. and lxvi. It is safer to regard these two chapters as one continuous discourse, complete in itself, and having no special reference to what immediately precedes.

The situation presupposed by this chapter and the next presents many features of great interest and importance. On the whole the impression is confirmed that in this part of the book we have to do with prophecies delivered in Palestine, at a time subsequent to the Restoration. The notes will supply some indications of this; and there appears to be nothing which really countenances the idea that the author lived among the exiles in Babylon. The most important fact is the sharp division of parties, already referred to, which runs through the prophecy. This fact may be explained in two ways: (1) It may be merely the distinction, which always existed in Israel, between the godly kernel of the nation and the great mass who were addicted to heathen practices. The antithesis in this case would be largely ideal, being obvious from the point of view of the prophet and those who shared his faith, but not recognised by their opponents. But this conception hardly corresponds to the state of things revealed by the allusions of the prophecy. The separation is open and acknowledged on both sides; each party excommunicates the other (lxvi. 5); and the apostates maintain an attitude of opposition to the Temple at Jerusalem (lxv. 11). (2) The second theory may better enable us to comprehend this situation. It is the same as was already suggested by ch. lvii. 3 ff., viz., that the schismatics referred to are the half-caste Samaritans and their adherents amongst the "people of the land," while the servants of Jehovah are the religious and strictly legal party which is known to have existed in the time of Malachi, and had been reinforced by the arrival of Ezra and his company from Babylon (Ezra ix. 1—4). Some points in favour of this view are (*a*) the Hebrew extraction of the party denounced (lxvi. 5; see on lvii. 3); (*b*) their separation from the Temple service (lxvi. 11); (*c*) the peculiar and revolting heathen rites to which they were addicted (lxv. 3—5, 11, lxvi. 3, 17) implying a degree of religious degeneracy not easy to conceive in a properly Jewish society; (*d*) their perpetuation of the illegal worship of the "high places" (lxv. 7); and (*e*) the manner in which they are addressed as a distinct and well-known body (lxv. 5, 11, lxvi. 5). These circumstances do not of course amount to a demonstration

I said, Behold me, behold me,
Unto a nation *that* was not called by my name.
2 I have spread out mine hands all the day unto
  a rebellious people,
Which walketh *in* a way *that was* not good, after their
own thoughts;
3 A people that provoketh me to anger continually to
my face;

of the hypothesis, although in conjunction with the presumption of post-exilic authorship they invest it with a certain degree of probability.
    1, 2. Jehovah's overtures have been rejected by an obdurate people.
    1. Render: **I was to be enquired of by those that** asked not, **I was to be found by them that** sought me not, etc. The first verb in each line is of the form *Niphal*, which is to be understood not as a simple passive, but in its *tolerative* sense: "I let myself be enquired of," i.e. "I was ready to answer," exactly as Ezek. xiv. 3, xx. 3, 31, xxxvi. 37: "I let myself be found," as ch. lv. 6. Jehovah's readiness to hear is contrasted with the people's unwillingness to pray.
    Behold me, behold me] Cf. ch. xl. 9, xli. 27, lii. 6, lviii. 9.
    that was not called by my name] We should read, changing the vowels in accordance with the Old Versions: **that did not call on my name**.
    2. *spread out mine hands*] The attitude of supplication; cf. Prov. i. 24.
    a rebellious (**refractory**, Hos. iv. 16) *people*] LXX. has; λαὸν ἀπειθοῦντα καὶ ἀντιλέγοντα; and so the citation Rom. x. 21.
    a way that was *not good*] "A not-good way" (litotes). The same phrase in Ps. xxxvi. 4; Prov. xvi. 29.
    The people referred to here are necessarily the same as those described in the sequel. If these be the paganised Israelites of the North who had not shared the Captivity the two verses reveal an important fact not otherwise recorded. The prophetic representatives of Jehovah in the post-exilic community must, in that case, have sought to win over these outcasts to the pure worship of Jehovah, and the acceptance of the Law. This might appear to be inconsistent with what is told in Ezra iv. 1—3, where the friendly advances of the Samaritans are met with a stern refusal on the part of the Jews. But the contradiction is perhaps only apparent. The Jewish leaders might very well have declined the co-operation of these people while they maintained their impure religion, and at the same time been eager to incorporate them in the Theocracy on the terms offered to foreigners in ch. lvi. 6 f.
    In Rom. x. 20, 21, St Paul quotes parts of these verses, applying *v.* 1 to the conversion of the Gentiles and *v.* 2 to the unbelief of Israel. Possibly this exegesis may have been traditional in the Apostle's time (Delitzsch), although the primary sense of the passage is that the same persons are referred to throughout.
    3—5. Description of their illegal and superstitious cults.

That sacrificeth in gardens, and burneth incense upon
   altars of brick;
Which remain among the graves,   4
And lodge in the monuments,
Which eat swine's flesh,
And broth of abominable *things is in* their vessels;
Which say, Stand by thyself,   5
Come not near to me; for I am holier than thou.

3. *that sacrificeth in* the *gardens*] Cf. ch. lxvi. 17, and see on i. 29.
burneth incense upon altars of brick] Strictly **on the bricks** (R.V.),
or tiles. We have no key to the meaning of the expression. Some
think the "tiles" denote the roofs of the houses, where sacrifices were
sometimes offered to false gods (see 2 Ki. xxiii. 12; Jer. xix. 13; Zeph.
i. 5); others (like A.V.) suppose that altars made of bricks are referred
to. Why the custom should be specially Babylonian (Del.) does not
appear. The word for "burn incense" may mean simply "burn sacrifice"; see on ch. i. 13.
   4. The first two lines read:
      Who sit in the **graves**,
      and pass the **night in secret** (lit. guarded) **places**.
The practice of "sitting in graves" is undoubtedly rooted in the worship
of ancestors (Schwally, *Das Leben nach dem Tode*, pp. 68, 71), and the
object probably was to obtain oracles from the dead. The phrase "pass
the night" seems to point to the custom known to the ancients as *incubation*: "ubi stratis pellibus hostiarum *incubare* soliti erant, ut somniis
futura cognoscerent" (Jerome). This idea is expressed by the LXX.
(which runs the two clauses into one): κοιμῶνται διὰ ἐνύπνια; i.e. for the
purpose of obtaining dream-oracles. But whether the "secret places"
are connected with the "graves" is uncertain.
   which eat swine's flesh] in sacrificial meals; in any case a violation of
the Law (Deut. xiv. 8; Lev. xi. 7). From the fact that wild pigs are
mentioned in the cuneiform inscriptions (Jensen, *Zeitschrift für Assyrio-
logie*, Vol. I. pp. 306 ff.) it has been inferred that the Jews were tempted
into this during the Exile. But the swine was "forbidden food to all
the Semites," being sacred to more than one deity, and used in sacrifice
only in some exceptional rites (W. R. Smith, *Religion of the Semites*[2],
pp. 218, 290 f., 351). It is probably such mystic sacrifices that are
here referred to; and there was no place where lax Jews were more
likely to be enticed into them than in their own land.
   broth of abominable things] Such creatures as are enumerated in lxvi.
17. The "sacrifices are boiled and yield a magical hell-broth" (W. R.
Smith, *Marriage and Kinship*, p. 310). "Broth" is the rendering of
the Qĕrē (*mārāq*, Jud. vi. 19 f.); the *Kĕthîb* has a word (*pārāq*) which
might mean "piece" (sing.), although it does not occur elsewhere.
   5. *Stand by thyself*] Lit. "Draw near to thyself." Cf. xlix. 20.
for I am holier than thou] This construction of the accus. suffix is
hardly admissible. The verb is to be pointed as *Piel*, and the clause

These *are* a smoke in my nose,
A fire that burneth all the day.
6 Behold, *it is* written before me:
I will not keep silence, but will recompense,
Even recompense into their bosom,

rendered: **else I sanctify thee** (cf. the similar use of the perf. in 1 Sam. ii. 16). The words express no Pharisaic sense of superior virtue; they are addressed by a Mystagogue (see on lxvi. 17), or at least a member of a special religious fellowship, to the uninitiated, warning them against the dangerous degree of holiness (taboo) which would be incurred by contact with the initiated (cf. Ezek. xliv. 19). (See *Rel. of Sem.*[2] pp. 343, 357—368). It is true we have no further evidence of the existence of such mystic societies in Palestine at any time. But the whole passage (*vv.* 3—5) is unique, and furnishes a startling revelation of a state of things without parallel in the O.T., although something similar may be inferred from Ezek. viii. 10. Its emergence at this particular period is no doubt to be explained by the collapse of the old national religions, which was the inevitable result of the Assyrian and Babylonian conquests. This naturally led to a recrudescence of primitive superstitions which had been handed down in obscure circles, but had been kept in check so long as the public religion of the state retained its vitality (*Rel. of Sem.*[2] pp. 357 f.). But while this general explanation may be sufficient, the situation becomes perhaps still more intelligible if we suppose the description to apply to descendants of the colonists settled by Assyrian kings in Samaria (Cheyne, *Introd.* p. 369).

these are *a smoke in my nose*] If the clause stood alone it would be interpreted as a figurative expression of the idea of *v.* 3 *a*,—a smoke entering into and irritating the nostrils. The parallel clause, however, has led nearly all commentators to understand the "smoke" as a symbol of the Divine anger (cf. Ps. xviii. 8); and to paraphrase the line thus: "these are (the cause of) a smoke (proceeding from) my nostrils." This is certainly very unnatural. Why should not the second line be subordinate to the first,—the continually burning fire being the source of the "smoke" as the emblem of provocation?

a fire that burneth all the day] Probably a citation from Jer. xvii. 4; cf. Deut. xxxii. 22.

6, 7. Sentence is now pronounced on the reprobates, who by their persistent idolatries have served themselves heirs to the guilt of their fathers.

it is *written before me*] The sins mentioned above stand recorded in the heavenly books, calling constantly for punishment (cf. Jer. xvii. 1). Another interpretation, according to which the subject of the sentence is the Divine decree of judgement, is less acceptable, because the following words can hardly be taken as the contents of such a decree.

I will not keep silence **until I have recompensed**] For the construction cf. Gen. xxxii. 26; Lev. xxii. 6, &c.

even recompense &c.] **and I will recompense** *into their bosom*,—a

Your iniquities, and the iniquities of your fathers to- 7
gether, saith the LORD,
Which have burnt incense upon the mountains,
And blasphemed me upon the hills:
Therefore will I measure their former work into their bosom.

Thus saith the LORD, 8
As the new wine is found in the cluster,

new sentence, as is shown by the Hebr. pointing of the verb as consec. perf. Cf. Jer. xxxii. 18; Ps. lxxix. 12.

7. *Your iniquities...your fathers*] The change from 3rd to 2nd pers. is extremely awkward, unless the verse could be detached from the preceding and regarded (down to "hills") as an exclamation. This is far from natural; the better construction is that of the E.V. which makes "iniquities" the obj. to "recompense." It is probably necessary (with the LXX.) to read "their" in both cases. The iniquities of the fathers are indicated in the following words.

which have burnt incense (**have sacrificed**,—see on i. 13) *upon the mountains*] The reference is obviously to the illegal worship of the "high places" or local sanctuaries, which is denounced in similar terms in Hos. iv. 13; Ezek. vi. 13; cf. Ezek. xviii. 6 (if the text be right,—see Davidson on the passage in *Camb. Bible for Schools*). That this form of idolatry was *also* practised by those here spoken of is in every way probable (see ch. lvii. 7); on the other hand their ancestors, the pre-exilic Israelites, could not be charged with the more heinous offences described in *vv.* 3—5. These last, however, were the outcome of the same idolatrous tendency which formerly shewed itself in the worship at the high places, and the judgement now about to descend on the children is called forth both by their own guilt and by that of their fathers.

therefore will I measure their former work] Rather: **and I will first measure their** reward. The word for "former" (*rī'shônāh*) if an adj., ought to have the art., and moreover the thought expressed by this translation would be unsuitable, since it passes by in silence the recompense due to the sins of the children themselves. It must therefore be rendered as an adverb, as in Jer. xvi. 18 ("and first I will recompense their iniquity" &c.). So R.V.

into their bosom] as *v.* 6.

8—10. In spite of the gross idolatries denounced in the preceding section there is that in Israel which makes it precious in the sight of Jehovah, and ensures for it a brilliant future.

8. In the figure, the grape-cluster represents the nation as a whole, including many unworthy members, the "new wine" (*tīrôsh*, "must") is the spiritual kernel of the nation, here called "my servants"; and the truth taught is that for the sake of the latter "the whole" shall not be annihilated in the judgement that is to come. It is an application to new circumstances of Isaiah's doctrine of the Remnant (ch. vi. 13).

And *one* saith, Destroy it not; for a blessing *is* in it:
So will I do for my servants' sakes,
That *I* may not destroy them all.

9 And I will bring forth a seed out of Jacob,
And out of Judah an inheritor of my mountains:
And mine elect shall inherit it,
And my servants shall dwell there.

10 And Sharon shall be a fold of flocks,
And the valley of Achor a place for the herds to lie down in,
For my people that have sought me.

11 But ye *are* they that forsake the LORD,

The words *Destroy it not, for a blessing* is *in it* have been thought, from their rhythm, to be the first line of one of the vintage songs often referred to in Scripture (cf. Jud. ix. 27; Isa. xvi. 10; Jer. xxv. 30, xlviii. 33, &c.). It has further been conjectured that the words "Destroy not" (*'al tashḥēth*) in the headings of four psalms (lvii., lviii., lix., lxxv.) refer to this song, naming its melody as the tune to which these Psalms were to be sung (W. R. Smith, *O. T. in Jewish Church*², p. 209).

that I may not &c.] (so as) **not to destroy the whole.**

9. When a separation is effected the true Israelites shall possess the land (ch. lvii. 13, lx. 21).

a seed] Cf. ch. vi. 13, liii. 10.

my mountains] the mountain land of Palestine, an Isaianic phrase (ch. xiv. 25). *shall inherit it*] i.e. the land.

shall dwell there] Dillmann infers from the adv. "there" that neither the prophet nor his hearers lived in Palestine; but the argument cannot be sustained. "There" may be said of a place just mentioned, irrespective of the speaker's relation to it. Thus in ch. xxxvii. 33 Isaiah says that the king of Assyria "shall not shoot an arrow *there*," referring to Jerusalem ("this city") where he was living.

10. *Sharon*] (in Hebr. always with the art.) the northern part of the Maritime Plain, from near Carmel to Joppa, varying in breadth from 6 to 12 miles. (For a description see G. A. Smith, *Hist. Geogr.* pp. 147 f.)

the valley of Achor] Josh. vii. 24, xv. 7; Hos. ii. 15. One of the valleys (not identified) running up into the mountains from the Jordan-depression somewhere near Jericho. The names are mentioned as the extreme limits, W. and E., of the land to be inherited by the servants of Jehovah.

for my people that have **inquired of me**] in contrast to those spoken of in *v.* 1.

11, 12. A renewed threat against the apostates, with a further allusion to their idolatry.

But ye are *they that forsake &c.*] Render: **But as for you** that

That forget my holy mountain,
That prepare a table for *that* troop,
And that furnish the drink offering unto *that* number.

forsake Jehovah (ch. i. 4) &c. The whole verse is a descriptive anticipation of the object of the verb "destine" in *v.* 12 (see R.V.).

that forget my holy mountain] The phrase may denote either simple indifference to the welfare of Zion (cf. Ps. cxxxvii. 5), or deliberate abstention from the Temple ritual. The second view implies residence in Palestine at a time when the Temple services were in full operation; hence the other is necessarily adopted by all who hold the prophecy to have been written in Babylon. It is perhaps impossible to decide which is right, although those who recognise a Palestinian colouring throughout the chapter will naturally prefer the second as the more forcible interpretation, and find in it some confirmation of their theory.

that prepare a table &c.] Better: **that spread a table for Gad, and fill up mixed wine** (see ch. v. 22) **to Meni**. The rites described are the *lectisternia*, well known throughout the ancient world, in which a table was spread, furnished with meats and drinks as a meal for the gods (Liv. v. 13; Herodot. 1. 183; Ep. of Jeremiah, *vv.* 27 f.; Bel and the Dragon, *v.* 11; cf. Jer. vii. 18, xix. 13, xliv. 17, 1 Cor. x. 21). A parallel in the O.T. religion is the Shewbread in the Temple (or Tabernacle), Ex. xxv. 30 &c. Gesenius remarks that the description of the complete *lectisternium* extends over both members of the parallelism, and infers that the two deities were worshipped together. This is probable, being in accordance with ancient custom (Liv. v. 13), but the laws of Hebrew parallelism hardly permit us to say that this must be the meaning.

That Gad and Meni are divine proper names is universally acknowledged, although neither has quite lost its appellative signification and both are here pointed with the article. Gad means "good fortune"; he is personified luck. [The rendering "troop" in A.V. is a mistake. Cf. Gen. xxx. 11. where "A troop cometh" should be "With fortune!" as R.V. marg. In Gen. xlix. 19, where a different etymology is supposed, the word for "troop" is not *gad* but *gĕdûd*.] The existence of a Syrian god of this name (or the Greek equivalent Τύχη) is well established, and his worship is proved to have extended over a very wide area (see Baethgen, *Beiträge zur Sem. Rel.-Gesch.* pp. 76—80). It appears that the evidence is most copious amongst the Greek inscriptions of the Hauran (note the proximity to the Hebrew tribe of Gad) where there must have been numerous temples in his honour. But the name occurs also in Phœnician and Palmyrene inscriptions, and on coins of several cities, including Ashkelon, while a temple to the "Fortune" of Gaza is known to have existed in that city (Baethgen, p. 66). The place-names Baal-Gad (at the foot of Hermon, Josh. xi. 17, xii. 7, xiii. 5) and Migdal-Gad (in Judah, Josh. xv. 37) seem to shew that his worship was practised in Palestine proper. There are besides frequent references in Syriac and later Jewish literature; a Syriac writer of the 5th century mentions that *lectisternia* were still prepared for Gad in his time. The

12   Therefore will I number you to the sword,
And ye shall all bow down to the slaughter:
Because when I called, ye did not answer;
When I spake, ye did not hear;
But did evil before mine eyes,
And did choose *that* wherein I delighted not.
13   Therefore thus saith the Lord GOD,
Behold, my servants shall eat, but ye shall be hungry:
Behold, my servants shall drink, but ye shall be thirsty:
Behold, my servants shall rejoice, but ye shall be ashamed:
14   Behold, my servants shall sing for joy of heart,
But ye shall cry for sorrow of heart,
And shall howl for vexation of spirit.
15   And ye shall leave your name for a curse unto my chosen:

Jewish interpreters identified Gad with the planet Jupiter, called by the Arabs "the greater Luck," but this association may be more recent than our passage (Baethgen). Meni (*Mĕnî*) has left fewer traces. He is possibly identical with the goddess *Manât*, one of the three chief divinities of the pre-Mohammedan Arabs (Koran, Sura liii. 19—23). A personal name '*Abdmenî* (= Servant of Meni?) has been found on coins of the Achæmenidæ, but the accuracy of this is doubted by some (Delitzsch, Schrader in Riehm's *Handwörterbuch*). The meaning of the word is "Destiny," and the god has been identified with the planet Venus, "the lesser Luck" of the Arabs. It is quite as likely, however, that Meni is the antithesis of Gad,—the god of *evil* destiny. [Observe that in the LXX. Gad is Δαιμόνιον and Meni Τύχη.] Nothing has yet been discovered to connect these deities with the Babylonian pantheon. Some think they may be Hebrew equivalents of Babylonian names (Dillmann), others that their worship was transported from Syria to Babylon (Baethgen). These are speculations, but the actual evidence points to Western Asia as the natural environment of this cult.

12.   Render with R.V. **I will destine you to the sword** &c. There is a play upon words between the verb for "destine" (*mānāh*) and *Mĕnî* in *v.* 11.

because when I called &c.] Cf. *vv.* 1, 2.
but did evil before mine eyes &c.] Exactly as ch. lxvi. 4.

13—16.   Contrast between the fate of these idolaters and that of Jehovah's servants.

14.   *joy of heart*] Cf. Deut. xxviii. 47.

vexation of spirit] lit. **breaking** of spirit; contrast the different sense of "broken of heart" (ch. lxi. 1).

15.   Their names shall be used in a formula of imprecation. Comp. in illustration Jer. xxix. 22: "And from them shall be taken a curse for

For the Lord GOD shall slay thee,
And call his servants by another name:
That he who blesseth himself in the earth shall bless 16
himself in the God of truth;
And he that sweareth in the earth shall swear by the
God of truth;
Because the former troubles are forgotten,
And because they are hid from mine eyes.

all the captivity of Judah...saying, 'Jehovah make thee like Zedekiah and like Ahab, whom the king of Babylon roasted in the fire!'." Have we such a formula quoted in the clause following, "and the Lord Jehovah shall slay thee"? It is objected (1) that the formula would be incomplete, the essential words—"like so-and-so"—being omitted; (2) the "and" is unaccounted for, while to remove it would leave a perf. with a precative sense, a usage which is very doubtful in Hebr. (Driver, *Tenses*, § 20). On the other hand, the use of 2nd pers. sing. rather favours the view that the words are meant as a specimen of the curse.

and call his servants by another name] The LXX. (Cod. Vat.), with slight modifications of the text, reads: "And on my servants shall be called a new name" (τοῖς δὲ δουλεύουσί μοι κληθήσεται ὄνομα καινόν). The καινόν is no doubt a slip; but the change of "his" to "my" is an obvious improvement, and may safely be adopted. The promise must not be taken too literally, nor too closely connected with the preceding threat. It is hardly conceivable that the prophet contemplates the abrogation of the name "Israel," because it has been degraded by unworthy Israelites (Cheyne, *Comm.*). This would be implied only if the name "Israel" were that which is to remain for a curse, which is again a too violent interpretation. The "other name" is contrasted, not with that which both parties had borne in common, but with names such as "Forsaken," which describe the present condition of the true believers. Cf. ch. lxii. 2, 4, 12.

16. *That*] R.V., **So that** (as Gen. xi. 7; Ps. xcv. 11; Mal. iv. 1, &c.).

he who blesseth himself in the **land**] i.e. "who invokes a blessing on himself"; cf. Gen. xxii. 18, xxvi. 4, xlviii. 20; Jer. iv. 2.

shall bless himself **by** *the God of truth*] using such expressions as, "May the God of truth bless me." By the fulfilment both of His threatenings and His promises Jehovah will have shewn Himself to be the God of truth, so that a blessing uttered in His name is certainly effective. *God of truth* is strictly "God of the Amen" (cf. 2 Cor. i. 20; Rev. iii. 14), but this is a too artificial phrase for so early a period. Read *'ōmen* (= "truth," "fidelity").

swear by the God of truth] Cf. ch. xlviii. 1.

the former troubles are forgotten] See Rev. xxi. 4. *hid from mine eyes*] a reminiscence probably of Hos. xiii. 14.

17 For, behold, I create new heavens and a new earth:
And the former shall not be remembered, nor come into mind.
18 But be you glad and rejoice for ever *in that* which I create:
For behold, I create Jerusalem a rejoicing, and her people a joy.
19 And I will rejoice in Jerusalem, and joy in my people:
And the voice of weeping shall be no more heard in her, nor the voice of crying.
20 There shall be no more thence an infant of days,

17—25. The last sentence of *v.* 16 inspires the loftiest flight of the prophet's imagination. The "former troubles shall be forgotten" in the glories of a new creation, in which all things minister to the welfare of Jehovah's regenerate people.

17. *new heavens and a new earth*] i.e. a new universe, Hebrew having no single word for the Cosmos (cf. ch. lxvi. 22; 2 Pet. iii. 13; Rev. xxi. 1). The phrase sums up a whole aspect of the prophetic theology. The idea of a transformation of nature so as to be in harmony with a renewed humanity has met us several times in the earlier part of the book (ch. xi. 6—9, xxix. 17, xxx. 23 ff., xxxii. 15, xxxv., &c.), and is a frequent theme of prophecy, but the thought of a new creation is nowhere expressed so absolutely as here. It may have been suggested to the prophet by ch. li. 6, where it is said that the present universe shall be dissolved, although it is doubtful if that verse contains more than a metaphorical expression of the transitoriness of the material in contrast with the spiritual. Here there can be no doubt that the words are to be interpreted literally. At the same time the new creation preserves as it were the form of the old, for the next verse shews that a new Jerusalem is the centre of the renovated earth.

the former] R.V. **the former things.** The reference may be specifically to the "former troubles" of *v.* 16, or generally to the old state of things which shall have vanished for ever.

nor come into mind] Lit. "come up on the heart," as Jer. iii. 16, vii. 31, &c.

18. *I create Jerusalem a rejoicing &c.*] i.e. either an object in which one may rejoice (*v.* 19, ch. lx. 15) or an abode of joy (ch. li. 3, lxi. 7).

19. God Himself rejoices in the new city and people; cf. lxii. 5.

and the voice of weeping &c.] Cf. ch. xxv. 8, xxxv. 10.

20. Amongst the blessings of the new people of God the chief shall be a miraculous extension of the term of human life. This is the dominant idea down to the end of *v.* 22. The expression of the thought is unaccountably laboured and obscure.

an infant of days] must mean one who lives only a few days.

Nor an old man that hath not filled his days:
For the child shall die an hundred years old;
But the sinner *being* an hundred years old shall be accursed.
And they shall build houses, and inhabit *them*; 21
And they shall plant vineyards, and eat the fruit of them.
They shall not build, and another inhabit; 22
They shall not plant, and another eat:
For as the days of a tree *are* the days of my people,
And mine elect shall long enjoy the work of their hands.
They shall not labour in vain, 23
Nor bring forth for trouble;

nor an old man...days] (cf. Gen. xxv. 8; Ex. xxiii. 26; Job v. 26), i.e. none shall become prematurely old; each shall attain the allotted measure of life according to the standard which shall then be normal.

for the **youth** *shall die an hundred years old &c.*] These two cases must be regarded as hypothetical merely. Death at the age of 100 years (if such a thing took place) would be looked on as an untimely death in extreme youth, and as a special mark of the Divine anger on a career of wickedness (Job xv. 32, xx. 5.). The possibility of a hardened sinner being actually found in the Messianic community cannot be seriously contemplated (see ch. lx. 21).

It is evident that the idea of immortal life is unknown to the writer. He looks forward to a restriction of the power of death, but not to its entire cessation. The same idea is probably implied in a prophecy of the early post-exilic period (Zech. viii. 4; see on ch. xxv. 8); and a conception precisely similar is characteristic of the first section of the Book of Enoch. See Charles, *Book of Enoch*, pp. 26, 55, 98. Comp. En. v. 9: "And [the elect] will not be punished all the days of their life, nor will they die of plagues or visitations of wrath, but they will complete the full number of the days of their life, and their lives will grow old in peace, and the years of their joy will be many, in eternal happiness and peace all the days of their life." Cf. also x. 17 and xxv. 4, 5.

21, 22. In consequence of this extension of the term of life, each man shall enjoy the fruit of his own labour (cf. Deut. xxviii. 30). The idea is therefore somewhat different from that of ch. lxii. 8, 9.

as the days of a tree] Cf. Ps. xcii. 12, 13.

mine elect (= **my chosen**, *v.* 15) *shall long enjoy &c.*] lit. "shall wear out," "use up" (Job xxi. 13).

23. *They shall not* **weary themselves for vanity**] ch. xlix. 4; Hab. ii. 13; because God's blessing rests on them.

nor bring forth (sc. **children**) *for* **sudden destruction**] Jer. xv. 8; Ps. lxxviii. 33.

For they *are* the seed of the blessed of the LORD,
And their offspring with them.
24 And it shall come to pass, that before they call, I will answer;
And whiles they are yet speaking, I will hear.
25 The wolf and the lamb shall feed together,
And the lion shall eat straw like the bullock:
And dust *shall be* the serpent's meat.
They shall not hurt nor destroy in all my holy mountain, saith the LORD.

and their offspring with them] Better perhaps as a complete sentence: **and their offspring shall be with them** (R.V. marg.); many generations living together. Cf. Job xxi. 8.
24. Cf. Dan. ix. 21.
25. A last feature of the new earth is the peace which shall reign in the animal world. See on ch. xi. 6—9, from which this verse is quoted. The second and fourth lines are cited literally from xi. 7, 9, the first is a condensation of xi. 6, 7 a. The only clause not represented in the original passage is the third line: *and dust* shall be *the serpent's meat*, an allusion to Gen. iii. 14. Duhm, partly on metrical grounds, rejects these words as a gloss.

CH. LXVI. THE ETERNAL BLESSEDNESS OF THE TRUE ISRAEL; THE DOOM OF THE APOSTATES.

This chapter continues the antithesis that runs through ch. lxv., carrying it onward to its eschatological issues. The connexion of ideas is frequently extremely difficult to trace, and no two critics are agreed as to where the different sections begin and end. The contents of the passage, however, may be exhibited as follows:
i. *vv.* 1—4. The chapter begins with a remarkable declaration against a formal and unspiritual ceremonial. Addressing those who contemplate the erection of a Temple in His honour, Jehovah points out how inadequate any earthly house must necessarily be to His majesty, and reminds them that the only worship acceptable in His sight is that which proceeds from a humble, contrite and reverent spirit (*vv.* 1, 2). How little this condition is fulfilled by those referred to is shewn by a rapid survey of the superstitious practices which, in direct defiance of the Divine Law, they seek to combine with the service of Jehovah (*v.* 3). Sentence is pronounced against them on account of their disobedience (*v.* 4).
ii. *vv.* 5—9. Turning from these, Jehovah speaks to those who comply with the requirement of *v.* 2, assuring them of a speedy triumph over their insolent persecutors, and announcing, under the figure of a new birth, a sudden and marvellous increase of the population of Zion.

Thus saith the LORD, 66
The heaven *is* my throne, and the earth *is* my
   footstool:
Where *is* the house that ye build unto me?
And where *is* the place of my rest?
For all those *things* hath mine hand made, 2
And all those *things* have been, saith the LORD:
But to this *man* will I look,
Even to *him that is* poor and of a contrite spirit,

   iii. *vv.* 10—14. Peace and joy shall reign in the new Jerusalem, and those who sympathise with and mourn for her present distress are invited to share in her future consolation.
   iv. *vv.* 15—17. A renewed description of the judgement (expanding the thought of *v.* 6). The judgement is universal ("with all flesh"), but special emphasis is laid on the fate of the apostates so often appearing in the last two chapters (*v.* 17).
   v. *vv.* 18—22. The judgement is followed by a manifestation of Jehovah's glory to all nations (*v.* 18). The survivors of the nearer nations, who have witnessed the catastrophe, shall be sent as messengers to the more distant countries (*v.* 19); these shall then voluntarily bring back to Zion the dispersed Israelites (*v.* 20); and from amongst them (the restored exiles or the converted heathen?) some shall be chosen as ministers of the sanctuary (*v.* 21). Israel, thus reconstituted, shall be as enduring as the new heavens and earth which Jehovah is about to create (*v.* 22).
   vi. *vv.* 23, 24. The universality of the true religion, expressed inadequately in terms of the old dispensation as a monthly and weekly pilgrimage of all nations to the sanctuary at Jerusalem (*v.* 23); with a closing reference to the appalling fate reserved for the impenitent rebels against Jehovah (*v.* 24).
   1, 2. Jehovah, who fills and has created heaven and earth, "dwelleth not in temples made with hands." Comp. the citation in Acts vii. 48 ff., also 1 Ki. viii. 27; Jer. xxiii. 24.
   The heaven is *my throne*] Ps. xi. 4, ciii. 19.
   the earth is *my footstool*] Hence the Temple itself (or the ark) is spoken of as Jehovah's footstool; Lam. ii. 1; Ps. xcix. 5, cxxxii. 7; 1 Chr. xxviii. 2.
   where is *the house &c.*] Render: **what manner of house will ye build unto me? and what manner of place is my resting place** (Ps. cxxxii. 8, 14)?
   2. *all* **these** things] i.e. the heavens and the earth, the whole visible creation. That the phrase refers to the Jewish community with its religious institutions (Duhm) is a thoroughly unnatural supposition. For *have been* read **have come into being**.
   but to this man *will I look* (**have regard**) *&c.*] Cf. ch. lvii. 15.
   contrite is lit. "smitten"; it is the same word which is rendered

And trembleth at my word.

"broken" or "wounded" (of the spirit) in Prov. xv. 13, xvii. 22, xviii. 14. In all the other passages where "contrite" is found in the E.V. (ch. lvii. 15; Ps. xxxiv. 18, li. 17) it represents a formation from another root, meaning "to be crushed."

trembleth at my word] Cf. *v.* 5; Ezra ix. 4, x. 3.

These two verses contain one of the most explicit declarations of the spirituality of religion to be found in the O.T., anticipating the principle enunciated by our Lord in John iv. 24. It is not surprising that commentators have differed widely as to their precise significance in their present connexion. (1) The opinion of a few writers, that the prophet enters a protest against the rebuilding of the Temple at Jerusalem and desiderates a pure spiritual worship without sanctuary or sacrifice, is quite untenable. It is certain that no conception that would lead to a disparaging estimate of the Temple and its services can be attributed either to the second Isaiah or to any of his successors. (See to the contrary, ch. xliv. 28, lvi. 5, 7, lx. 7, lxvi. 6, 20 f. &c.) The idea suggested lies entirely beyond the most spiritual writers in the O.T.; and in the passages most nearly akin to this (e.g. Ps. xl. 6, l. 8—15, li. 16 f.) there is no suggestion that a material sanctuary and ritual could be dispensed with. (2) Hitzig and some others have supposed a reference to a project entertained by some of the exiles to erect a Temple of Jehovah in Babylonia. Not only, however, is the assumption absolutely destitute of historical evidence, but it is almost incredible that such an intention should have entered the thoughts of any Jews in exile. (3) If the passage was written in the near prospect of a return to Palestine, there is but one explanation which is at all plausible. The prophet is thinking of the *character* of the mass of the people who are eagerly looking forward to the restoration of the national worship; and he warns them that Jehovah *needs* no temple, and that their whole service of Him will be vitiated by the want of a right religious disposition. In other words, the polemic is directed not against the existence of the Temple in itself, but against the building of it being undertaken by such men as those addressed. (4) If, on the other hand, the prophecy was written some time after the restoration, it seems impossible to evade the conclusion reached by Duhm and Cheyne, that the reference is to a design of the Samaritans to erect a rival temple to that of Jerusalem. This theory is perhaps less improbable than it may at first sight appear. In the first place we know that such a temple was actually erected on Mt. Gerizim some time after Nehemiah's second reformation in Judæa (see Ryle's note on Neh. xiii. 28); and it is to be supposed that the project had been talked of for some time previously. Nor is it any formidable objection to say that the argument here employed would tell equally against the pretensions of the sanctuary at Jerusalem. The prophet's assertion must in any case be qualified by the fundamental principle of the Jewish religion that the validity of every act of worship rests on the positive enactment of Jehovah. While Jehovah needs no human service, He is graciously pleased to accept it if rendered in accordance with His expressed will. Now this sanction

He that killeth an ox *is as if* he slew a man;   3
He that sacrificeth a lamb, *as if* he cut off a dog's neck;

had been bestowed on the one sanctuary at Jerusalem, but could not possibly belong to any temple built elsewhere. The erection of such a temple could only be justified on the assumption that man could arbitrarily assign a dwelling-place to the Most High, and to show the futility of this assumption is the purpose of the prophet's lofty declaration. The question turns largely on the interpretation of *v*. 3. If that verse is rightly understood to mean that the worship of the parties spoken of was really infected by degrading superstitions, it may well be that the persons described are the Samaritans, and in that case it will follow almost of necessity that these are also addressed in *v*. 1. At the same time, it must be admitted that if the erection of a schismatic Temple were referred to, we should have expected a much more explicit and vigorous condemnation of the project.

3. The first part of the verse runs literally thus: "The slaughterer of the ox, a slayer of a man; the sacrificer of the sheep, a breaker of a dog's neck; the offerer of an oblation,—swine's blood; the maker of a memorial of incense, one that blesseth vanity (i.e. an idol)";—four legitimate sacrificial acts being bracketed with four detestable idolatrous rites. The first member of each pair is probably to be taken as subj., the second as pred., of a sentence. But this leaves open a choice between two interpretations. (*a*) That the legal sacrificial action is as hateful in the sight of God as the idolatrous rite, so long as it is performed by unspiritual worshippers. (*b*) That he who does the first series of actions *does also* the second, i.e. combines the service of Jehovah with the most hateful idolatries. It is extremely difficult to decide which is the true sense. The words "as if" in E.V. are of course supplied by the translators, but the rendering is a perfectly fair one. The one fact that favours the second explanation (*b*) is that the latter part of the verse speaks of those who "delight in their abominations." Unless there be a complete break in the middle of the verse, which is unlikely, this would seem to imply that the abominations enumerated were actually practised by certain persons, who at the same time claimed to be worshippers of Jehovah. Cf. *v*. 17, lxv. 3—5, lvii. 3—9.

as if *he slew a man*] The reference may be either to murder merely or to human sacrifice; most probably the latter, since every other member of the sentence expresses a religious act. That human sacrifice was actually perpetrated by those spoken of may be safely inferred from ch. lvii. 5.

breaketh *a dog's neck*] "This sacrifice...seems...to be alluded to as a Punic rite in Justin XVIII. 1. 10, where we read that Darius sent a message to the Carthaginians forbidding them *to sacrifice human victims and to eat the flesh of dogs*: in the connexion a religious meal must be understood." (W. R. Smith, *Rel. of the Semites*², p. 291.) The whole paragraph should be consulted for other important references to

> He that offereth an oblation, *as if he offered* swine's blood;
> He that burneth incense, *as if* he blessed an idol.
> Yea, they have chosen their own ways,
> And their soul delighteth in their abominations.
>
> 4 I also will choose their delusions,
> And will bring their fears upon them;
> Because when I called, none did answer;
> When I spake, they did not hear:
> But they did evil before mine eyes,
> And chose *that* in which I delighted not.
>
> 5 Hear the word of the LORD, ye that tremble at his word;
> Your brethren that hated you,

the sacredness of the dog amongst the Semites. See also the note in Cheyne's *Commentary*.

he that offereth an oblation (see on ch. i. 13) (**offereth**) *swine's blood*] See on ch. lxv. 4.

burneth incense] R.V. marg. **maketh a memorial of incense**. The Hebr. verb (*hizkîr*) is connected with *'azkārāh*, the technical name of the part of the meal offering which had to be burned with incense on the altar (cf. Lev. ii. 2, xxiv. 7).

blesseth *an idol*] Lit. "vanity," but the rendering rightly expresses the sense; cf. ch. xli. 29.

Yea, they have chosen &c.] These clauses form the protasis to *v.* 4. Render: **As they have chosen**...(*v.* 4) **so will I choose** &c.

I also will choose] with the same shade of meaning as in *v.* 3 ("will find satisfaction in"). "The Orientals are fond of such antitheses" (Gesenius).

4. *delusions*] Perhaps **insults**; see on ch. iii. 4. Cheyne renders expressively "freaks of fortune," remarking, "the word is very peculiar: it represents calamity under the figure of a petulant child."

their fears] i.e. "that which they fear," and strive to avert by their magical rites.

because when I called &c.] Repeated from ch. lxv. 12.

5, 6. A promise to the believing Jews, that they shall speedily witness the discomfiture of their enemies and persecutors.

ye that tremble at his word]—thus fulfilling the condition of *v.* 2. The "word" of the Lord is that spoken by the prophets, and the "trembling" of these devout hearers expresses their scrupulous anxiety to conform with its requirements.

your brethren] men of the same stock with yourselves. The term could not be applied to the known leaders of the Samaritan community, like Sanballat and Tobiah (Neh. ii. 10 &c.), but might be used

That cast you out for my name's sake, said,
Let the LORD be glorified:
But he *shall* appear to your joy, and they shall be ashamed.
A voice of noise from the city, a voice from the temple, 6
A voice of the LORD that rendereth recompence to his enemies.
Before she travailed, she brought forth; 7
Before her pain came, she was delivered of a man child.
Who hath heard such *a thing?* who hath seen such things? 8
Shall the earth be made to bring forth in one day?

of the community as a whole, composed as it largely was of men of Israelitish descent and, in part, probably of Jews who had been spared in the general deportation of the people.

that hate *you*] as R.V. Cf. ch. lvii. 4.

that cast you out] Perhaps "that put you far away" (in aversion). Comp. the use of the word in Am. vi. 3 ("that put far away the evil day"). In later Hebr. it means to excommunicate.

said, Let the LORD &c.] Render: **have said, Let Jehovah shew Himself glorious** (pointing the verb as *Niph.*) **that we may see your joy** (cf. R.V.),—a sarcastic allusion to the enthusiastic hopes entertained by the pious Jews of a manifestation of Jehovah to their joy. Cf. ch. v. 19.

but *they shall be ashamed*] Ch. lxv. 13.

6. Description of the sudden outbreak of Jehovah's destructive might from His city and sanctuary (cf. Am. i. 2; Joel iii. 16; ch. xxxiii. 14). **A noise of uproar from the city! A noise from the temple! The noise of Jehovah rendering recompence** (see on lix. 18) **to His enemies!** (those referred to in *v.* 5). That these words presuppose the existence of the Temple is certainly the most natural interpretation. The thought of the verse is resumed in *vv.* 15, 16; the verses immediately following pass abruptly to a different subject.

7—9. The sudden repopulation of the city by her children. The figure is taken from ch. xlix. 17—21, liv. 1; the fact set forth being the instantaneous return of the exiled Israelites, by which, without effort, the poor and struggling Jewish community becomes at once a great nation.

8. *Shall the earth &c.*] Render: **Shall** (the people of) **a land be travailed with in one day?** For "land" in the sense of "population" there do not seem to be any real parallels; Judg. xviii. 30 is hardly a case in point. Possibly the word for "people" (*'am*) should be inserted (Duhm).

> *Or* shall a nation be born at once?
> For as soon as Zion travailed, she brought forth her children.

9 Shall I bring to the birth, and not cause to bring forth? saith the LORD:
Shall I cause to bring forth, and shut *the womb?* saith thy God.

10 Rejoice ye with Jerusalem, and be glad with her, all ye that love her:
Rejoice for joy with her, all ye that mourn for her:

11 That ye may suck, and be satisfied with the breasts of her consolations;
That ye may milk out, and be delighted with the abundance of her glory.

12 For thus saith the LORD,
Behold, I will extend peace to her like a river,
And the glory of the Gentiles like a flowing stream:
Then shall ye suck, ye shall be borne upon *her* sides,
And be dandled upon *her* knees.

9. Comp. ch. xxxvii. 3; "the children are come to the birth, and there is not strength to bring forth." But in this crisis Jehovah Himself is present, and what He begins He will carry on to its marvellous issue.

The second half of the verse should be rendered as in R.V. **shall I that cause to bring forth shut** the womb? &c.

10, 11. Invitation to the sorrowing children of Zion to rejoice in their mother's consolation.

10. *that mourn for her*] Cf. ch. lvii. 18, lxi. 2, 3.

11. Comp. ch. lx. 16.

abundance] The Heb. word (*zîz*) is of uncertain interpretation. It is found again only in Ps. l. 11, lxxx. 13 in the phrase "beast of the field" (*zîz sāday*). It is doubtful, however, if the word there be identical with that in this verse. A perfect parallelism (with "breast") would be obtained if we might translate by "udder." Ewald and Cheyne adopt this translation, Ewald without remark, Cheyne with a reference to the Assyrian and the vulgar Arabic, where a word *zîzāh* is said to mean "udder" (see his *Comm.* p. 174, and *Origin of the Psalter*, pp. 471f.).

12—14. A promise of prosperity to Jerusalem and her inhabitants.

12. *I will extend* (cf. Gen. xxxix. 21) *peace...like a river*] See ch. xlviii. 18.

the glory of the Gentiles] **the wealth of nations.** Cf. ch. lx. 5, lxi. 6.

borne upon **the side** (see on lx. 4)...**the** *knees*] So R.V. The insertion of "her" is misleading. As in lx. 4 (xlix. 22) the children of Zion are represented as carried and nursed by the Gentiles.

As one whom his mother comforteth, so will I comfort 13
you;
And ye shall be comforted in Jerusalem.
And when ye see *this*, your heart shall rejoice, 14
And your bones shall flourish like an herb:
And the hand of the LORD shall be known towards
his servants,
And *his* indignation towards his enemies.
For behold, the LORD will come with fire, 15
And with his chariots like a whirlwind,
To render his anger with fury,
And his rebuke with flames of fire.
For by fire and by his sword will the LORD plead 16
with all flesh:
And the slain of the LORD shall be many.

dandled] the passive of the verb rendered "play" in ch. xi. 8; "delight" in ch. v. 7 (R.V. marg.) is a cognate noun.
13. A still finer image, "the grown man coming back with wounds and weariness upon him to be comforted of his mother" (G. A. Smith).
14. R.V. **And ye shall see** (it) **and your heart** &c.; recalling ch. lx. 5. *your bones shall flourish like* **the tender grass** (R.V.)] i.e. shall be fresh and full of sap (cf. Job xxi. 24; Prov. xv. 30). So when the strength is exhausted by sickness, the bones are said to be consumed or burn (Ps. xxxi. 10, xxxii. 3, cii. 3; Lam. i. 13).
and his *indignation*] Strictly: **and he will have indignation** (as R.V.). A.V. would be a better construction if we might supply the suffix for "his" (so Duhm).
15, 16. In fire and tempest—the accompaniments of the theophany—Jehovah will appear to take vengeance on His enemies. There is a connexion with the last clause of *v.* 14; but the passage reads like a continuation of *v.* 6. Comp. ch. xxix. 6, xxx. 27 ff.; Ps. l. 3.
15. *with fire*] **in fire**. Cf. Deut. v. 22 ff.
and his chariots **shall be** *like* **the** *whirlwind* (R.V.)] Cf. Hab. iii. 8; Ps. lxviii. 17. The image is derived from the storm-clouds on which Jehovah rides; ch. xix. 1; Ps. xviii. 10, lxviii. 33; Deut. xxxiii. 26. The phrase is applied in Jer. iv. 13 to the Chaldæans (or Scythians).
16. *by his sword*] See ch. xxvii. 1, xxxiv. 5, 6.
plead] i.e. "enter into judgement," as Ezek. xxxviii. 22; Joel iii. 2.
the slain of the LORD shall be many] Cf. Jer. xxv. 33; Zeph. ii. 12 (Hebr.).
17. A renewed description of the apostates, in terms similar to *v.* 3, lxv. 3—5, 11. Although the judgement is "with all flesh" it has a special significance for these reprobates. The connexion of *v.* 17 with *v.* 16 is not, however, beyond suspicion.

17 They that sanctify themselves, and purify themselves in the gardens
Behind one *tree* in the midst,
Eating swine's flesh, and the abomination, and the mouse,
Shall be consumed together, saith the LORD.
18 For I *know* their works and their thoughts:

in the gardens] **for the gardens**, i.e. in order to go into the sacred gardens (ch. lxv. 3) where the illegal rites were to be consummated ("ad sacra in lucis obeunda").

behind one tree *in the midst*] A difficult and much disputed phrase. The insertion of the word "tree" is purely gratuitous, and indefensible. If the consonantal text be sound the best rendering by far is **after one in the midst**; i.e. following the actions of a hierophant or mystagogue, who stands in the midst of the brotherhood and regulates the important ceremony of purification. Comp. Ezek. viii. 11,"...seventy men of the elders of the house of Israel, and *in the midst* of them stood Jaazaniah the son of Shaphan, with every man his censer in his hand." There does not appear to be any valid objection to this interpretation, although it is not supported by any ancient authority. The Massoretes substitute the fem. of "one" for the masc., thinking apparently of the image of some goddess as the central object. (The Babylonian Codex and the Soncino Bible have the fem. in the text.) Many commentators, guided by a faulty reference in Macrobius (*Saturn.* I. 23), have supposed that the word for "one" (אֶחָד) contains the name of a deity; but this view, although revived by Lagarde, finds little favour among modern scholars. Several ancient versions (Pesh., Sym., Theod.) render "one after another" (Targ. "company after company"), which would be possible if we might insert an additional אַחַר (אַחַד אַחַר אַחַד), but it leaves "in the midst" unexplained. Cheyne (*Introd.* p. 370) reads with Klostermann אַחַד אַחַר בתנך—"one (consecrating) the other on the tip of the ear"; an ingenious emendation, but hardly yielding an easier sense than the received (consonantal) text as understood above.

swine's flesh] ch. lxv. 4.

the abomination] Hebr. *shéqeç*, the general name for unclean animals; Lev. vii. 21; xi. 10 ff. (*passim*); cf. Ezek. viii. 10. (Duhm reads *shéreç*, "vermin," creeping or swarming creatures).

the mouse] an unclean animal according to Lev. xi. 29. Of the 23 species of small rodents included under the name in Palestine, several are esteemed edible by the Arabs (Tristram, *Nat. Hist.*, pp. 122 ff.). The allusion here without doubt is to sacrificial meals, the mouse being a sacred animal in the same sense as the swine and the dog. See W. R. Smith, *Rel. of Sem.*[2] p. 293; who mentions a statement of Maimonides that the Harrₐnians sacrificed field-mice.

shall be consumed] **shall come to an end**; see on next verse.

It shall come, that *I* will gather all nations and tongues;
And they shall come, and see my glory.
And I will set a sign among them, 19
And I will send those that escape of them unto the nations,
To Tarshish, Pul, and Lud, that draw the bow,

18—22. The extension of the knowledge of Jehovah's power to the outlying nations, and the consequent voluntary surrender of the Israelites exiled among them.

The first sentence of *v*. 18 is untranslateable as it stands, and the text is certainly corrupt. A good suggestion is made by Duhm. He transfers the phrase "their works and their thoughts" to the last clause of *v*. 17 ("their works and their thoughts together shall come to an end"); then dropping the fem. term. of the participle the remaining sentence reads, **And I am coming to gather all the nations and tongues.** Both verses are thus improved, and the new section beginning here is disentangled from its misleading association with the idea of judgement.

all nations and tongues] An expression characteristic of the Aramaic part of the Book of Daniel (ch. iii. 4 and parallels); cf. also Zech. viii. 23.

they shall come, and see my glory] i.e., probably, the visible supernatural glory of Jehovah as He dwells in the Temple. See Ezek. xliii. 1—4. (The section contains many traces of the influence of the book of Ezekiel.) The idea that the nations shall assemble to be destroyed by Jehovah (Zech. xiv. 2, 12 ff.; Joel iii. 2; Zeph. iii. 8) is alien to the tenor of the verse and is not necessarily implied by *v*. 19.

19. *I will set a sign among them*] i.e. perform a miracle (ch. vii. 11) that shall convince them of Jehovah's divinity.

I will send...them] **I will send from them escaped ones**, survivors (cf. xlv. 20) of the judgement depicted in *v*. 16. The purpose is to spread the tidings of Jehovah's glory.

to *Tarshish...Javan*] All these names are taken from the book of Ezekiel; see xxvii. 10, 12 f., xxxviii. 1, xxxix. 1. So Duhm, who thinks the whole line is a gloss. *Tarshish* = Tartessus; see on ch. ii. 16. A name *Pul* occurs nowhere else, and it is doubtless here a clerical error for **Put** (so LXX. Φούδ). Phut and Lud are mentioned together in Jer. xlvi. 9; Ezek. xxvii. 10, xxx. 5; and in Gen. x. 6, 13 both peoples are connected genealogically with Mizraim (Egypt). Probably therefore two African nations are denoted.

that draw the bow] The bow is mentioned as the weapon of the Lydians (Lud) in Jer. xlvi. 9. The LXX. reads Μόσοχ (Meshech). This is attractive, because of the resemblance to *mōshĕkē* (drawing), and because Meshech and Tubal are nearly always associated (Gen. x. 2; Ezek. xxvii. 13, xxxii. 26, &c.). They are the Moschi and Tibareni of classical writers, the Muski and Tabal of the Assyrian monuments, tribes lying south and south-east of the Black Sea (Schrader, *Cun. Inscr.*

To Tubal, and Javan, *to* the isles afar off,
That have not heard my fame, neither have seen my glory;
And they shall declare my glory among the Gentiles.
20 And they shall bring all your brethren *for* an offering unto the LORD out of all nations
Upon horses, and in chariots, and in litters, and upon mules, and upon swift beasts,
To my holy mountain Jerusalem, saith the LORD,
As the children of Israel bring an offering
In a clean vessel *into* the house of the LORD.

pp. 82, 84). If the reading of the LXX. be adopted it will be necessary to find an equivalent for *qésheth* (bow); and Duhm suggests *Rosh* from Ezek. xxxviii. 1, xxxix. 1 (see Davidson's Note).

Javan (='Ιάƒων) the Ionians, is the Hebrew name for the Greek race.

the isles (**coastlands**, ch. xl. 15) *afar off, that have not heard my fame &c.*] This distinction between the nearer nations who have experienced something of the greatness of Jehovah, through contact with His people Israel, and the remoter nations who have not heard His name, originates with the prophet Ezekiel. It underlies the conception of the invasion of Gog's host and its destruction as described in ch. xxxviii. f. Gog is the leader and representative of the outlying nations of the earth, and the demonstration of Jehovah's power against them falls at a time subsequent to the peaceful settlement of Israel in its own land, and long after judgement has been executed on the neighbouring states which had been in contact with Israel throughout its history (see Davidson, *Camb. Bible, Ezekiel*, pp. 273 ff.). But while the distinction is common to the two prophets, the development of the idea is strikingly different. In Ezekiel Gog's ignorance of Jehovah tempts him to an act of sacrilege on the land of Israel, which is avenged by the annihilation of him and his host. The spirit of this passage is more evangelical. Jehovah sends missionaries from the nearer nations to those who have not heard His fame nor seen His glory; and the report carries conviction to their minds, so that they restore the Israelites exiled amongst them, as an offering to the Lord.

20. The subject of the sentence is the nations. Cf. ch. xlix. 22, lx. 9, xiv. 2.

litters] Elsewhere only in Num. vii. 3 (in the phrase "covered wagons").

swift beasts] **dromedaries** (R.V. marg.).

21. **And of them also will I take** &c. (R.V.). Commentators differ in opinion as to whether the ministers of the sanctuary are to be taken from the restored exiles or from the Gentiles who bring them back; the language is consistent with either supposition. The latter is thought by some to be excluded by lvi. 6 f. (shewing the utmost limit of concession

And I will also take of them for priests *and* for 21
Levites, saith the LORD.
For as the new heavens and the new earth, which I 22
will make,
Shall remain before me, saith the LORD,
So shall your seed and your name remain.
And it shall come to pass, *that* from one new moon 23
to another,
And from one sabbath to another,
Shall all flesh come to worship before me, saith the
LORD.
And they shall go forth, and look 24
Upon the carcases of the men that have transgressed
against me:

to foreigners), and lxi. 6 (where a priestly standing is assigned to the Jews). These considerations, however, are not decisive; and the emphasis of the statement is perhaps better explained by the bolder conception. In any case the prophet seems to contemplate a suspension of the provisions of the Law, for the words "I will take" suggest something more than that those who are priests and Levites by birth shall be permitted to exercise their hereditary functions.

for priests and *for Levites*] Strictly, "for the priests, for the Levites," implying that they were to be given for the service of the priests and Levites. But the article should probably be omitted, and the rendering of E.V. retained. The conjunction "and" is supplied by all the Versions and some MSS. The duplication of the preposition distinguishes the expression from a characteristic phrase of Deuteronomy (see Driver on Deut. xviii. 1), so that we cannot (without a change of text) render "for Levitical priests." Nothing would be gained by such an alteration, for the adj. "Levitical" in this connexion would be a meaningless addition.

22. Comp. Jer. xxxi. 35 f., xxxiii. 25 f.
the new heavens and the new earth] ch. lxv. 17.

23, 24. Month by month and week by week all flesh shall come to Jerusalem to worship, while the dead bodies of the rebellious Israelites shall remain as a fearful spectacle and an abhorring to all flesh.

23. Comp. Zech. xiv. 16. *from one new moon to another, &c.*] Lit. "as often as (ch. xxviii. 19) there is a new-moon on its new-moon &c.," i.e. apparently "at each separate new-moon &c.,"—a peculiar idiom found also in Num. xxviii. 10, 14.

24. *And they* (the worshippers) *shall go forth*] to some place in the vicinity of Jerusalem, no doubt the Valley of Hinnom, Neh. xi. 30; cf. Josh. xv. 8, xviii. 16; 2 Chr. xxviii. 3; Jer. vii. 32; 2 Ki. xxiii. 10. (See below.)

the men that **rebelled** *against me*] The apostates so often referred to in the last two chapters.

For their worm shall not die,
Neither shall their fire be quenched;
And they shall be an abhorring unto all flesh.

for their worm shall not die, &c.] (see below) Judith xvi. 17; Ecclus. vii. 17; Mark ix. 44 ff.

an abhorring] The Hebrew word (*dêrā'ôn*) occurs again only in Dan. xii. 2.

This verse is the basis of the later Jewish conception of Gehenna as the place of everlasting punishment (see Salmond, *Christian Doctrine of Immortality*, pp. 355—360). Gehenna is the Hebrew *Gê-Hinnôm* (Valley of Hinnom), the place where of old human sacrifices were offered to Molech (Jer. vii. 31 f., *et passim*), and for this reason desecrated by king Josiah (2 Ki. xxiii. 10). Afterwards it became a receptacle for filth and refuse, and Rabbinical tradition asserts that it was the custom to cast out unclean corpses there, to be burned or to undergo decomposition. This is in all probability the scene which had imprinted itself on the imagination of the writer, and which was afterwards projected into the unseen world as an image of endless retribution. The Talmudic theology locates the mouth of hell in the Valley of Hinnom. But how much of the later theology lies in this passage it is difficult to say. Nothing is expressly said of torment endured by the dead, but only of the loathsome spectacle they present to the living; although the former idea may be implied and is suggested by a comparison with ch. l. 11. "If this passage is of too early a date, as Dillmann thinks, to admit of a reference to the horrors of the Valley of Gehinnom, the double figure of the worm and the fire may be due to the two ways of disposing of the dead, by interment and by cremation. The immediate object of the description of the worm as never dying and the fire as never being quenched, appears to be to mark the destination of those men as a perpetual witness to the consuming judgements of God, and one which all flesh may see. The incongruity of the idea of a fire burning a dead body and never going out, is supposed, however, to point to something more.... It may be that the dead body is poetically conceived to be conscious of the pains of the worm and the fire, as Dillmann supposes [cf. Job xiv. 22]. But even that goes beyond the immediate object, which is to present the men in question as a perpetual spectacle of shame to all beholders" (Salmond, *l.c.* p. 212). The view thus expressed is reasonable if the passage was written by the author of the preceding chapters. But there is much to be said for the opinion (of Duhm and Cheyne) that the last two verses are an appendix to the prophecy, written at a later time, so that the language may to some extent be saturated with the ideas which were afterwards associated with the word Gehenna.

In Heb. Bibles and MSS. part of *v.* 23 is repeated (without the vowel signs) after *v.* 24, in accordance with a Massoretic direction, so that the reading in the Synagogue might "close with words of comfort." The same practice was followed in the reading of the "Twelve" (Minor) Prophets, Lamentations, and Ecclesiastes. See Ginsburg's *Introduction*, p. 850.

APPENDIX.

NOTE I.

THE "SERVANT OF JEHOVAH" IN CH. XL.—LV.

THE conception of the "Servant of Jehovah" in this prophecy is so difficult, and is the subject of so much controversy, that it may be useful to examine, more systematically than was possible in the Notes, the various theories that have been advanced. It hardly needs to be said how greatly the basis of discussion is affected by the tendency of some recent critics to isolate the four "Servant-passages" (ch. xlii. 1—4, xlix. 1—6, l. 4—9, and lii. 13—liii. 12) and treat them as interpolations (see Introd. p. liv). Except in these places (and the appendices to two of them, xlii. 5—7 and xlix. 7—12) there is not the least doubt that the Servant of the Lord represents the people of Israel. Again, one of the principal arguments against the view that the Servant is ever an individual is the unlikelihood that the term should be used by the same writer in two different senses (Introd. p. xxxiii f.). But if the passages in question have no organic connexion with the rest of the prophecy, it becomes quite conceivable that we have to do with two distinct conceptions of the Servant, one being that of the second Isaiah himself, and the other that of the unknown author of the interpolated sections. It is therefore of some importance to ascertain, by an independent examination of the Servant-passages, whether this is the case. The writer of these pages does not indeed accept the hypothesis of interpolation; although he would admit that a radical divergence of view with regard to the Servant of Jehovah would be a strong argument in its favour. If, on the other hand, it should be found that the conception which prevails in the rest of the book is consistent with the teaching of these passages, this result will undoubtedly strengthen the presumption that they form an integral part of the prophecy.

The theories to be considered fall naturally into two clauses: (i) those which explain the Servant as a *collective* idea, representing either the nation of Israel or some smaller community within it; and (ii) those which regard the Servant as an *individual*. Both of these can in one form or another be traced back to ancient times, and each has points of contact in the recognised usage of the O.T. The individual explanation might be based on the application of the name to the great religious personalities of the O.T., such as Moses (Deut. xxxiv. 5, &c.), David (Ps. lxxxix. 3, 20, &c.), Isaiah (Is. xx. 3), Job (i. 8, &c.) or the prophets generally (Am. iii. 7; Jer. vii. 25, &c.); while the collective theories are justified by its application to Israel in Ezek. xxviii. 25, &c.

i. That the Servant of Jehovah denotes *Israel* in some sense is the oldest interpretation for which literary evidence can be produced. Its antiquity is proved by the LXX., which inserts the words "Jacob" and "Israel" in its translation of ch. xlii. 1. And if the word "Israel" in the Heb. text of xlix. 3 be a gloss, it is at all events a very ancient gloss (being found in the LXX.); and both facts together shew how naturally the minds of early readers adopted the national interpretation of at least two of the Servant-passages. But this general view that the Servant is Israel is capable of several modifications, which it is necessary to consider separately.

(1) The simplest form of the theory is that generally maintained by the Jewish interpreters, although it has also been advocated by some Christian scholars (Hitzig, Reuss, Giesebrecht and others). In the view of these writers the Servant of Jehovah represents the whole *people of Israel* as it actually existed in history. The nation is of course personified and to a certain extent idealised, but there is no distinction in the prophet's mind between the historical Israel and an ideal Israel; the conception is merely a poetic presentation of the destinies of the historic Israel, and the idealisation proceeds no further than in other parts of the second Isaiah. The chief recommendation of the theory, indeed, is that it attaches the same significance to the expression "Servant of Jehovah" wherever it occurs throughout the prophecy.

The difficulties of this interpretation appear when we apply it to the principal passage, ch. lii. 13 ff. It is necessary to assume that those who speak in liii. 1—6 are the Gentile nations, at whose hands Israel has suffered grievous wrongs, who have misjudged and despised it, but who now perceive that it has borne the chastisement of their sins. The whole passage becomes a parable of the history and destiny of the people of Jehovah. The death of the Servant denotes the Exile, which was the death of the nation; and his resurrection is a figure for the glorious restoration of Israel, which is followed by the conversion of the heathen to the true God. It is not to be denied that many features of the conception are satisfactorily explained by this hypothesis. That the idea of Israel suffering for the good of the world is foreign to the O.T. is not perhaps a decisive argument against it, for there is a truth in the idea (see Rom. xi. 11 f.), and on any view of the Servant the passage contains thoughts more profound than are expressed elsewhere in the O.T. But the insuperable objection to this explanation is the unnaturalness of the assumption that the speakers in liii. 1 ff. are the heathen. There is nothing in the language to suggest this; and the religious attitude expressed in these verses is such as no prophet could have attributed to the heathen world. When the pressure of the theory is relaxed, it is impossible to escape the impression that the speakers are Israelites, from which it necessarily follows that the Servant and the actual nation of Israel are not identical. And this inference is confirmed and put beyond all reasonable doubt by ch. xlix. 1—6, where the idea that the Servant has a mission to discharge towards Israel shews that some distinction must be recognised between the Servant and the historical nation. This view, therefore, although it may contain elements of truth, does not satisfy all the conditions involved in the problem.

(2) A modified form of the national interpretation is that the Servant of Jehovah is a personification, not of Israel as a whole, but of the *spiritual Israel*, the religious kernel of the nation, on whom the sufferings of the Exile fell most severely, and in whom the hope of the future lay (Knobel, &c.). Much that is said of the Servant no doubt finds an explanation in the experience of this faithful minority of the people. It was their mission—and they were doubtless partly conscious of it—to bring their nation to repentance, and ultimately to extend the knowledge of God to the Gentiles. It is conceivable that in the discharge of this mission they suffered persecution at the hands of their own countrymen during the Exile. But it is difficult to think that there can have been such a difference between the mass of the exiles and the believing remnant as would account for the language of ch. liii. Although the national calamity was felt with peculiar severity by those who recognised it to be the just punishment of the sin of Israel, there was nothing in their outward lot that could have given rise to the impression that they were in a special degree the objects of the divine wrath. Moreover, the Servant is described as one who has died and is destined to be raised again from the dead. This has a meaning if the subject be Israel, which as a nation ceased to exist at the Exile; but it could not be said that the spiritual Israel died in the captivity. And even if this theory could be successfully carried through the Servant-passages, it would not be consistent with the teaching of the rest of the book. The people of Israel and the spiritual Israel are distinct subjects, and it is not likely that the same writer included both under a common designation.

(3) All these objections apply with equal force to a view advocated by Gesenius and a few others, that by the Servant is meant *the prophetic order*. This interpretation derives whatever plausibility it possesses from the prophetic traits in the delineation of the Servant's person and work. But these are features inseparable from his function as the organ of Jehovah's revelation, and can be explained on any interpretation of the title. Otherwise there is almost nothing to be said for this now discredited theory.

(4) There remains the view for which a preference is expressed in this volume, that the Servant of the Lord is *the ideal Israel*. The advantage of this definition is that, while harmonising the various references to the Servant which occur throughout the prophecy, it enables us to combine in a single conception the aspects of truth represented by other interpretations. The Servant is first of all a personification of Israel as it exists in the mind and purpose of God, of the ideal for the sake of which the nation has been chosen and towards which its history is being fashioned. This ideal has never yet been realised in the earthly Israel, and hence it is described (as in ch. xlii. 1 ff.) in language which could not be used of any section of the historic people. But on the other hand, since the ideal is inseparably associated with the nation, it is intelligible that the significant facts of the history should be introduced into the portrait of the Servant, and that he should thus be spoken of as one who has passed through certain experiences and has still a career before him (xlix. 1 ff., l. 4 ff., lii. 13 ff.). On the same principle we can understand how the character and life of the Servant should reflect the

experience of the spiritually-minded Israelites, who had become conscious of the nation's destiny and mission; these formed an inner circle of religious fellowship, approximating more closely to the ideal than the nation as a whole had ever done. Again, it is natural to suppose that the concrete details of the picture (especially in ch. liii.) were partly suggested by the fate of some eminent servant of God, such as Jeremiah, or, as others think, an unknown saint and martyr of the Exile. Finally, although this probably goes beyond the writer's conscious meaning, the personification of the ideal Israel easily passes into the conception of the ideal Israelite, and thus the figure of the Servant becomes in a real sense an indirect prophecy of Jesus Christ. Israel, in fact, was a type of Christ, and Christ fulfilled the mission of Israel.

Some of the difficulties involved in this interpretation are dealt with in the Introduction (p. xxxiv) and these need not be referred to here. Amongst others which may occur to the reader perhaps the most important arises from the description of the Servant as a sacrifice in ch. liii. How, it will be asked, can the ideal Israel be said to suffer for the sins of individual Israelites? It is a question not easy to answer, but if the general conception be accepted the answer must be somewhat as follows. The fact of vicarious suffering was brought home to the mind of the prophet by what he observed in the spiritual history of his time. In the calamity of the Exile the greatest sufferers were necessarily those most loyal to Jehovah; and there may have been individuals, who might be considered innocent, whose tragic and inexplicable fate caused the greatest perplexity to believers in the justice of God. The problem of retribution was in the air, and was kept alive by facts like these. It may therefore be supposed that the prophet, with all this before him, was led further to perceive that the suffering of the righteous for the guilty is a divinely appointed law of the spiritual life, that it is a soteriological principle, and that this principle is so essentially bound up with the vocation of Israel that the Divine purpose of salvation could only be effected through its operation. If this was his thought, it was natural that it should find expression in his conception of the Servant of Jehovah, who embodies all that is of religious significance in the true idea of Israel. The sufferings of all the righteous men who bore on their hearts the burden of Israel's guilt, are transferred to the ideal figure in whom Israel's character and destiny are reflected; and thus Jehovah's Servant is the meek and patient martyr and the sinless sacrifice for his people. Such a view is in perfect harmony with the Christological reference of the prophecy in the sense stated above. It is one of the marvels of the Old Testament that the idea of vicarious suffering, which was but imperfectly illustrated in the history of Israel, is so clearly and profoundly apprehended by this prophet that only "the immeasurable step of the Incarnation" could reveal the perfect life in which his creation is realised.

ii. The opinion that the Servant is an *individual* is maintained in two very different forms: (1) that he was an actual historical person, a contemporary of the writer of the passages which relate to him; (2) that he is an ideal man whose appearance in the future is predicted.

(1) Of the first view, the most consistent exposition ever given is perhaps to be found in the Commentary of Duhm. He holds that the Servant of Jehovah was a religious teacher (a *Thora-Lehrer*), who lived in the early post-exilic period, before the date of Trito-Isaiah; and that the Servant-passages were composed by one who was his disciple. The description of his sufferings and death is to be taken literally; he was a man disfigured by leprosy, spurned and persecuted by his generation, one who, after being cut off by his disease, was laid in a dishonoured grave. Yet the impression made on his adherents by his character and teaching was such as to produce the expectation that he would rise from the dead and carry his work to a successful and glorious issue. The improbabilities of this theory are so manifest as almost to place it beyond possibility of belief. (*a*) It is hardly credible that an individual such as is supposed could have existed and exerted the profound spiritual influence attributed to him, without leaving some trace in the history of the time or in the subsequent literature. (*b*) The lofty and world-wide mission of the Servant, as well as his altogether unique relation to Jehovah, would be inconceivable from the O.T. standpoint if the subject were a private individual. (*c*) A still more serious difficulty is presented by the idea of a personal resurrection. Nothing urged by Duhm relieves the objections to supposing that such an expectation should have been entertained by a writer of this period (see on ch. lxv. 20).

(2) The alternative form of the individual interpretation is that the passages in question are a Messianic prophecy in either the definite or the more general sense of the expression. It is represented by the Targum (on xlii. 1 and lii. 13) where the reference is explicitly said to be to the Messiah. It has of course been the prevalent view in the Christian Church, which has always regarded the conception as a direct and conscious prophecy of Christ. The chief arguments against it are those stated in the Introduction (p. xxxv), and proceed on the assumption that a consistent usage must be maintained throughout the prophecy. But even if it were admitted that the Servant-passages represent an independent point of view, there are still some difficulties which cannot be ignored. In the first place it is surely remarkable that the language is *never* that of prediction. The Servant is invariably spoken of as having a present existence; what is foretold concerning him is not his appearance in a future age, but his exaltation, which is the result of his past labours and sufferings. The occurrence of the word "Israel" in ch. xlix. 3 would also, if genuine, appear to be irreconcileable with this hypothesis. And even if these objections should be disposed of, it would still remain a question whether the *rôle* assigned to the Servant is not too great to be sustained by any individual, however exalted, according to Old Testament modes of thought (see Introd. p. xxxvi).

At all events, it will probably be felt that the choice lies between i. (4) and ii. (2). Either the ideal Israel or an ideal Israelite must be assumed as the subject in the prophet's mind when he speaks of the Servant of Jehovah. Many of the best expositors (such as Delitzsch and G. A. Smith) think that neither suffices alone to set forth all that is meant by the expression. The idea is supposed to expand and contract in the mind of the writer, being sometimes so large as to include the whole of Israel, and at other times concentrating itself on the person of an ideal man whom the prophet expects to arise and fulfil the mission in which Israel failed. This is of course a correct explanation of how the ideal was fulfilled, but whether it is true to the prophet's conception is another question. While admitting the truth of the collective interpretation it does not remove a single difficulty of the alternative view. Its only recommendation is that it does justice to those features of the picture which naturally suggest a human personality; but this advantage is gained at the expense of the principle that the subjects to which the name is applied must be presumed to be essentially identical.

NOTE II.

On the Meaning of "Righteousness" in Ch. XL.—LXVI.

The variety of senses which it is necessary to assign to the words "righteousness," "righteous" &c., in different passages of this prophecy is apt to cause perplexity to the reader. It will not be supposed that the ambiguity arises from any laxity in the prophet's use of words; it lies in the idea itself as it is unfolded in the general usage of the O.T. Hence a brief statement of the applications most frequently occurring may help the reader to judge for himself what meaning is intended to be conveyed in each particular passage.

The first thing to be noted is that "the ideas of right and wrong among the Hebrews are forensic ideas; that is, the Hebrew always thinks of the right and the wrong as if they were to be settled before a judge. Righteousness is to the Hebrew not so much a moral quality as a legal status. The word 'righteous' (*ṣaddîq*) means simply 'in the right,' and the word 'wicked' (*rāshā'*) means 'in the wrong'" (W. R. Smith, *Prophets of Israel*², pp. 71 f.). Comp. Ex. ix. 27: "Jehovah is *in the right*, and I and my people are *in the wrong*"; Gen. xxxviii. 26: "she is *in the right as against me*," &c. It is not asserted that this was the primary idea of the root; and there may be a few instances in the O.T. which point back to some simpler conception in which there was no reference to judicial procedure. But these instances are quite exceptional, if they exist at all; and the forensic aspect of the notion so nearly covers the whole field of O.T. usage that attention may here be confined to the important developments to which it gives rise.

In this forensic use of the group of words expressing the idea of righteousness three distinct applications are included:—

(*a*) Righteousness is the quality expected and required *in the judge* (or the king in his judicial capacity). His proper function is to "declare in the right" (*hiṣdîq*) him who *is* in the right (*ṣaddîq*) and to condemn him who is in the wrong (*rāshā'*); in the discharge of this duty he manifests the virtue of righteousness (*ṣédeq*). E.g. Deut. xvi. 18: "they (the judges) shall judge righteous judgement (*mishpaṭ ṣédeq*)";

i. 16: "judge righteousness (*ṣédeq*)." Cf. 2 Sam. xv. 4; Is. xi. 4, 5, xvi. 5 &c.

(*b*) The righteousness of the private citizen is such a course of conduct as will stand the scrutiny of an impartial judge. Originally, perhaps, the word was used of being in the right as against another person in a particular case; as in Gen. xxxviii. 26; 1 Sam. xxiv. 17; Prov. xviii. 17 ("He that pleadeth his cause first is in the right, but &c."); Deut. xxv. 1 &c.; or being innocent of a particular charge (2 Ki. x. 9). But by a natural extension of meaning it came to denote right moral conduct in general, especially when the implied reference is to the judgement of God (Job iv. 17; Ezek. xviii. 5; Ps. xv. 2; Prov. xvi. 8 &c.).

(*c*) Righteousness means further the legal status which results from a judicial sentence in one's favour. This sense is so far distinct from (*b*) that the Hebrews could speak of "removing the righteousness of the righteous from him" (Is. v. 23), i.e. depriving the man who is really in the right of the righteous standing which a just decision would have secured to him. Cf. Ezek. xviii. 20 ("the righteousness of the righteous shall be upon him") &c.

The social righteousness so much insisted on by the prophets is the ideal state of things in which the three aspects of the notion, just enumerated, are comprehended in a higher unity. It appears to be conceived as an attribute of the community rather than of individuals; its chief element is a sound administration of justice (*a*), maintaining a perfect correspondence between real (*b*), and legal (*c*), right. This is the case, *e.g.* in Is. i. 21, where Jerusalem is described as a "city in which righteousness used to dwell," as is clear from the contrast in *v.* 23. So also in Am. v. 7, 24 (cf. *v.* 15 "set up judgement in the gate" where the word used is *mishpaṭ*), vi. 12; Is. v. 7, xxxii. 16 f. &c. The same conception is found in ch. lix. 4, 14, where righteousness and judgement are personified as the qualities that ought to preside over judicial procedure (see under ii. 1, below).

Now these forensic analogies form the basis of the religious use of the terms which is most characteristic of the second part of the book of Isaiah. The subjects of which righteousness is most frequently predicated are Jehovah on the one hand and Israel on the other. The two ideas are correlative and either may be defined in terms of the other. Jehovah's righteousness is the quality exhibited in the vindication of Israel's right, and again the right of Israel depends upon its relation to the righteousness of Jehovah. These definitions would not be quite exhaustive, but in a great number of instances it may be said that the righteousness of Israel and that of Jehovah are the two sides of one idea, both resting on the truth that the cause of Israel and the cause of Jehovah are one.

i. The righteousness of God may be described as that attribute on which Israel can rely for the vindication of its right, although it is not easy to define the attribute. In some cases it is sufficient to think of it as the attribute belonging to Jehovah as the Judge of all the earth, in virtue of which He punishes wrong wherever it is perpetrated (see ch. li. 5 "mine arms shall judge the peoples"). But it is manifest that this conception is not wide enough to include all the forms in which the idea occurs. There are many passages which shew clearly that righteousness is an absolute quality of the divine character, revealing itself in ways that are independent of Jehovah's judicial action, or His special relation to Israel. The word in fact appears to embrace all that constitutes *trustworthiness* in personal relations,—truthfulness in speech, steadfastness of purpose, consistency of principle and method, &c. These essential qualities of Godhead, however, receive a specific determination through Jehovah's covenant with Israel, and hence righteousness may sometimes be equivalent to fidelity to the terms of the covenant. In other cases the trustworthiness ascribed to Jehovah is His rectitude as the Supreme Judge of men and nations. And finally the divine attribute of righteousness is conceived as embodied in the act of deliverance by which Israel's right is vindicated, and in the state of salvation which ensues.

The following passages will illustrate the different aspects of the idea of righteousness as predicated of Jehovah. (1) *Truthfulness or straightforwardness of speech* is the idea chiefly emphasised in ch. xlv. 19: "I am Jehovah, who speak righteousness, announce rightness"; perhaps also in v. 21: "a righteous and saving God." (In v. 23 the sense may rather be constancy of purpose;—see below.) Comp. also lxiii. 1. The meaning is slightly varied in xli. 26 ("that we may say, 'He is right'"), and xliii. 9 ("that they may be in the right");—both referring to the heathen deities directly, but indirectly to Jehovah. In these cases righteousness denotes correctness of prediction,—correspondence of the announcement with the fact. These closely related uses of the word are very rare in Hebrew, but common in Arabic where "*sidq* is by implication the agreeing of what is said with what is conceived in the mind, and with the thing told of, together" (Lane's *Lexicon*). (2) *Steadfastness and consistency of purpose* is expressed in xli. 10 ("I uphold thee with my right hand of righteousness), xlii. 6 ("called thee in righteousness"), xlv. 13 ("I have raised him [Cyrus] up in righteousness"). In the first two passages righteousness no doubt includes Jehovah's fidelity to His covenant with Israel; although this fidelity is not to be conceived as an obligation which He owes to Israel, but as the expression of His own essential character. In the same sense the word is probably to be understood in xlii. 21 ("it pleased Jehovah for His righteousness' sake to magnify revelation" &c.); the motive for the abundance of His revelation being His fixed purpose to make of Israel a people for Himself. (3) *Judicial* righteousness appears from the context to be the idea most prominent in l. 8 ("He that justifieth me"), and lix. 16 ("His righteousness upheld Him"). (4) The places where righteousness, as a divine attribute, occurs in parallelism with "salvation" are ch. xlvi. 13, li. 5, 6, 8, lvi. 1 *b*. Although the two ideas are practically identical the words are not strictly synonyms. Salvation is the outward act of deliverance and the state of things ushered in by it, while righteousness is the divine quality which is illustrated and embodied in the act. But the divine righteousness which thus assumes a concrete external form ceases to be a mere attribute of Jehovah; it becomes an objective fact, and hence, as we shall see, it may be spoken of indifferently as the manifestation of the righteousness of God or as the manifestation of the righteous standing which belongs to Israel.

ii. The righteousness of Israel is also a many-sided conception, combining elements which can only be elucidated from the peculiar religious situation caused by the Exile. First of all there was in the mind of the people the consciousness of being *in the right* as against the nations that oppressed them. Whatever might be the explanation of Israel's calamities, the sense of having suffered wrong and injustice at the hands of heathen conquerors could not be suppressed; and this fact constituted a claim on the righteousness of God for the vindication of Israel's right. The feeling is sometimes expressed by earlier prophets, especially by Habakkuk, who applies the epithets *ṣaddîq* and *rāshā‘* to Israel and the Chaldæans respectively (Hab. i. 4, 13). But along with this there went a profound conviction, produced by the teaching of prophecy, and enforced by the lesson of the Captivity, of being *in the wrong* before God. "History, to Israel, was God's supreme tribunal... But when the decision of history went against the nation, when they were threatened with expulsion from their land and with extinction as a people, that just meant that the Supreme Judge of men was giving His sentence against them. Israel had broken the terms of the Covenant. They had lost their right; they were no longer *righteous*" (G. A. Smith, *Exposition*, Vol. II. p. 218). Thus "Israel's unrighteousness is her state of discredit and disgrace under the hands of God; her righteousness, which she hopes for, is her restoral to her station and destiny as the elect people" (*ibid.* pp. 219 f.).

Now both these points of view are represented in this prophecy. The first appears in ch. xl. 27, where Israel complains that "my right (*mishpāṭ*) is passed over from my God" (comp. also xlix. 4, lii. 4). The second is most clearly expressed in the ironical challenge of xliii. 26 ("declare thou that thou mayest be pronounced in the right"), and is involved in the frequent confessions of national guilt which occur in the prophecy. In each case righteousness is a matter of legal standing, and it is not easy at first sight to see how the sense of demerit before God is consistent with the consciousness of a right whose vindication is hoped for from Jehovah. The reconciliation must be found in the larger view of the divine righteousness which includes Jehovah's steadfast adherence to the purpose He had in His choice of Israel. That purpose is exhibited in the figure of the ideal Servant of Jehovah, who is perfectly righteous (ch. liii. 11) and who by his unmerited sufferings and death procures forgiveness and a righteous relation to God for the whole nation. But besides denoting a legal status to be vindicated by Jehovah's judicial interposition, righteousness is also used ethically of the character and life which is right in the sight of God.

We may now attempt to classify the principal passages where righteousness is spoken of in connexion with Israel, although it must be premised that the precise shade of meaning conveyed is frequently indeterminate and the classification therefore somewhat uncertain. (1) The passages where the words are used of *civic* righteousness in the sense of the older prophets have already been referred to; viz., ch. lix. 4, 14. Other places where the same sense may possibly be intended, or at least included, are xlv. 8, liv. 14, lvi. 1*a*, lix. 9, lx. 17. (2) The *ethical* idea of righteousness, as equivalent to the possession of a right moral and religious character, appears to be implied in ch. liii. 11, lvi. 1*a*, lviii. 2. In these instances the subject is either Israel or the Servant of the Lord; of individual Israelites the word is used in li. 1, 7, lvii. 1, lx. 21, lxiv. 5, 6; in xlviii. 1 the word seems to have the narrower meaning of truthfulness. (3) On the other hand, the *forensic* idea (righteousness as a religious standing) predominates in xlvi. 12, liv. 17, lvii. 12. (4) Lastly, the forensic idea passes over into that of righteousness manifested in external prosperity and glory. This is the case in ch. lxi. 10, lxii. 1, where the parallel expression is "salvation" (cf. xlv. 8); in lviii. 8, lxii. 2 the parallel is "glory," in xlviii. 18, lx. 17, "peace"; cf. xlv. 24, 25. In these passages "righteousness" might be rendered "justification"; it denotes the blessings conferred on Israel in token that its right is acknowledged and declared by God (see under i. 4, above). To this class may be assigned two other passages, where righteousness is, as it were, *hypostatised* and spoken of as a state of things created on earth by Jehovah; viz., xlv. 8 (in parallelism with "salvation") and lxi. 11 ("righteousness and praise").

A somewhat peculiar use of the word is found in ch. xli. 2, where (if the translation given in the notes be correct) it is said of Cyrus that "righteousness attends him at every step." Here righteousness must be equivalent to "success" or "victory"; the idea being that the remarkable successes of Cyrus on the battle-field were decisions by the Almighty in his favour and the demonstration to all the world that his was the right cause. A sense closely approaching to "victory" is implied in xlv. 24 ("righteousnesses and strength"; cf. *v*. 25: "all the seed of Israel shall have right, and shall triumph").

NOTE III (p. lx).

SOME CRITICAL THEORIES OF THE COMPOSITION OF
CHS. XL.—LXVI.

In order to shew how complicated the problem of the literary structure of this prophecy has been felt to be, the views of some recent scholars may be briefly noticed. Ewald and Dillmann are the chief representatives of the school which recognizes the unity of the second Isaiah while admitting that the author has made use of earlier written material. Ewald holds that ch. xl. 1, 2, lii. 13—liii. 12, lvi. 9—lvii. 11, are passages borrowed from pre-exilic prophets, while lviii. 1—lix. 20 is taken from an exilic predecessor of the author. The first edition of the prophecies contained two books, ch. xl.—xlviii., xlix.—lx.; ch. lxi. 1—lxiii. 6 and lxiii. 7—lxvi. 25 are two additions made by the author himself.—Dillmann's position is somewhat similar. The influence of earlier prophets can be traced more or less clearly in the language of lii. 13—liii. 12, lvi. 9—lvii. 13, lviii. and lix.; and in other passages the possibility of later alterations is conceded. The original prophecy consisted of two books, xl.—xlviii. and xlix.—lxii.; and there are two appendices, lxiii. 1—6 and lxiii. 7—lxvi. 25. The whole, however, is held to have been completed before the end of the Exile.—Cheyne, who had previously convinced himself of the post-exilic origin of certain portions of the prophecy (lvi. 1—8, lviii., lix., lxiii.—lxvi.), now accepts the conclusions of Duhm, with some important modifications. While Duhm assigns the whole of ch. lvi.—lxvi. to a single author (to whom he gives the name of Trito-Isaiah) Cheyne carries the analysis further, and finds evidence that several hands have been engaged in the compilation of these discourses. The collection as a whole, however, is still regarded as a product of the age of Ezra and Nehemiah, the only important exception being lxiii. 7—lxiv. 12, which is brought down to the troubled period under Artaxerxes Ochus (see Vol. I. p. 204).—Kuenen (1889, *Onderzoek*, § 49) also divided the prophecy into two parts, one exilic and the other post-exilic. But to the exilic writer he assigned only ch. xl.—xlix., lii. 1—12, and possibly lii. 13—liii. 12. All the rest he considered to be the work of various prophets living in Palestine after the Return.—Cornill (1896, *Einleitung*[3] pp. 157—161) occupies a position intermediate between those of Dillmann and Kuenen. He holds that the two books, ch. xl.—xlviii., xlix.—lxii. were both written by the second Isaiah, the former in Babylonia before the close of the Exile, the latter in Palestine after the Restoration. The remaining chapters (lxiii.—lxvi.) cannot, he thinks, be ascribed at least in their present form to the author of xl.—lxii.—Kosters (*Theol. Tijdschrift*, 1896, pp. 577—623) agrees with Cheyne as to the composition of ch. lvi.—lxvi.; but differs from him with regard to xlix.—lv., which (following Kuenen) he considers to be another collection of prophecies delivered in Palestine. He advocates a very complicated theory of the origin of the four "Servant-passages"; and his view is partly influenced by his theory of the history of the restoration period (on which cf. Davidson, *The Exile &c.* p. 115).—A somewhat peculiar view is adopted by Bredenkamp (1887), of which the distinctive feature is that ch. xl.—lxvi. contain a nucleus of genuine Isaianic passages, which have been amplified and published by a prophet of the Exile period. See further, Driver, *Isaiah*[2] p. 211, and *Introduction*[6], pp. 244 ff.

Several of these theories suggest the enquiry how far the hypothesis of a post-exilic date for some of the chapters may be compatible with identity of authorship. If the writer of ch. xl.—xlviii. lived in Babylonia it is reasonable to suppose that he returned to Palestine with Zerubbabel and Joshua in 536; and if he was a very young man at the beginning of his work, his active career might nearly extend over the first half-century after the Restoration. Can the indications of post-exilic origin be satisfactorily explained on the assumption that the Palestinian discourses were written within that period and by the original author himself? The suggestion is not to be altogether disregarded, but the balance of probability would seem to be against it. Several of the passages appear to presuppose a longer experience of life in Palestine than can be reasonably attributed to a contemporary of Zerubbabel; the division of parties suits the age of Malachi better than that of Haggai and Zechariah; and the corruption of the ruling classes is not likely to have proceeded so far in the years immediately following the removal of Zerubbabel and Joshua. On the whole, it may be said that if the arguments for post-exilic authorship be valid at all, they point to the conclusion that the last division of the prophecy was written on the eve of the great reformation under Nehemiah (444).

INDEX.

'Abdment, 216
Aben Ezra, xxxix, 16
'ābîr (Mighty One), xlvii, 99
Abraham, xxxi, 15 f., 18 f., 45, 105 f., 198, 203
Absalom, 130; "A.'s hand," 149
abundance = wealth, 179; = zîz, 226
acacia, 21
Achor, Valley of, 214
'ādôm, 196
'Adônāi, 94; 'ădônîm, 137
adulterer, 151, 154
adultery, idolatry compared to, 156
adversaries of Jehovah, 175, 193
agates, 139
Ahriman, 60
Ahuramazda, 60
aliens, see strangers
'al tashḥēth, 214
Ammonites, lvii, 148; Milkom, god of the, 157
Amos, xxii, xxx
"angel of the Presence," 200
Annalistic Tablet, xviii, 57
"anoint," 186; "anointed," see Cyrus
Ansan, xvii
anthropomorphism, xxix, 31, 98 f., 119, 174, 194—197, 203, 227
antimony, 139
apostates, future of, xvii, 208 ff, 220—232
Aquila, Greek transl. of, 51, 102, 122
Arabia, Arabians, lvii, 44; A. Felix, 180
'ārîṣ, 98
arm of Jehovah, 84, 109 f., 123 f.; His holy —, xix, 119, 201
Arrian quoted, 119
Artaxerxes Ochus, 199, 243
artificer, 17
'ărûkah, 'ărîka, 166
ash, 51
ashes, 187
'astonied,' 121
astrologers, 78
Astyages, xvii, xix
Atonement, Day of, 162

audition, prophetic, 3
'azkārāh, 224
'ăṣûbāh, 191

Baal, 68, 155; "Face of," 200; bā'al (="marry" or "possess"), 191
Baal-Gad, 215
Babylon, her overthrow predicted, xiii, 35, 40; downfall of her state religion, xiv, 68—72; ode on the fall of, xiv, 73—79; personification of, ibid.; Cyrus and, xviii, 14—16, see Cyrus; the departure from, predicted, 118 f., 146; "mistress of kingdoms," 75; cosmology of, 39; her reliance on sorcery, 55, 77
Babylonia, allusions to, xvii f., 1 n., 3, 56 ff., 69, 76—79, 117, 154
bāṣîr, 196
Baethgeu referred to, 215 ff.
balance, xxv, 70
bāmāh, 131
Baptist, the, 159
bārā', see create
basilisks' eggs, 170
bassēr, 5, 118, 186
beasts, wild, = heathen nations, 151
Bel, 68
believers, future of, xvii
bērîth, 28
Bertholet referred to, 148
Bēth essentiae, 6
Beulah, 191
Bleek referred to, xxxix
blind, spiritually, xxxii, 32, 35, 37, 152
Blue Nile, 36
Borsippa, 68
bow, 229 f.
box-tree, 21, 182
Bozrah, 195
'branch of my planting,' 184, 187
branding slaves, custom of, 47
Brandt referred to, 46
Bredenkamp referred to, 243
brier, 1, 146
Buussen referred to, xxxix, 1
burnt-offerings, 43

ṣaddîq, ṣĕdāqāh, ṣédeq, xlvii, 16, 61, 98, 238—242
calamus odoratus, 44
Calvin referred to, 16
ṣāmaḥ, xlix
Cambyses, 36
camels, 179, 230
Canaanitish heathenism, 154
ṣār, 175
caravans, 180
carbuncles, 139
carpenter, 17, 51
Carthage, Carthaginians, 200, 223
ṣĕ'ĕṣā'îm, xlix
cedar, 21, 51
Chaldæa, Chaldæan, Chaldæans, xx, xxii, xxxi, xl, 6, 40, 73, 83, 86, 111, 117, 199, 207, 227, 241
chalîl ullah, 19
characteristic expressions of Isaiah, xlix f.; of II Isaiah, xlvii—xlix
Charles referred to, 219
'chastisement,' of the Servant, 127—134; of Israel, 75, 151, 160
Cheyne quoted or referred to, xlvi, lv, 14, 20, 23, 34, 62, 80, 85, 98, 127, 170, 177, 199, 212, 222, 243
children, Eastern mode of carrying, 178
China, 93
ṣîr, 200
'circle of the earth,' xxv, 11
circumcision, 148
'cities of the wilderness,' 30
Clericus referred to, 23
'clifts of the rock,' 154 f.
coast-lands, see isles
cockatrice' eggs, 170
'coming things,' see 'new things'
'condole, to,' 114
confession, prayer and, xvi, 162, 166, 172 f., 197—208
confusion, see vanity
controversy, Jehovah's, with the nations, 14—18, 35—39, 66 f.; with the idols, 22—24, 38—40, 49—53
Cornill referred to, 243
Cosmos, 218
'covenant of the people,' 28 f., 92; New C., 136, 141, 143, 149, 176, 188
covetousness, 152, 161
create, use of the word, xxiv f., xlviii, 12, 28, 36, 59 f., 62, 65, 82, 140, 218
Crœsus, xviii f., 14, 58
cry=prophesy, 4
cuneiform inscriptions, references to, xviii, 39 f., 57, 59 f., 68 ff., 106, 153, 180, 211, 215, 229
curtains, 136
cypress, 21, 51, 146
Cyrus, anointed instrument of Jehovah, x f., xiii, xix f., xxii f., xxvi, xxxvii f., 14—16, 23, 36, 54—68; oracles concerning his mission, xiii, 54—68; career and historical relation to the prophecy,

xvii—xix; prophecies fulfilled by his appearance, xx, 24, 29, 38, 66, 71; his progressive relation to Jehovah, 23, 58 f.; honorific titles, 56, 59, 84; compensated for Israel, 36, 63; raised up in righteousness, xxvii, 62; rejectors of, xxiii, 54; original form of the word, 56

Dalman referred to, 99
David, 233; house of, 141, 143; "Last Words of," 'mercies of,' ib.
Davidson quoted or referred to, x, xxiv, xxix, xxxvi f., xxxix, liv, lx, 6 f., 33, 53, 59, 85, 109, 111, 114, 121, 129 f., 143, 155, 161, 172, 182 f., 213, 230 f., 243
death, O.T. feeling regarding, 153
Delitzsch quoted or referred to, xl, 19, 22, 29 f., 49, 56, 59, 61, 85, 130, 166, 188, 195, 216, 237
Delitzsch, Friedrich, quoted, 69
deliverance from Babylon, xiii, xxiii, xxviii, 1, 35 f., 40—42, 55, 94, 116, et passim; see redeem
dĕrā'ôn, 232
desert, march through the, 1, 3, 6, 15, 21, 31, 35, 41, 87, 92 f., 146; 'region of darkness,' 31; distinguished from 'wilderness,' 42
Deuteronomy, 231; D. law, 149
devastation and destruction, 114, 171, 183
Dillmann quoted or referred to, 10, 23, 46, 53, 73 f., 83 f., 86, 92, 98, 128, 132, 146, 152, 175 f., 214, 216, 232, 242
dîn (Arab.), 27
'direct'=regulate, 8
Dispersion, the, lvi; ingathering of, xxi, 37, 93, 150, 193
diviners, influence of, in Babylon, 55, 77
divorcement, bill of, 99
Döderlein referred to, xxxix
dogs, dumb, =prophets, 152
Dooseh, ceremony of, 115
dôr, 129
Douglas referred to, xl
doves, ships compared to, 180
dragons, 42; the Dragon, 109
Drechsler referred to, xl
Driver quoted or referred to, xxviii, xxxix, xliv, xlvi, xlviii, 2, 19 f., 23, 38, 45, 85, 87, 92, 143, 204, 217, 231, 243
dromedaries, 179, 230
Duhm quoted or referred to, l, liv, lvii, lix, 3, 34, 50, 53, 73, 80, 85, 88, 128, 155, 170, 174, 177, 199, 222, 229, 237, 243

eagle, 14
Edom, Day of Vengeance in, 194—197

INDEX.

Egypt, xxx f., l, 3, 19, 36, 63, 93, 109, 148, 229
'ēl, 10; hā-'ēl, 28
Elam, xvii, 23
'ĕleph, 184
'ĕlīlīm, xlix
elm, 21
embassies, political, 157
'end' or 'ends of the earth,' xlviii, 19, 29
Enoch, Book of, 219
Ephah, 179
'ephes, xlviii
Eshmunazar, 153
Ethiopia, xxx, 36, 63
eunuchs, admission of, to covenant blessings, xvi, 147 ff.
Euphrates, 40, 86
Euting referred to, 200
'Evangelist of the O.T.,' ix
evangelists, see messengers
evil, moral and physical, 60
Ewald quoted or referred to, xxxix, l, liv, 16, 20, 48, 113, 124, 132, 226, 242
'exactors,' 183
Exodus, the, xxxi, 3, 19, 35, 41, 119; the New, xiii, 40, 86, 119, 146, 193
'eye to eye,' 118
Ezekiel, xxxi, l, 79, 82, 117, 230
Ezra, lvi, 204, 209

"Face," of Jehovah, 169, 200; of Baal, 200
fast-days, fasting, 162—165
Fatherhood of God, 198, 203, 207
fetishes, 155
fire, fire-brands, 104
firmament, ancient conception of, 108
'First, the, and the Last,' xxvi, 17, 48, 83
fir tree, 21, 146, 182
fleabane, 146
flock = Israel, 150 ff., 201
footstool of Jehovah, 221
foreigners, admission to covenant blessings, xvi, 147—150, 181, 192, 231
forgiveness, 1, 3, 44, 53, 160
form, *forma*, 125
'former things,' xxi, 22, 29, 35, 38, 41, 71, 79, 218
'fruit of the lips,' 161
fury, divine, 113, 115, 127, 227; in other connexions, 111, 114

gā'al, xlviii, see redeem
Gad, 215 f.
Galli, mutilation of, 148
gardens, sacred, 211, 228
garland, 186, 189
Gaza, "Fortune" of, 215
gēdūd, 215
Gehenna, Jewish conception of, 232
Gentiles, the, subservience of, xvi, xxv, xxxviii, 97, 179, 181 f., 187, 226; God's purpose towards, xxx, xxxvii—xxxix,

29, 65 ff., 91; 'light of,' xxxvi, 29, 91
Gerizim, Mt, 222
Gesenius referred to, xxxix, 50, 53, 98, 115, 117, 152, 166, 172, 215, 224, 235
Giesebrecht referred to, 112, 234
Ginsburg referred to, 232 n.
girdle, 96
glory = wealth, 226; use in Isaiah, xlix
gnats, 108
Gō'ēl, 20, see redeem
Gospel, message of the, foreshadowed, 142
grape-cluster, figure of the, 208, 213
grasshoppers, xxv, 11
graves, custom of sitting in, 211
guilt-offering, 132
Gunkel referred to, 109

ḥadarīya (Arab.), villagers, 30
Hadramant, 44
"hand," Absalom's, 149
hā-rī'shōnōth, 22
Harranians, 228
ḥārūṣ, 20
Hauran, Greek inscriptions of the, 215
Hävernick, xl
ḥēleq, ḥalqē, 155
Hengstenberg referred to, xi
ḥēphes, xlviii, 56, 71, 84, 132, 164, 168
Hephzibah, 191
Herodotus referred to, xviii, 36, 40, 56, 58, 215
'high and lofty One,' 160
'high places,' 21, 209, 213
hillēl, tĕhillāh, xlix
Hinnom, Valley of, 231 f.
Hitzig quoted or referred to, xxxix, 16, 70, 205, 222, 234
holm-oak, 51
'holy city,' xlix, 80, 115
'Holy One of Israel,' xlvi, 74, 92, 137, 182
holy Spirit, 201
'holy, of Jehovah' (of the Sabbath), 168
Horace quoted, 51, 172
Hosts, Lord of, see Jehovah
Husband of Zion, Jehovah as, xv, 135—137

idolatry, polemic against, xi, xiii, xxvi, 7, 9—11, 17, 49—53, 70 f.; prevalent among the exiles, 81; compared to adultery, 156; household—, ibid.; nations renounce, xxiii, 63 ff.; idols, flight of, xiv, 68 f.; manufacture of, 49—53; challenged by Jehovah, 22—24, 38—40, 49—53; idolaters, confusion of, 32, 64; future of, 208 f., 213; idolatrous rites, 151, 154—159, 210—215, 223 f., 228
image, graven, 10, 24, 49, 66, 69
immortality, idea of, 219
incense, 44, 223 f.

incomparableness of Jehovah, xxv, 6, 9, 12, 70
incubation, custom of, 211
infinity of Jehovah, see Jehovah
'inhabitants of the rock,' 30
inscriptions, see cuneiform
instrument, threshing, 20; smith's —, 140
isles, islands, 9, 15, 30 f., 89, 108, 175, 180, 230
'*iṣma* (Arab.), 22
Israel, mission and place in history, xxiv, xxvi, xxx—xxxix, 2, 33 f., 107, 112, 187, *et passim*; two-fold personification of, 2; blessedness of, 184, 186, 189 f., 220, 226 f.; external prosperity, 138 f., 179—183, 187, 226; social evils, xvi, 168—173
'*iyyîm*, xlviii

jackals, 42
Jacob, 22, 45, 47, 208
Jarchi quoted, 44
Jashar, book of, 46
Javan, 229
jealousy, 30, 203
Jehovah,—of Hosts, 12, 48, 63, 74, 112, 137; —Creator, xxiv f., 28, 59 f., 62, 65, 82, 140, 218; everlasting, 13; incomparable, xxv, 6, 9, 12, 70; infinity of, xi, 7—14; Qâdôsh (Holy), xxvi, xlvi, 12, 74, 92, 137, 182; as Redeemer, see redeem; as Shepherd, xxiii, xxix, 6; the First and the Last, xxvi, 17, 48, 83; unique Godhead of, xxvi, 39, 49, 59, 64—67, 71; as Warrior, 30, 98 f., 119, 174; righteousness of, xxvii, 19, 24, 28, 62, 65, 67, 72, 108, 239 ff.
Jensen referred to, 211
Jeremiah, xxii, xxxi, lii, 56, 103 f., 111, 142, 166, 202
Jerome referred to, 10, 205, 211
Jerusalem, "good tidings to," xi, 5 f., 118, 180; deliverance foretold, xiii, xxiii, xxviii, 1, 35 f., 40—42, 55, 94, 116; personification of, 2, 94—101, 113, 115, 118, 135—141; holy city, 80, 115; glory and prosperity of the New, 177 —194; see Zion
Jeshîmôn, 42
Jeshurun, 46
Jesus, son of Sirach, l
Job, 2, 13, 122, 125 ff., 134, 153, 233
Josephus quoted or referred to, li, 36, 57, 63
Jubilee, 186
Judah, 'out of the waters of,' 80
judgement = right, 13, 90, 171; = judicial process, 16; = religion, 26 f., 107; in other connections, 129, 172, 174
Jupiter, 68; planet, 215
justice = righteousness, 147, 163, 172 f., abuses of, 168, 170

Kay referred to, xl

Kedar, 30, 180
kên, kinnâh, kinnîm, 108
king, Messianic, xliv f., 57, 144
Kirkpatrick referred to, xl, l f.
Klostermann referred to, 228
Knobel referred to, xxxix, 129, 235
König referred to, xxxix, xlvii, 167
Koran referred to, 99, 216
Kosters referred to, liv, 243
Kuenen referred to, xxxix, 199, 243
kunya (Arab.), 47

Lagarde referred to, 10, 71, 228
land = population, 225
Lane quoted or referred to, 90, 115, 139, 179, 240
law, see *tôrâh*
law-suits, 170
leader = prince, 144; unworthy spiritual leaders, 150 ff.
Lebanon, 9, 181
lĕbônâh, 44
lectisternia, 215
Lenormant referred to, 77
leper, leprosy, 125 ff., 130, 206, 237
Levites, 187, 231
'liars, tokens of the,' 55
'liberty,' use of word in O.T., 186
light, emblem of salvation, 165, 178; of the New Jerusalem, 183; of the nations, xxxvi, 29, 91
litters, 230
Livy referred to, 215
Lowth referred to, 30, 51, 56, 74, 167, 206
Lucan quoted, 117
"Luck, the greater and the lesser," 26
Lud, Lydia, Lydians, xviii, 14, 229

Madian, city of, 179
magic, Babylonian, 77
Mal'ak Yahveh, 200
Manasseh, age of, xlii, liv; mother of, 191
Manât, 216
mârâq, 211
mâshîaḥ, 57
matmôn, 58
mĕbassēr, mĕbassĕreth, see *bassēr*
Media, xviii, 14, 23
Melek, 157
memorial, 146, 149, 156, 224
Meni, 215 f.
merchants, 79
Merodach, xviii, 40, 57, 68
Meroë, 36
Meshech, Moschi, Muski, 229
mĕshullâm, 33
messengers, xi, xv, 1, 5, 32, 56, 118, 200
Messiah, personal, xxxv f., 57, 144, 237; see Cyrus
mĕṣukkân, 10
'meted out,' xxv, 7 f.

INDEX.

Michaelis, J. D., referred to, 93
midbār, 42
Midianites, 179
Migdal-Gad, 215
Milkom, 157
Milton quoted, 58
'minister,' 149, 180 f., 187
mirage, 93
mishpāṭ, 8, 16, 26, 238 f.
'mistress of kingdoms,' 75
Moabites, 148
Moabite Stone, 165
Molech, 155, 232
monument (to eunuchs), 147, 149
mōrāg, 20
Moses, 109, 180, 201 f., 233; M. law, 99 f.
moshḥāth, 121
moslim, 'the surrendered one,' 33
moth, 104, 109
mourning, of the dove, 172; garb of, 101; mourners, 161, 184, 186, 226
mouse, the, in sacrificial meals, 228
Muir referred to, 178
musukkânu (Ass.), 10
myrtle, 21, 146

nābî, 68
Nabonidus, xviii
Nägelsbach, xl, 24
nāgîd, 144
nations, see Gentiles
Nebajoth, Nabataeans, 180
Nebo, 68
Nebuchadnezzar, 57, 72, 118
Nehemiah, lvi, 222, 244; governorship of, 177
'new things,' xxi, 22, 29, 35, 41, 79, 83
Noah, covenant of, 136, 138
'nursing fathers,' 97

oaks, 155, 187
oath, Jehovah's, to Noah, 136, 138
oblation, 156, 223 f.
Oehler referred to, xxxix
offerings, 43; guilt-, 132; meal-, 224; meat-, 156
'officers,' 183
'oil tree' (=oleaster), 21
Oort referred to, 48, 74
oracles, selling of, 152
Orelli referred to, xxxix
'ōren, 51
ostriches, 42
Ovid referred to, 58
owls, 42

Palestine, tree-worship in, 155; invaded by Midianites, 179; mystic societies in, 212; "waste and ruined," xx, xxi n., 92, 96, 107, 118, 167, 187, 191, 207; prophecies written in, l n., lviii, 209
parag, 211

paronomasia, 138, 187, 216
pastors = rulers, 152
Peace, personified, 173, 183
Pelusium, 93
pĕ‘ullāh = recompence, xlvii, 6, 90
pĕgahqōah, 186
Persia, xvii
pésel, 10
Peshitto referred to, 98, 121, 166, 175, 207, 228
Petra, 30
Phut, 229
pilgrimages, 157
pine tree, 51, 182
'place' = monument, 149
plain, 4
plane tree, 21
'planting the heavens,' 112
Pliny referred to, 44, 180
poplars, 46
potter, 207
praise, 30, 42, 187; praises = praiseworthy deeds, 180, 199; see *hillēl*, xlix
priests, lvii, 2, 119, 151, 187, 231
'prognosticators,' 78; see diviners
prophecy, argument from, xi ff., xx f., 35, 47 ff.; spirit of, 201
prophets, function of, 163; hireling, lvii, 152; = watchmen, 151 f.
proselytes, admission to covenant blessings, 147 ff.; sacrifices of, 150, 181
Ptolemy, 179
pûkh, 139
Pul, 229
pûrāh, 196

Qādôsh, xxvi, xlvi, 12, 74, 92, 137, 182
gānâh, gāneh, 44, 70
qînāh, 113
qishshurîm, 96
qubba‘ath, 113

Rahab, 109 f.
ransom, xxx, 36, 63
rā‘āh, 53
rāshā‘, 238, 241
recompence, see *pĕ‘ullāh*
redeem, redeemer, xxiii, xxviii, 20, 35 f., 40, 42, 55, 116, 137
'remembrance,' see *zikkârôn*
Renan referred to, 46
'report,' 123
Reuss referred to, xxxix, 234
rî shônāh, as adverb, 213
Riehm referred to, 216
righteousness, see Appendix, Note II
rites, heathen, 151, 155—158, 210—215, 223 f., 228
ritual, 42, 215
'rough places,' 4
rubies, 139
Rückert referred to, x n.
rulers, denunciation of, 151—153

Rutgers referred to, xl
Ryle referred to, 59, 199, 222

Sabæans, 63 f.
Sabbath-observance, lv, 147 ff., 167 f.
sacrifices, 42 f.; of proselytes, 150; human, in Israel, 55
ṣāgad, 42, 70
ṣāgān, 23
Salmond referred to, 232
salvation, herald of, xi, xv, 5 f., 118, 184 ff.; history of the idea of, xxxviii *n.*; hindrances to Israel's, 168 ff.; =welfare, 61; =victory, 119; =righteousness, 72, 107 ff., 146, 240, 242; universal, xxiii, xxvi, xxx, xxxviii, 2, 33 f., 65 ff., 107, 112, *et passim*; day of, 92, 145; highway of, 159, 193
Samaritans, lvii, lix, 154, 157 ff., 199, 209 f., 222 f.; attitude towards Jews, 155, 224 f.
Sanballat, 224
Sardis, xviii, 58
ṣāṣ, 109
Sayce referred to, xvii f., 59, 78
scales, xxv, 8
Schrader referred to, 39 f., 69, 180, 216, 229
Schwally referred to, 211
Scythians, 227
Seba, xxx, 36
Secker referred to, 80, 167
seers, 152
Seetzen referred to, 47
Sela, 30
Semites, cultus of, 157
Sennacherib, 40, 69
Servant of Jehovah; ideal, xii, 24—27; xiv f., 87—91; xv, 101—104; xv, 120—135; xxxii f., xxxiv—xxxvii, App. Note I 235 f.—Israel as, xii, 32—34; xxx—xxxii, xxxiii f., 18, 28 f., 37 ff., 45 f., 53, 59, 69 f., 86 f., App. Note I 233—235
Servant-passages, genuineness of, liii—lv.
servants of Jehovah = prophets, 56; = worshippers, xxxi, 149; the ideal servant reproduced in individuals, 141
'serve,' Jehovah, 149, 180 f., 187
service, religious, of the people, 162
Shakespeare quoted, 153, 164
shaknu (Ass.), 23
Sharon, plain of, 214
Sheba, 179 f.
shéçeph qéçeph, 138
sheep-dogs, 152
Shemaiah, 152
Sheol, 158
shepherd, see Jehovah; as honorific title=ruler, 56, 59; unworthy, 150 ff.; referring to Moses, 201
'ships of rejoicing,' 40
shittah tree, 21
Sin (Pelusium), 93

Sinim, 93
Sirach, son of, l
sirocco, 4, 93
ṣirpād, 146
slavery, slaves, lvii, 47, 63, 99, 113, 164
smith, 50, 140
Smith, G. A., quoted or referred to, x, xl, 4, 22, 194, 214, 227, 237, 241
Smith, Payne, referred to, 86
Smith, W. R., quoted or referred to, 148, 157, 211 f., 214, 223, 228, 238
Soncino Bible, 197, 228
soothsaying, overthrow of, 55
sorceress, sorcery, 55, 77, 154
soul, spirit, the principle of life, 28, 160, 46
span, xxv, 7
spirituality of religion, 222
'spoil, divide,' 133
'sprinkle many nations,' 122
stakes, 136
'standard, lift up,' 176
Stier referred to, xl f.
'stouthearted,' xxiii, 72
strangers admitted to covenant blessings, xvi, 147—150, 181, 192, 231
stroke (of God's hand), 126, 129
sūs, masôs, sāsôn, xlviii
Syene, 93
Symmachus, Greek transl. of, 228
Synagogue, reading in the, 232 *n.*

Tablet, Annalistic, xviii, 57
Tadmor, centre of caravan trade, 30
Tanit, 200
tannîn, 110
ta'ănîth, 164
Targum referred to, 2, 10, 14, 16, 93, 121 f., 175, 178, 185, 188, 107, 207, 228, 237
Tarshish (Tartessus), ships of, 181, 229
tĕ'asshûr, 21
tĕhôm, 110, 202
Temple, the, house of prayer, 150; destruction of, 199, 207; shew-bread in, 215; ritual, lv, 42, 215; rebuilding of, 54, 57; 'stones of antimony' for, 139; existence presupposed, 150, 180, 192, 214 f., 225
tĕmûnāh, 10
tent, 136
terebinths, 154 f., 187
tĕrûmāh, 10
Theodotion, Greek transl. of, 51, 122, 229
Theophany, prayer for a, 204 f., 227
thorn, l, 146
threshing-instrument, 20
throne, Jehovah's, 221
Tiāmat, 110
tidhar, 21
tîrôsh, 213
tirzāh, 51

Tobiah, 224
tôhû = chaos, xxv, xlviii. 9, 12, 24, 49, 65, 170
tôrâh, xlvi, 33, 107
trees, memorial, 141 f.; for the Temple, 181; of righteousness, 187
tree-worship 155
Tribes, the Ten, 70
Tristram referred to, 228
Trito-Isaiah, 237, 243
Tubal, Tibareni, Tabal, 229
turban, 186
Tylor referred to, 156

Umbreit referred to, xxxix
unguents, 157
utensils, sacred, 119
'*ûth*, 102

vanity = nothingness, see *tôhû*; = idol, xxv, 159, 223 f.
vengeance, day of, 186; on the Edomites, 194—197
Vergil quoted, 50 f.
'vex' (of the Spirit), 201
vices of prophets and priests, 152
vintage songs, 213
viper, 171
Vitringa referred to, 56
Vulgate referred to, 3 f., 10, 14, 16, 51, 93, 102, 122, 126, 158, 172, 178, 195

wabariya (= nomads, Arab.), 30
wadis, 86, 154 f.
warrior, Jehovah as, see Jehovah, and anthropomorphism
wasî'a (Arab.), xxviii
'wasting and destruction,' 114, 171, 183
watchmen, city, 118; = prophets, 151 f.; = invisible guards, 191
water-sellers, 142
Weir referred to, 167

well, access to a, 142; 'wells of salvation,' ibid.
Wette, de, referred to, xxxix
White Nile, 36
wife, Zion the—of Jehovah, 135 ff.
wife of youth, 137 f.
wild beasts, heathen compared to, 151
willows, 46
wine-press, 194, 196 f.
wisdom of Jehovah, xi, 8; of the Servant, 121
witchcraft, 154
witness, David as, to the nations, 143 f.
work, recompence, see *pe'ullâh*
workman, 17, 50
worm, 109
worship, ordinances of, 148; tree-, 155
wrath, divine, 113, 115, 127, 138, 161, 227

Xenophon referred to, 36, 58, 72

yaḥad, yaḥdâv, xlviii
Yahveh, 114
yâshâr, 46
Yemen, 180
yeshaʻ, xxviii n. 61,
Yeshûrûn, 46

zeal, 30, 203
Zechariah, xxii n., lii, lvi, 162, 244
Zerubbabel, l, 199, 207, 243 f.
zikkârôn, 156
Zion, glorification of, xiv f.; consolation of, 94—101; personification of, 5, 94—101, 113, 115 f., 118; felicity of, 112—119, 135—141, 177—184; "good tidings" to, xi, 5, 118, 180; population of, 94 f., 135 f., 225 f.
zîz, 226
zodiac, 78
Zoroastrianism, 60

THE PITT PRESS SERIES.
COMPLETE LIST.

1. GREEK.

Author	Work	Editor	Price
Aeschylus	Prometheus Vinctus	Rackham	*In the Press*
Aristophanes	Aves—Plutus—Ranae	Green	3/6 *each*
,,	Vespae	Graves	3/6
,,	Nubes	,,	*In the Press*
Demosthenes	Olynthiacs	Glover	2/6
Euripides	Heracleidae	Beck & Headlam	3/6
,,	Hercules Furens	Gray & Hutchinson	2/-
,,	Hippolytus	Hadley	2/-
,,	Iphigeneia in Aulis	Headlam	2/-
,,	Medea	,,	2/6
,,	Hecuba	Hadley	2/6
,,	Alcestis	,,	2/6
,,	Orestes	Wedd	4/6
Herodotus	Book V	Shuckburgh	3/-
,,	,, VI, VIII, IX	,,	4/- *each*
,,	,, VIII 1—90, IX 1—89	,,	2/6 *each*
Homer	Odyssey IX, X	Edwards	2/6 *each*
,,	,, XXI	,,	2/-
,,	Iliad VI, XXII, XXIII, XXIV	,,	2/- *each*
Lucian	Somnium, Charon, etc.	Heitland	3/6
,,	Menippus and Timon	Mackie	3/6
Plato	Apologia Socratis	Adam	3/6
,,	Crito	,,	2/6
,,	Euthyphro	,,	2/6
,,	Protagoras	J. & A. M. Adam	4/6
Plutarch	Demosthenes	Holden	4/6
,,	Gracchi	,,	6/-
,,	Nicias	,,	5/-
,,	Sulla	,,	6/-
,,	Timoleon	,,	6/-
Sophocles	Oedipus Tyrannus	Jebb	4/-
Thucydides	Book III	Spratt	5/-
,,	Book VII	Holden	5/-
Xenophon	Agesilaus	Hailstone	2/6
,,	Anabasis Vol. I. Text.	Pretor	3/-
,,	,, Vol. II. Notes.	,,	4/6
,,	,, I, II	,,	4/-
,,	,, I, III, IV, V	,,	2/- *each*
,,	,, II, VI, VII	,,	2/6 *each*
,,	,, II	Edwards	1/6
,,	,, III	,,	1/6
,,	Cyropaedeia I, II (2 vols.)	Holden	6/-
,,	,, III, IV, V	,,	5/-
,,	,, VI, VII, VIII	,,	5/-

THE PITT PRESS SERIES.

2. LATIN.

Author	Work	Editor	Price
Caesar	De Bello Gallico Com. I, III, VI, VIII	Peskett	1/6 each
,,	,, II–III, and VII	,,	2/- each
,,	,, I–III	,,	3/-
,,	,, IV–V	,,	1/6
,,	De Bello Gallico I ch. 1–29	Shuckburgh	1/6
,,	,, ,, II Belgic War	,,	1/6
,,	De Bello Civili. Com. I	Peskett	3/-
,,	,, ,, Com. III	,,	In the Press
Cicero	Actio Prima in C. Verrem	Cowie	1/6
,,	De Amicitia	Reid	3/6
,,	De Senectute	,,	3/6
,,	Div. in Q. Caec. et Actio Prima in C. Verrem	Heitland & Cowie	3/-
,,	Philippica Secunda	Peskett	3/6
,,	Pro Archia Poeta	Reid	2/-
,,	,, Balbo	,,	1/6
,,	,, Milone	,,	2/6
,,	,, Murena	Heitland	3/-
,,	,, Plancio	Holden	4/6
,,	,, Sulla	Reid	3/6
,,	Somnium Scipionis	Pearman	2/-
Cornelius Nepos	Miltiades, Themistocles, &c.	Shuckburgh	1/6
,,	Hannibal, Cato, Atticus	,,	1/6
,,	Lysander, Alcibiades, &c.	,,	1/6
,,	Timotheus, Phocion, &c.	,,	1/6
Horace	Epistles. Bk I	,,	2/6
,,	Odes and Epodes	Gow	5/-
,,	Odes. Books I, III	,,	2/- each
,,	,, Book II, IV	,,	1/6 each
,,	Epodes	,,	1/6
Juvenal	Satires	Duff	In the Press
Livy	Books IV, VI, IX, XXVII	Stephenson	2/6 each
,,	,, V	Whibley	2/6
,,	,, XXI, XXII	Dimsdale	2/6 each
Lucan	Pharsalia. Bk I	Heitland & Haskins	1/6
,,	De Bello Civili. Bk VII	Postgate	2/-
Lucretius	Book V	Duff	2/-
Ovid	Fasti. Book VI	Sidgwick	1/6
,,	Metamorphoses, Bk I	Dowdall	1/6
Plautus	Epidicus	Gray	3/-
,,	Stichus	Fennell	2/6
,,	Trinummus	Gray	3/6
Quintus Curtius	Alexander in India	Heitland & Raven	3/6
Tacitus	Agricola and Germania	Stephenson	3/-
,,	Hist. Bk I	Davies	2/6
Terence	Hautontimorumenos	Gray	3/-
Vergil	Aeneid I to XII	Sidgwick	1/6 each
,,	Bucolics	,,	1/6
,,	Georgics I, II, and III, IV	,,	2/- each
,,	Complete Works, Vol. I, Text	,,	3/6
,,	,, ,, Vol. II, Notes	,,	4/6

THE PITT PRESS SERIES.

3. FRENCH.

Author	Work	Editor	Price
About	Le Roi des Montagnes	Ropes	2/-
Biart	Quand j'étais petit, Pts I, II	Boïelle	2/- each
Corneille	La Suite du Menteur	Masson	2/-
,,	Polyeucte	Braunholtz	2/-
De Bonnechose	Lazare Hoche	Colbeck	2/-
,,	Bertrand du Guesclin	Leathes	2/-
,,	,, Part II (*With Vocabulary*) ,,		1/6
Delavigne	Louis XI	Eve	2/-
,,	Les Enfants d'Edouard	,,	2/-
D'Harleville	Le Vieux Célibataire	Masson	2/-
De Lamartine	Jeanne d'Arc	Clapin & Ropes	1/6
De Vigny	La Canne de Jonc	Eve	1/6
Dumas	La Fortune de D'Artagnan	Ropes	2/-
Erckmann-Chatrian	La Guerre	Clapin	3/-
Guizot	Discours sur l'Histoire de la Révolution d'Angleterre	Eve	2/6
Lemercier	Frédégonde et Brunehaut	Masson	2/-
Mme de Staël	Le Directoire	Masson & Prothero	2/-
,,	Dix Années d'Exil	,,	2/-
Malot	Remi et ses Amis	Verrall	2/-
Mérimée	Colomba	Ropes	2/-
Michelet	Louis XI & Charles the Bold	,,	2/6
Molière	Le Bourgeois Gentilhomme	Clapin	1/6
,,	L'École des Femmes	Saintsbury	2/6
,,	Les Précieuses ridicules	Braunholtz	2/-
,,	,, (*Abridged Edition*)	,,	1/-
,,	Le Misanthrope	,,	2/6
,,	L'Avare	,,	2/6
Perrault	Fairy Tales	Rippmann	1/6
Piron	La Métromanie	Masson	2/-
Ponsard	Charlotte Corday	Ropes	2/-
Racine	Les Plaideurs	Braunholtz	2/-
,,	,, (*Abridged Edition*)	,,	1/-
Sainte-Beuve	M. Daru	Masson	2/-
Saintine	Picciola	Clapin	2/-
Scribe & Legouvé	Bataille de Dames	Bull	2/-
Scribe	Le Verre d'Eau	Colbeck	2/-
Sédaine	Le Philosophe sans le savoir	Bull	2/-
Souvestre	Un Philosophe sous les Toits	Eve	2/-
,,	Le Serf & Le Chevrier de Lorraine	Ropes	2/-
,,	Le Serf (*With Vocabulary*)	,,	1/6
Thierry	Lettres sur l'histoire de France (XIII—XXIV)	Masson & Prothero	2/6
,,	Récits des Temps Mérovingiens, I—III	Masson & Ropes	3/-
Villemain	Lascaris ou les Grecs du XVe Siècle	Masson	2/-
Voltaire	Histoire du Siècle de Louis XIV, in three parts	Masson & Prothero	2/6 each
Xavier de Maistre	La Jeune Sibérienne. Le Lépreux de la Cité d'Aoste	Masson	1/6

THE PITT PRESS SERIES.

4. GERMAN.

Author	Work	Editor	Price
Andersen	Six Fairy Tales	Rippmann	2/6
	Ballads on German History	Wagner	2/-
Benedix	Dr Wespe	Breul	3/-
Freytag	Der Staat Friedrichs des Grossen	Wagner	2/-
	German Dactylic Poetry	,,	3/-
Goethe	Knabenjahre (1749—1761)	Wagner & Cartmell	2/-
	Hermann und Dorothea	,, ,,	3/6
,,	Iphigenie	Breul	*In the Press*
Grimm	Selected Tales	Rippmann	3/-
Gutzkow	Zopf und Schwert	Wolstenholme	3/6
Hackländer	Der geheime Agent	E. L. Milner Barry	3/-
Hauff	Das Bild des Kaisers	Breul	3/-
,,	Das Wirthshaus im Spessart	Schlottmann & Cartmell	3/-
,,	Die Karavane	Schlottmann	3/-
Immermann	Der Oberhof	Wagner	3/-
Klee	Die deutschen Heldensagen	Wolstenholme	3/-
Kohlrausch	Das Jahr 1813	,,	2/-
Lessing	Minna von Barnhelm	Wolstenholme	3/-
Lessing & Gellert	Selected Fables	Breul	3/-
Mendelssohn	Selected Letters	Sime	3/-
Raumer	Der erste Kreuzzug	Wagner	2/-
Riehl	Culturgeschichtliche Novellen	Wolstenholme	3/-
,,	Die Ganerben & Die Gerechtigkeit Gottes	,,	3/-
Schiller	Wilhelm Tell	Breul	2/6
,,	,, (*Abridged Edition*)	,,	1/6
,,	Geschichte des dreissigjährigen Kriegs Book III.	,,	3/-
,,	Maria Stuart	,,	3/6
,,	Wallenstein I. (Lager and Piccolomini)	,,	3/6
,,	Wallenstein II. (Tod)	,,	3/6
Uhland	Ernst, Herzog von Schwaben	Wolstenholme	3/6

5. ENGLISH.

Author	Work	Editor	Price
Bacon	History of the Reign of King Henry VII	Lumby	3/-
,,	Essays	West	3/6 & 5/-
Cowley	Essays	Lumby	4/-
Earle	Microcosmography	West	3/-
Gray	Poems	Tovey	*In the Press*
Lamb	Tales from Shakespeare	Flather	1/6
Macaulay	Lord Clive	Innes	1/6
,,	Warren Hastings	,,	1/6
,,	William Pitt and Earl of Chatham	,,	2/6
Mayor	A Sketch of Ancient Philosophy from Thales to Cicero		3/6
More	History of King Richard III	Lumby	3/6
,,	Utopia	,,	3/6
Milton	Arcades and Comus	Verity	3/-
,,	Ode on the Nativity, L'Allegro, Il Penseroso & Lycidas	,,	2/6
,,	Samson Agonistes	,,	2/6
,,	Paradise Lost, Bks I, II	,,	2/-
,,	,, Bks III, IV	,,	2/-
,,	,, Bks V, VI	,,	2/-
,,	,, Bks VII, VIII	,,	2/-
,,	,, Bks IX, X	,,	2/-
,,	,, Bks XI, XII	,,	2/-
Pope	Essay on Criticism	West	2/-
Scott	Marmion	Masterman	2/6
,,	Lady of the Lake	,,	2/6
,,	Lay of the last Minstrel	Flather	2/-
,,	Legend of Montrose	Simpson	2/6
Shakespeare	A Midsummer-Night's Dream	Verity	1/6
,,	Twelfth Night	,,	1/6
,,	Julius Caesar	,,	1/6
,,	The Tempest	,,	1/6
,,	King Lear	,,	1/6
,,	Merchant of Venice	,,	1/6
Shakespeare & Fletcher	Two Noble Kinsmen	Skeat	3/6
Sidney	An Apologie for Poetrie	Shuckburgh	3/-
Wallace	Outlines of the Philosophy of Aristotle		4/6
West	Elements of English Grammar		2/6
,,	English Grammar for Beginners		1/-
Carlos	Short History of British India		1/-
Mill	Elementary Commercial Geography		1/6
Bartholomew	Atlas of Commercial Geography		3/-
Robinson	Church Catechism Explained		2/-

THE PITT PRESS SERIES.

6. EDUCATIONAL SCIENCE.

Author	Work	Editor	Price
Colbeck	Lectures on the Teaching of Modern Languages		2/-
Comenius	Life and Educational Works	Laurie	3/6
	Three Lectures on the Practice of Education		
Eve	I. On Marking		
Sidgwick	II. On Stimulus	} 1 Vol.	2/-
Abbott	III. On the teaching of Latin Verse Composition		
Farrar	General Aims of the Teacher	} 1 Vol.	1/6
Poole	Form Management		
Locke	Thoughts on Education	Quick	3/6
Milton	Tractate on Education	Browning	2/-
Sidgwick	On Stimulus		1/-
Thring	Theory and Practice of Teaching		4/6

7. MATHEMATICS.

Author	Work	Editor	Price
Ball	Elementary Algebra		4/6
Euclid	Books I—VI, XI, XII	Taylor	5/-
,,	Books I—VI	,,	4/-
,,	Books I—IV	,,	3/-
	Also separately		
,,	Books I, & II; III, & IV; V, & VI; XI, & XII		1/6 each
,,	Solutions to Exercises in Taylor's Euclid	W. W. Taylor	10/6
	And separately		
,,	Solutions to Bks I—IV	,,	6/-
,,	Solutions to Books VI. XI	,,	6/-
Hobson & Jessop	Elementary Plane Trigonometry		4/6
Loney	Elements of Statics and Dynamics		7/6
	Part I. Elements of Statics		4/6
	,, II. Elements of Dynamics		3/6
,,	Solutions of Examples, Statics and Dynamics		7/6
,,	Mechanics and Hydrostatics		4/6
Smith, C.	Arithmetic for Schools, with or without answers		3/6
,,	Part I. Chapters I—VIII. Elementary, with or without answers		2/-
,,	Part II. Chapters IX—XX, with or without answers		2/-
Hale, G.	Key to Smith's Arithmetic		7/6

LONDON: C. J. CLAY AND SONS,
CAMBRIDGE UNIVERSITY PRESS WAREHOUSE,
AVE MARIA LANE.
GLASGOW: 263, ARGYLE STREET.

The Cambridge Bible for Schools and Colleges.

GENERAL EDITORS:
J. J. S. PEROWNE, D.D., BISHOP OF WORCESTER,
A. F. KIRKPATRICK, D.D., REGIUS PROFESSOR OF HEBREW.

Extra Fcap. 8vo. cloth, with Maps when required.

Book of Joshua. Rev. G. F. MACLEAR, D.D. 2s. 6d.
Book of Judges. Rev. J. J. LIAS, M.A. 3s. 6d.
First Book of Samuel. Prof. KIRKPATRICK, D.D. 3s. 6d.
Second **Book of Samuel.** Prof. KIRKPATRICK, D.D. 3s. 6d.
First & **Second Books of Kings.** Prof. LUMBY, D.D. 5s., and separately 3s. 6d. each.
Books of Ezra & Nehemiah. Prof. RYLE, D.D. 4s. 6d.
Book of Job. Prof. DAVIDSON, D.D. 5s.
Psalms. Book I. Prof. KIRKPATRICK, D.D. 3s. 6d.
Psalms. Books II and III. Prof. KIRKPATRICK, D.D. 3s. 6d.
Book of Ecclesiastes. Very Rev. E. H. PLUMPTRE, D.D. 5s.
Book of Isaiah. Chaps. I.–XXXIX. Rev. J. SKINNER, D.D. 4s.
—— Chaps. XL.–LXVI. Rev. J. SKINNER, D.D. *In the Press*
Book of Jeremiah. Rev. A. W. STREANE, D.D. 4s. 6d.
Book of Ezekiel. Prof. DAVIDSON, D.D. 5s.
Book of Hosea. Rev. T. K. CHEYNE, M.A., D.D. 3s.
Books of Joel and Amos. Rev. S. R. DRIVER, D.D. 3s. 6d.
Books of Obadiah and Jonah. Arch. PEROWNE. 2s. 6d.
Book of Micah. Rev. T. K. CHEYNE, M.A., D.D. 1s. 6d.
Nahum, Habakkuk & Zephaniah. Prof. DAVIDSON, D.D. 3s.
Books of Haggai, Zechariah & Malachi. Arch. PEROWNE. 3s. 6d.
Book of Malachi. Archdeacon PEROWNE. 1s.
First Book of Maccabees. Rev. W. FAIRWEATHER and Rev. J. S. BLACK, LL.D. 3s. 6d.
Gospel according to St Matthew. Rev. A. CARR, M.A. 2s. 6d.
Gospel according to St Mark. Rev. G. F. MACLEAR, D.D. 2s. 6d.
Gospel acc. to St Luke. Very Rev. F. W. FARRAR, D.D. 4s. 6d.
Gospel according to St John. Rev. A. PLUMMER, D.D. 4s. 6d.
Acts of the Apostles. Prof. LUMBY, D.D. 4s. 6d.
Epistle to the Romans. Rev. H. C. G. MOULE, D.D. 3s. 6d.
First and Second Corinthians. Rev. J. J. LIAS, M.A. 2s. each.
Epistle to the Galatians. Rev. E. H. PEROWNE, D.D. 1s. 6d.
Epistle to the Ephesians. Rev. H. C. G. MOULE, D.D. 2s. 6d.
Epistle to the Philippians. Rev. H. C. G. MOULE, D.D. 2s. 6d.
Colossians and Philemon. Rev. H. C. G. MOULE, D.D. 2s.
Epistles to the Thessalonians. Rev. G. G. FINDLAY, B.A. 2s.
Epistles to Timothy & Titus. Rev. A. E. HUMPHREYS, M.A. 3s.
Epistle to the Hebrews. Very Rev. F. W. FARRAR, D.D. 3s. 6d.
Epistle of St James. Very Rev. E. H. PLUMPTRE, D.D. 1s. 6d.
St Peter and St Jude. Very Rev. E. H. PLUMPTRE, D.D. 2s. 6d.
Epistles of St John. Rev. A. PLUMMER, D.D. 3s. 6d.
Book of Revelation. Rev. W. H. SIMCOX, M.A. 3s.

Other Volumes Preparing.

LONDON: C. J. CLAY AND SONS,
CAMBRIDGE UNIVERSITY PRESS WAREHOUSE,
AVE MARIA LANE.

The Smaller Cambridge Bible for Schools.

Now Ready. With Maps. Price 1s. each volume.

Book of Joshua. Rev. J. S. BLACK, LL.D.
Book of Judges. Rev. J. S. BLACK, LL.D.
First Book of Samuel. Prof. KIRKPATRICK, D.D.
Second Book of Samuel. Prof. KIRKPATRICK, D.D.
First Book of Kings. Prof. LUMBY, D.D.
Second Book of Kings. Prof. LUMBY, D.D.
Ezra & Nehemiah. Prof. RYLE, D.D.
Gospel according to St Matthew. Rev. A. CARR, M.A.
Gospel according to St Mark. Rev. G. F. MACLEAR, D.D.
Gospel according to St Luke. Very Rev. F. W. FARRAR, D.D.
Gospel according to St John. Rev. A. PLUMMER, D.D.
Acts of the Apostles. Prof. LUMBY, D.D.

The Cambridge Greek Testament
for Schools and Colleges

GENERAL EDITOR: J. J. S. PEROWNE, D.D.

Gospel according to St Matthew. Rev. A. CARR, M.A. With 4 Maps. 4s. 6d.
Gospel according to St Mark. Rev. G. F. MACLEAR, D.D. With 3 Maps. 4s. 6d.
Gospel according to St Luke. Very Rev. F. W. FARRAR. With 4 Maps. 6s.
Gospel according to St John. Rev. A. PLUMMER, D.D. With 4 Maps. 6s.
Acts of the Apostles. Prof. LUMBY, D.D. 4 Maps. 6s.
First Epistle to the Corinthians. Rev. J. J. LIAS, M.A. 3s.
Second Epistle to the Corinthians. Rev. J. J. LIAS, M.A. 3s.
Epistle to the Hebrews. Very Rev. F. W. FARRAR, D.D. 3s. 6d.
Epistles of St John. Rev. A. PLUMMER, D.D. 4s.

GENERAL EDITOR: Prof. J. A. ROBINSON, D.D.

Epistle to the Philippians. Rev. H. C. G. MOULE, D.D. 2s. 6d.
Epistle of St James. Rev. A. CARR, M.A. 2s. 6d.
Pastoral Epistles. Rev. J. H. BERNARD, D.D. [*In Preparation*
Book of Revelation. Rev. W. H. SIMCOX, M.A. 5s.

London: C. J. CLAY AND SONS,
CAMBRIDGE WAREHOUSE, AVE MARIA LANE.
Glasgow: 263, ARGYLE STREET.
Leipzig: F. A. BROCKHAUS.
New York: THE MACMILLAN COMPANY.

THE CAMBRIDGE BIBLE FOR SCHOOLS AND COLLEGES.

General Editors:

J. J. S. PEROWNE, D.D., *Bishop of Worcester.*

A. F. KIRKPATRICK, D.D., *Regius Professor of Hebrew.*

Opinions of the Press.

Guardian.—"*It is difficult to commend too highly this excellent series.*"

Academy.—"*The modesty of the general title of this series has, we believe, led many to misunderstand its character and underrate its value. The books are well suited for study in the upper forms of our best schools, but not the less are they adapted to the wants of all Bible students who are not specialists. We doubt, indeed, whether any of the numerous popular commentaries recently issued in this country will be found more serviceable for general use.*"

Baptist Magazine.—"*One of the most popular and useful literary enterprises of the nineteenth century.*"

Sword and Trowel.—"*Of great value. The whole series of comments for schools is highly esteemed by students capable of forming a judgment. The books are scholarly without being pretentious: and information is so given as to be easily understood.*"

Sunday School Chronicle.—"*There are no better books in exposition of the different parts of Scripture than those contained in the Cambridge Bible for Schools and Colleges. The series has long since established its claim to an honourable place in the front rank of first-rate commentaries; and the teacher or preacher who masters its volumes will be, like Apollos, 'mighty in the Scriptures.' All conscientious and earnest students of the Scriptures owe an immense debt to the Cambridge University Press for its Bible for Schools and Colleges. Take it for all in all, it is probably the most useful commentary alike on the Old Testament and on the New that has been given us in recent years.*"

II. Samuel. *Academy.*—"Small as this work is in mere dimensions, it is every way the best on its subject and for its purpose that we know of. The opening sections at once prove the thorough competence of the writer for dealing with questions of criticism in an earnest, faithful and devout spirit; and the appendices discuss a few special difficulties with a full knowledge of the data, and a judicial reserve, which contrast most favourably with the superficial dogmatism which has too often made the exegesis of the Old Testament a field for the play of unlimited paradox and the ostentation of personal infallibility. The notes are always clear and suggestive; never trifling or irrelevant; and they everywhere demonstrate the great difference in value between the work of a commentator who is also a Hebraist, and that of one who has to depend for his Hebrew upon secondhand sources."

I. Kings and Ephesians. *Sword and Trowel.*—"With great heartiness we commend these most valuable little commentaries. We had rather purchase these than nine out of ten of the big blown up expositions. Quality is far better than quantity, and we have it here."

Ezra and Nehemiah. *Guardian.*—"Professor Ryle's Commentary is quite the best work on these books accessible to the English reader."

Christian World.—"This book should be in the library of every Bible Student."

The Book of Job. *Spectator.*—"Able and scholarly as the Introduction is, it is far surpassed by the detailed exegesis of the book. In this Dr DAVIDSON's strength is at its greatest. His linguistic knowledge, his artistic habit, his scientific insight, and his literary power have full scope when he comes to exegesis."

Methodist Recorder.—"Already we have frequently called attention to this exceedingly valuable work as its volumes have successively appeared. But we have never done so with greater pleasure, very seldom with so great pleasure, as we now refer to the last published volume, that on the **Book of Job**, by Dr DAVIDSON, of Edinburgh....We cordially commend the volume to all our readers. The least instructed will understand and enjoy it; and mature scholars will learn from it."

Psalms. Book I. *Church Times.*—"It seems in every way a most valuable little book, containing a mass of information, well-assorted, and well-digested, and will be useful not only to students preparing for examinations, but to many who want a handy volume of explanation to much that is difficult in the Psalter.......We owe a great debt of gratitude to Professor Kirkpatrick for his scholarly and interesting volume."

Literary Churchman.—"In this volume thoughtful exegesis founded on nice critical scholarship and due regard for the opinions of various writers, combine, under the influence of a devout spirit, to render this commentary a source of much valuable assistance. The notes are 'though deep yet clear,' for they seem to put in a concentrated form the very pith and marrow of all the best that has been hitherto said on the subject, with striking freedom from anything like pressure of personal views. Throughout the work care and pains are as conspicuous as scholarship."

Psalms. Books II. and III. *Critical Review.*—"The second volume of Professor KIRKPATRICK's Commentary on the Book of Psalms has all the excellent qualities which characterised the first....It gives what is best in the philology of the subject. Its notes furnish what is most needed and most useful. Its literary style is attractive. It furnishes all that is of real value in the form of introduction, and it has a studious regard for the devout as well as intelligent understanding of the Psalms."

Baptist.—"This volume of the Cambridge Bible for schools and colleges is a very valuable contribution to the expository literature of the Old Testament. The introduction, which occupies some 70 pages, is a compact compendium of explanatory and critical information upon the whole Psalter. The notes are brief, but full, and very suggestive."

Job—Hosea. *Guardian.*—"It is difficult to commend too highly this excellent series, the volumes of which are now becoming numerous. The two books before us, small as they are in size, comprise almost everything that the young student can reasonably expect to find in the way of helps towards such general knowledge of their subjects as may be gained without an attempt to grapple with the Hebrew; and even the learned scholar can hardly read without interest and benefit the very able introductory matter which both these commentators have prefixed to their volumes."

Isaiah. **Chapters I—XXXIX.** Professor W. H. Bennett in the *British Weekly.*—"Dr Skinner's name on the title-page of this book is a guarantee for extensive and exact scholarship and for careful and accurate treatment of the subject. This little volume will more than sustain the high reputation of the series in which it appears...readers will look forward with much interest to Dr Skinner's second volume on chapters xl—lxvi."

School Guardian.—"This last addition to 'The Cambridge Bible for Schools and Colleges,' is a most valuable one, and will go far to increase the usefulness of what we have no hesitation in calling the most useful commentary for school purposes. There ought to be two copies, at least, of this in every parish—one in the clergyman's and the other in the teacher's library."

Jeremiah. *Church Quarterly Review.*—"The arrangement of the book is well treated on pp. xxx., 396, and the question of Baruch's relations with its composition on pp. xxvii., xxxiv., 317. The illustrations from English literature, history, monuments, works on botany, topography, etc., are good and plentiful, as indeed they are in other volumes of this series."

Ezekiel. *Guardian.*—"No book of the Old Testament stands more in need of a commentator than this, and no scholar in England or Scotland is better qualified to comment upon it than Dr A. B. Davidson. With sound scholarship and excellent judgement he combines an insight into Oriental modes of thought which renders him a specially trustworthy guide to a book such as this....His commentary may be safely recommended as the best that has yet appeared. Nor is it unlikely that it will remain the best for some time to come."

Nahum, **Habakkuk and Zephaniah.** *Literary World.*—"An admirable little book, worthy of Dr A. B. Davidson's high scholarship and of the excellent series to which it belongs. The introductions are so comprehensive and thorough, and the notes so entirely useful, that one feels the book is all that can be required for the study of these prophecies by most biblical students, and by many Christian ministers."

Guardian.—"Prof. Davidson has laid all students of the Old Testament under a fresh debt of gratitude by the publication of this scholarly little volume. It is quite the best commentary on these books that has yet appeared....Small as it is, the volume is well worthy to take its place by the side of the same author's invaluable commentaries on Job and Ezekiel."

Spectator.—"We may say without hesitation that Professor Davidson's guidance is amply satisfactory. The theological student or the preacher who may have to deal with the subject cannot do better than consult him."

Malachi. *Academy.*—"Archdeacon Perowne has already edited

Jonah and Zechariah for this series. Malachi presents comparatively few difficulties and the Editor's treatment leaves nothing to be desired. His introduction is clear and scholarly and his commentary sufficient. We may instance the notes on ii. 15 and iv. 2 as examples of careful arrangement, clear exposition and graceful expression."

The Gospel according to St Matthew. *English Churchman.*—"The introduction is able, scholarly, and eminently practical, as it bears on the authorship and contents of the Gospel, and the original form in which it is supposed to have been written. It is well illustrated by two excellent maps of the Holy Land and of the Sea of Galilee."

St Mark. *Expositor.*—"Into this small volume Dr Maclear, besides a clear and able Introduction to the Gospel, and the text of St Mark, has compressed many hundreds of valuable and helpful notes. In short, he has given us a capital manual of the kind required—containing all that is needed to illustrate the text, i.e. all that can be drawn from the history, geography, customs, and manners of the time. But as a handbook, giving in a clear and succinct form the information which a lad requires in order to stand an examination in the Gospel, it is admirable......I can very heartily commend it, not only to the senior boys and girls in our High Schools, but also to Sunday-school teachers, who may get from it the very kind of knowledge they often find it hardest to get."

St Luke. *Spectator.*—"Canon FARRAR has supplied students of the Gospel with an admirable manual in this volume. It has all that copious variety of illustration, ingenuity of suggestion, and general soundness of interpretation which readers are accustomed to expect from the learned and eloquent editor. Anyone who has been accustomed to associate the idea of 'dryness' with a commentary, should go to Canon Farrar's St Luke for a more correct impression. He will find that a commentary may be made interesting in the highest degree, and that without losing anything of its solid value....But, so to speak, it is *too good* for some of the readers for whom it is intended."

The Gospel according to St John. *English Churchman.*—"The notes are extremely scholarly and valuable, and in most cases exhaustive, bringing to the elucidation of the text all that is best in commentaries, ancient and modern."

Acts. *School Guardian.*—"We do not know of any other volume where so much help is given to the complete understanding of one of the most important and, in many respects, difficult books of the New Testament."

Epistle to the Romans. *Expositor.*—"The 'Notes' are very good, and lean, as the notes of a School Bible should, to the most commonly accepted and orthodox view of the inspired author's meaning; while the Introduction, and especially the Sketch of the Life of St Paul, is a model of condensation. It is as lively and pleasant to read as if two or three facts had not been crowded into well-nigh every sentence."

Galatians. *Modern Church.*—"Dr PEROWNE deals throughout in a very thorough manner with every real difficulty in the text, and in this respect he has faithfully followed the noble example set him in the exegetical masterpiece, his indebtedness to which he frankly acknowledges."

English Churchman.—"This little work, like all of the series, is a scholarly production; but we can also unreservedly recommend it from a doctrinal standpoint; Dr E. H. PEROWNE is one who has grasped the distinctive teaching of the Epistle, and expounds it with clearness and definiteness. In an appendix, he ably maintains the correctness of the A. V. as against the R. V. in the translation of II. 16, a point of no small importance."

Ephesians. *Baptist Magazine.*—"It seems to us the model of a School and College Commentary—comprehensive, but not cumbersome; scholarly, but not pedantic."

Guardian.—"It supplies matter which is evidently the outcome of deep study pursued with a devotional mind."

Philippians. *Record.*—"There are few series more valued by theological students than 'The Cambridge Bible for Schools and Colleges,' and there will be no number of it more esteemed than that by Mr H. C. G. MOULE on the *Epistle to the Philippians.*"

Colossians. *Record.*—"Those who have already used with pleasure and profit Mr Moule's volumes of the same series on Ephesians and Philippians will open this little book with the highest expectations. They will not be disappointed.......No more complete or trustworthy volume has been contributed to this series."

Expository Times.—"This is now the Commentary on Colossians and Philemon to have at your hand, whether you are schoolboy or scholar, layman or clergyman."

Thessalonians. *Academy.*—"Mr FINDLAY maintains the high level of the series to which he has become contributor. Some parts of his introduction to the Epistles to the Thessalonians could scarcely be bettered. The account of Thessalonica, the description of the style and character of the Epistles, and the analysis of them are excellent in style and scholarly care. The notes are possibly too voluminous; but there is so much matter in them, and the matter is arranged and handled so ably, that we are ready to forgive their fulness....Mr FINDLAY'S commentary is a valuable addition to what has been written on the letters to the Thessalonian Church."

Baptist Magazine.—"Mr FINDLAY has fulfilled in this volume a task which Dr Moulton was compelled to decline, though he has rendered valuable aid in its preparation. The commentary is in its own way a model—clear, forceful, scholarly—such as young students will welcome as a really useful guide, and old ones will acknowledge as giving in brief space the substance of all that they knew."

Timothy and Titus. *The Christian.*—"The series includes many volumes of sterling worth, and this last may rank among the most valuable. The pages evince careful scholarship and a thorough acquaintance with expository literature; and the work should promote a more general and practical study of the Pastoral Epistles."

Hebrews. *Baptist Magazine.*—"Like his (Canon Farrar's) commentary on Luke it possesses all the best characteristics of his writing. It is a work not only of an accomplished scholar, but of a skilled teacher."

James. *Expositor.*—"It is, so far as I know, by far the best exposition of the Epistle of St James in the English language. Not schoolboys or students going in for an examination alone, but ministers and preachers of the Word, may get more real help from it than from the most costly and elaborate commentaries."

The Epistles of St John. *Churchman.*—"This forms an admirable companion to the 'Commentary on the Gospel according to St John,' which was reviewed in *The Churchman* as soon as it appeared. Dr Plummer has some of the highest qualifications for such a task; and these two volumes, their size being considered, will bear comparison with the best Commentaries of the time."

Revelation. *Guardian.*—"This volume contains evidence of much careful labour. It is a scholarly production, as might be expected from the pen of the late Mr W. H. SIMCOX....The notes throw light upon many passages of this difficult book, and are extremely suggestive. It is an advantage that they sometimes set before the student various interpretations without exactly guiding him to a choice."

Wesleyan Methodist Sunday-School Record.—"We cannot speak too highly of this excellent little volume. The introduction is of the greatest possible value to the student, and accurate scholarship is combined with true loyalty to the inspired Word. There is much more matter of practical utility compressed into this volume of pp. 174 than is contained in many a portentous tome."

The Smaller Cambridge Bible for Schools.

Sunday-School Chronicle.—"*We can only repeat what we have already said of this admirable series, containing, as it does, the scholarship of the larger work. For scholars in our elder classes, and for those preparing for Scripture examinations, no better commentaries can be put into their hands.*"

Record.—"*Despite their small size, these volumes give the substance of the admirable pieces of work on which they are founded. We can only hope that in many schools the class-teaching will proceed on the lines these commentators suggest.*"

Educational Review.—"*The Smaller Cambridge Bible for Schools is unique in its combination of small compass with great scholarship.... For use in lower forms, in Sunday-schools and in the family, we cannot suggest better little manuals than these.*"

Literary World.—"*All that is necessary to be known and learned by pupils in junior and elementary schools is to be found in this series. Indeed, much more is provided than should be required by the examiners. We do not know what more could be done to provide sensible, interesting, and solid Scriptural instruction for boys and girls. The Syndics of the*

Cambridge University Press are rendering great services both to teachers and to scholars by the publication of such a valuable series of books, in which slipshod work could not have a place."

Christian Leader.—*"For the student of the sacred oracles who utilizes hours of travel or moments of waiting in the perusal of the Bible there is nothing so handy, and, at the same time, so satisfying as these little books..... Nor let anyone suppose that, because these are school-books, therefore they are beneath the adult reader. They contain the very ripest results of the best Biblical scholarship, and that in the very simplest form."*

Joshua. *School Guardian.*—"This little book is a model of what editorial work, intended for the use of young students, should be; and we could scarcely praise it more highly than by saying that it is in every way worthy of the volumes that have gone before it."

Schoolmistress.—"A most useful little manual for students or teachers."

Judges. *Educational News* (Edinburgh).—"The book makes available for teaching purposes the results of ripe scholarship, varied knowledge, and religious insight."

Schoolmaster.—"The work shows first-rate workmanship, and may be adopted without hesitation."

Samuel I. and II. *Saturday Review.*—"Professor KIRKPATRICK'S two tiny volumes on the First and Second Books of Samuel are quite model school-books; the notes elucidate every possible difficulty with scholarly brevity and clearness and a perfect knowledge of the subject."

Kings I. *Wesleyan Methodist Sunday-School Record.*—"Equally useful for teachers of young men's Bible classes and for earnest Bible students themselves. This series supplies a great need. It contains much valuable instruction in small compass."

St Mark. St Luke. *Guardian.*—"We have received the volumes of St Mark and St Luke in this series....The two volumes seem, on the whole, well adapted for school use, are well and carefully printed, and have maps and good, though necessarily brief, introductions. There is little doubt that this series will be found as popular and useful as the well-known larger series, of which they are abbreviated editions."

St Luke. *Wesleyan Methodist Sunday-School Record.*—"We cannot too highly commend this handy little book to all teachers."

St John. *Methodist Times.*—"A model of condensation, losing nothing of its clearness and force from its condensation into a small compass. Many who have long since completed their college curriculum will find it an invaluable handbook."

Acts. *Literary World.*—"The notes are very brief, but exceedingly comprehensive, comprising as much detail in the way of explanation as would be needed by young students of the Scriptures preparing for examination. We again give the opinion that this series furnishes as much real help as would usually satisfy students for the Christian ministry, or even ministers themselves."

THE CAMBRIDGE GREEK TESTAMENT
FOR SCHOOLS AND COLLEGES

with a Revised Text, based on the most recent critical authorities, and English Notes.

Expositor.—"*Has achieved an excellence which puts it above criticism.*"

Expository Times.—"*We could not point out better handbooks for the student of the Greek.*"

St Luke. *Methodist Recorder.*—"It gives us in clear and beautiful language the best results of modern scholarship....For young students and those who are not disposed to buy or to study the much more costly work of Godet, this seems to us to be the best book on the Greek Text of the Third Gospel."

St John. *Methodist Recorder.*—"We take this opportunity of recommending to ministers on probation, the very excellent volume of the same series on this part of the New Testament. We hope that most or all of our young ministers will prefer to study the volume in the *Cambridge Greek Testament for Schools.*"

II. Corinthians. *Guardian.*—"The work is scholarlike, and maintains the high level attained by so many volumes of this series."

London Quarterly Review.—"Young students will not easily find a more helpful introduction to the study of this Epistle than this....There is everything that a student of the Epistle needs in this little volume. It deals clearly and thoroughly with every point, and is written in a style that stimulates attention."

St James. *Athenæum.*—"This is altogether an admirable text-book. The notes are exactly what is wanted. They shew scholarship, wide reading, clear thinking. They are calculated in a high degree to stimulate pupils to inquiry both into the language and the teaching of the Epistle."

The Epistles of St John. *Scotsman.*—"In the very useful and well annotated series of the Cambridge Greek Testament the volume on the Epistles of St John must hold a high position....The notes are brief, well informed and intelligent."

Revelation. *Journal of Education.*—"Absolute candour, a feeling for Church tradition, and the combination of a free and graceful style of historical illustration with minute scholarship characterise this work. We wish we had more work of the same kind in the present day, and venture to think that a mastery of this unpretentious edition would prove to many a means of permanently enlarging the scope of their studies in sacred literature."

Guardian.—"The volume is well worthy of its place in the admirable series to which it belongs."

www.ingramcontent.com/pod-product-compliance
Lightning Source LLC
Chambersburg PA
CBHW030728230426
43667CB00007B/637